'This book makes a new and significant contribution to the literature on the critical relationship between Saudi Arabia and the United States. Paradoxically, the writer has been able to use US documents to present a distinctively Saudi perspective on the relationship. The rationale of Saudi policy, and the strong but controlled sense of betrayal when expectations were not fulfilled, is conveyed lucidly in the text. The Saudi establishment finds itself, as Naif bin Hethlain shows, caught between its private security concerns and the requirements and interests of its regional and Islamic roles.'

Professor Tim Niblock
Institute of Arab and Islamic Studies, University of Exeter

Naif bin Hethlain

Saudi Arabia and the US since 1962
Allies in Conflict

SAQI

ISBN: 978-0-86356-465-9

© Naif bin Hethlain, 2010

All rights reserved. No part of this book may be reproduced or transmitted in any form or by any means, electronic or mechanical, including photocopying, recording or by any information storage and retrieval system, without permission in writing from the publisher.

This book is sold subject to the condition that it shall not, by way of trade or otherwise, be lent, resold, hired out, or otherwise circulated without the publisher's prior consent in any form of binding or cover other than that in which it is published and without a similar condition including this condition being imposed on the subsequent purchaser.

A full CIP record for this book is available from the British Library.
A full CIP record for this book is available from the Library of Congress.

Printed and bound by Thomson Press Ltd (India)

SAQI

26 Westbourne Grove, London W2 5RH, UK
2398 Doswell Avenue, Saint Paul, Minnesota, 55108, US
Verdun, Beirut, Lebanon
www.saqibooks.com

This book is dedicated to a man who has devoted his life to the service of others, and has not received the appreciation he deserves.

Contents

List of Abbreviations	9
Introduction	13
1. The Faisal Era (1962–79): Mutual Collaboration, Different Agendas	31
2. The First Fahd Era (1979–90): From Reserved Cooperation to Far-Reaching Dependence	117
3. The Later Fahd Legacy (1990–2001): From Reliance to Mutual Liability	196
4. The 'Abdullah Era (2001–6): Confrontation, Mutual Accusation and Disappointment	264
Conclusion: Future Prospects	309
Postscript: Obama – Continuation or Change?	315
Bibliography	325
Index	365

List of Abbreviations

ACC – Arab Cooperation Council
AFP – Agence France-Presse
AIPAC – American-Israel Public Affairs Committee
APRF – Archive of the President, Russian Federation
ARAMCO – Arabian American Oil Company (now Saudi Aramco)
ATA – Anti-Terrorism Assistance Program (CIA)
AUSA – Association of the US Army
AWACS – Airborne Warning and Control System
AWF – Ann Whitman File
CALTEX – California Texas Oil Company
CAOC – Combat Air Operations Centre
CASOC – California Arabian Standard Oil Company
CCC – Commodity Credit Cooperation
CENTCOM – Central Command
CFR – Council on Foreign Relations
CIA – Central Intelligence Agency (US)
CINCCENT – Commander-in-Chief, US Central Command
CINCSTRIKE – Commander-in-Chief, Strike Command
CRS – Congressional Research Service (Library of Congress, Washington, DC)
CSG – Counterterrorism Security Group
CSIS – Center for Strategic and International Studies (Washington DC)
CTC – Counter-Terrorism Center (CIA)
CWIHP – Cold War International History Project
DCA – Defense Cooperative Agreement
DCI – Director of Central Intelligence
DDL – Dwight D. Eisenhower Library
DIA – Defense Intelligence Agency

DPG – Defense Planning Guidance
FATF – Financial Action Task Force
FBI – Federal Bureau of Investigation
FBIS – Foreign Broadcast and Information Service
FRS – Sandinista Revolutionary Front
FRUS – Foreign Relations of the United States
GBPL – George Bush Presidential Library
GCC – Gulf Cooperation Council
GID – General Intelligence Department (Saudi Arabia)
IHT – *International Herald Tribune*
IIM – Interagency Intelligence Memorandum
IISS – International Institute of Strategic Studies (London)
IMF – International Monetary Fund
INR – Intelligence and Research Bureau (US State Department)
INSS – Institute for National Strategic Studies
ISI – Inter-Services Intelligence (Pakistan)
JCS – Joint Chiefs of Staff
JDOP – US–Saudi Joint Directorate of Planning
JFKL – John F. Kennedy Presidential Library
KTO – Kuwaiti Theatre of Operation
LJL – Lyndon Johnson Library
mbd – million barrels per day (of oil)
MECS – *Middle East Contemporary Survey*
MEES – *Middle East Economic Survey*
MEFTA – US-Middle East Free Trade Area
MEPI – Middle East Peace Initiative
MERIP – Middle East Research and Information Project
MoN – Memorandum of Notification
NAM – Non-Aligned Movement
NARA – National Archives and Record Administration
NEA – Bureau of Near Eastern Affairs (US)
NEPD – National Energy Policy Development Group
NGO – Non-Governmental Organization
NIE – National Intelligence Estimate (US)
NPMP – Nixon Presidential Materials Project
NSA – National Security Archives
NSC – National Security Council (US)
NSDD – National Security Decision Directive

List of Abbreviations

NSF – National Security Files
NSPG – National Security Planning Group
NSS – National Security Strategy
OAPEC – Organization of Arab Petroleum Exporting Countries
OH – Oral Histories
OIC – Organization of the Islamic Conference
OPEC – Organization of Petroleum Exporting Countries
OPLAN – Operation Plans (CENTCOM)
ORHA – Office of Reconstruction and Humanitarian Assistance
PDPA – People's Democratic Party of Afghanistan
PDRY – People's Democratic Republic of Yemen
PLO – Palestine Liberation Organization
PNA – Palestine National Authority
PNAC – Project for the New American Century
PNC – Palestinian National Council
PPP – Public Papers of the Presidents
RDJTF – Rapid Deployment Joint Task Force
RRPL – Ronald Reagan Presidential Library
SAMs – Surface-to-Air Missiles
SCC – Special Coordination Committee
SEIB – Senior Executive Intelligence Brief
SIG – Interagency Working Group
SN – Subject–Numeric (files)
SOCAL – Standard Oil of California
TIFA – Trade and Investment Framework Agreement
TsKhSD – Centre for the Storage of Contemporary Documentation (Russia)
UAE – United Arab Emirates
UAR – United Arab Republic
UNSC(R) – United Nations Security Council (Resolution)
UNYOM – United Nations Yemen Observation Mission
USAF – United States Air Force
USMTM – US Military Training Mission
VOA – Voice of America
WMD – Weapons of Mass Destruction
WSAG – Washington Special Action Group
WTC – World Trade Center
WTO – World Trade Organization
YAR – Yemen Arab Republic

Introduction

This book examines the relationship between the Kingdom of Saudi Arabia and the United States from 1962 to the present day. Although the two countries have a history of strategic cooperation, their association has also involved an often complex diplomatic balancing act – particularly on the part of Saudi Arabia, which has always tried to maintain good relations with its regional neighbours as well as with the world's superpowers. Indeed, the relationship has sometimes been a difficult one: US policies have often overridden subtle attempts by the Kingdom to avoid conflict through mediation and by maintaining principled behaviour towards its neighbours.

Most previous studies have relied on US sources and express only US points of view. Rachel Bronson's study *Thicker than Oil*, from 2006, employs only US documentation, for instance; Anthony Cave Brown bases his *Oil, God and Gold* (1999) mainly on US accounts of events; and Anthony Cordesman's 2003 appraisal of Saudi Arabia in the twenty-first century is conceived solely from a Western perspective and focuses more on the military-strategic relationship than on diplomatic and political connections. One excellent work is Nadav Safran's *Saudi Arabia: The Ceaseless Quest for Security*, written in 1988; however, it predates both Gulf Wars and the events of 11 September 2001.[1] The present account has striven for greater balance in its documentation, and aims to

---

1. Rachel Bronson, *Thicker Than Oil: America's Uneasy Relationship with Saudi Arabia* (Oxford: Oxford University Press, 2006); Anthony Cave Brown, *Oil, God, and Gold* (New York: Houghton Mifflin, 1999); Anthony H. Cordesman, *Saudi Arabia Enters the Twenty-first Century: The Political, Foreign Policy, Economic, and Energy Dimensions* (Westport, CT: Praeger/Greenwood, 2003); Nadav Safran, *Saudi Arabia: The Ceaseless Quest for Security* (Ithaca: Cornell University Press, 1988).

present a more objective analysis of the relationship while highlighting Saudi Arabia's perspective on events.

Documentary sources for the Kingdom are limited in scope and not easily accessible, but I have made extensive use of reports from reliable media sources as well as from biographical works. It had been my intention to carry out extensive interviews with key figures on the Saudi side, as interviews can yield rich, insightful material unobtainable any other way. Unhappily, when I began to schedule appointments and provide outlines of the sorts of questions I wished to pursue, many of these potential sources – who had warmly promised interviews – found that they were no longer available to talk to me. This was disappointing and frustrating, though this kind of behaviour among senior officials is not an uncommon situation in the Middle Eastern context. However, those who did agree to be interviewed provided me with valuable insight, for which I am most grateful.

The Saudi-US Relationship in Context

The Arab Middle East is marked by a highly incongruous mix of sub-national, trans-national and supra-national identities on one hand, and territorial state sovereignties on the other. The state system imposed on the region after World War I fragmented it arbitrarily into competing units based on the interests of the Great Powers. Permanent boundaries were defined that protected these proto-nations from absorption, and endowed them with ruling elites and state apparatuses.[1] One consequence was that loyalties often remained attached to pre-existing 'sub-state' identities, which frequently spilled across the imposed boundaries – the states thereby became 'trans-states', giving rise to irredentism.[2] A second consequence was the enduring power of 'supra-state' identities, expressive of lost cultural unity: the ideologies of both Arab nationalism and pan-Islamism challenged the legitimacy of the individual states and spawned movements that promoted regional unity as a cure for the fragmentation of the community.[3]

1. Iliya Harik, "The Origins of the Arab State System", in Ghassan Salame, ed., *The Foundation of the Arab State* (London: Croom Helm, 1987), pp. 19–46.
2. M. Ayoob, *The Third World Security Predicament: State Making, Regional Conflict and the International System* (Boulder, CO: Lynne Rienner Publishers, 1995), pp. 47–70.
3. Bahgat Korany, "Alien and Besieged Yet Here to Stay: The Contradictions of

Introduction

Many scholars argue that imperialism transformed the Middle East, making the new states dependent on external powers. First, a multitude of relatively weak and artificial states was created. According to Brown, this fragmentation produced a regional power struggle as insecure states sought external patrons and resources.[1] Second, a classic dependent economy was created, marked by the production and export of raw materials and the import of manufactured products and technology. This economic dependency shattered regional economic interdependence, and made these states responsive to the demands of global powers.[2]

Third, by implanting "client elites", shared economic interests were created between the metropolitan states and dominant local classes. Galtung notes that the establishment of these elites at "the centre of the periphery nation for the joint benefit of both" was to sustain the region's subordination to the core.[3] Fourth, as a means of perpetuating this subjection, the core powers used economic punishment – e.g. withdrawal of aid, economic sanctions – against regional states. As a last resort, the imperialist powers periodically used military force. Such intervention is consistent with Wallerstein's view that world capitalism needs a dominant state (a "hegemon") that defends, maintains and expands the system.[4]

Other scholars with realism-centred views contest the notion that core-periphery relations are static, claiming that the foreign policy of regional states enjoys some autonomy. First, superpower rivalry gave regional states leverage over their patrons on regional issues. Young argues that regional autonomy increases when great powers are unable fully to control a regional subsystem, or are not interested in doing so.[5] Second, according to Thompson, the lack of

---

the Arab Territorial State", in Salame, ed., pp. 54–5; see also P. J. Vatikiotis, *Islam and the State* (London: Routledge, 1987), pp. 42–4.

1. Carl L. Brown, *International Politics and the Middle East: Old Rules, Dangerous Game* (Princeton: Princeton University Press, 1984), pp. 3–5.
2. Bruce Moon, "The State in Foreign and Domestic Policy", in L. Neack, J. Hey and P. Haney, eds, *Foreign Policy Analysis: Continuity and Change in Its Second Generation* (Englewood Cliffs, NJ: Prentice Hall, 1995), pp. 197–8.
3. Johan Galtung, "A Structural Theory of Imperialism", *Journal of Peace Research*, vol. 8, no. 2 (1971), pp. 81–98.
4. Immanuel Wallerstein, "The Rise and Future Demise of the World Capitalist System: Concepts for Comparative Analysis", *Comparative Studies in History and Society*, vol. 16, no. 4 (1974), pp. 387–415.
5. Oran Young, "Political Discontinuities in the International System", *World Politics*, vol. 20, no. 3 (April 1968).

regional economic ties has not prevented trans-state cultural and political ties.[1] Third, regional states endeavoured to reduce their dependence on the core. Some turned to Soviet markets and technology to diversify their dependence and enhance their power capabilities, while others, interested in enhancing their autonomy within the global system, played a moderating role in stabilizing oil prices. This role allowed Saudi Arabia, for example, to transform dependency into asymmetrical interdependence.[2] With the collapse of the Soviet Union and the resulting unchecked US hegemony, however, autonomy narrowed for many of the regional states.

As oligarchies or dynasties, regional states were, therefore, highly susceptible to penetration by the core powers. The main threat to the system was instability within the individual states. The desire to defend and legitimize regimes ultimately exceeded aims to deter external threats. David maintains that a regime will align with an external power to contain an internal threat. Where the threat is external, a regime may seek alliance with similarly threatened states.[3] Revolutionary regimes threaten those that are wedded to the status quo, which then look Westward for protection.

In practice, threats from nearby states are of greater concern than threats from the strongest powers in the international system. Middle Eastern politics are renowned for contending leadership bids by Arab states; shifting alliances; a steady stream of crises; occasional wars; and the ongoing pursuit of security and survival in a very aggressive environment. Realists would expect that Arab states attempt, in such an environment, to increase security by accumulating arms. Arab states have indeed spent heavily on defence, but their primary focus has been on securing support through military alliances. According to Walt, Arab states have allied to protect their image, not in response to shifts in military power: "The Arab states have balanced one another not by adding up armies but by adding up votes."[4] Arab states have deployed symbolic power, not military power, to enhance their security and influence each other's foreign policy.

---

1. William R. Thompson, "The Arab Sub-System and the Feudal Pattern of Interaction: 1965", *Journal of Peace Research*, vol. 7 (1970), pp. 15–67.
2. Raymond Hinnebusch and Anoushiravan Ehteshami, eds, *The Foreign Policies of Middle East States* (Boulder, CO: Lynne Rienner Publishers, 2002), pp. 5–6.
3. Steven David, "Explaining Third World Alignment", *World Politics*, vol. 43, no. 2 (1991), pp. 233–56.
4. Stephen M. Walt, *The Origins of Alliances* (Ithaca, NY: Cornell University Press, 1987), p. 149.

Cooperation between the region's states has often been frail and transient. Forming alliances has reflected internal and external power balances, and has tended to be perfunctory. There are deep inclinations to cooperation, but suspicion and rivalry – along with regime insecurity and external intervention – overlie attempts to create any regional community. The Arab-Israeli conflict and the Gulf conflicts have shaped the region's politics, dictated intra-Arab relations and dominated the domestic agenda in the Arab world. They also helped introduce the superpowers into the region on opposing sides; arms transfers from the US and USSR escalated the level of militarization in Arab states. The imperatives of survival within the system have tended to shape its parts – individual states have needed to "balance" against threats, to use Walt's term. Walt maintains that, when confronted by external threats, states either "balance" or "bandwagon": "*Balancing* is defined as allying with others against the prevailing threat; *bandwagoning* refers to alignment with the source of danger."[1] He also claims that when a state is more secure, it chooses to balance; when security is scarce, bandwagoning is preferred.

States choose to balance for two main reasons. First, they do so to curb a potential hegemony before it becomes too strong. According to Vattel,[2] "... the surest means of preserving this balance of power would be to bring it about that no State should be much superior to the other ..." However, if one state has become stronger than another, then it is best, in Vattel's view, to form alliances, "in order to make a stand against a very powerful sovereign and prevent him from dominating."[3] Second, the need of the weaker side for assistance increases the influence that a new member can wield in an alliance, given that its support will be needed.[4]

Bandwagoning is more widespread a choice among states. It was a recurring theme throughout the Cold War. As Henry Kissinger claimed, "if leaders around the world ... assume that the US lacked either the forces or the will ... they will accommodate themselves to what they will regard as the dominant

---

1. Ibid., p. 17.
2. Emerich de Vattel (1714–67) was a Swiss philosopher, diplomat and legal expert whose theories were influential to the founding of modern international law and political philosophy.
3. Cited in Edward V. Gulick, *Europe's Classical Balance of Power* (New York: Norton, 1955), p. 60.
4. Walt, *The Origins of Alliances*, pp. 18–9.

trend."[1] States will ally themselves with a power on the basis of the latter's strength and will to demonstrate this.

There are two motives for a state to bandwagon. First, it chooses bandwagoning for defensive reasons – to preserve its independence in the face of a potential threat. Second, it chooses to do so in order to share the benefits of victory. According to Walt, these two elements can be framed thus: "Balancing is alignment with the weaker side, bandwagoning with the stronger."[2] The importance of alliances is based on the domestic and international credibility that is attached to them, rather than the actual enhancement of a state's concrete power. In the realist view, alliances are a key component in maintaining the balance of power. Morgenthau argues that nations with weak power capabilities can be of great value to a large power if they have strategic resources or occupy a geographically strategic position.[3]

As a weak, rich, pro-Western state, Saudi Arabia has faced significant security threats and has had to become highly dependent on the US for protection. According to Walt, "states ally to balance against threats rather than against power alone", while the level of threat is also affected by "geographic proximity, offensive capabilities and perceived intentions".[4] Saudi Arabia fits well with Walt's argument in that it needs US protection to deter regional threats. David contends that Third World leaders will "appease – that is, align with – secondary adversaries so that they can focus their resources on prime adversaries." Hence Saudi Arabia's alignment with Iraq against Iran. David also maintains that "omni-balancing" incorporates the appeasement of secondary adversaries, and enables leaders "to balance against internal and external threats in order to survive in power"; he suggests that the need for Third World leaders to counter threats explains their alignment decisions.[5] David's argument accounts for the Saudi decision to invite the US and others to defend the Kingdom against Iraq in 1990. Furthermore, Saudi Arabia's foreign relations are designed to protect itself from internal as well as external

---

1. US House of Representatives, Committee on Foreign Affairs, "The Soviet Union and the Third World: Watershed in Great Power Policy", 97th Cong., 1st sess., 1977, pp. 157–8.
2. Walt, *The Origins of Alliance*, pp. 20–1.
3. Hans J. Morgenthau, *Politics Among Nations: The Struggle for Power and Peace* (New York: Alfred A. Knopf, 1978), pp. 192–3.
4. Walt, *The Origins of Alliances*, p. 5.
5. David, "Explaining Third World Alignment", pp. 233–56.

threats. Saudi omni-balancing is influenced by the need for religious and Arab acceptance (if not support).

Saudi Arabia's foreign policy is shaped by four clear determinants. First, with regard to the international system, the Kingdom's close cooperation with the US clearly affects foreign policy. Although some analysts depict this relationship as one of classical dependence, the record shows that the Kingdom has retained a fair amount of autonomy. In the international system, it plays a role that is more one of asymmetric interdependence than of dependence. Oil has helped preserve the state's independence and the regime's stability.

Second, within the regional system the Kingdom must react not only to political threats but also to shifts in military and economic strength. Saudi foreign policy has been complicated by conventional power as well as by ideologies confronting and challenging the country. Thus the Kingdom has attempted to avoid close identification with the US, and prefers to keep US assistance "over the horizon".

The third determinant relates to state formation and domestic politics. King Ibn Saud welded the country into existence, not merely by territorial conquest but by constructing a viable polity based on strong political, ideological, traditional-tribal and personal foundations. However, the Kingdom's strong sense of regional identity meant that the regime was particularly worried about regional powers meddling in its domestic affairs. To keep his realm together, King Ibn Saud relied on the distribution of benefits, and during the 1970s oil money was used to maintain stability through such supplementary payments. Regionalism, as a threat to Saudi Arabia's integrity and security, was thus eliminated by the country's oil revenues. This had two important consequences for the Kingdom's foreign policy. First, for the social services system to continue, the oil policy had to provide the government with funds. Second, with regard to security, Saudi citizens expected the regime to defend the state without requesting military service from them. The Kingdom has therefore had to rely on its security ties with the US, which in turn has made it less assertive in the regional politics of the Middle East.[1]

The fourth determinant is the role of Islam. Islam serves both to legitimize the regime domestically and to assert its leading political role among Muslim states. This leadership function has been used by the Kingdom as a tool and as a

---

1. F. Gregory Gause III, "The Foreign Policy of Saudi Arabia", in Hinnebusch and Ehteshami, eds, *Foreign Policies of Middle East States*, pp. 193–208.

constraint in dealing with the US, but domestically it can expose it to criticism. On the one hand, Saudi Arabia has been the preserver and protector of Islam; on the other, the regime has been completely dependent on the US for the country's security and continued wealth. Therefore, according to Hinnebusch, Saudi Arabia's foreign policy has come under contradictory pressures: "the first drove it to distance itself, even oppose aspects of US policy connected with Israel; the second dictated a close partnership with Washington."[1]

Saudi Arabia has, from the outset, been sufficiently secure in its Islamic identity and autonomy to pursue close and mutually beneficial relations with the West. Islamic solidarity is a major legitimizing force for Saudi foreign policy, and the Kingdom's status as guardian of the holy cities enables it to secure a position of moral leadership in the Islamic world. This leadership, in turn, serves the domestic security interests of the regime. Saudi Arabia's dependence on the US has sometimes run counter to its desire to maintain its Islamic credentials, while relations between the two have become enmeshed in dependencies.

In order to reconcile this contradiction, Saudi Arabia has had to focus on its Islamic credentials, and on building an Arab consensus. The Kingdom used its Islamic identity to combat communism, for example, and justified its US connection on this basis. The Arab defeat of 1967 presented Saudi Arabia with an opportunity to lead the Arab world and moderate the radical Arab regimes. As a swing oil producer, the Kingdom had leverage over the West with which to promote Arab interests; this position enabled Saudi Arabia to assume inter-Arab leadership. However, the country's growing dependency on the US, and its declining oil revenues, checked its rise to leadership.

In many ways Saudi Arabia is limited in its alignment choices by the bounds of Islamic (and Arab) respectability. Religion, however, is not the guiding light of Saudi foreign policy according to Landau, who claims that "policy decisions have generally been made and implemented in the light of national, rather than religious, considerations."[2]

During the Cold War, the US – as a superpower in a bipolar system – had

---

1. Raymond Hinnebusch, *The International Politics of the Middle East* (Manchester, UK: Manchester University Press, 2003), p. 131.
2. Jacob M. Landau, *The Politics of Pan-Islam: Ideology and Organization* (Oxford: Clarendon Press, 1990), p. 253.

Introduction

to adopt a policy in the Middle East that revolved around three factors, as follows:[1]

1. Geo-strategy: To contain the Soviet Union and its allies in the Middle East, the US considered that the entrenchment of Soviet power in the region would constitute a decisive shift in the global balance. Throughout the Cold War, it therefore had to balance its international and regional interests when formulating and implementing policies towards the Middle East generally and Saudi Arabia in particular. The end of the bipolar system and the 1991 Gulf War left the US as the predominant external actor in the region, and US strategy during the 1990s was designed primarily to maintain regional stability by containing Iraq and Iran. The 11 September attacks on New York in 2001 altered the US perception of "threat" to that posed by terrorist groups and their state sponsors. It duly formulated a strategy that drew on all available diplomatic, economic, military and political means.[2]

2. Geo-economics: During World War II the US administration became aware that oil supplies in the Western World would not be sufficient to meet consumer demand. This realization led to increased commercial and military linkages between the US and Saudi Arabia. These commercial ties also led to increased US military presence in the Gulf – first, to guarantee US access to the region's natural resources, and second, to guarantee the security of the Saudi regime.[3] Access to oil at a stable price has been of vital interest to the US, and it is thus advantageous for the US to remain in a largely hegemonic position regionally.[4] Historically, Great Britain played the role of hegemon after World War II, and was superseded by the US. From the Truman and Eisenhower Doctrines to

---

1. Leon Hadar, *Sandstorm: Policy Failure in the Middle East* (New York: Palgrave Macmillan, 2005), p. 5.
2. Robert J. Pauly, Jr., *US Foreign Policy and the Persian Gulf: Safeguarding American Interests through Selective Multilateralism* (Aldershot, UK: Ashgate Publishing, 2005), ch. 2.
3. Michael A. Palmer, *Guardians of the Gulf: A History of America's Expanding Role in the Persian Gulf, 1893–1992* (New York: Macmillan, 1992), pp. 48–9.
4. Daniel J. Graeber, "The United States and Israel: The Implications of Alignment", in Jack Covarrubias and Tom Lansford, eds, *Strategic Interests in the Middle East: Opposition or Support for US Foreign Policy* (Aldershot, UK: Ashgate Publishing, 2007), ch. 8.

the administrations of Nixon, Carter and Reagan, controlling Middle Eastern oil was seen as central to US national interests.

3. Geo-ideology: Since the establishment of Israel, the US has emphasized its historic and moral commitment to ensuring the survival of the Jewish state. US support is, to a large extent, rooted in domestic politics, as American Jewish community support for Israel is well organized and focused. Sentiment, values, politics and guilt have all propelled the US to help the Jewish state, and to some extent US foreign policy in the Middle East is driven by Israel's regional policies. Opinion in the Arab community holds that Israel is an extension of Western imperialism.[1]

US foreign policy overall is shaped by two determinants: US national interests and US domestic politics. The national interests of the US must be seen within the context of US values projected into the international arena. It is possible to identify five fundamental beliefs that define the US role in the international system:

1. The right of self-determination;
2. The inherent worth of any individual;
3. Rulers owe their power to the people and are accountable to them;
4. Any political system professing similar values and trying to function according to US principles must be protected and nurtured;
5. US values are grounded in the Judeo-Christian heritage.

The US political system derives its nature from such fundamental values.[2] However, there are many cases in which the US chooses, for strategic reasons, to support regimes evincing none of these values. Morgenthau argues that nations ought to pursue "power" and "national interest" rather than abstract moral or legal principles.[3]

The broad goals of US national interests have included the maintenance

---

1. Ibid.
2. Eugene R. Wittkopf, *The Domestic Sources of American Foreign Policy: Insights and Evidence*, 2nd ed. (New York: St. Martin's Press, 1994).
3. Hans J. Morgenthau, "Defining the National Interest – Again: Old Superstitions,

Introduction

of world peace in order to strengthen the economic and political stability of US allies by containing the influence of those opposed to the US system and values, and, more importantly, the protection of US access to foreign markets and sources of critical supplies by maintaining an open global economy.[1]

The interests of the US in the Third World encompass national security as well as economic issues. In the Middle East, there is a multiplicity of interests – complex, overlapping, often even conflicting with US interests. In many cases, however, there is almost no agreement on what these interests mean in term of concrete policies. Often strategic policy concerns come first, and then the interests are found to justify the policy. To protect a range of US interests in the Middle East, potentially at variance with each other, the policy of promoting the Arab-Israeli peace process was adopted in the belief that, if peace could be achieved, regional stability would be enhanced and oil supplies would be more secure.

The nature of US interests does not predetermine a single course of action. Many choices do exist on most issues, despite the constraints imposed by the international system and domestic politics. In addition, crises may increase the importance of an individual interest, and lead to alterations in policy. President John F. Kennedy changed US policy towards Egypt, which was threatening Saudi Arabia, but his commitment to maintaining Saudi Arabia's integrity did not waver.[2]

Domestic politics shaping US foreign policy in the Middle East comprise five factors: the president; the executive branch; the legislative branch (Congress); interest groups; and public opinion:

1. The president and his staff are pre-eminent in the foreign policy-making process, and the majority of the population feels that strong presidential leadership is needed in foreign policy. The president can invoke a broad, open-ended mandate based on a wide range of actions – such as executive agreements and executive orders – in order to carry out foreign policy. More

---

New Realities", in Charles W. Kegley, Jr., and Eugene R. Wittkopf, eds, *Perspectives on American Foreign Policy* (New York: St. Martin's Press, 1983), pp. 32–9.

1. John W. Sewell and John A. Mathieson. *The Third World: Exploring US Interests*, Headline Series no. 259 (New York: Foreign Policy Association, May 1982).
2. William B. Quandt, *Peace Process: American Diplomacy and the Arab-Israel Conflict since 1967* (Washington, DC: Brookings Institution Press, 2005), pp. 11–20.

important are his skills as a practised politician. For example, President Ronald Reagan, in order to win Senate approval for the sale in 1981 of AWACS aircraft to Saudi Arabia, doled out funds for a new hospital in a state represented by one senator and for a coal-fired power plant in another, for another; he also appointed the friend of a third senator US Attorney.[1]

The president is the key actor in shaping Middle East policy. He defines and articulates US interests, and Congress usually responds to what the president has communicated. Several US presidents have stated that Saudi Arabia and the Gulf region are of crucial interest to the US, from Franklin D. Roosevelt's declaration that Saudi Arabia was fundamental to the defence of the US to Jimmy Carter's warning that any attempt to gain control of the Gulf would be regarded as an assault on his nation's vital interests.

Presidential styles or decisions can set precedents that succeeding presidents will follow. Under pressure from supporters of Israel and by the four-year cycle of presidential elections, most US presidents have adopted policies favourable toward the Jewish state.

2. The president heads the executive branch of government, along with its various departments and agencies. Major foreign policy decisions are made in a hierarchical, structured and orderly manner, although in practice the dynamics of decision-making and policy implementation have tended to be less strictly hierarchical, less neatly structured and much more disorderly.[2]

Presidential advisers include the "big four": the national security adviser, the secretary of state, the secretary of defence and the director of the CIA (who became, post-2004, the Director of National Intelligence). While consensus among them does not necessarily mean perfect harmony, it does indicate a prevailing sense of teamwork and collegiality. However, too much consensus among senior advisers can lead to pressure for unanimity that works against individual thinking. (An often-cited example is the disastrous 1961 "Bay of Pigs" invasion of Cuba.) Disagreements can mean the dismissal or consignment to bureaucratic purgatory of ideas that

---

1. James M. Lindsay, *Congress and the Politics of US Foreign Policy* (Baltimore: Johns Hopkins University Press, 1994), p. 90.
2. Bruce W. Jentleson, *American Foreign Policy: The Dynamics of Choice in the 21st Century*, 3rd ed. (New York: W. W. Norton & Company, 2007), pp. 35–6.

are good on their merits (which occurred under the administration of George W. Bush).[1] The state department, in shaping Middle East policy, must contend with the Israel lobby, along with elements in Congress who consider certain policies as anti-Israel.

3. The relationship between Congress (the legislative branch) and the president is one in which the separate institutions share powers. Legislative power gives Congress a great deal of influence over foreign policy. Henkin asserts that there is no part of foreign policy "that is not subject to legislation by Congress".[2] Among Congress's prerogatives is its power of appropriation, which can be used to influence more basic policy decisions. Many in the US believe Congress pays more attention to the views of the public than the president does. Congress is thus willed to be a major partner in policy-making with the president, and a check on presidential decisions. It is involved in making foreign policy, and has increasingly imposed its own goals on the executive. Since 11 September 2001, however, a sense has prevailed that power has tended to drift away from Congress to the White House. Describing the relative balance between Congress and the president in determining the nation's foreign policy, Cronin notes: "Congress has regained some of its own lost power and it has very correctly tried to curb the misuse and abuse of power – but it has not weakened the presidency."[3]

There is a high level of support for Israel in Congress because of active pro-Israel lobbies, and many members of Congress must consider their domestic re-election strategies when taking a position on the Arab-Israeli conflict. Congress regularly authorizes massive financial aid to Israel, blocks arms sales to Arab governments and criticizes the Palestinian leadership.

4. US Middle East policy is guided by the trans-national manipulation of US domestic politics. It is heavily influenced by a coalition of pro-Israel forces, for instance, and in some cases, by well-funded lobbyists representing Arab oil states. Policy-makers may pre-empt the desires of their domestic constituencies and, in order to avoid pressure by their domestic

---

1. Ibid., pp. 38–9.
2. James M. McCormick, *American Foreign Policy and Process* (Itasca, IL: F. E. Peacock Publishers, 1992), p. 268.
3. Thomas E. Cronin, "A Resurgent Congress and the Imperial Presidency", *Political Science Quarterly* 95 (Summer 1980), pp. 209–37.

interest groups, may change their stance.[1] The US foreign policy process is especially vulnerable to certain groups. Zionists, for example, are well positioned in the US bureaucracy and in the press, and it is dangerous for US politicians to be thought to be offending this lobby.

Among the most influential interest groups are, or have been, the American-Israel Public Affairs Committee (AIPAC) and the Project for the New American Century (PNAC). PNAC, which has not been active since 2006, argued that US security was best protected by promoting political and economic freedom abroad. These principles played a major role in guiding policy, especially after the attacks of 11 September 2001, and explain the decision to invade Iraq in 2003. AIPAC, meanwhile, campaigns vigorously to provide Israel with the US support it needs to guarantee its security.

Each pressure group pursues its own particular interests and petitions the government on behalf of the shared concerns and values of its members. The mass media itself can be viewed as a kind of interest group. In an article on US security policy, Cohen explores the influence of the media and interest groups in the case of the 1981 sale of AWACS (Airborne Early Warning and Control System) aircraft to Saudi Arabia, emphasizing that the media paid attention to those who tried to block the sale, and identified around 150 Jewish groups that were engaged in public activity to influence US foreign policy in the Middle East. He quotes Representative Dan Rostenkowski as saying that voting for the sale of AWACS "would have been the right vote but I did not want Jewish groups coming down on me".[2]

5. Public opinion is closely involved with decision-making. Decision-makers are usually guided by multiple motives in the foreign policy choices they make. In fact, many of these choices often result from domestic factors rather than international considerations. Public opinion limits the range of permissible foreign policy options from which decision-makers can choose, and sets the boundaries within which they are permitted to operate. However, more often than not decision-makers make their choices

---

1. Robert Trice, "Congress and the Arab-Israeli Conflict: Support for Israel in the US Senate, 1970–73", *Political Science Quarterly* 92 (Summer 1977), p. 456.
2. Bernard C. Cohen, "The Influence of Special-Interest Groups and Mass Media on Security Policy in the United States", in Kegley, Jr., and Wittkopf, eds, *Perspectives on American Foreign Policy*, pp. 232–4.

first and then use their considerable resources to mould public opinion in support of their policies.[1]

Potentially, the mass media has the power to shape public preferences on specific policy issues. Free and Watts point to the US public's cautious vision of its country's role in the world, noting that "the Soviet invasion of Afghanistan, coming on top of the seizure of American hostages in Iran ... brought about a sea change in the attitudes of the American people toward the world around them."[2] A growing mistrust of government contributed to the emergence and development of organizations claiming to represent the public interest.

The relationship between Saudi Arabia and the US may be expressed as one of "mutual dependence", where each side has become increasingly dependent on assets controlled by the other. Even so, this mutual dependence did not, for example, prevent direct Saudi involvement in wars against Israel, the 1973 oil embargo, the Kingdom's disapproval of the Egypt-Israel peace treaty, the missile deal with China and the debate in the late 1990s over policy towards Iraq. Similarly, the US, despite Saudi opposition, recognized the republican regime in Yemen in 1962, increased its aid to Israel and invaded Iraq. Walt notes that the essence of the Saudi-US relationship can be defined as one of "symbiosis rather than dependence".[3]

Many of Saudi Arabia's foreign-policy goals complement those of the US, and can be used to justify an alliance between the two countries. These common objectives provide Riyadh with leverage over Washington. Saudi Arabia is critical to US interests in the region, and the latter's failure to acquiesce to Saudi requests could lead the Saudis to turn away from promoting US interests regionally and in the Third World. Relationship dilemmas do arise in certain policy areas, including:

1. Saudi domestic pressures to reduce oil production;
2. Saudi concern over the Palestinian issue and especially the fate of East Jerusalem;

---

1. Kegley, Jr., and Wittkopf, eds, *Perspectives on American Foreign Policy*, pp. 169–73.
2. Lloyd Free and William Watts, "Internationalism Comes of Age ... Again", *Public Opinion* 3 (April/May 1980), pp. 46–50.
3. Walt, *The Origins of Alliances*, pp. 234–5.

3. Other US policy goals in the region;
4. US political commitment to building up Saudi armed forces.[1]

The determinants above shall recur as themes throughout this book, while the Saudi-US relationship will be investigated by dividing the overall period covered by the study into four phases: 1962–79, 1979–90, 1990–2001 and 2001–6. Before doing so, however, it is important to review the foundations of the relationship in the period up to 1962.

Saudi-US Relations Before 1962

Saudi Arabia as a place of strategic importance first entered the US consciousness in 1943. As the US moved from being a net exporter to a net importer of oil during the 1940s, and as the US government realized that the vast oil reserves of Saudi Arabia were under concession to an American oil company, its oil policy towards Saudi Arabia began to emerge.

On 29 May 1933, Saudi Arabia had granted an oil concession to the Standard Oil Company of California (SOCAL), essentially covering the eastern half of Saudi Arabia. A supplementary agreement was also signed in which the company was accorded preference rights to oil concessions covering certain other areas in Saudi Arabia. By November 1933 the concession had been assigned to a SOCAL subsidiary, the California Arabian Standard Oil Company (CASOC). In 1936 the Texas Oil Company became a half-partner in CASOC, and in July of that year an additional agreement was concluded that established the California Texas Oil Company (CALTEX) as a marketing subsidiary. The size of the concession was subsequently increased in 1939, but then decreased in 1947 and 1963, with further relinquishments of underdevelopment areas at five-year intervals thereafter.[2]

The US government played no role in the original Saudi concession. The gaining of the concessions by US companies would inevitably begin to change

---

1. US House of Representatives, Committee on International Affairs, Subcommittee on Europe and the Middle East, "Saudi Arabia and the United States: The New Context in an Evolving Special Relationship", Staff Report by Richard M. Preece, 97th Cong., 1st sess., Aug. 1981, pp. 69–70.
2. Arabian American Oil Company (ARAMCO), *ARAMCO Handbook: Oil and the Middle East*, rev. ed. (Dhahran, SA: Arabian American Oil Company, 1969), p. 122.

the web of political interests in the region; although Washington was slow to realize this, Britain's loss was indeed to be the US's gain.

Due to the position of King 'Abdulaziz Ibn Abdul Rahman Al-Saud (Ibn Saud) as one of the great leaders of the Arab world, and to geopolitical factors such as the problem of Palestine, and because of diminishing oil resources in the US, President Franklin D. Roosevelt decided to meet Ibn Saud. This meeting was held aboard the US cruiser *Quincy* on the Great Bitter Lake of the Suez Canal, on 14 February 1945. The king questioned the president about US reliability in the future, pointing out that the British had assured him that his security and economic stability were bound up with British foreign policy and that after the war "America will return to its preoccupations in the Western Hemisphere". The two leaders also discussed the conflict in Palestine. The king insisted that Arabs should not pay for the misdeeds of others, and Roosevelt promised him that the US would make no change in its basic policy. He assured Ibn Saud that he "... would do nothing to assist the Jews against the Arabs and would make no move hostile to the Arab people."[1]

During a joint session of Congress in March 1945, Roosevelt departed from his text to add: "I learned more about the whole problem of Arabia – the Muslims, the Jewish problem – by talking to Ibn Saud for five minutes than I could have learned in the exchange of two or three dozen of letters."[2] On 5 April he sent Ibn Saud a letter in which he promised not to do anything that might be hostile to the Arabs. He also guaranteed that there would be no fundamental change in the US policy over Palestine without consulting both Jews and Arabs. However, Roosevelt's successor, Harry S. Truman, did not keep that promise.

By the end of World War II, Ibn Saud had emerged on the international scene as the single most powerful and prestigious Arab and Islamic leader. The Arab Muslim world acclaimed him as such, and the US and Great Britain also recognized his tremendous prestige in the region. US interest in obtaining permission to construct an airfield base in the Kingdom, initially for use during the war and later as part of the US effort to develop a series of strategically

---

1. United States Department of State, Foreign Relations of the United States [hereafter FRUS], 1945, vol. 8, "Great Bitter Lake Conversation", Memorandum of Conversation Between the King of Saudi Arabia (Abdul Aziz al Saud) and President Roosevelt, 14 February 1945.
2. William A. Eddy, *FDR Meets Ibn Saud* (New York: American Friends of the Middle East, 1945), p. 5.

located bases throughout the world, reflected the importance assigned to Saudi Arabia. Meanwhile, Saudi Arabia strove to bring in the US as a counterweight to the British and as an alternative support for the Kingdom's security. More specifically Ibn Saud wanted the US to pressure the British to restrain the Hashemites.[1] He also requested arms from the US, and even wished to conclude a full-fledged treaty of alliance.

The post-war Soviet threat in the Middle East created a mutual Saudi-US security interest that remained as the backbone of political relations between the two countries for almost forty years. Between 1947 and 1950, US strategic planners, particularly the naval tacticians, became deeply concerned about the possibility of losing Middle Eastern oil resources to a powerful Soviet enemy in the event of war. The Joint Chiefs of Staff duly developed a plan (codenamed "Pincher") for defending the Gulf oil fields. By 1949 oil production was already enhancing the Kingdom's strategic importance; thus oilfield security, along with suspicions about Soviet-sponsored regional instability, had become dominant interests for both the Kingdom and the US. Saudi Arabia's strategic importance, together with the increasing value of its oil, challenged the US to strengthen the Kingdom and keep it firmly aligned with the West. To these ends, the US and the Kingdom signed a Mutual Defence Assistance Agreement that led to the establishment of the US Military Training Mission on 27 June 1953.[2]

The collapse of British and French influence in the Middle East following the Suez fiasco in 1956 left a power vacuum for the Soviet Union to fill. In response, the US developed what became popularly known as the Eisenhower Doctrine. (This policy held that any state coming under the threat of aggression by another could request US economic or military assistance.) While managing the shift from British to US dominance in the region, this policy was confined largely to coping with the growing Arab nationalist movement.

---

1. The Hashemites, who trace their ancestry to the Prophet Muhammad, ruled the Hejaz until Ibn Saud annexed it in 1925, sending the dynasty into exile. In 1921, the British transplanted the Hashemites to the thrones of both Iraq and Transjordan, over which Britain had been granted a mandate. After World War II, the British encouraged various schemes to protect their sphere of influence in the Middle East, among them the Hashemite visions of "Greater Syria" and "The Fertile Crescent Plan" – both alarming to Saudi Arabia.
2. Benson Lee Grayson, *Saudi-American Relations* (Washington, DC: University Press of America, 1982), p. 83.

CHAPTER ONE

The Faisal Era (1962–79): Mutual Collaboration, Different Agendas

During the period from 1962 to 1979, Saudi-US relations were shaped by King Faisal's strategic thinking. Even after the king's death in 1975, the line of policy that he had developed continued to mould the relationship.

In order to understand policy-making by the West during this time, its perceptions of the threat of Arab nationalism need to be placed in the context of Western objectives aimed at securing Middle Eastern petroleum resources. The emergence of nationalist movements throughout the 1950s had alarmed Western policy-makers because they threatened to alter the uneven balance of power and profit between developing countries and Western business interests and/or governments. Pan-Arabism had earlier been an empty rallying cry in the region, but Egypt's Gamal Abdel Nasser took the first tangible step with the creation of the United Arab Republic (UAR) in 1958. One leader could now control both the Suez Canal and the oil pipelines that ran through Syria; as a result, Nasser was now a significant player in Middle Eastern petroleum politics.

The need to maintain a political and economic environment in the region favourable to Western interests and to protect oil and oil transport systems explains the interventionist character of US diplomacy that developed at this time. Anglo-American oil policy planners devoted considerable attention to this problem in the mid-1950s.

As part of a Middle East policy review, the US administration of President Dwight D. Eisenhower re-examined its attitude toward Arab nationalism, and both Eisenhower and Secretary of State John Foster Dulles expressed interest in making a cautious overture to Nasser. Meeting on 4 November 1957, the National Security Council (NSC) planning board considered US sponsorship of a plan for Arab unity and a regional economic organization. Eisenhower's advisors, Under-Secretary of State for Middle Eastern Affairs Herbert Hoover, Jr. and former Deputy Secretary of Defense Robert B. Anderson discussed a regional development organization funded by a 10 percent tax on oil revenues, to which oil-producing countries would also publicly subscribe. United Nations Secretary General Dag Hammarskjöld sent Dulles a proposal for a Middle East development fund to be managed by Arab states, the World Bank and the UN. However, faced with antagonistic relationships between the oil companies and oil-producing countries, the US resolved to preserve the status quo and prevented these plans from becoming reality. During a meeting with Selwyn Lloyd, the British Foreign Secretary, Dulles stressed that the plans contained "inherent dangers for the oil companies".[1]

The administration's new policy paper on the Middle East (NSC 5801, 24 January 1958) conveyed US support for Arab unity in terms of strengthening ties among Saudi Arabia, Jordan and Iraq, and bolstering these moderate Arab states against Egypt. In response to the creation of the UAR, the administration also encouraged Saudi involvement in an Iraqi-Jordanian Arab union. However, King Saud of Saudi Arabia was unenthusiastic about confronting Nasser's brand of revolutionary Arab nationalism.

An assessment on the situation in the Middle East prepared by the Departments of State and Defense as well as the CIA was received by Dulles on 24 March 1958 and suggested that Nasser's latest actions threatened to jeopardize access to petroleum. In April, CIA director Allen Dulles informed the NSC that certain intelligence reports predicted the nationalization of the Arabian American Oil Company (ARAMCO – the renamed CASOC) as well as a takeover of Saudi Arabia by Nasser.[2] Meanwhile, an Anglo-American study group (established following the 1943 Bermuda Conference) finalized its report on the oil-transport crisis on 13 May. It concluded that closure of the Suez Canal and of Middle East pipelines would deprive Europe of about

---

1. FRUS, 1958–60, vol. 12, "Memorandum of conversation by Reinhardt", 30 January 1958, p.35
2. Dwight D. Eisenhower Library (DDEL), ACW, NSC Series, Box 10, "Memorandum of Discussion at the 363rd Meeting of the NSC," 24 April 1958.

a third of its oil, and that European countries would have to make up the shortfall by purchasing Western hemisphere petroleum.[1]

US officials were prevented by concerns over Arab nationalism from seizing the opportunity to make economic development of the region a higher priority, from attempting to address the tremendous disparities in wealth among the Arab states and from indicating a willingness to depart from an oil diplomacy based mainly on supporting private investment. For the Saudi government, the period following the Suez war marked the beginning of political and economic reform that would lay the foundations of the modern Saudi state.

Containing Nasserism

Egypt's willingness to purchase arms from the Soviet bloc in 1955 was a significant step along the road to a policy of radical nonalignment. This exercise of sovereignty by an Arab state enhanced Egypt's and Nasser's leadership in the Arab region; a year later, Nasser succeeded in turning Egypt's struggle against aggression into a struggle of Arab nationalism against its enemies. British and French actions over the Suez Canal in 1956 had the effect of strengthening Egyptian leadership and accelerating the nationalist tide. By the end of 1956, Nasser's influence in the Arab world had become so pronounced that the term "Nasserism" came to be applied generally to that form of nationalism.

Prior to the Suez war, Saudi-Egyptian relations had been amiable. King Saud had concluded a mutual defence treaty with Egypt in October 1955, and cooperated with Nasser in attempts to isolate Iraq – which subscribed to the Baghdad Pact – and prevent Syria and Jordan from joining the Pact. (Saudi Arabia's opposition to the Baghdad Pact was based on the Saudis' traditional rivalry with the Hashemites, a feud with the British over disputed claims to the Buraimi Oasis and a desire to defuse revolutionary sentiment in the Kingdom itself.[2] Therefore, King Saud chose to forego the Baghdad Pact in favour of an all-Arab alliance with Egypt.)

The Egyptian-Syrian-Saudi alliance constituted a decisive rejection of Iraq's

---

1. FRUS, 1958–60, vol. 12, Deputy Under-Secretary of State Douglas Dillon to the Acting Sec. Christian Herter, 30 June 1958, and attachment "Transport of Oil from the Middle East (Joint Report by US-UK officials)", 12 May 1958, pp. 64–71.
2. David Holden and Richard Johns, *The House of Saud* (London, UK: Sidgwick & Jackson, 1981), pp. 184–7.

plans to link the Arab world to the Western powers, and a solid endorsement of Nasser's own proposal for a unified, independent Arab policy. Nasser proposed a collective security pact and Arab non-alignment.[1] Similarly, Saudi Arabia did not want to become involved directly in superpower confrontation, preferring a more informal relationship with implicit guarantees of US support.[2]

King Saud had supported Egypt's anti-Baghdad Pact campaign since early 1955, echoed Nasser's anti-imperialist rhetoric and even defended Egypt's decision to purchase arms from the Soviet bloc. By March 1956, the State Department's Bureau of Near Eastern Affairs (NEA) was proposing a sustained effort to detach Saudi Arabia from Egyptian influence.

Eisenhower tried to promote Saud as an anti-Nasserist, pan-Arab leader, but although separating Saud from Nasser was a feasible objective, building him up as a pan-Arab rival to Nasser was not. Few US officials shared Eisenhower's enthusiasm for pitting Saud against Nasser, but the more modest goal of separating the two leaders was widely supported within the administration – a task that was facilitated by the Suez crisis. By August 1956, Saud was rethinking the alliance with Egypt. Nasser seemed to have embarked on an increasingly revolutionary course, and had developed the habit of taking drastic decisions without consulting his allies or considering the effect of his decisions on them. Saud's move to mend fences with Iraq, encouraged by both the US and the UK, was an indication of his displeasure with Egyptian policy.

In late August, Eisenhower sent Robert B. Anderson on a secret mission to Saudi Arabia. At a meeting with King Saud and Crown Prince Faisal, Anderson warned that Nasser's behaviour over Suez was damaging the West's confidence in the canal as a reliable shipping route, and that it would seek alternative shipping routes; that would drive up the price of Middle Eastern oil, creating an incentive to purchase oil elsewhere. Anderson hinted that the West might even be forced to explore new sources of energy. Faisal, whose suspicions of US motives far exceeded those of Saud, dismissed the notion. Anderson also urged the Saudi government to try to persuade Egypt to negotiate on the basis of the proposals that had been developed at the August conference on the Suez crisis convened in London and attended by the US, Britain, France and Egypt. The proposals involved developing a formula for the international

---

1. Fawaz Gerges, *The Superpowers and the Middle East: Regional and International Politics, 1955–1967* (Boulder, CO: Westview Press, 1994), pp 21–40.
2. Anthony H. Cordesman, *The Gulf and the Search for Strategic Stability* (Boulder, CO: Westview Press, 1984), pp. 102–3.

administration of the canal that would be acceptable to Egypt and the major maritime nations.[1] Saud's advisor Yusuf Yassin was dispatched to Cairo, but was unable to move the Egyptians toward a negotiated compromise.

On 7 September Saud wrote to Nasser, offering to intercede with the US to find a resolution to the crisis compatible with Egyptian interests. On 23 September Nasser went to Saudi Arabia to warn Saud of US efforts to drive a wedge between Egypt and Saudi Arabia. Saud joined Nasser in a public communiqué that supported Egypt's stand in the Suez crisis.[2]

The Suez war began on 29 October. Convinced that the US would lose standing in the world if it failed to uphold Egypt's sovereignty, the Eisenhower administration strongly opposed the tripartite attack against Egypt by Britain, France and Israel and introduced a resolution in the UN General Assembly (rather than the Security Council, to avoid British and French vetoes), demanding immediate cessation of hostilities by the aggressors and withdrawal by Israel behind armistice lines.[3] With the ceasefire in place, Nasser was hailed throughout the Arab world as a heroic resister of Great Power aggression.

On 3 December, Britain and France finally yielded to US pressure and agreed to an unconditional withdrawal from Egypt. However, Israel refused to vacate the Sinai Peninsula and the Gaza Strip, and did not begin withdrawing its forces until late in February 1957, completing the process by 11 March.[4]

The resulting reduction in British power and influence created a diplomatic, political and military vacuum in the Arab world. However, the US had gained considerable prestige by opposing aggression in the Suez war, and Eisenhower was confident that once the dispute over the Suez Canal was resolved and foreign forces had departed Egypt, the Arab states could be persuaded to keep the Soviets at arm's length. For Nasser, there was the simple recognition that US action had helped frustrate an attempt to destroy the Egyptian regime. However, Arab gratitude was not enough to ensure lasting support for US policy in the region.

---

1. Salim Yaqub, *Containing Arab Nationalism: The Eisenhower Doctrine and the Middle East* (Chapel Hill, NC: University of North Carolina Press, 2004), p. 47.
2. Penelope Tuson and Anita Burdett, eds, "Joint Saudi-Egyptian-Syrian Communiqué, 24 September 1956", *Records of Saudi Arabia 1902–1960* (London: Archive Editions, March 1992), pp. 290–1. The Syrian president also attended this meeting.
3. Keith Kyle, *Suez* (New York: St. Martin's Press, 1991), p. 386.
4. Yaqub, *Containing Arab Nationalism*, p. 111.

Arab nationalism under Nasser took the liquidation of Western economic and political domination – or, at least, its gradual phasing out – as its point of departure; the failure of other regimes to take up similar policies brought their legitimacy into question. In late November, Egyptian military attachés were implicated in violent subversive activities in other Arab countries, and Radio Cairo stepped up its propaganda war against Nasser's conservative Arab rivals. Nasser appealed to the Arab masses, and all constraints on whatever new initiatives he chose appeared to collapse. Faced with this situation, Saud tried to revitalize the US connection as a security asset against Nasser, and to reinforce the Saudi relationship with the Hashemites. At the same time, US officials were losing patience with Nasser, and State Department planners called for attempts to isolate and undermine the Egyptian leader.

When the Eisenhower Doctrine was unveiled in early January 1957, Egypt avoided its outright rejection: doing so could have ruled out future US economic assistance and forced Egypt into a position of utter dependence on the Soviets. Although Saud remained uncommitted to the Doctrine, he was being pulled in two directions. On the one hand, the Suez war had confirmed many of his worst misgivings about Nasser; moreover, the Saudis' close economic and military ties to the US, and their opposition to communism, forced him to look favourably upon the Eisenhower Doctrine. On the other hand, it was clear that embracing the Doctrine could be politically costly, and Saud could not afford to be perceived as opposing Nasser. The Doctrine revealed both the US preoccupation with the Soviet Union and its lingering concern over Nasser's aims and sympathies. US policy now focused on limiting Nasser's influence. The US did not appreciate the extent to which Arab fears of Israel and desire for real independence were more important than any remote Soviet threat.[1]

At the Cairo Conference, which took place on 26–7 February and at which Saud was in attendance, Nasser referred to the economic pressure being placed on Egypt by the Western powers, including the US. The communiqué issuing the resolutions of the conference endorsed the principle of non-alignment in the Cold War, criticized the West for failing to distinguish between nationalism and communism and claimed that Egypt's strengthening ties to the Soviets were the result of Western economic pressure.[2] In late April, Egypt finally rejected the Eisenhower Doctrine.

---

1. L. Carl Brown, *International Politics and the Middle East: Old Rules, Dangerous Game* (Princeton, NJ: Princeton University Press, 1984), p. 176.
2. DDEL, AWF, International Series, Box 46, Folder: "Saudi Arabia, King Saud

During the summer of 1957, King Saud further reassessed his position on Egypt. Nasser appeared to be the sole custodian of the Arab nationalist mantle, which he invoked at will to appeal to Arab mass opinion over the heads of their rulers. This added to Saud's misgivings about Nasser, which had developed with Nasser's practice of acting without consultation; with suspicions of Egyptian involvement in sabotaging Saudi military factories at Al-Kharj on 4 October 1956; and, finally, with events (on 19 April 1957) that led to the expulsion of an Egyptian diplomat suspected of involvement in a plot to assassinate Saud himself.

In combating the destabilizing impact of radical Arab nationalism, Saud finally decided that the long-standing and often bitter rivalry between the Saudis and the Hashemites had to end. He therefore resumed and intensified efforts to come to a rapprochement with Iraq, which included a state visit to that country in May 1957, and a visit by Iraq's King Faisal to Saudi Arabia at the beginning of December 1957. The US was also seeking to weaken Nasserism, and adopted a two-part strategy that sought to discredit Nasser for not recognizing the threat of communism while trying to encourage and unite conservative Arab leaders.[1]

Nasser's soaring prestige gave Egypt the power to threaten other Arab states. Saudi Arabia initially sought to appease him by "bandwagoning", but when appeasement proved unsuccessful it shifted to a "balancing" alignment with Iraq and the US. Egypt's emergence as a dominant regional actor led Saudi Arabia to seek both regional and Western allies to defend its interests.

During summer 1957, contrary trends began to take shape in the Arab world. Although Jordanian and Lebanese relations with Egypt and Syria remained hostile, Iraq and Saudi Arabia enjoyed a modest reconciliation with the radical camp. The disagreement between Saudi Arabia and the US over the Gulf of Aqaba also permitted a rapprochement between Saudi Arabia and Egypt,[2] and on 8 July 1957, Yassin declared that Saudi Arabia would avoid all foreign pacts and follow Egypt's policy of "active neutralism".[3]

In late August 1957, US pressure was directed against an increasingly

---

1957 (1)", US Embassy, Cairo, to State Dept., 28 February 1957.
1. Yaqub, *Containing Arab Nationalism*, p. 145.
2. To gain Israeli withdrawal from Sinai, Eisenhower pledged to support Israeli maritime rights in the Gulf of Aqaba. Saud thought that this pledge was tantamount to rewarding Israel for its aggression against Egypt. Saud also argued that Israel's use of the Gulf threatened the pilgrimage route to Mecca.
3. Yaqub, *Containing Arab Nationalism*, p. 148

factionalized Syria. The Syrian chief of staff, a moderate, had been replaced on 15 August 1957 by an openly pro-Soviet officer, and Robert Strong, the US *chargé d'affaires*, predicted that Syria would "undertake a major subversive effort [to] topple King Saud and establish a regime similar to that in Syria".[1] Egypt's initial response was to attempt to use its influence to stabilize the situation. Nasser believed that the Syrians had gone too far in courting the Soviets, but as the crisis developed into a Cold War confrontation Egypt was compelled to take a public position. In a press interview with the newspaper *Al-Ahram* on 9 September, Nasser declared that "Egypt stands on Syria's side unconditionally",[2] a position dictated in part by its rivalry with Saudi Arabia. Egypt distanced itself from Saud's effort to mediate a peaceful resolution to the crisis, and Nasser declared that direct Syrian-US negotiations were required to defuse the situation.[3]

Egyptian-Saudi relations worsened over the course of 1957. Nasser's pre-eminent position in the Arab world in the wake of the Suez crisis came to be perceived as a threat to the stability of the Saudi monarchy, and the atmosphere was further poisoned by mutual accusations of subversion. Furthermore, while Saud was trying to mediate a solution, Nasser sent a contingent of Egyptian troops to Syria without consulting him.

The formation of the UAR on 1 February 1958 precipitated an open crisis between Saudi Arabia and the new union. Saudi Arabia was accused of attempting to instigate a Syrian military coup aimed at preventing its implementation, and Nasser told a crowd of supporters in Damascus on 5 March 1958 that Saud's involvement in an attempt to sabotage the Egyptian-Syrian union had just been exposed. Saud had, in fact, acted against a US warning of entrapment on the part of the Syrian officials. Saudi accounts of the affair do not deny contact with, and payment of money to, the Syrian intelligence director 'Abd al-Hamid Sarraj, but maintain that the initiative had come from Sarraj prior to the creation of the UAR.[4]

1. United States Department of State Records, Central Files (783.00/8-2357), Strong to State, 19 August 1957.
2. Muhammed Hassanain Heikal, *Sanawat al-ghalayan* (Cairo: Al-Ahram Centre for Political and Strategic Studies, 1988), pp. 266–9.
3. David W. Lesch, *Syria and the United States: Eisenhower's Cold War in the Middle East* (Boulder, CO: Westview Press, 1992), p. 180.
4. Sarah Yizraeli, *The Remaking of Saudi Arabia: The Struggle Between King Saud and Crown Prince Faysal, 1953–1962* (Tel Aviv: Moshe Dayan Center, 1998), pp. 68–9.

On 6 March 1958, Dulles informed the NSC of the abortive plot in Syria and the predictable reaction it had provoked. According to Dulles, "Nasser was fully engaged in an all-out battle with the remaining pro-Western Arab leaders."[1] At a meeting of the NSC on 13 March, Dulles reported that the entire Western position in the Middle East was on the verge of collapse, and that Nasser had now caught the imagination of the masses throughout the region.

The years after the Suez war seemed to represent a steady march towards greater integration among the Arab states. Arab nationalism appeared to be an unstoppable tide, and the demand for unification was growing. Dulles observed that the US could only contain the threat it posed to US interests until it subsided.[2]

The irresponsibility demonstrated by Saud resulted in a serious loss of prestige for the monarch, both at home and abroad. Regionally, Saudi Arabia had attempted to subvert the formation of the UAR; its humiliating failure was yet another victory for Nasserism in the battle for Arab opinion.

Following his assumption of power as prime minister in March 1958, Faisal quickly distanced Saudi Arabia from other pro-Western monarchies and sought a propaganda truce with the UAR. In a private interview with US Ambassador Donald R. Heath on 11 August, he expressed his view that the US had erred in wanting Arab states to declare themselves in either the Western or Eastern camp, and that it was in the interests of both the US and the Arabs that the Middle East become truly neutral. He explicitly declared Saudi Arabia to be neutral itself, claiming the Saudis as "Arabs among Arabs".[3] The ambassador then delivered a statement from Dulles recognizing the desire and the right of Arab nations for closer association with each other, in accordance with the freely expressed will of the peoples of these countries.

During this meeting, the ambassador asked for Faisal's assessment of Nasser and whether or not he feared Nasser's designs on Saudi Arabia. Faisal replied that Nasser was a profoundly intelligent and ambitious man who unquestionably had a tremendous hold on the Arab masses, including many sections of the Saudi population. He added that he was not afraid of Nasser

---

1. DDEL, AWF, NSC Series, Box 9, "Memorandum of Discussion at the 357th Meeting of the National Security Council", 6 March 1958.
2. Malik Mufti, *Sovereign Creations: Pan-Arabism and Political Order in Syria and Iraq* (Ithaca, NY: Cornell University Press, 1996), pp. 180–93.
3. United States Department of State Records, Central Files (786A.11/8-1258), US Embassy, Jeddah, to State Dept., 12 August 1958.

inciting revolution in Saudi Arabia as, regardless of the Egyptian's popularity, the Saudis did not want Nasser or Egypt to rule over them. On the other hand, Faisal explained that if the present Saudi government "failed to meet the needs of the people, Nasser or anyone else could easily start a successful revolution here".[1] Faisal thought the US could and should develop friendly relations with Nasser by giving him some support.

A joint Saudi-UAR communiqué issued at the end of a visit by Faisal to Cairo on 15 August stated that a policy of non-alignment and positive neutrality was one of the bases of Arab nationalism. The two states declared that they did not approve of the presence of foreign troops on the soil of any Arab country, and condemned intervention by any foreign state in the affairs of another state. The main reason for the visit was that Iraq's revolutionary leader, 'Abd al-Karim Qasim, had allied himself with Iraqi communists and shown sympathy for communists in the UAR, prompting Nasser to seek a rapprochement with both the US and Saudi Arabia. Nasser's warmer relations with Saudi Arabia were being facilitated by Faisal's relative acceptance of the Egyptian general's primacy among Arab leaders.

Ironically, US military intervention in Lebanon in July 1958 contributed to the growing détente between the US and the UAR – quick withdrawal by the former easing Nasser's obsessive fears for his own security.

Egypt was now enjoying seemingly cordial relations with Saudi Arabia, and in addition was receiving considerable support from both superpowers.

In November 1958 an American paper on the Middle East predicted that US accommodation of revolutionary Arab politics would imply the abandoning of conservative allies such as Saudi Arabia and Jordan, the relinquishing of Western oil assets and military bases in the Middle East and endorsement of Nasser's regional ambitions. The paper supported cooperation with Nasser as head of the UAR, but not as paramount Arab leader, and also stated that the US should establish a working relationship with Arab nationalism while seeking to contain its outward thrust.

On 1 December, having been approached by the Egyptians, American ambassador to Egypt Raymond Hare encouraged the State Department to approve the sale of wheat to the UAR under PL480, the Agricultural Trade Development Assistance Act (some years later President Kennedy would

---

1. United States Department of State Records, Central Files (786A.11/8-1258), US Ambassador, Jeddah, to Sec. of State, 12 August 1958.

rename PL480 "Food for Peace"). The State Department accepted Hare's recommendation. In response, Nasser arrested some communist dissidents, and at the same time sought to improve relations with conservative Arab states. Only once Assistant Secretary of State William Rountree returned in December from the Middle East did US officials fully grasp the significance of the hostility between Nasser and Qasim, concluding that Nasser's growing antagonism toward the latter represented a positive development in the US campaign to manage Arab nationalism and contain communism.

By late January 1959, the UAR was feuding with the Soviet Union. The dispute intensified in March when Iraqi Nasserist officers tried to seize the army garrison at Mosul, in a revolt crushed by pro-government paramilitary units.[1] Nasser stated publicly that Iraq had fallen under a "red dictatorship"; Soviet Premier Nikita Khrushchev retorted in turn that Nasser was now indulging in "the language of imperialists".[2] The US welcomed Nasser's growing hostility toward the Soviet Union. In a cable sent by Ambassador Hare to the State Department on 1 April, Hare advised that "it must be recognized that Nasser has dealt body blows to both the communists and the Soviets recently", and recommended that Nasser be rewarded.[3] The State Department duly authorized an additional sale of PL480 wheat to Egypt, and later that month approved a proposal by the International Bank for Reconstruction and Development (IBRD) to provide a loan of US $100 million to the UAR.

Having won the 1960 election, John F. Kennedy and his advisers were intent on improving the US relationship with Egypt, and were intrigued by the idea of finding a way to entice Nasser away from the Soviet Union even if he could not be lured all the way into the Western camp. The overture to Nasser represented a sharp break with previous US policies in the Middle East. By the time Kennedy took office, the Arab monarchs were feeling menaced by Nasserism, and suspected that Cairo's pan-Arab nationalism was a pretext for knocking them off their thrones. Kennedy reached out to Nasser in an attempt to gain a Cold War advantage, but by 1961 the Arabs were plunging

---

1. Hanna Batatu, *The Old Social Classes and the Revolutionary Movements of Iraq: A Study of Iraq's Old Landed and Commercial Classes and of Its Communists, Baathists, and Free Officers* (Princeton, NJ: Princeton University Press, 1978), pp. 866–89.
2. Ibid., p. 863.
3. FRUS, 1958–60, vol. 12, US Embassy, Cairo, to State Dept., 1 April 1959, p. 522.

into a Cold War of their own, in which the forces of conservatism squared off against the forces of revolution. This basic split was becoming the central dynamic of inter-Arab politics.

Nasser's repeated attacks on "Arab reactionaries" encouraged the latter to ally themselves against Egypt, despite their traditional dynastic rivalries. These alliances were more the result of Nasser's actions than of the independent power of monarchical solidarity. The Arab monarchies based their legitimacy on traditional values and allegiances, and the implicit ideological basis of monarchical alliance reinforced the sovereignty of each monarch. Arab mutual accusation led to the vanishing of unification from the agenda. Arab states came to operate according to the norms of sovereignty, and accepted the territorial status quo.

Nasser's ability to mobilize trans-state support had allowed the assertion of Egyptian hegemony in the region. This induced anti-hegemonic balancing, which undermined pan-Arab solidarity. Alliance formation and power-balancing blunted Egyptian ambitions and preserved the states-system.

NSC staff, led by McGeorge Bundy and Walt Rostow, preached the virtues of Third World development and formulated a series of diplomatic nettles for the new administration to grasp. Among their key suggestions was the question of reappraising US relations with Nasser.[1]

Having criticized Eisenhower for being reactive, the new administration sought to seize the initiative in the Middle East. On 11 May 1961 Kennedy sent letters to six major Arab heads of state: Nasser, Lebanese President Fuad Chehab, King Saud, King Hussein of Jordan, Prime Minister Qasim of Iraq and Imam Ahmad of Yemen. The State Department hoped the letters would reassure Arab leaders as to the administration's impartiality in Arab-Israeli affairs. (It should be noted that King Saud had retaken control of Saudi foreign policy from Faisal at this time.)

The king's sour reply, on 25 June, hinted that Saudi Arabia was wary of the administration even before it had begun to reach out to Nasser. He was strongly critical of US support for Israel, and of the US position on the Arab-Israeli dispute – particularly the stand it had adopted during a recent UN General Assembly debate on Palestinian refugees. He insisted that the only basis for considering the Palestine question was that the Arabs were the legal possessors

---

1. John F. Kennedy Library (JFKL) Oral Histories (OH), Robert W. Komer, NSC *chargé* of Middle Eastern affairs, 16 July 1964, p. 2.

of Palestine and had a right to live there. To Saud, Israel was a usurper and an aggressor, established with the political assistance of the US.

On 27 June 1961 the administration unveiled a new National Intelligence Estimate (NIE) – a formal assessment designed to guide policy-makers on "Nasser and the future of Arab Nationalism".[1] The new NIE represented an abrupt departure from the Eisenhower era, with the analysis predicting: "Militant nationalism will continue to be the most dynamic force in Arab political affairs, and Nasser is likely to remain its foremost leader and symbol for the foreseeable future." The NIE believed the appeal of Arab unity was not as strong as it had been. "Nasser probably now appreciates the practical obstacles involved in seeking to establish such a union," it stated. It also emphasized that the UAR would make strong efforts to achieve progress in economic development, but would not attain significant economic growth without substantial and continued foreign aid. Robert W. Komer, an NSC staff member who wrote to Rostow in support of the NIE, recommended "not trying to outbid the Soviets, not deluding ourselves with any idea we can bring him [Nasser] into the Western camp, but merely that we must live with him and he must live with us". He pointed out that one of the key things the US had to offer was "assistance in economic development. In turn, however, we must let Nasser know that we expect a compensatory quid pro quo in a less antagonistic policy on his part."[2] Komer proposed a major shift in policy toward Nasser, with aid being utilized to lure Cairo away from Moscow.

The US had cut off foreign aid to Egypt in 1956 because of Suez, but the previous administration had renewed the programme on a project-by-project basis. The Kennedy administration now concluded that "while it is not feasible to expect significant help from Nasser in solving major international problems, much can be done to push the pendulum of US-UAR relations."[3] It felt that the best course was to continue its constant probing of the UAR on important issues, while fostering personal contacts with Nasser and his senior advisors and continuing modest economic assistance. This policy was designed for three main purposes:

1. FRUS, 1961–3, vol. 17, NIE 36-61, 27 June 1961, pp. 164–6.
2. JFKL, NSF, UAR, 7/61-10/61, Memorandum from Komer to Rostow, 30 June 1961.
3. United States Department of State Records, PPS Files: Lot 67D 548, Egypt, Talbot to McGhee, 30 May 1961.

1. To demonstrate US sympathy for the massive challenges of industrialization and overpopulation facing the UAR;
2. To make clear that the UAR did not need to rely fully on Communist Bloc assistance;
3. To develop a US position that would permit timely exploitation of Soviet errors and periodic tensions in UAR-USSR relations.[1]

On 27 May 1961 the administration concluded a PL480 supplemental agreement with the UAR, covering additional shipments of 200,000 tons of wheat and flour, and a request from the UAR for even more such assistance for fiscal year 1962 was submitted to the administration. The Under-Secretary of State for Political Affairs, George McGhee, concurred with the conclusion reached by the NEA about forcing the pace.

In late September 1961, a new anti-Nasser regime came to power in Syria, backed by conservatives as well as army officers. It promptly departed from the UAR. The US pointedly tried not to worsen Nasser's embarrassment, even warning its traditional friends in the region to contain their enthusiasm over their arch-enemy's discomfiture. Nasser blamed the coup on the jealous kings. The termination of the union with Syria ended Nasser's second bid for hegemony.

On 16 October, Bundy asked the State Department for a policy recommendation on Egypt and Syria. Komer noted, on 3 November: "I am convinced that recent events may present us with the best opportunity since 1954 for a limited marriage of convenience with the guy who I think is still, and will remain, the Mister Big of the Arab world."[2] Because the superpowers were so ready to balance against each other, states could reap ample rewards by threatening to shift their allegiances. Here, the absence of significant superpower collaboration in Middle East diplomacy reinforced the tendency for each superpower to act primarily to limit possible gains by the other. On 1 December, Mustafa Kamel, the Egyptian ambassador, told Phillips Talbot, Assistant Secretary of State for NEA, that he had received orders from Nasser himself to convey that the UAR would be happy to rely on the US for its

---
1. Ibid.
2. JFKL, NSF, Meeting and Memoranda Series, Staff Memoranda, Robert W. Komer (11/61-12/61), 3 November 1961.

economic development. With the food aid package tied to a six-month renewal, the Egyptians were left under the impression that they were on probation until the next tranche of aid had been approved. On 8 December, Komer proposed that a long-term food aid package should be offered to Egypt. "The time may be ripe for a more positive initiative," he wrote, emphasizing nevertheless that too many issues remained between the two sides for them to have anything other than what he had described as a "limited marriage of convenience". His rationale for the new initiative was that it would give Nasser "the impression we're opening a new chapter, using as bait the very substantial aid we're probably going to give him anyway".[1]

But while the State Department, the NSC and the Egyptian embassy were pushing for a major shift in policy toward Nasser, Kennedy remained cautious. Speaking to Carl Kaysen, an NSC staff member, he remarked that "it seemed too much aid was being given to the UAR".[2] His reservations were strengthened when France tried to block aid to Egypt from the International Monetary Fund (IMF), and after King Saud had commented, during a meeting with Kennedy in Washington on 13 February 1962, that recent nationalization and sequestration measures had revealed Nasser as "a Communist who presents a real danger to the Arab World".[3]

On 27 March the Syrian army installed a new government in place of the conservatives who had taken the country out of the UAR. The following day the Kennedy administration's intelligence agencies prepared a new NIE assessing Nasser's prospects. The document argued that he would continue to scowl at the Arab conservatives, but would have to keep his connections to both superpowers significantly less hostile because of his heavy dependence on the US for food and on the Soviets for military and development aid.[4]

The Egyptian leader now initiated a new campaign against conservative forces in the Arab world. The rationale for this policy was straightforward.

---

1. JFKL, NSF, UAR, 11/61-12/61, Memo from Komer to Bundy and its attachment Memorandum for the President "A Shift in Policy Toward Nasser", 8 December 1961.
2. JFKL, NSC, Meetings and Memoranda, Staff Memoranda, Robert W. Komer, Memorandum from Komer to Kennedy "Aid to the UAR", 15 February 1962.
3. United States Department of State Records, Central Files, (786A. 11/2–1362), Memorandum of Conversation between King Saud and President Kennedy, 13 February 1962.
4. FRUS, 1961–3, vol. 17, Special National Intelligence Estimate (SNIE) 36.1-62, 28 March 1962, pp. 549–50.

Nasser argued that true Arab unity could be achieved only if all Arab states had compatible political systems. The end result was once again to divide the Middle East into two distinct groups, with inevitable effects on relations between regional states and the superpowers as well.[1] Nasser's efforts created more enemies than allies, threatening his potential partners – his various attempts to implement an Arab union quickly became a struggle for hegemony.

The Saudis immediately saw Nasser's growing influence and aggressive tactics as a source of considerable danger. With Egypt presenting an ever more imminent threat, and with the US offering increased support for the Kingdom, realignment against Nasser was in order. A common thread running through US foreign policy had consistently been not to permit Third World nationalism to frustrate the wishes of the dominant Western power. On this basis, the administration carried on with its step-by-step approach of rewarding Egypt with economic cooperation for improved behaviour. Meanwhile, Saudi Arabia did its best to cool any new US enthusiasm for Nasser. A State Department memo in June 1962 warned the White House: "The Saudis now appear to feel our aid to the UAR implies a lessening of US concern for Saudi Arabia."[2]

US policy toward Nasser was designed to turn him inward and to increase US leverage over him so that the US could encourage policies that were less antagonistic to US interests and those of its friends. Certainly, the administration believed that withholding aid from the UAR would afford the Soviets renewed opportunities for exploitation in the Middle East, and would force the UAR to take more extreme positions internally and externally to the detriment of US interests and those of other states in the area.

Saudi Arabia defined its position during a meeting on 27 September 1962 between US Secretary of State Dean Rusk and Faisal, who stated that no Arab would wish to deny any Arab people the kind of support the UAR was receiving from the US. However, since the UAR had evidently chosen to attack Saudi Arabia with the sole aim of destroying it, given current conditions US aid would damage Saudi interests. Faisal would have preferred the US to conduct normal relations with the UAR, economic aid included, provided

---

1. Ali Abdel Rahman Rahmy, *The Egyptian Policy in the Arab World: The Intervention in Yemen, 1962–1967: A Case Study* (Washington, DC: University Press of America, 1983), pp. 33–5.
2. United States Department of State Records, Central Files, (611.86A/6-462), Memorandum from the Dept. of State Executive, William Brubeck, to Bundy, 4 June 1962.

that US influence could be used to deter the UAR from its intransigent and subversive policy towards other Arab countries.

On 21 June 1962 Nasser wrote Kennedy the warmest letter of their entire correspondence. He told the president that when he was asked at press conferences or by US diplomats what he wanted from the US, he always replied: "… All we seek and desire is understanding … of course, outside forces would continue to cause tensions."[1] While Nasser's letter served as a simple note of thanks for the aid given, its unprecedented warmth and subtext delighted the State Department. The NSC was equally enthusiastic: "We've made a score on relations with the key guy in the Arab world," Komer wrote to Bundy.[2] But Nasser would prove incapable of taking full advantage of Kennedy's overture. The collapse of the union with Syria did not force him to focus on the home front, but rather drove him to increased militancy in his foreign policy.

The Yemen War

On 26 September 1962, Imam Muhammad al-Badr of Yemen was overthrown by a military coup after the death of his father, Imam Ahmad. The coup was led by Colonel 'Abdallah al-Sallal and a group of fellow officers; all were Nasser's men. Nasser had not tried to conceal his desire to bring about change, and a call for revolution had been broadcast from Cairo the previous winter, so angering Imam Ahmad that the Yemeni ruler had expelled the Egyptian ambassador. Within days of the coup, Egyptian paratroopers landed in Yemen to spearhead a combined expeditionary force. De Gaury claims that Egyptian troops arrived in the Red Sea before the coup on 24 September, reaching Sana'a immediately after it.[3] Certainly, the speed and scope of the Egyptian intervention clearly indicated Nasser's prior knowledge of and preparation for the coup.

A note from Roger Hilsman at the State Department's Intelligence and Research bureau (INR) to the Acting Secretary on 27 September, titled "Turmoil in Prospect in the Yemen", noted that UAR involvement in Yemen

---

1. JFKL, Nasser Correspondence, NSF, Box 169, UAR, Nasser letter to Kennedy, 21 June 1961.
2. JFKL, White House Memoranda, NSF, Komer papers, UAR 1961-62, Komer memo to Bundy, 10 July 1962.
3. Gerald de Gaury, *Faisal: King of Saudi Arabia* (London: The Trinity Press, 1966), p. 110; Fathi Al-Deeb, *'Abd al-Nasser wa harakat al-teharere al-yemeni* (Cairo: Dar Al-Mustaqbal al-'Arabi, 1990), pp. 82–90.

was suspected and that the UAR strongly supported the new regime; it also predicted: "If the UAR is clearly seen to be directing affairs in the Yemen, conservatives' internal resistance to the new regime will increase. The UK, Saudi Arabia, and the [Soviet] Bloc will be disposed to oppose UAR control over the Yemen."[1] The expectation that the Soviet Bloc would also oppose UAR control was perhaps surprising. A telegram from the State Department on 27 September stated: "Reports now clearly indicate revolutionaries working with UAR."[2]

The nationalist officers who carried out the coup were ideologically formed by Arab nationalism, and Egyptian officers brought to Yemen had contributed to politicizing the officer corps. Muhammad 'Abdul Wahhad, the Egyptian *chargé d'affaires* in Sana'a, was in contact with al-Sallal and the officer group and had, in fact, warned al-Badr on 25 September that al-Sallal and fifteen other officers were preparing a revolution. According to Schmidt, 'Abdul Wahhad aimed to cover himself and his government if the coup failed, to galvanize the plotters into action and to drive the other plotters and al-Sallal together into a single conspiratorial effort. He also wanted to enable al-Sallal to convince Imam al-Badr that Yemen's small force should be concentrated around Sana'a so as to be ready to cope with any challenge.[3]

When the revolutionaries in Sana'a declared the Yemen Arab Republic (YAR) – the first republic in the Arabian Peninsula – they announced that it believed in Arab reunification and Arab nationalism.[4] Faisal was in the US at

---

1. JFKL, NSF, Countries Series, Yemen, 8/61-9/62.
2. United States Department of State Records, Central Files (786H. 00/9-6, 2762), Circular telegram from the State Dept. to Certain Posts, 27 September 1962.
3. Dana Adams Schmidt, *Yemen: The Unknown War* (New York: Holt, Rinehart and Winston, 1968), pp. 23–5. As the Imam's Chief of Staff and principal confidant, Sallal had for a long time held a special place in Imam Al-Badr's life, and the Imam, unable to believe any charges against him, allowed himself to accept Sallal's denial. When al-Sallal had been accused of plotting against the Imamate at the time of Imam Ahmed, Al-Badr had insisted on his innocence and loyalty. Sallal, when confronted, again reassured the Imam: "you know my loyalty to you." Concerning the other plotters, he said that these charges were probably also baseless, and that he would disperse them quietly to distant posts to eliminate any possibility of trouble. Years later, the Imam justified his lack of action by saying, "My father killed many men, I did not want to be like him, I did not want to start my reign with bloodshed. I thought that if I gave the people what they wanted they would believe in me."
4. Ahmed Noman and Kassim Al Madhagi, *Yemen and the U.S.: A Study of a Small*

the time, and used his visit to try to enlist Kennedy to the Kingdom's defence. Over a working luncheon with the president on 5 October, he warned Kennedy that the UAR and the Soviet Union were supporting the new Yemeni regime, and that it would be wise to go slow over recognition, noting: "Saudi Arabia's concern is that, unless the situation in Yemen is reversed, fertile ground for the entrenchment and spread of Communism and its attendant subversive activities will be provided in the area."[1] Linking US assistance to Egypt to the Yemen crisis, Faisal warned that it would wind up being used to undermine Nasser's neighbours, especially Saudi Arabia. After lunch, Kennedy offered such reassurances as moving a few US Navy destroyers into Saudi ports as a display of friendship, and expediting the pending sale of F-5A fighters. In preparation for this meeting, Faisal's special aide Rashad Fir'wan had underlined Saudi Arabia's concern over the situation in Yemen to Phillips Talbot on 3 October, noting that the coup in Yemen "was obviously the result of intrigues and planning indulged in by the UAR and the communists".[2]

A memorandum on the Yemen situation dated 8 October was sent from the CIA's Office of National Estimates to John McCone, the CIA director, and stressed that the establishment of a republican, pro-Nasser regime in Yemen would significantly increase the pressures against Saudi Arabia, Jordan and Britain's position in Aden. It would, it added, also not be particularly conducive to the spread of communist influence in the area; nor would it necessarily be detrimental to US interests. The State Department was also convinced that the new Yemeni regime was definitely in control, and that the UAR was committed to keeping it there.

Saudi Arabia was faced with a threefold threat as a result of the coup and the Egyptian intervention. First, the Saudi government was presented with a persistent security threat that could encourage dissidents in Saudi Arabia to follow the Yemeni example. Second, there were signs that the events in Yemen were causing problems in the armed forces, and when several Saudi

---

Power and Super-State Relationship, 1962–1994 (London: Tauris Academic Studies, 1996), pp. 28–9.
1. JFKL, NSF, Box 443, Komer Papers, Saudi Arabia, Faysal Visit 10/4/62-10/8/62, (Folder 1 of 3), Memorandum of Conversation between Crown Prince Faysal and the President, 5 October 1962.
2. JFKL, NSF, Box 443, Komer Papers, Saudi Arabia, Faysal Visit 10/4/62-10/8/62, (Folder 1 of 3), Memorandum of Conversation between Talbot and Dr. Fir'awn, 3 October 1962.

pilots defected with their planes and cargoes to the Egyptian side, the regime's mistrust of them intensified. Third, there was the possibility of an Egyptian-initiated invasion of the country.[1]

Faisal evolved a three-point strategy to deal with these Egyptian-Yemeni threats. First, in order to avoid direct Saudi military intervention at any cost, he adopted a strategy of supporting the loyalists, believing that this would create a situation of unrest in Yemen that would lead to negotiations (whereas direct Saudi intervention would give the Egyptians an excuse to extend the war to Saudi Arabia itself). Second, he decided to drop all pretence of non-alignment and to incur the liability of seeking help from the US and Britain. The third element involved a plan to reinforce the home front. On 6 November 1962, Faisal's impressive ten-point reform and development programme was also announced.[2]

By October 1962, the situation on the ground in Yemen had become complex. The British, assuming that al-Badr was dead, and in order to safeguard their Aden Protectorate, supported Prince Hassan Hamid al-Din, the head of the Yemeni delegation to the UN who had left New York and was commanding royalist troops. Nasser's troops were already in Sana'a and in the western port town of Hodeida, and Yemeni tribes were choosing sides. Faced with the Egyptian presence in Yemen, the Saudi government started massing troops along the Saudi-Yemeni border. The Jordanian government sent technical advisors to help Prince Hassan. All this put the US-Egyptian rapprochement at risk. While Yemen was heading towards civil war, the State Department finally wanted to conclude an expanded, multi-year PL480 aid agreement for Egypt, and the new aid package was signed on 8 October with minimum publicity.

On 10 October, Mohamed Hassanein Heikal, editor of *Al-Ahram* and Nasser's closest confidant, delivered a personal communication from Nasser to US Ambassador John S. Badeau that sought to explain Nasser's intervention. Heikal maintained that the UAR had positive evidence of Saudi meddling in Yemen, and followed this claim with various points that were a direct message from the Egyptian leader: Nasser had no intention of embarrassing the US with the UAR's Yemen policy; the UAR insisted on there being no foreign military intervention; the UAR would not allow the new regime to be

1. Safran, *Saudi Arabia: The Ceaseless Quest for Security*, p. 94
2. Ibid., pp. 95–7.

defeated, and it was hoped that US recognition would soon be forthcoming. Heikal also noted the discontent in a Saudi Arabia considered ripe for revolt. If the royal regime were to be toppled, he advised, the only result would be a prolonged period of chaos that would be against the interests of both the UAR and the US. When Badeau and Anwar Sadat, President of the UAR National Assembly, met the following day, Sadat confirmed that the message had come from Nasser and that US recognition would be a major factor in stabilizing the situation.

Yemen was fast becoming a no-win situation for the US. Although Kennedy found the new progressive regime more appealing than its predecessors, he also shared Saudi fears for its own stability and British concerns for Aden. Thus began a long, frustrating quest for a way out of the Yemen chaos. Badeau was directed to use Heikal as a back channel and to emphasize that the US government concurred with Heikal's approach as it offered an opportunity to work out an accommodation according to which a new Yemeni regime, friendly to the UAR and to the West, would be legitimized. Meanwhile, US, UK, Saudi and Jordanian interests would be safeguarded by the UAR applying pressure and offering inducements to the Yemeni regime to dissuade it from activism in Aden. Notwithstanding the UAR's "Arab Socialism" doctrine and its eagerness to destroy "reactionaries", it would be required to choose between the vast benefits of economic "cooperation" with the West and direct confrontation with vital US-UK interests in Saudi Arabia and Aden.[1]

In its plan for restoring order in Yemen, the US maintained its position that it would recognize the new regime provided the UAR promised not to menace Aden and Saudi Arabia; however, the most immediate question was whether or not to recognize the new regime. On 17 October 1962, the Office in Charge of Arabian Peninsula Affairs at the State Department indicated that there were "overriding factors" militating against early action. It saw no advantage in permitting the UAR, whose complicity in planning the Yemen revolt was now apparent on the basis of recent intelligence, to undertake similar adventures elsewhere in the Arabian Peninsula, and recognized that such action would be viewed as a concession to Nasser and as an indication of a lessening of US concern for "our friend's interests in the area".[2]

---

1. United States Department of State Records, Central Files, (786H. 00/10-1062), State Dept. to US Embassy, Cairo, 13 October 1962.
2. Ibid., (786H. 02/10-1762), Paper by the Office in Charge of Arabian Peninsula Affairs, State Department's division of NEA, Talcott Seelye, 17 October 1962. The

On 18 October Komer sent Kennedy a memorandum outlining the reasons why the new Yemeni regime was not yet recognized:

1. The YAR regime was stronger than the royalists, but by no means fully in control;
2. In order to promote compromise with Nasser, the US needed to keep recognition as a major lever;
3. The UK, Jordan and Saudi Arabia were opposed to it;
4. Only twenty countries had so far recognized the YAR;
5. Recognition would be "inconsistent with our non-intervention posture at this point".

Komer concluded: "We're not under great pressure yet. Instead, let's hold out as one means of getting UAR and YAR to provide reassurances to Saud, the UK, and Jordan."[1]

Kennedy then sent Faisal a letter on 25 October 1962, pledging full US support "for the maintenance of Saudi Arabia's integrity", and stating that the US had "a deep and abiding interest in the stability and progress of Saudi Arabia".[2] The purpose of the letter was to reassure Faisal of US support, to encourage his path of modernization and reform and to serve as non-provocative notice to Cairo of the US commitment to Saudi Arabia.[3] These assurances were designed to protect US interests in Saudi Arabia; however, there was a certain tendency within the Saudi government to overestimate US

---

paper prepared by the Office, entitled "United States Position on Recognition of Yemen Arab Republic", expressed hopes that the US would be in a position to extend recognition to the new regime, following (a) a démarche being made to Nasser to limit his involvement in Yemen and to desist from his subversion against Saudi Arabia and Jordan; (b) face-saving moves to enable Saudi Arabia and Jordan to withdraw gracefully from their support of royalist forces; and (c) satisfactory reassurances to Saudi Arabia and Jordan of "our intention to stand by them and to circumscribe Nasser's influences in the Arabian Peninsula".

1. JFKL, NSF, Meeting and Memoranda Series, Staff Memoranda, Komer papers, Komer memo to Kennedy, 18 October 1962.
2. United States Department of State Records, Central Files (786A. 11/10-2562), State Dept. to US Embassy, Jeddah, 2 November 1962.
3. Ibid. (786A. 11/11-162), Memorandum from William Brubeck, State Dept., Executive Sec. to Bundy, 1 November 1962.

commitment. According to a US document, which clearly explains the US position: "Our statements have been vaguely worded ... Our assurances to the Saudis have never been submitted for Congressional consideration."[1]

On 3 November the Saudi government issued a communiqué expressing concern about UAR intervention in the internal affairs of Yemen and noting that several Saudi localities had been attacked the previous day by combat aircraft supplied by the UAR to the Yemeni insurrectionists. On the evening of 3 November, Omar Saqqaf, Minister of State for Foreign Affairs, called the attacks "savage acts against Saudi Arabia" and announced that his country held the UAR responsible for such aggressive actions and reserved the right of response. Saqqaf also asked the US ambassador, Parker T. Hart, where the US stood concerning this aggression. On 4 November Saudi Defence Minister Prince Sultan Bin 'Abdul 'Aziz summoned Colonel W. W. Wilson, Commander of the Second Air Division's Dhahran contingent and Chief of the US Military Training Mission, to inform him that the Saudi government would soon formally request US assistance in establishing an active air defence system for the maintenance of internal security.

Prince Sultan summoned Wilson again on 7 November and asked him to convey a request for a US show of force in Saudi Arabia. The Saudi government did not want US forces to participate in the defence of Saudi Arabia, but the appearance of US air and naval forces would provide convincing evidence to the Saudi people and others of the depth of US interest in and support for Saudi Arabia. On 15 November US aircraft flew sorties over major Saudi cities in a demonstration of support, but it became clear to the Saudi government that such support did not extend to Saudi territories close to the Yemeni border, where Egyptian attacks continued with impunity. In fact, it was becoming clear that US protection extended only to the oil facilities.

On 16 November Kennedy sent a letter to the key regional players – the new Yemeni regime, the Jordanians, the Egyptians, and the Saudis – spelling out his peace plan, which proposed the following:

1. Termination of external support to royalists;
2. Phased withdrawal of UAR forces from Yemen;

---

1. Lyndon Johnson Library (LJL), National Security File (NSF), Country Files, Saudi Arabia, Faisal Visit Briefing Book 6/21 – 27/66, Background Paper Prepared in the Dep. of State, 7 June 1966.

3. Withdrawal of Saudi-Jordanian forces from the vicinity of the Yemen border;
4. A public statement by the YAR reaffirming its intention to honour international obligations and seek normalization of relations with neighbouring states;
5. US recognition of the UAR in return for the above conditions.[1]

At a meeting on 19 November, an astonished Faisal asked Ambassador Hart how the US could propose so one-sided a programme, in effect liquidating the royalists. He remarked to Hart: "This thing is actually what Nasser wants." Faisal was adamant that his government would never agree to US recognition of the revolutionaries until there had been a clear and comprehensive withdrawal of all external forces from Yemen, and objected bitterly to US recognition in advance of the total withdrawal of UAR troops: "I plead with you not to trust Nasser and not to accord your recognition before they have withdrawn all their forces."[2]

But despite the Saudi protest, the US did not change its policy. The rationale behind its Yemen strategy held that there were doubts about the royalists' ability to conquer the principal centres, and that the republican regime and the heavily committed UAR would both be prepared to seek Soviet assistance if necessary. The stability of Saudi Arabia and Jordan had also been affected. Obtaining public commitments from the UAR and the republican regime would give the US leverage over both parties while achieving a measure of stability that could act as the prelude for a total withdrawal of UAR forces. Stability in Saudi Arabia would thereby be safeguarded, and serious pressure on the British base at Aden lessened; at the same time, the situation in Yemen would be normalized, enhancing regional stability. Furthermore, the US would increase its support for Saudi Arabia to avoid any harmful effects on the Kingdom.

Several weeks of wrangling now ensued over the content of the statements from Nasser and al-Sallal. On 18 December Yemen released its communiqué, and Egypt followed suit on 19 December – the day the State Department

---

1. United States Department of State Records, Central Files (786H. 00/11-1062), State Dept. to US Embassy, Jeddah, 10 November 1962.
2. Ibid., Central Files, (786H. 00/11-2062), Telegram from US Embassy, Jeddah, to State Dept., 19 November 1962.

announced US recognition of the new republic in Yemen. According to Ambassador Badeau, the decision to extend recognition despite Saudi Arabia's vehement opposition was due to expectations of a rapid republican victory, and concern that any delay might provide the Soviets with another regional ally.[1]

To Faisal, Washington's recognition of the new regime in Yemen seemed to reflect a disturbing tilt toward Nasser and acceptance of an outcome that Faisal had sought desperately to avoid. He continued to oppose any recognition of the new regime in Yemen and demanded a supervised consultation of the Yemeni people once all foreign intervention had ceased.

At the very end of 1962, a fighter from the UAR attacked a supposed royalist supply site at Najran, just over the Saudi side of the Saudi-Yemeni border. Nasser's excuse was that Najran was being used to stockpile arms for the royalists. Ambassador Badeau was instructed to register the Kennedy administration's strongest protest to date by stating to the highest available UAR authority that the US "had repeatedly made clear the importance it attaches to the integrity of Saudi Arabia and that it would consider any attack on that integrity as damaging to direct US interests".[2] Despite the objections of the State Department, the NSC began pushing for a tougher line with Nasser. Komer told Bundy on 2 January 1963: "I'd like to see us threaten him [Nasser] a bit ... but State fears we may just make him sore."[3]

At this point Faisal demanded four courses of action from the US government:

1. Issuing a public declaration of support for the Saudi government;
2. Dispatching US Air Force planes to Saudi Arabia;
3. Providing the Saudi government with necessary military equipment;
4. Considering taking the matter back to the UN Security Council.[4]

---

1. John S. Badeau, *The American Approach to the Arab World* (New York: Harper & Row, 1968), pp. 132–48.
2. United States Department of State Records, State Dept., US Embassy, Cairo, 31 December 1962.
3. JFKL, NSF, Box 169, UAR, Memorandum from Komer to Bundy, 2 January 1963.
4. United States Department of State Records, Central Files, (686A.86B/12-3162),

The US emphasized its determination to do everything possible to check the spread of the conflict, and urged Faisal not to be drawn into action that would expand the hostilities. As for Faisal's four requests, it proposed the following: First, if Faisal would release the text of Kennedy's 25 October letter for publication, the US would issue a public announcement in Washington supporting Saudi Arabia's integrity along the lines of that letter. Second, subject to Faisal's approval, the US would announce planned Saudi-US military exercises in early 1963. Third, the US would ship certain arms and process the rest of the previously submitted order as swiftly as possible; fourth, the US believed that at that juncture it was inadvisable to take the matter to the Security Council, and that the best present course was through US government representatives in Cairo.

Ambassador Hart was instructed to inform Faisal that the US had "no intention of being drawn into hostilities between Saudi Arabia and the UAR", and to point out that it could not serve as a shield protecting Saudi Arabia while the Saudi government stoked "the fires of war" by supplying weapons and ammunition to royalists.[1]

As a result of Saudi Arabia's stepping up supplies to the royalist forces and a worsening of the YAR/UAR military situation, an Egyptian aircraft again bombed Najran three times on 7 January 1963. At a meeting with Egyptian Foreign Minister Mahmoud Fawzi, Badeau emphasized the need for constructive UAR action to forestall a worsening of US-UAR relations. The US government considered that the UAR was making reciprocal action more difficult by the way it issued propaganda as well as a stream of insults, carried warfare across Saudi Arabia's border, violated its pledges to the US and continued its destructive activities in the Middle East. Badeau was therefore ordered, on 19 January 1963, to deliver a steely toned letter from President Kennedy warning that misunderstanding over the Yemen affair "may prejudice our growing rapport."[2] It was hoped that this letter would help dispel suspicion within the UAR while directing it toward courses of action the US deemed desirable.

Memorandum of Conversation between Khayyal and Talbot, 31 December 1962.

1. Ibid., (786A. 5486B/12-1362), State Dept. to US Embassy, Jeddah, 31 December 1962.
2. Ibid., Central Files (786H. 02/1-1963), State Dept. to US Embassy, Cairo, 19 January 1963.

Meanwhile, on 11 January 1963, the UK informed the US that it had decided to defer its decision on recognition of the YAR because of concerns over Aden, and announced on 16 January that it was resuming diplomatic relations with Saudi Arabia. Once relations were restored, the UK cooperated with Faisal in every possible way, supporting the royalists and Saudi defence plans.[1]

It was clear in February that Nasser was more encouraged by US recognition of the YAR than he was discouraged by Kennedy's January reprimand. He still had around 40,000 troops in Yemen. On 18 February 5,000 men set off in what became known as the "Ramadan Offensive". The Egyptians swept eastward into the desert, then back westward into the royalist-held mountains, recapturing the towns of Marib and Harib and then advancing some distance north into the mountains. On 23 February, Faisal sent a letter to Kennedy in which he maintained that recent US demands for Saudi Arabia to cease supplying the Yemeni royalists contradicted the president's October 1962 assurances of unconditional US assistance to the Kingdom to help maintain its security, stability and progress. Faisal noted that the US position had come as a huge shock to him, and vowed that Saudi Arabia would continue to take measures to ensure its safety and security. After the Egyptian successes, the Saudi government increased its aid to the royalists, particularly in terms of supplying funds to buy tribal loyalties.[2]

Simultaneously, Nasser's position in the Arab world was enhanced by events in Iraq and Syria. Qasim's regime was toppled by pro-Nasser elements of the Ba'th Party on 8 February 1963, followed by the overthrow of the Syrian regime on 8 March. Both governments pledged to work for Arab unity with Nasser. The Egyptian leader exploited the situation to offset his earlier defeat in Syria and to bolster his recent success in the Yemen. Saudi Arabia was now surrounded by "liberated states".

During a US presidential meeting dealing with Yemen on 25 February 1963, Talbot explained that Faisal was unhappy about the Iraqi coup, and that the Egyptians were running a major offensive, claiming they would win in three weeks. However, although the Egyptians had resumed bombings and sent in paratroopers, Talbot saw no evidence that they would actually invade Saudi Arabia. When Kennedy queried why Faisal seemed so determined to fight on in Yemen, Talbot replied: "Faisal took the position of the royalists as part

---

1. Safran, *Saudi Arabia*, p. 97.
2. Edgar O'Ballance, *The War in Yemen* (Hamden, CN.: Archon Books, 1971), pp. 108–9.

of the defense of Saudi Arabia ... [and] we couldn't ask him to turn it off."[1] Realizing that Faisal would not stop aiding the royalists, Kennedy accepted the State Department's suggestion that former US ambassador to India Ellsworth Bunker be sent to ask Faisal to suspend aid to the royalists in exchange for the US air protection Saudi Arabia had requested on 31 December 1962.[2]

Bunker was to offer US assistance in expediting the build-up of Saudi Arabia's own air defence capabilities, at Saudi expense. He would also try to convince Faisal to use the visit of a UN mediator as a means of promoting simultaneous UAR and Saudi disengagement with honour, and inform Faisal that if he accepted the offer, the US would press Nasser to withdraw an initial contingent from Yemen simultaneously with Saudi suspension of aid. Bunker would also carry a message from the president to Faisal, expressing Kennedy's deep concern over the recent course of events. "What is involved here is a difference over means, not objectives," Kennedy's letter stated.[3]

Badeau met Nasser on 4 March 1963 to deliver Kennedy's message that "... there is real risk that events might lead to a collision involving the interests of our two countries."[4] Badeau also emphasized US concern over UAR attacks on Saudi Arabia and the detrimental implications of continued UAR military

---

1. JFKL, NSF, Yemen, Memorandum for the Record: Presidential Meeting on Yemen, 25 February 1963.
2. United States Department of State Records, Central Files, (686A. 86B/12-3162), Memorandum of Conversation between Talbot and Saudi Ambassador, Washington, Ibrahim Khayyal, 31 December 1962. Kennedy decided to send Bunker to reassure Faisal of US interest in Saudi Arabia, to convince him of the importance of disengaging from Yemen, and to explain how the US thought this could be done without loss of face. Bunker was authorized to tell Faisal that the US would consider the temporary stationing of a token air defence squadron with associated ground support in Western Saudi Arabia to deter UAR air operations. This would be wholly contingent on a firm Saudi undertaking simultaneously to suspend aid to the royalists and not to use Saudi territory for air operations against the YAR/UAR. The offer would be provisional so that the US would have a chance to consider it further before final agreement, and would be for a two-month period only, on the understanding that the US would be prepared to keep the squadron there longer if the situation required. If Saudi Arabia resumed aid to the royalists without concurrence, the squadron would be withdrawn.
3. JFKL, NSF, Countries Files, Yemen, Bunker/Bunche Missions. Letter from Kennedy to Faisal, 1 March 1963.
4. United States Department of State Records, Central Files, (POL 26 YEMEN), State to US Embassy, Cairo, 2 March 1963.

involvement in Yemen for the disengagement process and for US Congressional support for economic assistance to the UAR.

Bunker then met Faisal at Dammam, Saudi Arabia, on 6, 7 and 8 March, and presented his disengagement programme. His approach centred on US recognition of the dangers confronting Saudi Arabia and the desire of the US to be helpful. However, he pointed out, if American forces were actually sent to Saudi Arabia, the Saudi policy of aid to the royalists would make the US an accomplice in action against the YAR, which it had recognized. Bunker also stated that the US believed it was possible to have simultaneous Egyptian withdrawal and Saudi government suspension of aid to the royalists, and that great pressures could be marshalled thereafter to ensure the completion of Egyptian withdrawal – which would actually be initiated as soon as neutral observers along the northern Yemeni border had verified that supply activities had been suspended. Faisal indicated that he was prepared in principle to accept the suspension of aid, provided he could be assured that UAR forces would indeed leave Yemen.

According to an undated memorandum from Talbot to Secretary of State Rusk, Faisal wished for consideration be given to the stopping of all UAR raids and all other acts of aggression on Saudi territory, and to the cessation of all military action by the UAR in Yemen at the time of agreement on simultaneous disengagement. Pending withdrawal, which would include officers, men and all equipment, UAR forces would return to base from field activities in Yemen. In addition, there was to be a time limit on the withdrawal of foreign forces from Yemen.

On 11 March, Kennedy and several top aides including the recently returned Bunker met to discuss the Yemen crisis. Reporting Faisal's worries that he was being abandoned by the US, Bunker expressed his view that both sides should withdraw and leave the Yemenis to settle their own affairs. His impression, based on Faisal's acceptance of his proposal, was that the job of disengagement could be done. At the end of the discussions, Kennedy remarked: "If we got Faisal turned off, we have got a good line with Nasser." He was anxious for Faisal to suspend aid and suggested that he write again to Faisal or send Bunker.[1]

On 17 March 1963, Bunker delivered a message from Kennedy to Faisal in which the president reflected that events in Iraq and Syria had established

---

1. JFKL, NSF, White House Memoranda, Box 44, Komer Files, Yemen, 1961–64, Memcon: JFK meeting on Yemen, 11 March 1963.

a new atmosphere in the Arab world "which can only give new confidence to your opponents and bring new pressure on your Government". Kennedy urged Faisal to accept Bunker's proposal to arrange a suspension of aid to the royalists "without conditions or reservations", and at the same time requested the UAR to begin its withdrawal "by moving a unit out of Yemen" – reaffirming that this would "permit Saudi Arabia, with our help, to meet the gathering threats to its interests".[1] Faisal replied that he detected in the message an attempt to intimidate him into accepting set conditions. He characterized the US government's estimation of events in and around Saudi Arabia as faulty at best, adding: "I regret to say these reports of trouble within the country can usually be traced to American sources." Bunker assured Faisal that intimidation was not on the president's mind, and explained that Kennedy regarded Faisal's additional points as essentially procedural detail that would fall logically into place after disengagement had begun. He also pointed out that proceeding with disengagement would not only satisfy Faisal's points but allow him to reap substantial advantages at the same time.

According to Bunker, Faisal's private assurance to suspend aid – thereby permitting Nasser to initiate troop drawdown – would enable the US to place the full weight of its influence on the UAR to begin disengagement; to come unequivocally and effectively to the defence of Saudi Arabia by bringing in air units, which would deter further incursion on Saudi soil; and to initiate an expanded air defence training programme. He also emphasized that "the US government has linked itself closely with Faisal's regime in its dedication to internal development and the last thing the President wishes is sullying Faisal's honor."

Faisal again called attention to the US's inactivity in the face of the UAR attacks, and emphasized the paramount importance of "freedom and dignity". He said that "he would not continue [to] rule Saudi Arabia if [the] people do not want him", and asked Bunker to inform the president that he was motivated by honour and conviction. Bunker again repeated: "We want to help you but you must make it possible for us to help." Agreeing that the present situation was fraught with urgency, Faisal reiterated that Nasser wished to crush him. Writing from Lebanon to the State Department, Bunker concluded that if the US could secure a definite commitment from Nasser, he believed one or

---

1. United States Department of State Records, Central Files, (POL 7 US/BUNKER), State to US Embassy, Jeddah, 14 March 1963.

two talks with Faisal would secure the latter's agreement to suspend aid on the basis of the US proposal; but he claimed that "Arab pride and Faisal's own appraisal of the situation had not quite brought him to point."[1]

On 1 April 1963, Nasser met Bunker, who was carrying a message from Kennedy pointing out the administration's even-handed concern for the integrity of both Saudi Arabia and the YAR, as well as for Aden's security and Egypt's position. Bunker also stated the president's hope that Nasser would explore "avenues for containing the Yemen conflict and bringing it to early close".[2] He had a second meeting on 2 April with Nasser and Ali Sabri, UAR Deputy Prime Minister and Minister for Presidential Affairs, and at their final meeting on 3 April they had further discussion on the disengagement proposal. In light of these meetings, Bunker revised the proposal to ensure Nasser's acceptance; at Bunker's urging, Nasser agreed, as a token of goodwill, to withdraw one to two companies simultaneously with the Saudi government's suspension of aid.[3]

Bunker met Faisal again on 5, 6 and 9 April 1963 to discuss the revised proposal. Faisal called attention to the concessions he had already made, and said he had done so from a desire to be reasonable and because of his appreciation of the position of "our friends the Americans and their noble objective". Adding minor changes to the proposal, Faisal commented that as a gesture of confidence in the US president, he was prepared to acquiesce to the fullest extent in the proposal as presented and amended. With Bunker's assurances, Faisal stated: "This country's rulers have demonstrated their nobility of purpose by deeds rather than words."[4]

On 10 April Nasser and Faisal finally agreed to pull their forces out of

---

1. Ibid. (POL 26 YEMEN), US Embassy, Lebanon, to State, 19 March 1963.
2. Ibid. (POL 7 US/Bunker), State to US Embassy, Cairo, 18 March 1963.
3. Ibid., (POL 16 YEMEN), US Embassy, Cairo, 3 April 1963. The revised proposal included: 1) suspension by the Saudi government of its support to the royalists on a date to be determined; 2) prevention by the Saudi government of efforts by the Imam's adherents to continue the struggle from Saudi territory; 3) cessation of UAR attacks on Saudi territory; 4) establishment of a demilitarized zone extending for 20 kilometres on either side of the Saudi Arabian-Yemeni border; 5) within 15 days of Saudi suspension of aid to the royalists, UAR was to begin withdrawal of its troops; 6) stationing of impartial observers on both sides of the border; 7) cooperation of all with UN or other mutually acceptable mediators in reaching agreement on the process and verification of disengagement; and 8) Sallal to treat his neighbours responsibly.
4. Ibid., (POL 27 YEMEN), US Embassy, Jeddah, to State, 7 April 1963.

Yemen simultaneously and to make room for a UN-supervised demilitarized zone of 20 kilometres on each side of the Saudi-Yemeni border. On 12 April 1963, Bunker met with U Thant, the UN Secretary General, and urged the UN to proceed rapidly in setting up for verification of the disengagement. Thant agreed to move quickly once he had al-Sallal's concurrence, but was encouraged by Bunker not to seek Yemen's formal adherence to the agreement because Saudi Arabia would object – Yemen could acquiesce verbally. Thant duly reported to the Security Council on 29 April that Saudi Arabia, the UAR and Yemen had confirmed their acceptance of the disengagement agreement.

Egypt's acceptance of the plan was based on a misreading of the situation in Yemen. The success of the Ramadan Offensive had deluded Cairo into thinking that the YAR's position was secure.[1] Saudi Arabia's acceptance was based on the belief that if the Egyptians complied, the major threat to Saudi security would have been removed. Even if the Egyptians were not to be trusted, the US had made Saudi Arabia's acceptance a condition for further aid in the Saudi defence build-up. However, Soviet stalling tactics at the UN prevented the positioning of UN observers as well as the formal commencement of disengagement, and therefore also the sending of a US Air Force squadron to Saudi Arabia.

Meanwhile, the UAR resumed air attacks on 8 June against towns that were well within Saudi Arabia. Faisal pleaded with the US that the situation had become intolerable, and that he could no longer depend on promises made. The NSC forwarded Faisal's message to Kennedy with a recommendation that the US should continue to withhold dispatch of the flight squadron until UN observers were on the ground in Yemen. On 9 June Hart delivered a message from Kennedy to Faisal blaming the Soviets: "Soviet stalling is behind the last-minute delay." Hart assured Faisal that the president was clear: "We do not back out on our promises, and our squadron is ready." He further stated that the US had made strong representation to the UAR about its raids into Saudi territory. Faisal expressed great disappointment that the US had not implemented its pledge to send the squadron.[2]

The Pentagon remained unenthusiastic about this plan, warning the State Department that while the squadron might deter the UAR from carrying out air operations over Saudi Arabia, it lacked the military capability to provide

---

1. Ahmad Yusif Ahmad, *Al-Dur al-masri fi al-yaman* (Cairo: Al-Hay'a al-Masriyya al-Amma li al-Kitab, 1981), pp. 238–9.
2. United States Department of State Records, Central Files, (POL 27 SAUD-UAR), US Embassy, Jeddah, to State, 10 June 1963.

an adequate air defence of Saudi Arabia. However, both Rusk and Komer urged the president to send the squadron in an attempt both to deter Nasser and to calm Faisal. Rusk told Kennedy that, in his view, unless the squadron was moved to Saudi Arabia there was a real danger that Saudi-US relations, already seriously deteriorating, would "reach a dangerous low point".[1] On 13 June the president, using the code phrase "Hard Surface", approved the deployment of an air unit to Saudi Arabia consisting of eight F-100 tactical fighter planes and one transport-type command support aircraft. The State Department instructed the US embassy to remind the Saudi government that sending the air unit was predicated on the complete cessation of all forms of Saudi assistance to the Yemeni royalists.

On 14 June, Saqqaf summoned Ambassador Hart to convey Faisal's demand that the US publicly denounce a statement made by Congressman Emanuel Celler, Chairman of the House Judiciary Committee, that "Jews were no[t] included in US elements in Saudi Arabia"[2] and stressed Faisal's decision not to let any US serviceman enter the Kingdom until he had received a US response to this demand. Acting under detailed State Department instructions, Hart tried to persuade Faisal to withdraw the ultimatum; but when he failed to resolve the matter, the State Department proposed that Saudi Arabia should retain its visa policy respecting persons of Jewish faith. Hart negotiated the content of the statement with Saqqaf, and Faisal's approval was finally obtained on 27 June. On 29 June, in conjunction with a proposal to alleviate Faisal's concerns through an announcement that the US would be sending a training mission, "Operation Hard Surface", to Saudi Arabia, the State Department's spokesman affirmed that the Kingdom had not altered its visa policy with respect to persons of Jewish faith and retained its sovereign right to screen applicants for visas on the basis of its own policies. In response to a question, the spokesman said: "As regards US air units which have undertaken or will undertake joint training exercises with Saudi forces no problem has arisen with respect to their entry into Saudi Arabia on a transient basis."[3]

Faisal's fears of communist penetration in Yemen were becoming a reality. An assessment of Soviet Bloc activity in Yemen by Brigadier General Robert Glass, Acting Chief of Staff of the US Defense Intelligence Agency (DIA), was

---

1. Ibid., (POL 27-5 US), Memorandum from Rusk to Kennedy, 12 June 1963.
2. *New York Times*, 10 June 1963.
3. United States Department of State Records, (DEF 19-2 SAUD-US), Circular Telegram, 29 June 1963.

presented on 21 June 1963 to William P. Bundy, Deputy Assistant Secretary of Defense for International Affairs, and provided interesting details about Soviet technical and infrastructural projects. Another estimate of Soviet involvement in Yemen, prepared by the CIA's Office of National Estimates on 24 July 1963, concluded that in the absence of effective competition the Soviets had established an imposing presence in that country: "Unless they make serious blunders in their relations with the Yemenis, the Soviets stand to have a favorable image and a friendly atmosphere in which to operate for years to come."[1]

In a letter to Kennedy on 2 July 1963, Komer remarked: "Unless we send the fighters promptly, Faysal may again accuse us of breaking promises." He informed the president that the main UN element would arrive in Yemen on 3 July and was scheduled to deploy on 5 July, and indicated his agreement with State/Defense opinion that the US should finally go ahead with the deployment.[2] On 3 July the Joint Chiefs of Staff, on the order of the president, instructed the Commander in Chief of Strike Command and other departments to proceed with deployment to Dhahran but to go no further unless authorized.

1. JFKL, NSF, Countries Series, Yemen, 7/63, "Estimate of Soviet Involvement in Yemen" by the Office of National Estimates of CIA, 24 July 1963. The assessment contained the following information: (a) immediately following the revolution, the Soviet Union assisted Nasser in meeting the military requirements of the new regime and apparently provided some military equipment directly to the YAR; (b) Soviet and Eastern Bloc influence in Yemen was being enhanced by a growing number of instructors and technicians; (c) in late May 1963, at least 500 Soviet personnel began construction of a jet airfield north of Sana'a. It was also reported that construction would begin at Hodeida on a 700-unit housing project and an electricity generating station, plus the completion of an artesian well system. Other economic aid projects were reported to be under construction; (d) the Yemeni revolution had provided a made-to-order opportunity for the Soviet Union to identify itself with a revolutionary cause. The Soviet Union had been willing to supply military and economic assistance even though the activities of local Yemeni communists were strictly curtailed. Yemen had an added strategic significance for the Soviet Union because of its proximity to Aden, the Horn of Africa and the southern entrance of the Red Sea; and (e) from the Egyptian viewpoint, Soviet and UAR interests in Yemen coincided at that moment. Both wished to protect and secure the revolutionary regime and were cooperating toward that end.
2. JFKL, NSF, Countries Series, Saudi Arabia, 7/63-8/63, Memo from Komer to Kennedy, 2 July 1963.

Concurrently, al-Sallal's position had been somewhat eroded; tribal discontent was flaring up; and the UAR, which was engaged in quelling resistance in the northwest and around the city of Sa'ada, was facing the prospect of costly and inconclusive guerrilla operations. Saudi support for the royalists had ceased, a letter from Faisal having been sent to Imam al-Badr informing him of the decision to withdraw Saudi support at the beginning of July 1963.

US Deputy Assistant Secretary of State for Politico-Military Affairs Jeffrey Kitchen sent a memorandum on 5 July 1963 to Ural Alexis Johnson, Deputy Under-Secretary of State for Political Affairs, concerning a variety of reports (mostly from journalists) claiming that the UAR had been using toxic chemical bombs against the royalist forces since late May. Badeau registered strong concern on 6 July with Ali Sabri over these reports and strongly urged "their discontinuance as imperiling disengagement and generating grave fears in US".[1] When he raised the issue with Nasser on 11 July, the Egyptian president claimed that a napalm bomb called "Opal" was being used against crops and some villages, and it was this that had given rise to reported poison gas. Badeau insisted that his report suggested it might be anything from phosphorus to mustard gas, to which Nasser replied that a bomb that had been manufactured in UAR was being used but he did not know the precise chemical content. Badeau urged that gas was "self-defeating" in Yemen and "aroused deep concern in the US government".[2] On 12 July the deputy director of the CIA, Richard Helms, transmitted an intelligence report to McGeorge Bundy revealing that the UAR had used ammunition in Yemen that contained a chemical warfare agent.

Nasser had also told Badeau during their meeting on 11 July that the conditions of disengagement on which the UAR withdrawal was promised had not yet been met. Saudi aid, either official or unofficial, had continued, and al-Badr and his family were still in the Jizan area. Nasser's objective was to bring home a full battalion of troops in August, by which time he hoped northern tribal resistance would have ended. On 12 July 1963, Komer informed Kennedy that the Saudi government had finally turned off aid. Now the problem was to encourage the UAR to start carrying out its end of the bargain. He stressed that "Nasser's promise to start withdrawing troops in August is

---

1. United States Department of State Records, Central Files, (POL 27 SAUD-UAR), US Embassy, Cairo, to State, 6 July 1963.
2. Ibid., (POL 27 UAR-YEMEN), US Embassy, Cairo, to State, 11 July 1963.

good but not good enough", and noted that the State Department believed the cessation of Saudi aid was increasingly strangling the royalists and that war would gradually subside to the level of tribal bickering, which had always characterized the Yemeni scene. "I think we're getting Yemen under control," he told the president.[1]

All these factors led Komer to believe that that the strategic gain from sticking to the new policy towards Nasser was real, as Nasser had listened to the US on Yemen and other issues and had been brought by the US from a pro-Soviet position to one where the Soviets had as much trouble with him as did the US. Other gains were harder to pin down, but probably amounted largely to what Nasser had not done that he could have done.

In a lengthy discussion with Kennedy on 19 July 1963, Ambassador Mustafa Kamel of Egypt stressed that the UAR had agreed to the US disengagement proposal in Yemen, but that Nasser could not be pushed into immediate withdrawal: this would leave Yemen in chaos, he argued, and lead to hard questions from the Egyptian people as to why Nasser had sent 30,000 soldiers to Yemen and why around 5,000 had died. He emphasized that disengagement would occur, but time was needed. Kennedy persisted in saying that an early gesture on disengagement in Yemen was needed.

On 24 July 1963, the State Department tried to arrange direct talks between Saudi Arabia and the UAR in a neutral capital, with the aim of generating further détente between the two countries. It also wished to gain their agreement to a reconstitution of the Yemeni regime that, while preserving the republican form of government, would draw in moderate elements, reduce tribal dissidence and lead to eventual Saudi recognition. On 1 August 1963, Saqqaf conveyed Faisal's reply that if contact were to be established, the UAR must make the first move, and that there could be no contact until the UAR had carried out the Bunker agreement and disengaged from Yemen. On 9 August 1963, the UAR accepted the proposal for quiet talks with Saudi officials.

Nasser eventually started moving a few thousand troops out of Yemen, although many remained. On 13 August 1963, in light of the Egyptian move, Hart conveyed Faisal's agreement in principle for Saudi Arabia to hold discussions with the UAR. However, Faisal's insistence on a prior UAR gesture made it impossible to hold direct talks between the two sides. Nicholas Thacher, NEA Deputy Chief of Mission in Tehran, informed the State Department

---

1. JFKL, NSF, Countries Series, Yemen, 7/63, Komer to Kennedy, 12 July 1963.

on 20 August 1963 that Faisal could not hold talks with the UAR while it continued its propaganda attacks on Saudi Arabia.

Meanwhile, the UN agreement could have led to a major Saudi-royalist split, but the speed with which Egypt's unwillingness to withdraw became apparent made the UN effort singularly short-lived and unsuccessful. General Carl von Horn, Commander of the United Nations Yemen Observation Mission (UNYOM), resigned on 21 August 1963, citing the impossibility of the task and the lack of support he had received.[1]

After Faisal's rejection of the US proposal for informal, unconditional, exploratory talks between the Saudi and Egyptian governments, the US was adamant in telling Faisal that disengagement alone could not resolve the conflict: it was necessary to create a proper atmosphere for the restoration of peace, in which the Yemenis could exercise self-determination. Both parties, it maintained, should therefore bury past grievances and seek a *modus vivendi*, and the proposed talks offered an opening in this direction. However, the Saudi government continued to cite UAR propaganda attacks as their reason for refusing to participate. The US was quite prepared to try to persuade the UAR to moderate its propaganda, but Saudi government practices – such as permitting Yemeni royalists to use Mecca radio to broadcast reported victories over UAR troops and make scurrilous attacks against the UAR – jeopardized any chance of success. Moreover, such practices were inconsistent with the Saudi government's undertaking to suspend support to the royalists, and with earlier affirmations that it was indifferent as to who ruled Yemen so long as Yemenis made the choice freely. When Thacher conveyed this message on 30 August 1963, Faisal replied: "We are glad to have this assurance that American policy is unchanged toward disengagement."[2]

On 20 September 1963, Komer prepared a paper titled "The Next Round in Yemen", in which he acknowledged that disengagement had not worked because the US and Nasser had both miscalculated how long and how much it would take to pull Yemen together. It was easy to seize all the towns, but controlling the mountain tribes was another matter. Saudi gold and arms had kept the tribal pot boiling, and even when UNYOM arrived and Saudi aid was cut back, some assistance was still going in. As Komer remarked

---

1. United Nations, Department of Public Information, *The Blue Helmets: A Review of United Nations Peace-Keeping* (New York: UN, 1985), pp. 188–97.
2. United States Department of State Records, Central Files, (POL 27 YEMEN), US Embassy, Jeddah, to State, 30 August 1963.

speculatively: "Faysal may even be conning us, or at least turning a blind eye."[1] He described Nasser's position as well: "Nasser is trapped in Yemen. It's bleeding him, but he can't afford either the sharp loss of face in letting go or (we hope) the risk of confronting us." The paper suggested that to influence the short-term outcome, the US should continue to press for disengagement and try to keep UNYOM in place as an indispensable buffer. It also needed to press the Saudi government to halt any remaining covert aid, to make the cost to Nasser clear to him if he resumed bombing and to seek some form of compromise in reshuffling the YAR regime.

The paper offered four recommendations for the continuation of disengagement. First, the US needed to make it very clear to Nasser personally that "we've not tried to snooker him" and to impress on him that disengagement was "in his best interest". If he agreed, he should be told he was expected to make a gradual withdrawal with absolutely no bombing raids. If he disagreed, the US had to inform him that it would be "compelled to reassess our policy". Second, the US would have to take a harder line toward the Saudi government about obvious aid leakage. Faisal should be reminded that "if disengagement fails we will withdraw our squadron", leaving him to "slug it out with Nasser". The third recommendation was for the US to actively promote a compromise in reshuffling the YAR regime by bringing in some of the royalist elements. The paper emphasized that Faisal should be told that "we're flatly opposed to restoration of the Imamate, but tell Nasser he can't have it all his way either." Fourth, the US needed to convince Thant to keep UNYOM in existence and, if possible, enlarge it. Thant had to be reminded "that the UN's prestige as well as ours is tied up in this affair".[2]

Officially, the Kennedy administration was determined to stick with the UN agreement. For this agreement to work and for UN observers to return, Faisal would have to "stay out, and Nasser to get out".[3] To initiate the sequence, an explicit linkage between Yemen and continued US aid was finally forged by the administration, and in late September Rusk made it clear to 'Abd al-Moneim Kaissouni, the Egyptian economic minister, that further US aid

---

1. JFKL, NSF, Countries Series, Yemen, 9/63, Paper by Komer, "The Next Round in Yemen", 20 September 1963.
2. Ibid.
3. United States Department of State Records, S/S-NSC Files: Lot 72 D 316, NSAM 262, National Security Action Memo No. 262, "Yemen Disengagement", 10 October 1963.

to Egypt was dependent upon satisfactory performance in Yemen. On 20 October Badeau delivered a message from Kennedy to Nasser blaming him for not living up to his part of the bargain while Saudi aid had almost halted, and adding that Yemen had complicated US efforts to carry forward a policy of friendly collaboration.

The US needed UNYOM to continue beyond the 4 November termination date to preserve the disengagement as well as restrain Faisal from resuming active support for the royalists. These steps, in turn, depended heavily not only on Nasser reaffirming his intention of carrying out withdrawal commitments, but also on an immediate and convincing action by the UAR. The message Badeau had delivered to Nasser on 20 October had indicated that the US government considered that the UAR had failed to match the Saudi government in fulfilling its disengagement responsibilities. In addition, it was impossible to obtain Faisal's support for a continued UNYOM presence without a public and dramatic UAR disengagement before 1 November. Without a formal request from the Saudi government, the Secretary General was unlikely to support any extension of UNYOM.

Badeau urged Nasser to announce and begin major troop withdrawals before that date. Nasser, however, feared that as the Saudi government had only partially fulfilled the disengagement requirements, and that as long as its support for the royalists continued, any major troop withdrawal would trigger an immediate expansion of royalist activities that would necessitate a slow, costly operation to return troops to Yemen. Badeau stressed that the vital question was not who was at fault but how to obtain action and that this, in effect, meant making a gesture that would enable the US to elicit Faisal's support for the continuance of UNYOM. Nasser then confirmed that some troop withdrawals had in fact been made. If that was the case, Badeau said, it was very much in the UAR's interests to make this fact publicly known before 1 November; meanwhile the Secretary General should be directly informed of troop withdrawals to date and plans for further major troop pull-outs.

In line with this strategy, Hart spent three hours on 23 October 1963 arguing with Faisal, who did not want to be blamed for the failure of UNYOM but who also did not want to stop helping the royalists. He promised to weigh the question of the extension of UNYOM's mandate. He realized that "Operation Hard Surface" could be withdrawn if aid to the royalists resumed and that, under certain circumstances, he could not rely on the US for the defence of his country. Consequently he had to address whether the defence of Saudi Arabia could be obtained by other means and from other sources. (Clearly, he had in mind the purchase of planes and the hiring of mercenary pilots.) Hart did indeed warn Faisal that "Hard Surface" could be withdrawn.

On 28 October 1963, Hart was asked by the State Department to tell Faisal that Nasser had informed Thant that, as well as the announced withdrawal of 6,000 troops, he intended to withdraw another 5,000 by the end of the year. He was also to inform Faisal that the Secretary General intended to publish his report shortly, which would probably announce the termination of UNYOM and place primary responsibility on Saudi unwillingness to agree to its continuance. Faisal also had to be told that if he continued to support UNYOM, the president was prepared to leave "Hard Surface" in place until the end of the year. Hart met Faisal again on 30 October 1963, and Faisal agreed to an extension of UNYOM's mandate for two more months, but asked for additional US pressure to obtain a UAR withdrawal. On 9 November 1963, the Joint Chiefs of Staff extended the deployment of "Hard Surface" until 31 December 1963.

At another meeting on 6 November 1963, Talbot and Mustafa Kamel discussed how the deadlock in Yemen could be broken. Talbot urged the UAR to moderate its propaganda, broaden the government in Yemen, expand cooperation with UNYOM, cease rotating UAR units into Yemen, evacuate the demilitarized zone and stop the bombings. On 20 November 1963, the State Department asked Badeau to request immediate action to expedite disengagement from Yemen. In this connection, the US noted that:

1. UAR forces in Yemen remained around 30,000 in number, contrary to Nasser's assurances that they would be reduced to 26,000 by 1 November;
2. Bombing of royalist bases continued;
3. Bombing of Saudi territory had resumed.[1]

Talbot's six recommendation points to Kamel were also noted.

Kennedy was assassinated in Dallas, Texas, on 22 November 1963, and all the overtures he had made were stopped. The new administration of Lyndon

---

1. Ibid., (POL 32-1 SAUD-UAR), US Embassy, Jeddah, to State, 19 November 1963.

B. Johnson estimated that despite Nasser's promise to withdraw 6,000 UAR troops by 1 November, and his suggestion that another 5,000 would depart by 1 January 1964, UAR troop numbers remained – and seemed likely to remain – at about 32,000. The administration therefore informed Faisal that the Bunker agreement had succeeded in preventing a Saudi-Egyptian military confrontation. However, various factors beyond its control had obstructed its undertaking to Faisal to obtain "expeditious" withdrawal of UAR troops during the six-month period of UNYOM's official presence. In view of the foregoing and of Faisal's decision to resume aid to the royalists on 4 January 1964, as conveyed by Faisal's aide Rashad Fir'wan to Talbot on 18 November, the US considered Faisal to be relieved of his commitment to the US. The time had now come to develop a new strategy.

Faisal's decision to resume aid to the royalists had prompted the US to decide to withdraw "Hard Surface" in late December 1963, the better to avoid being placed in an unacceptable position. However, on 9 December 1963, the State Department informed the Saudi government of its decision to leave "Hard Surface" in the Kingdom until the end of January 1964, provided the Saudis did not continue support to the royalists: a Joint Chiefs of Staff meeting on 24 December 1963 felt that if "Hard Surface" was withdrawn after Faisal resumed aid to the royalists, it would clearly signal to the UAR that the US had withdrawn support for Saudi Arabia – which would be an open invitation for further UAR aggression.

In January 1964 there was heavy fighting between Egyptian and royalist troops along the Sana'a–Hodeida road, and battlefield failure at this time led Nasser to seek to repair relations with the Saudis. However, this initiative became caught up in an intra-family power struggle in Saudi Arabia. Saud had returned to the Kingdom in September 1963 after a long period abroad (ostensibly for medical reasons), and had immediately requested recovery of the powers Faisal had acquired during his absence.[1] A political struggle ensued. "Every time I treat a wound, another one opens," complained Faisal.[2] When Nasser called for an Arab summit in Alexandria to deal with Israel's diversion of the waters of the Jordan River, Saud insisted that he should represent the

---

1. Early in 1963, Saud had in fact left Saudi Arabia for medical reasons. Faisal began removing Saud's loyalists and appointing like-minded princes in key military and security positions. Alexei O. Vassiliev, *The History of Saudi Arabia* (London: Saqi Books, 1998), pp. 366–7).
2. De Gaury, *Faisal*, p. 132.

Kingdom. The dispute that developed was resolved only when Saudi Arabia's Grand Mufti intervened with the suggestion that Faisal maintain effective power and Saud remain sovereign. Therefore, Saud would represent the Kingdom at the summit.

During his talks with Nasser, Saud paved the way for peace negotiations to be undertaken with Faisal. It was agreed that a conciliation commission would visit Riyadh in February 1964, followed by an Egyptian peace delegation headed by Vice President 'Abd al-Hakim Amer. When they finally met on 3 March 1964, the Egyptians conceded to the notion of letting the Yemenis determine the future of their country. However, Faisal insisted on putting off further negotiations until a meeting between himself and Nasser could take place. Therefore, when Saud wrote to Faisal on 13 March 1964 asking him to resign, the peace negotiations became caught up in the family disputes.[1]

As the internal crisis in Saudi Arabia reached its climax, fighting continued in Yemen. A major Egyptian offensive in June–August 1964 forced Imam al-Badr to abandon his headquarters in Yemen and retreat to Saudi Arabia. During this offensive the royalists sought to broaden the scope of their foreign support. Faisal responded by cutting off his direct subvention, renewing it only on the condition that the royalists would cooperate with dissident republicans and tribes who, while not royalist, were anti-Egyptian.[2]

On 17 August 1964, Hart met Faisal and was told that UAR planes had invaded Saudi airspace twice in the previous few days; moreover, the Saudi government had received a report from inside Yemen that UAR troops were moving northward toward the Saudi border. Faisal had therefore decided to send weapons and troops to defend the border, and wanted to know where the US would stand should war break out between Saudi Arabia and the UAR. Hart reminded Faisal of the US position on helping Saudi Arabia against unprovoked attack, but pointed out that aid to the royalists would be considered by the US as provocation. On 22 August 1964, the State Department instructed Hart to urge Faisal to avoid the appearance of becoming re-involved in the Yemen conflict, and suggested he limit the Saudi mobilization on the frontier in order to avoid any mistaken or hasty UAR reaction. Hart noted that Faisal was not thinking of sending forces across the frontier or renewing aid to the royalists before the Arab summit in September, and also recommended

---

1. Safran, *Saudi Arabia*, pp. 100–1.
2. Rahmy, *The Egyptian Policy in the Arab World*, p. 152.

consultation with the UK on strengthening US-UK cooperation in the Arabian Peninsula.

Meanwhile, Denis Greenhill, the British *chargé d'affaires* to the US, called on Rusk on 21 August 1964 to discuss an urgent letter from Foreign Secretary Richard Butler concerning the threatened increase of friction between the UAR and Saudi Arabia in Yemen. In his letter, Butler appealed for the coordination of US and UK policies and requested that the US urge Nasser to reach a political arrangement with Faisal in Alexandria. In his reply on 28 August, Rusk echoed this, stressing that the US was impressing on both "the importance for everyone that Faisal and Nasser reach an agreement on Yemen at their forthcoming meeting". Rusk concurred with Butler on Faisal's isolated position in the Arab world: "His aiding the royalists tends to increase that isolation and encourages the threat to his regime from both within and from outside Saudi Arabia." He also pointed out to Butler that encouraging Faisal to increase his aid to the royalists would appear dangerous "for all of our interests in the area".[1]

The summer offensive of 1964 strengthened the Egyptian-YAR position on the ground. Faisal, having reaffirmed his dominance at home, was once again willing to attempt to negotiate away the Egyptian presence in Yemen; at the September summit in Alexandria, Faisal and Nasser announced an initiative to seek a peaceful solution. Their joint communiqué declared that the two countries intended to cooperate fully in resolving differences between the various parties in Yemen, and that steps would be taken to establish the necessary contacts with the interested parties.[2]

On 2 November, Yemeni republican and royalist representatives meeting in Erkowit, Sudan, concluded an agreement providing for a ceasefire in Yemen beginning on 8 November, and announced a national conference in Yemen beginning 23 November. The preliminary conference in Erkowit suggested that the royalists and republicans could reach a compromise without much trouble. However, the Saudi government subsequently refused to accept the designation of "Republic" for the future state of Yemen, claiming it would prejudice the outcome of the proposed talks. The republicans, some of whom had been excluded from the Erkowit talks, then quarrelled among themselves

1. National Archives and Records Administration (NARA), RG59, Central Files 1964–66, (POL 1 SAUD-UAR), State to the US Embassy in the UK, 28 August 1964.
2. Amin Said, *Tarikh al-dawla al-sa'udiyya*, vol. 3 (Beirut: Dar al-Katib al-'Arabi, 1965), pp. 362–3.

over the make-up of their delegation, while the Egyptians attempted to control its composition. The upshot was that the plenary conference did not convene and the ceasefire, which had been fairly widely observed, broke down. With the failure to hold the agreed-upon national conference, fighting resumed in late November. The royalists took the offensive, seeking to regain territory lost to the Egyptians in the summer, and the republicans, with Egyptian help, repelled the attack. Once again a stalemate set in.[1]

Faisal (now King Faisal) continued to use Yemeni tribal proxy forces to lever the Egyptians out of the country and at least tame the republican regime. Nasser came to Jeddah on 22–4 August 1965 to confer with Faisal, and the two reached an agreement similar to their joint communiqué at the September summit. The Jeddah Agreement called for a ceasefire; for a popular plebiscite to be held in Yemen no later than 23 November 1966; and for UAR-Saudi cooperation in setting up an interim conference of Yemeni republicans and royalists to be convened on 23 November 1965 in Harad, Yemen, to negotiate arrangements for a transitional government and for the plebiscite. UAR military forces were to be withdrawn within ten months from 23 November 1965, and Saudi agreement was sought to put an immediate stop to any form of military assistance to the royalists and to the use of Saudi territory for action against Yemen.

As a result of the agreement, the Saudi government ceased military and material assistance to the Yemeni royalists. This time, the royalists and republicans were actually brought together the following November, in Harad, to work out a constitution and a government. The Saudis made every effort to ensure that the royalists would be responsive to finding a peaceful solution, but Nasser failed to exert similar control over the republicans. Most sources blame republican intransigence for the failure of the conference. Subsequently, however, Nasser went to Moscow, and developments took a different turn. Radio Sana'a violently attacked the agreement; the Yemeni prime minister travelled to the Soviet Union and China; and arms were brought into Yemen from various sources. (Three Soviet ships unloaded arms and equipment in Hodeida.)

When the British government announced in February 1966 that it intended to withdraw from Aden and South Yemen by 1968, the prospect of using the Yemen base to extend his influence gave Nasser an added incentive; the Yemen

---

1. Badeep, *The Saudi-Egyptian Conflict Over North Yemen*, p. 81.

conflict then suddenly accelerated towards greater violence. Nasser tore up the Jeddah Agreement, and in March reinforced Egyptian units launched the biggest offensive yet in an attempt to crush the royalists. The royalists launched a counterattack during the summer, which also eventually faltered, resulting in yet another stalemate in the field. However, Nasser did not return to negotiations. Instead, he withdrew his forces from outlying areas, concentrated them in a triangle based on the cities of Ta'iz, Sana'a and Hodeida, and used air power, sabotage and subversion to try to break the enemy's will. Egyptian-supported groups, mostly comprising Yemeni expatriates, executed a series of sabotage-bombings against targets throughout Saudi Arabia,[1] and on at least two occasions (January and May 1967) the Egyptians even used poison gas.

Faisal's response was to redouble his efforts along already established lines. He visited the US in June 1966 to confer with President Johnson and obtain renewed assurances of US support.[2] He also patched up a disagreement that had developed between him and the royalist leadership and increased his support, supplying funds and armaments.

The solution that Faisal had been unable to bring about on the battlefield or at the negotiating table was finally imposed upon Egypt from the outside. Nasser's crushing defeat at the hands of Israel in the war of June 1967 made his position in Yemen untenable. The failure of the unity schemes, along with the 1967 defeat, shattered the ideological hegemony of Arab nationalism. (Yemen itself became two countries in November 1967, with Sana'a and the northwest comprising the YAR, and Aden and the south/east declared the People's Republic of South Yemen [PRSY].)

Pan-Islamism vs Pan-Arabism

The years 1964–7 saw another dimension of confrontation between Nasser and Faisal in addition to Yemen: the ideological conflict between Faisal's pan-Islamism and secularist Arab nationalism. As Faisal sought to involve the US in his struggle against secularist Arab nationalism, the issue became important in Saudi-US relations. US decision-makers calculated that the Kingdom provided a counterweight to radical forces, such that Saudi Arabia could exert political

---

1. Safran, *Saudi Arabia*, p. 121.
2. LJL, NSF, Country Files, Saudi Arabia, Memos, vol. I, 12/63-4/67, Memorandum of Conversation, "President's Meeting with King Faisal", 21 June 1966.

leadership in the Arab world and use its religious legitimacy to gain support for US policy in the region.

Radical Arab hopes were boosted by the 1963 Ba'th victories in Syria and Iraq, giving rise to the prospect of a new and stronger UAR. During a meeting on 15 May 1964 in Washington, DC between Rusk and Saqqaf, the former expressed the US government's disapproval of Arab unity if it came about as a result of force, although the US could not object if it was attained by free choice. Saqqaf commented that every Arab wanted unity, but in his own way. He alleged that had Nasser acted in the right manner he could have "had the Arab world" after the Suez crisis, but had failed because Arabs as a whole, "by nature and by religion, are opposed to Socialism".[1] On 11 December 1964, Saqqaf expressed his government's concern about the dangers of anarchy and communist activity in Yemen, claiming that virtually all facets of international communism were at work in Yemen.

Faced with Arab radicalism and communist activity in the Middle East, Faisal adopted a counter-strategy in the form of an appeal for Pan-Islamic solidarity. He needed to engender broader intergovernmental cooperation among Islamic states, not only to bring the Muslim nations together for mutual benefit, but also to curtail the spread of radicalism in the Arab world.

Pan-Arabism is a classic example of how an ideology that calls for its members to form a centralized movement is likely to produce precisely the opposite result. Khadduri notes that, as an ideology, "... Arab Socialism was intended to be a unifying rather than a disruptive factor in the movement towards Arab unity. But no sooner had the nucleus of an Arab union been achieved – the United Arab Republic – than several variants began to develop, stemming partly from parochial and partly from personal and procedural differences."[2]

On 19 February 1966, Hermann Eilts, US Ambassador to Saudi Arabia, held lengthy discussions with Faisal, who worried about the growing communist threat in the Middle East. Remarking on the large number of Soviet and Chinese communist technicians in the area, Faisal reiterated his belief that the UAR was providing a protective screen behind which Soviet influence could gain a foothold and spread, and pointed out that unless they "were

---

1. NARA, RG59, Central Files 1964–66 (POL 7 SAUD), Memorandum of Conversation, 15 May 1964.
2. Majid Khadduri, *Political Trends in the Arab World* (Baltimore, MD: Johns Hopkins University Press, 1970), pp. 171–2.

nipped in the bud now", the capability of these countries would "steadily grow" until they were able to subvert Western interests in the Middle East as well as governments friendly to the West. Eilts told Faisal the US might be worried about the UAR's tolerance of the Soviet and Chinese presence and of communists in various parts of the Middle East including Yemen, but had no real evidence to justify the assertion that the UAR was deliberately furthering communist objectives. Faisal disagreed, insisting he was unable to understand why the US seemed to ignore the fact that Nasser and the Egyptians had been largely responsible for introducing the Soviet and the Chinese presence into the Middle East. Eilts warned Faisal not to accept exaggerated estimates of the numbers or activities of Soviets or Chinese in the region. While their activities, particularly in the Red Sea area, might indeed be reaching a point where they required closer surveillance, they had also to be kept in perspective in terms of magnitude and the intentions of the governments of the area.

On 21 February 1966, Saudi Defence Minister Prince Sultan met President Johnson with a message from Faisal, in which the king expressed his appreciation for the US effort in the face of the communist tide and explained: "We fight on religious grounds what you fight for doctrinaire reasons." He offered to coordinate efforts to "put an end to the spread of Communism in the world, as a first step toward eliminating it".[1] Johnson replied that he welcomed the opportunity "to share our analysis of the present and the potential threat of Communism in the near East" and told Faisal that after further study of his views he would request that Eilts discuss the subject with him in detail.[2]

At a meeting on 23 February 1966, Sultan told Rusk that the Saudi government considered the spread of communism in the Middle East its biggest threat. The Saudis were endeavouring to combat communism on the basis of their religion, believing Islam to be the strongest shield against it. Sultan emphasized the importance of working closely together to improve mutual understanding of communist activities in the area. Rusk responded that the US was sensitive to any communist moves to increase control, and believed it was very important to have a close and systematic exchange of views on the subject with the Saudi government. Raymond Hare, Assistant Secretary for NEA, was asked to work out a technique for implementing such an exchange.

1. LJL, NSF, Country Files, Saudi Arabia, Memos, vol. I, 12/63-4/67, Memorandum of Conversation, 21 February 1966.
2. NARA, RG59, Central Files 1964–66 (POL 23-7 NEAR E.), State to US Embassy, Jeddah, 26 February 1966.

Eilts and Saqqaf met on 9 April, and the ambassador stressed that the most important stage lay ahead: the development of programmes the two countries might undertake separately and jointly to counter the threat. They met again on 4 May, and Eilts submitted an analysis of the communist threat in the Middle East; Saqqaf noted that the overall estimate was much lower than had been suggested by Faisal. When Eilts asked about Faisal's sources, Saqqaf replied somewhat laconically that it had been obtained "from the Syrians around him".[1]

In his call for Islamic solidarity, Faisal's views were shaped by a number of factors. He believed any cooperation between Muslims would only enhance the prestige of the Arab nation. In his opinion, without Islam the Arab lands would not have become a nation; without the Qur'an, the Arabic language would not have been preserved; and without Islamic values and concepts there would have been no Arab modes of thought, customs or characteristics. Faisal also considered that in the past, insistence on the national factor had exhausted and distorted the Islamic state. Similarly, he asserted that the departure of the Arabs from the path of their religion had weakened them, torn their homeland apart and brought them under the domination of imperialism.[2]

To emphasize the significance of his Pan-Islamic call, Faisal began a series of state visits to Muslim countries in which he appealed for Pan-Islamic unity. Visiting Iran in December 1965, he said: "We, the Muslims, take responsibility first of all for studying and learning our religion and our *shari'a*. If we understand the essence of our Islamic *shari'a*, it will save us the confusion caused by … dominant ideologies and trends." Speaking during a visit to Sudan in January 1966, he said: "We know the forces that oppose what we are doing today. They are the powers of colonialism, Zionism and communism." During a visit to Pakistan in April 1966, he explained the dimensions of Islamic solidarity that he called on the Islamic world to adopt: "We seek peace … seek understanding … but this does not mean that we sacrifice our basic principles, our belief, our religion, for the sake of the fraternity and understanding that is sought." In a joint Pakistani-Saudi statement, he spoke of "the solidarity of the Islamic countries", attributing to them "significant power" in helping to "creat[e] a righteous international order [and] … to secure better lives for all people.

---

1. NARA, RG59, Central Files 1964–66 (POL 23-7 NEAR E.), US Embassy, Jeddah, to State, 4 May 1966.
2. Ahmed Assah, *Miracle of the Desert Kingdom* (London: Johnson, 1969), pp. 97–8.

It provides, particularly for the Islamic world, perfect integrated economic unity."[1]

Faisal also addressed the Tunisian Congress in September 1966, declaring: "If we want to achieve permanent stability for our nations and countries and provide them with full development, we must return to our rules ... we do not need to import any views, ideologies or laws from abroad."[2]

Nasser saw in Faisal's call for Islamic solidarity another US attempt to organize an alliance against him, and at a mass meeting on 22 February 1966 he claimed that the Islamic pact was "created by imperialism and reactionaries",[3] a US-British conspiracy aimed at dividing the Arab world and undermining Arab hopes for unity. However, Faisal repeatedly denied that the aim in calling for Islamic solidarity was to form a pact or a bloc against any other state in the Arab world, and in a speech on the occasion of honouring the heads of Hajj delegations on 27 March 1966, he denounced the allegation that this call was prompted by any foreign source:

> It has been said that we seek alliances, and that these alliances are directed by colonial entities. I hereby ... invite those who say this to ... participate with us ... to see whether or not this call derives from colonial incentives or whether it emanates from the hearts that are faithful to their Lord who calls Muslims to what is good for their religion and living.[4]

In May 1966, the State Department, concerned about Nasser's increasing claims that the US was sponsoring an Islamic alliance, issued a contingency guidance for background use with friendly diplomats, host governments and others. The document stated that the US had neither supported nor opposed the formation of any Islamic alliance, saw little likelihood of an effective Islamic alliance taking shape, doubted whether Islam still could serve as a force for Arab unity and wondered whether any action would not contribute to the polarization of the Arab world. A policy paper prepared on 1 June 1966 by the State Department in advance of a visit by Faisal to the US called for emphasizing to Faisal that polarization was dangerous for the Middle East; that the US would protect its mutual interests with all the states of the area,

---

1. Faisal's call for Islamic solidarity was reported in *Al-Manhal* (Saudi Arabia), vol. 33, no. 12, December 1972/January 1973, pp. 1,272–5, 1284.
2. See *Um al-Qura*, vol. 2,139, 23 September 1966.
3. *Al-Ahram*, 23 February 1966.
4. Quoted in *Al-Jazirah*, 29 March 1966.

and would not contribute to polarization; and that communist penetration was less problematic than Faisal's estimates. The implication throughout the paper was that Faisal was somehow a contributor to the area's tensions, and that he had not understood the potential consequences. It pointed out that, whatever Faisal's original intent, the Soviet Union had elected to distort the Islamic solidarity issue to suit its own purposes and anxieties and, for better or worse, "it had become an element in the growing schism between Egypt and Saudi Arabia."[1]

When Faisal met Johnson in Washington on 21 June 1966, he wished to discuss the danger communism presented for the Middle East that, in turn, could have great ramifications for the rest of the world. While he did not favour the principle of military intervention, he emphasized that the US should intervene in all areas to stop such problems in their infancy. He stated that Saudi cooperation with others in the region to obstruct communism, whether on the Arab or Islamic level, was intended to make people aware of this danger.

In December 1966, a National Intelligence Estimate concluded that the prospects were poor for real accommodation between Faisal and Nasser. Each would continue to work against the other, not only in the Arabian Peninsula but in the Arab and Muslim world generally. Though a meeting or pact between Islamic leaders was unlikely, Faisal would continue to promote the idea of Islamic solidarity as a means of countering Nasser's influence, and would seek support from the US and the West, while Nasser would look to the Soviet Union for help. In addition, both would blame the US for encouraging Faisal and would urge it to hold him back.

In a lengthy session with Eilts on 6 January 1967, Rashad Fir'wan conveyed his government's regrets at what it considered the US government's apparent reluctance to cooperate more closely with Saudi Arabia on matters of mutual interest. He spoke of the US's lukewarm view of Islamic solidarity and its failure to recognize the communist threat in the Middle East according to the dimensions in which the Saudi government saw it. Eilts replied that the US had been cooperating closely with Saudi Arabia on many matters of mutual concern, but that by definition Islamic solidarity was hardly a subject in which it could be directly involved. He acknowledged that Islamic solidarity was yet

1. NARA, RG59, S/S visit, Files: Lot 67 D 587, Visit of King Faisal of Saudi Arabia, 21–23 June 1966, vol. II, Memcons, Admin and Sub. Misc., "Proposed Strategy for Visit of King Faisal", 1 June 1966.

another factor contributing to current polarization in the Arab world and the resultant tensions, but noted that the US neither disapproved nor approved of the concept.

The State Department also instructed Eilts to inform the Saudi government that the US, as a non-Muslim country and not a state in the region, had not in the past felt it appropriate to comment on Islamic solidarity. The US questioned the Saudi gain from Arab polarization, concluding: "What might be a useful aim in tranquil times seems hardly have served to buttress the solidarity concept in the current charged atmosphere among key Islamic States."[1]

However, with the Israeli occupation of Jerusalem in June 1967, Faisal's notions of Pan-Islamic solidarity took on a new and compelling significance. He presented the Palestinian problem to the wider Muslim world as a Muslim issue, and called on the Islamic states to support the Arabs in the liberation of Jerusalem.[2] In a speech during the Hajj season, on 23 February 1968, he said:

> Jerusalem is calling you to save it from its distress; what are we waiting for, and for how long should we wait? We want an Islamic wrath and renaissance, not for people to embrace nationalism, or racism, or partism, but an Islamic call, a call for *jihad* in the cause of Allah. In the cause of our religion and our doctrine, in defence of our holy sites and our sanctuaries, I ask Allah almighty to make me die as martyr for the sake of Allah.[3]

The arson attempt on the al-Aqsa Mosque in Jerusalem in August 1969 sent a shockwave across the Islamic world. Faisal called for an Islamic summit, and Nasser had to publicly support Faisal's call, though he had little interest in the matter and did not attend in person.[4] One month later, the world's first Islamic summit was convened in Rabat, capital of Morocco. It declared the support of Islamic states for the Palestinian people, condemned the criminal act against the al-Aqsa Mosque and affirmed the Islamic states' need to promote cooperation and mutual assistance in all fields.[5]

---

1. NARA, RG59, Central Files 1967–69 (POL SAUD-US), State to US Embassy, Jeddah, 16 January 1967.
2. *The Islamic Review and Arab Affairs*, vol. 57, no. 2 (1969), p. 4.
3. Quoted in *Um al-Qura*, 7 March 1969.
4. *International Herald Tribune* (IHT), 1 September 1969.
5. Organization of the Islamic Conference (OIC), *Declarations and Resolutions of the Conference of the Organization of the Islamic Conference from Rabat to Kuala Lumpur* (Jeddah: OIC, General Secretariat, 1974), pp. 11–4.

The tide of radicalism in the Arab world was stemmed by Nasser's death in September 1970. His successor, Anwar Sadat, who had taken an early interest in pan-Islamism, began to move closer to Faisal and to appreciate his strategy. Syria started to moderate its position, Sudan reduced its militancy and Libya began to advocate its own version of pan-Islamism, thus reducing the number of radical Arab countries opposed to Faisal's pan-Islamist movement to Algeria and Iraq only.[1]

Faisal's sudden death in 1975 was a great loss to the pan-Islamist movement; he had become a spiritual leader for most of the Muslim world, as well as the representative of Islam and the guardian of its holiest shrine.

The Soviet Expulsion from Egypt

Exhausted by the war in Yemen, defeated by Israel and deprived of the Sinai Peninsula and of income from the Suez Canal, Egypt had to concentrate all its efforts on restoring its military capability. The more or less total destruction of the Egyptian armed forces in the Six-Day War and the post-war Egyptian policy of resisting any settlement involving territorial concessions to Israel implied a greatly increased dependence on the Soviet Union as an arms supplier and as a source of political and diplomatic support. The 1967 war opened the door to an increasing military dependency among regional states and growing superpower penetration.

Following the war, Nasser had turned to the Soviet Union for military assistance. In contrast to his earlier stance, he was now willing to accept the risk of some loss of autonomy that might accompany an increased Soviet presence.[2] According to Heikal, Nasser's strategy was to involve the Soviets more than ever in the Middle East, as he wanted to ensure "that they felt Egypt's defeat was their defeat, that their prestige was bound up with that of Egypt".[3] The Egyptians desperately needed – and therefore expected – a rapid, massive, but short-term Soviet involvement for the limited purpose of compelling Israel

---

1. Abdullah M. Sindi, "King Faisal and Pan-Islamism", in Willard A. Beling, ed., *King Faisal and the Modernization of Saudi Arabia* (Boulder, CO: Westview Press, 1980), p. 192.
2. Michael N. Barnett and Jack S. Levy, "Domestic Sources of Alliances and Alignments: The Case of Egypt 1962–73", *International Organization*, vol. 45, no. 3 (summer 1991), p. 384.
3. Mohamed H. Heikal, *The Sphinx and the Commissar: The Rise and Fall of Soviet Influence in the Arab World* (London: Collins, 1978), p. 191.

to accept Egypt's terms for a settlement. Despite tremendous growth in the Soviet-Egyptian relationship after 1967, Egypt's dependence on the USSR hardly made Nasser into a reliable tool. Rubinstein reports that Nasser defined Egypt's ties to the Soviets by saying: "We cannot dispense with the Russian experts as long as we are at war with Israel and as long as there is no peace."[1]

The paramount goal of the USSR, on the other hand, was to establish a permanent strategic military presence in Egypt to be employed for broad Soviet global and regional purposes. The resulting opportunities to secure general recognition by the West of Soviet hegemony in Eastern Europe, and the Sino-American rapprochement, meant that the Soviet Union was very serious about avoiding unnecessary antagonism in its relations with the US in the Middle East. It was unwilling to sacrifice its global interests by becoming engaged in a full-scale military operation aimed at Egypt's recovery of the Sinai Peninsula.[2] Therefore, in order to prevent Egypt from undertaking an offensive against Israel, the Soviets consistently refused to permit Egypt to use weapons to regain its territories; they kept their advanced weaponry under Soviet operational control; refused to supply sufficient quantities of ammunition and spare parts; and refused delivery of offensive weapons.[3]

However, by the end of 1970, despite the difficulties and aggravations that characterized Soviet-Egyptian relations, Egypt was host to more than 200 Soviet pilots flying the latest-model MiG-21J aircraft as well as an estimated 12–15,000 Soviet experts assigned to some eighty missile sites.[4]

Earlier in the year, President Richard M. Nixon's National Security Advisor Henry Kissinger had declared, at a background briefing on 24 June, that the continued presence of Soviet troops threatened US interests in the area. The idea was to expel the Soviet military presence in Egypt; Kissinger asserted that, contingent on serious Egyptian concessions, the US could put the heat on the Soviets and influence the Israelis. The Egyptians would wake up when

---

1. Alvin Z. Rubinstein, *Red Star on the Nile: The Soviet-Egyptian Influence Relationship since the June War* (Princeton, NJ: Princeton University Press, 1977), pp. 44–46, 117.
2. Oded Eran and Jerome Singer, "Exodus from Egypt and the Threat to Kremlin Leadership", *New Middle East* 40 (January 1972), pp. 21–5.
3. Dina R. Spechler, "The USSR and Third-World Conflicts: Domestic Debate and Soviet Policy in the Middle East, 1967–73", *World Politics*, vol. 38, no. 3 (April 1986), p. 437.
4. Walter Laqueur, *Confrontation: The Middle East and World Politics* (London: Wildwood House, 1974), p. 4.

they realized that the Soviets preferred détente with the US to a new war in the Middle East.[1]

In November 1970, a few weeks after Nasser's death,[2] Faisal sent Kamal Adham, the Saudi chief of intelligence, on a confidential mission to Cairo to explore the possibility of an understanding with President Sadat. Emphasizing Saudi concerns over the extent and influence of the Soviet presence in Egypt, Adham put forward Faisal's proposition that the withdrawal of Soviet military experts might encourage the US to adopt a more forceful and positive policy in the Middle East. After underlining Egypt's urgent need for Soviet assistance to counterbalance the weaponry being supplied to Israel by the US, Sadat produced a counter-suggestion: if Israel withdrew its forces from the east bank of the Suez Canal and allowed the canal to be cleared for shipping, he would then ask the Soviets to leave Egypt. Sadat confirmed that Faisal could convey this proposal to the US, and Adham was duly instructed by the king to deliver the message.[3] Adham made frequent trips to Egypt during 1970 and 1971, and in effect became Sadat's contact with the White House, to whom he passed on news of the Egyptian president's intention of reducing his dependence on the USSR as speedily as possible.[4]

During May 1971, Faisal watched the sequence of events in Cairo with concern. Sadat was engaged against a group within the ruling hierarchy opposed to any divergence from the already well-established alignment with the Soviet Union. Members of the group, termed "the Soviet agents" years later by Sadat, were arrested on 16 May.[5] On 27 May, hours before Faisal's arrival in Washington, Radio Cairo announced that Egypt and the USSR had signed a fifteen-year Treaty of Friendship and Cooperation. The White House talks centred around the treaty, but Faisal assured President Nixon that, whatever its links with the Soviet Union, Egypt would never be transformed into a communist state. Faisal expounded the theory that US bias toward Israel had only served to further the interests of communism, and urged the US to persist

---

1. Henry Kissinger, *The White House Years* (Boston: Little, Brown and Company, 1979), p. 578.
2. The Egyptian leader died on 28 September 1970.
3. Holden and Johns, *The House of Saud*, p. 292.
4. Ibid., p. 294.
5. Anwar El-Sadat, *In Search of Identity: An Autobiography* (London: Collins, 1978), p. 222.

in the effort to achieve an interim agreement. US Secretary of State William Rogers took on this task during the remainder of the year.[1]

Despite the Soviet-Egyptian treaty and all the exchanges of visits and joint communiqués, Sadat's relationship with the Soviets had from the outset been caught in a web of contradiction and mutual suspicion. He came to believe that the Soviets preferred the status quo, which kept Egypt dependent, and that détente had reduced their willingness to make commitments comparable to US support for Israel.[2] The Soviet Union would not deliver the weapons required by Egypt and was apparently either uninterested in, or incapable of, bringing about progress toward a diplomatic solution, thereby removing the handicap they had placed on Egypt's dealings with the US. The breaking point came in the wake of the US-Soviet summit in Moscow in May 1972 when the Soviets, in Sadat's opinion, formally endorsed the status quo. In the declarations signed at the end of the summit, the US and the USSR agreed to inform each other of potential local conflicts in order to dampen regional instability and limit any confrontation of their own. These declarations would clearly restrict Sadat's ability to consider war as long as Soviet troops were in Egypt.[3]

Sadat's decision to break with the Soviet Union was influenced by other major and equally compelling factors, among which was the need to reduce rising frustration over the Soviet presence inside Egypt. The armed forces were infuriated at being ordered about by the Soviets. Sadat also hoped to administer a shock to Moscow that would force it to reconsider its refusal to supply him with offensive weapons.[4]

With Faisal's encouragement and assurance of financial assistance, Sadat now thought more actively about breaking the "no-war-no-peace" deadlock by evicting the Soviet experts; on 18 July he reversed seventeen years of Egyptian policy and threw out some 21,000 Soviet military experts.[5] Unfortunately, the US regarded the expulsion as motivated by Sadat's desire to stabilize Egyptian

---

1. Safran, *Saudi Arabia*, p. 146.
2. Avraham Sela, *The Decline of the Arab-Israeli Conflict: Middle East Politics and the Quest for Regional Order* (Albany, New York: State University of New York Press, 1998), pp. 136–8.
3. Steven L. Spiegel, *The Other Arab-Israeli Conflict: Making America's Middle East Policy, from Truman to Reagan* (Chicago: University of Chicago Press, 1985), p. 214.
4. *US News and World Report*, 14 August 1972, p. 46.
5. Michael I. Handel, *The Diplomacy of Surprise* (Cambridge, MA: Harvard University Center for International Affairs, 1981), pp. 278–9.

politics and his own decision-making base – in other words, that it was done to placate the army. Its failure to understand Sadat's move can be attributed to cultural differences. In Egypt, good deeds or noble acts were performed unilaterally, but under such circumstances it was expected that the beneficiary would respond by rendering a service of commensurate magnitude. This gesture by Sadat accomplished everything he could have wished for. A huge success at home, it also worked wonders in attracting attention in Moscow, while thoroughly misleading both the Israelis and the Americans.

The expulsion of the experts brought immense relief to the Saudi government and opened the way for a solid strategic alliance between Saudi Arabia and Egypt. Eventually, the US would benefit from this opportunity to win Egypt over to its own camp, enabling the facilitation of a peace agreement between Egypt and Israel.

The October 1973 War and the Oil Embargo

After the Soviet expulsion, Kissinger and Hafiz Ismail, his Egyptian counterpart, had several secret meetings. At their last meeting before war broke out in October, held in Rochefort, France on 20 May 1973, Kissinger stated:

> If the status quo along the Canal is protracted indefinitely ... a point will be reached where that will develop its own ... It will simply become a part of the international landscape to which people have become accustomed. So that is the argument for getting some movement, because wherever the new movement will be, the advantage is that it will at least be new.[1]

According to Heikal, it was clear to the Egyptians that the US needed action from the Egyptian side to begin the process. Nothing meaningful would be achieved by dragging the Israelis toward peace unless they were forced to deal with a new, harsher reality.[2]

Faced with this political stalemate, Sadat believed that a military option was necessary to secure US political intervention and to facilitate negotiations. He

---

1. United States Department of State Records, Records of Henry Kissinger, Box 25, Cat C Arab-Israeli War, Memorandum of Conversation between Hafiz Ismail and Henry Kissinger, 20 May 1973.
2. Mohamed Heikal, *Autumn of Fury* (New York: Random House, 1983), pp. 49–50.

The Faisal Era (1962–79)

proclaimed in July 1971 that that year was to be the "year of decision", implying that Egypt would resort to war if no progress toward a political settlement was made.[1] Realizing that he needed partners to make a military option workable, he turned to Syrian President Hafiz al-Assad; Faisal, meanwhile, was a non-military ally, who promised to use the oil weapon against the US.[2] The 1967 war had signalled the decline of Egyptian hegemony, the cost of which had impoverished Egypt, while oil revenue decisively shifted the balance of economic power to the oil-rich conservatives. Recovery of Israeli-occupied territory was only possible through inter-Arab cooperation. Thus the "trilateral alliance" between Egypt, Syria and Saudi Arabia replaced Egyptian hegemony.[3]

In early spring 1973, Sadat had told *Newsweek* journalist Arnoud de Borchgrave that the time had come for a "shock", but no one at the time believed he had a plan for war.[4] During his Anniversary of the Revolution address on 23 July, he also spoke of the potential for future Arab leverage over the US growing out of the current world energy and monetary crisis. With an effective alliance now forged, Soviet support available at sufficient levels and the diplomatic front deadlocked, war was now Sadat's only real option. During a visit to Saudi Arabia on 23 August, he informed Faisal of his decision to go to war and was offered encouragement by the Saudi leader. Faisal pledged financial contribution as well as oil as leverage. According to Heikal, the king added "... But give us time. We don't want to use oil as a weapon in a battle that goes on for two or three days and then stops. We want to see a battle that goes on for a long enough time for world opinion to be mobilized."[5] However, Faisal was still reluctant to attack the US publicly or to link petroleum sales to politics without fair warning.

In April, Faisal had sent Saudi Oil Minister Ahmed Zaki Yamani to Washington with a message that Saudi Arabia would not continue to increase production to meet US needs unless the US made some movement toward

---

1. Mehran Kamrava, *The Modern Middle East: A Political History since the First World War* (Berkeley, CA: University of California Press, 2005), p. 127.
2. Kenneth Stein, *Heroic Diplomacy: Sadat, Kissinger, Carter, Begin, and the Quest for Arab-Israeli Peace* (New York: Routledge, 1999), pp. 4–67.
3. Alan Taylor, *The Arab Balance of Power* (Syracuse, NY: Syracuse University Press, 1982), pp. 49–56.
4. Arnoud de Borchgrave, "Next, a 'Shock' by Sadat?", *Newsweek*, 23 April 1973, pp. 36–7.
5. Mohamed Heikal, *The Road to Ramadan* (London: Collins, 1975), p. 275.

justice for the Palestinians and Israeli withdrawal from the territories occupied in 1967, including Jerusalem. On 23 May, Faisal met ARAMCO head Frank Jungers along with other oil company executives in Geneva. He explained that Saudi Arabia was in danger of being isolated among its Arab friends because of the failure of the US government to lend it positive support. Faisal stated that he was not going to let this happen, and declared: "You will lose everything."[1]

Despite such efforts, Faisal felt his message was not being heard or believed. He told *The Christian Science Monitor* on 6 July that the US should adopt a "more even-handed policy in the region" to enable Saudi Arabia to maintain friendly ties with it,[2] and gave his first-ever American television interview to the National Broadcasting Corporation (NBC), shown on 31 August. "We do not wish to place any restrictions on our oil exports to the US," he said during that interview, "but America's complete support of Zionism against the Arabs makes it extremely difficult for us to continue to supply US petroleum needs and even to maintain our friendly relations with America."[3]

No one in Washington believed that the Arabs were preparing for war. A report of 8 August 1973 from the State Department Bureau of Intelligence and Research underlined that "while his [Sadat's] threats of military action ring increasingly hollow, a mounting payment deficit is jeopardizing urgent domestic needs". It was also noted that the Egyptian president appeared to be receiving crucial assistance from Saudi Arabia, "but this won't solve Sadat's basic problem of dislodging Israel from the Sinai".[4] Washington's unresponsiveness was partly due to the fact that the Saudi government was at that time negotiating and concluding deals with the US to upgrade its military forces. Thus there was acknowledgement by all that a problem did exist, but disbelief that any drastic action was imminent. According to ARAMCO officials, "the impression was given that some believed Faisal was calling wolf, when no wolf exists except

1. US Congress, Senate Committee on Foreign Relations, Subcommittee on Multinational Corporations, "Multinational Petroleum Companies and Foreign Policy", 93rd Cong., 2nd sess., 20 and 21 February, 27 and 28 March 1974, p. 504.
2. *Middle East Journal* (MEJ), "Chronology" (Autumn 1973).
3. *Middle East Economic Survey* (MEES), supplement (7 September 1981), p. 2. Faisal gave similar warnings in an interview with *Newsweek* (10 September 1973).
4. United States Department of State Records, GR-State, Political-UAR, Egypt, 1970–1973, Entry 1613, Box 2250, Bureau of Intelligence and Research note, 30 August 1973.

in his imagination. Also, there is little or nothing the US government can do or will do on an urgent basis to affect the Arab-Israeli issue."[1]

The second Soviet-US summit took place in Washington in summer 1973, and both sides agreed on the need to avoid a superpower conflict in the Middle East. In Kissinger's view, by removing the danger of such a confrontation, the policy of preserving the status quo until the Arabs moderated their position was advisable.[2] Washington had been dismissing the likelihood of war on the grounds that Israel had no reason to open hostilities; nor would it dare launch a pre-emptive attack as it had done in 1967. As Israel was thought to wield military superiority, it appeared irrational for the Arabs to consider starting a war in which they would be badly beaten. In fact, however, Sadat had instructed his war minister back in October 1972 to prepare plans for a limited war devised to hold a bridgehead on the east bank of the Suez Canal and thus break the no-war-no-peace stalemate.[3] Sadat was intent on strategic surprise, and to that end had put considerable effort into deception. He had feinted at least twice before by appearing to prepare for war. Israel mobilized both times, at great cost and budgetary stress but to no purpose. The experience made it sceptical and complacent.

On 6 October 1973, the Jewish holy day of Yom Kippur, Egyptian forces attacked Israel; at the same time, Syrian troops were flooding the Golan Heights in a surprise offensive. The successful crossing of the Suez Canal and the penetration of Israel's line of defence was a brilliant military achievement. Sadat had set a very modest goal of advancing 10–15 kilometres east of the canal before halting.[4]

On the morning of 6 October, before the US learned that war had broken out, the Washington Special Action Group (WSAG) – an elite NSC unit – met, in Kissinger's absence, in the White House Situation Room. A document prepared by the NSC had tried to interpret the various signs of impending conflict. Possibly the evacuation of Soviet advisors the previous day meant that Moscow had heard war was imminent. Perhaps there had been a major crisis in Arab-Soviet relations. US intelligence, again downplaying the likelihood of an

1. US Congress, Senate, "Multinational Corporations and US Foreign Policy", Hearing, 94th Cong., 1st sess., 1975, 7:33, p. 509.
2. Safran, *Saudi Arabia*, p. 155.
3. Heikal, *The Road to Ramadan*, p. 181.
4. Kirk J. Beattie, *Egypt During the Sadat Years* (New York: Palgrave, 2000), pp. 134–5.

Arab attack on Israel, saw an Arab-Soviet crisis as a more plausible explanation. According to Stein, the US and Israel took the Egyptian deployment of forces in early October along the Suez Canal as another pretence of launching an attack.[1] But war did break out.

Israel had assumed that it had sufficient supplies to last for three weeks of war, a premise derived from the experience of the Six-Day War; but the Israelis now found themselves consuming materiel at an alarming rate. That miscalculation of requirements would prove grave for Israel, and would also lead directly to a Saudi-US confrontation that would have a tremendous effect on the oil prices.[2]

On 7 October, the US began secretly to send limited supplies to Israel. On 9 October, the Israelis pleaded urgently for more military assistance. Acknowledging the diplomatic implications of substantial US wartime aid, Kissinger (now Secretary of State) allowed unmarked El Al aircraft to go to the US for additional supplies, and also began pressing US commercial aircraft into shipping materiel, despite their reluctance to be involved in the conflict for fear of being targeted by Palestinian fanatics.

On 10 October, Yamani told oil company representatives that if the US made a misstep during the current hostilities – such as re-supplying Israel – Saudi Arabia would immediately reduce oil production. That day, Kenneth Rush, Deputy Secretary of State, met top executives from Exxon and Gulf Oil, who warned Washington to avoid action that could lead to moves against US oil interests.

On 11 October, Faisal sent a message to Nixon via the US embassy, urging him to take action to bring about an end to hostilities and to insist on Israel's withdrawal from the occupied territories. The Nixon administration was pleased to receive such a restrained message from Faisal. Meeting Saqqaf the next day, Kissinger explained that the US objective was "to bring about an end to hostilities and lay a basis for achieving a just settlement".[3] On 12 October the State Department similarly instructed the US embassy in Saudi Arabia to

---

1. Kenneth Stein, *Heroic Diplomacy: Sadat, Kissinger, Carter, Begin, and the Quest for Arab-Israeli Peace* (New York: Routledge, 1999), p. 68.
2. Daniel Yergin, *The Prize: The Epic Quest for Oil, Money and Power* (New York: Barnes & Noble, 1992), pp. 603–4.
3. United States Department of State Records, RG 59, SN 70-73, POL 15-1 US/ Nixon, Joseph Sisco, Assistant Secretary of State to Kissinger, "Proposed Presidential Message to King Faisal", 12 October 1973, Attachment Tab B.

deliver a message from Nixon to Faisal. Nixon stated that the US wanted to see the situation resolved in a manner that would contribute "to the attainment of our mutual objective of bringing a just and lasting peace to the Middle East", and reassured Faisal that "our policy at this time is not one-sided". The president concluded by emphasizing that it was essential to "work together to help bring about a restoration of an atmosphere in which we can renew effectively the search for a just and lasting political settlement."[1]

Meanwhile, Nixon, Kissinger, and Secretary of Defense James Schlesinger were beginning to make major decisions on the US supply operation. As noted, US commercial aircraft companies wanted no part of the conflict, and the Israelis were running low on ammunition. On 13 October Nixon ordered a major US military airlift to supply Israel. Kissinger justified this on the grounds that Egypt failed to support a ceasefire in place, which was an Egyptian blunder. He believed it was necessary to prolong the fighting to create a "situation in which the Arabs would have to ask for a ceasefire rather than we".[2]

As a US military airlift to Israel could not occur in secret, Kissinger and the State Department coordinated a diplomatic campaign to minimize the damage. Kissinger sent a private message to Faisal, playing up the anti-Soviet angle and suggesting that the reason behind the US decision was insufficient Soviet cooperation in the latest ceasefire along with the Soviets' having supplied Egypt and Syria – what he called a "massive airlift". (Kissinger acknowledged, years later, that the Soviet leaders had been pressing for a ceasefire from the beginning, and that the Soviet airlift was not comparable in scope or impact to the US's airlift to Israel.)[3] Moreover, Kissinger said that the US decision was necessary "if we are to remain in a position to use our influence to work for a just and lasting peace".[4] Although Faisal's response to Nixon remains classified, Prince Saud al-Faisal, the Saudi foreign minister, would say years later that the king was angry, and that his reply was strong and harsh.[5] However, the Saudis were careful to conceal any antagonism; US Ambassador James Akins informed

---

1. Ibid.
2. National Security Archive (NSA), Transcripts of Sec. of State Henry Kissinger, Staff Meetings, 1973–1977, Box 1, Transcript, "Secretary's Staff Meeting", 23 October 1973.
3. Henry Kissinger, *Diplomacy* (New York: Simon & Schuster, 1994), p. 739.
4. NPMP, NSCF, Box 1174, 1973 Middle East War, 15 October 1973, File No. 9, State Dept. to US Embassy, Jeddah, 14 October 1973.
5. Prince Saud al-Faisal, interview with the author, December 2005.

the State Department that "there was no visible anger at the US, but rather a genuine expression of sorrow that the US government move had set a course for inevitable divergence of interests of US and Saudi Arabia government."[1]

On 17 October a group of Arab foreign ministers headed by Omar Saqqaf met both Kissinger and Nixon. Saqqaf feared that "US-Arab relations could be damaged by the US re-supply of Israel", and called on Israel to "respect the resolutions of the UN" expressing concern at Israel's "intention to keep Arab territory". He added: "The US should support the integrity of the states of the Middle East, and this required Israeli withdrawal from the territory of Egypt, Jordan and Syria." Saqqaf also expressed Saudi Arabia's view that the Soviet Union was not interested in solving the Middle East problem, but in practice was seeking to take advantage of it to increase its own influence. Indirectly, the US, by supporting Israel, was helping the Soviets towards this goal. Finally, he insisted that no Arab leader could accept a return to the 6 October ceasefire lines. He repeated his hope that US-Arab relations would not suffer and in conclusion summarized the Arab position, which was that Israel must withdraw to pre-1967 lines and respect Palestinian rights. He also asked for a more balanced US position in dealing with Israel and the Arabs.

Kissinger replied that the US recognized how intolerable the pre-6 October situation was for the Arabs, and said that even without the war, the US was willing to try to improve the situation. Two problems had to be resolved: ending the war, and working for peace – and the US position was that "there should be a ceasefire based on present realities, to be followed rapidly by negotiations."[2] President Nixon reiterated Kissinger's theme, assuring the Arab foreign ministers: "You have a commitment from us. A commitment not just to obtain a ceasefire; what we are saying is that the ceasefire will be linked with a diplomatic initiative in which we will use our full weight."[3]

Meanwhile, members of the Organization of Arab Petroleum Exporting Countries (OAPEC) met on 17 October in Kuwait. The options available to

---

1. NPMP, NSCF, Box 1174, 1973 Middle East War, 16 October 1973, File No. 11, US Embassy, Jeddah, to State Dept., 16 October 1973.
2. United States Department of State Records, SN 70-73, POL 27 Arab-Isr, William B. Quandt to Kissinger, Memoranda of Conversation with Arab foreign ministers, 17 October 1973.
3. NPMP, NSCF, Box 664, Middle East War Memos & Misc., 6–17 October 1973, Memo of conversation between Nixon and Arab Foreign Ministers, 17 October 1973.

the Arab oil producers for wielding the oil weapon were limited. Expropriating the assets of US oil companies was ruled out as possibly counterproductive; if the companies then retaliated by withdrawing their personnel, production and oil movements would be adversely affected. Furthermore, while embargos could be imposed on specific destinations, there were considerable misgivings about monitoring the complex global distribution of crude. It was finally decided that, as overall Arab oil output could be cut by varying degrees or completely, this method would generally be simple to administer as well as adjustable.[1]

During this meeting the Saudi government resisted a proposal from Iraq for all-out economic warfare against the US, the consequences of which, as Yergin notes, would have been very uncertain for all parties concerned.[2] The oil ministers, except for Iraq's, then announced that average September output would be cut by 5 percent, with further cuts in production of 5 percent every month thereafter until Israel withdrew completely from Arab territories and until the legitimate rights of the Palestinians had been restored.[3] Production cuts against a single country would be more effective than an export ban, because oil could always be moved around; such cuts would also ensure that the absolute level of available oil went down. Meanwhile, the overall plan would maximize uncertainty, tension and rivalry within and among the oil-importing countries. Saudi Arabia announced on 18 October, that it was cutting production by 10 percent effective immediately.[4]

A WSAG meeting on 17 October had, meanwhile, recommended maintaining the airlift at the highest level and initiating an immediate sealift of equipment. A decision would be made on 19 October concerning a request for supplementary military assistance to Israel. "Without our airlift," said Kissinger, "Israel would be dead." He also remarked, during a review of plans for energy conservation in the event of an oil embargo, that his diplomatic strategy during the present war had eliminated the possibility of an Arab oil embargo.[5] Nixon, who telephoned during the meeting, said: "We can't allow a Soviet-supported operation to succeed against an American-supported

---

1. Holden and Jones, *The House of Saud*, p. 339.
2. Yergin, *The Prize*, p. 607.
3. *Ukaz*, 18 October 1973.
4. Saudi Press Agency, 18 October 1973.
5. NPMP, NSC Institutional Files, Box H-117, WSAG Minutes 10-2-73 to 7-23-74, Minutes of WSAG, 17 October 1973.

operation." He confirmed his belief that the airlift was essential for preserving US credibility everywhere, as well as for bringing Israel to a settlement.[1]

Faisal and Sadat were careful not to provoke Washington into committing itself to seeking an Israeli military victory, and were therefore satisfied with the assurances offered on 17 October by Nixon and Kissinger. But Nixon's request to Congress on 19 October for a US $2.2 billion appropriation for military assistance to Israel, along with sudden drastic changes in the military situation, put an altogether different light on the whole of Washington's policy. It was strongly suspected that when Nixon and Kissinger said they were striving to end the fighting and prevent its spread in preparation for negotiations, they had been deceiving the Arabs all along.[2] Faisal retaliated by going beyond the policy of cutbacks to an embargo of all shipments of oil to the US, and on 21 October the Saudi government instructed ARAMCO to stop sales to the US military.[3] ARAMCO officials were summoned to Washington to discuss the situation.

The US defence establishment was concerned about the operational capability of the US Sixth Fleet in the Mediterranean and the US Seventh Fleet in the Pacific and Indian Oceans. A memorandum from the Pentagon on 30 November 1973 informed the White House that the Department of Defense was facing a serious petroleum shortage, and unless the US found a way to meet its demand "we will soon be forced to begin standing down operational forces".[4] The defence establishment wanted to avoid official negotiations; therefore Deputy Secretary of Defense Bill Clement and ARAMCO CEO Frank Jungers met to consider how the Saudis might be influenced to allow ARAMCO to ship oil to the US military.

Jungers met Faisal shortly thereafter to explain the problem and the serious consequences to the Middle East of undermining US military capabilities, emphasizing that if and when a shift in US policy towards Israel occurred, it would certainly not happen straightaway. He urged the king to allow

---

1. NPMP, NSC Institutional Files, Box H-92, WSAG Meeting Middle East 10/17/73, Folder 6, Memcon, "WSAG Principles: Middle East War", 17 October 1973.
2. Safran, *Saudi Arabia*, pp. 156–60.
3. Saudi Press Agency, 21 October 1973.
4. NPMP, NSC Files, Subject Files, Box 321, Folder: "Energy Crisis, November 1973–74", Memorandum from Pentagon to the White House, 30 November 1973.

ARAMCO to provide necessary oil supplies to the US military. "Are you telling me, then," asked Faisal, "that this approach is not instigated by the oil companies?" Jungers explicitly replied: "No, it's not." Faisal agreed to not make an issue of it, but warned Jungers: "God help you if you get caught, or if it becomes a public issue."[1] ARAMCO then carried out emergency shipments of Saudi oil to US military bases all over the world, in violation of the embargo.

According to Faisal's strategic thinking, the danger of creating difficulties for the US military in its confrontation with Soviet military operations – which he saw as the ultimate threat to Saudi Arabia and to the Muslim world at large – was critical. It influenced his decision to allow emergency shipments of oil to the US military.

On 22 October, the Security Council passed Resolution 338, calling on the belligerents to end the fighting and immediately to start implementation of Resolution 242, which was passed in 1967 at the end of the Six-Day War and, among other things, called for Israeli withdrawal from occupied Palestine.[2]

Kissinger and Faisal met in Riyadh on 8 November. The secretary of state explained the difficulty the US was facing because of the embargo. Faisal demanded an immediate announcement by the US that "Israel must withdraw from the territories and allow the return of the Palestinians", and that if it failed to do so, that the US "will no longer support it". Kissinger emphasized that such announcement would create dramatic upheaval in the US. He urged Faisal to consider lifting the embargo "to make our task easier". He explained that opponents of the administration would mobilize public opinion with the view that "we are yielding to Arab blackmail". Faisal replied that this was the Arabs' own predicament: "The communists are accusing some Arab elements of going along with US pressure." At Kissinger's insistence, Faisal explained that, since the embargo had not been decided upon exclusively by the Saudis but was part of a joint decision, he needed a speedy public announcement, and would consult with and persuade his Arab colleagues. Later, Kissinger met

---

1. Frank Jungers, "From Construction Engineer to CEO and Chairman of Aramco, 1948–1978", an oral history conducted in 1992 by Carol Hicke, in *American Perspectives of Aramco, the Saudi-Arabian Oil-Producing Company, 1930s to 1980s* (Berkeley, CA: University of California, Bancroft Library, Regional Oral History Office, 1995), pp. 134–6.
2. Holden and Johns, *The House of Saud*, p. 343.

Saqqaf, who said: "We want to dispel the myth that there is no connection between oil and the problem in the Middle East."[1]

Kissinger and Faisal had another meeting on 14 December. According to US documentary sources, they again discussed the embargo, and Kissinger told the king: "We have had to reduce the military readiness of some of our forces to conserve petroleum. That weakens the defensive capability of the US, and that affects us both." He understood Faisal's action as retaliation for what had seemed like the US siding with the Arabs' enemies. "But now we have made a solemn promise," he added. Faisal repeated his previous demand for a public statement. Kissinger again played up the domestic angle and suggested a lifting of the embargo, which could be re-imposed at a later point if the negotiations failed. He claimed that "public blame would focus on the other side if the other side seemed to be the cause of the negotiations impasse." Once again Faisal insisted on a statement mentioning withdrawal, recognition of Palestinian rights and the fate of Jerusalem: "At the moment that is said, the faucets would open again." At the end of the meeting Faisal said he would be pleased to announce the lifting of the embargo the following day, but cautioned that, "as the American expression goes, it does take two [to tango] ... it should be a situation where you strengthen my hand and I strengthen yours."[2]

Despite the conclusion of ceasefire and disengagement agreements between Israel and Egypt on 18 January 1974, and notwithstanding attempts to initiate a comprehensive conference for settling the Middle East problem, the partial withdrawal of Israeli forces from post-1967 positions under UN forces supervision and Nixon's messages declaring his wish to announce the end of the embargo in his State of the Union address, no immediate reduction occurred in the total embargo of oil to the US. Kissinger then hinted that he might be obliged to release the texts of the commitments undertaken by Faisal, to which the Saudis responded by suggesting that they, too, might have some embarrassing messages to release.[3]

In Washington, meanwhile, certain parties had advocated the seizure of

---

1. NSA, State Dept. Records, (POL 7 US/KISSINGER), Memorandum of Conversation between Saqqaf and Kissinger, 8 November 1973.
2. NSA, State Dept. Records, (POL 27 ARAB-ISR), Memorandum of Conversation between Faisal and Kissinger, 14 December 1973.
3. William B Quandt, *Peace Process: American Diplomacy and the Arab-Israeli Conflict Since 1967*, (Washington, DC: Brookings Institution Press 2005), p. 466, n. 32.

Saudi oilfields. On 19 November 1973, Kissinger warned that if the embargo continued, "the US will have to consider what countermeasures it may have to take"; to which Yamani implied that Saudi Arabia would cut its oil production by 80 percent.[1] In December, Senator James Fulbright, Chairman of the Foreign Relations Committee, warned that consumers might move militarily against producers to obtain supplies.[2] At the end of December Saqqaf sent an open letter to the American people, which was published in *The New York Times* and *The Washington Post*. Having explained the motives behind the Saudi embargo, he asked the people for their understanding of the Arab view and concluded thus: "We offer Israel peace, but we don't offer our lands." He added that fair-minded people should not expect otherwise.[3] In January 1974, Secretary of Defense Schlesinger stated that if the embargo continued, public opinion might demand a show of force.[4] During a press conference on 25 February, Nixon threatened to stop US efforts to achieve peace, saying: "If the embargo is not lifted, it will naturally slow down the efforts that we are making on the peace front."[5]

Sadat had wanted to lift the embargo after the disengagement agreement, but Faisal refused – he believed it was much too early. On 11 February, the king arranged for a summit in Algiers with Sadat, Algerian President Houari Boumédienne and Assad.[6] Sadat argued for ending the embargo; Assad insisted on its continuation until an agreement on disengagement between Syria and Israel was achieved; and Faisal played a mediating role. The summit then sent Saqqaf and Egyptian Foreign Minister Ismail Fahmi to meet Kissinger on 17 February to discuss details for a proposed Syrian-Israeli disengagement.[7]

Saqqaf and Fahmi informed the US, in confidence, of the decision of the four leaders to lift the embargo at the next meeting of the Arab oil ministers, and conveyed the leaders' insistence – not as a condition, but rather as a strong request – that maximum effort should be made to bring about a Syrian-Israeli disengagement. They also requested that Nixon send Kissinger to the region to

---

1. *The New York Times*, 22 November 1973.
2. *The New York Times*, 10 December 1973.
3. Saudi Press Agency, 1 January 1974.
4. *The New York Times*, 23 January 1974.
5. Public Papers of the Presidents (PPP), Richard Nixon, The President's News Conference, 25 February 1974 (Washington DC: US Government Printing Office).
6. *Ukaz*, 11 February 1974.
7. *Ukaz*, 17 February 1974.

start the process. Saqqaf explained that the Saudi logic behind this decision was not to complicate the relationship with the US but to "help the administration to be strong and to take more measures".[1] During a meeting on 26 February, Kissinger and Assad discussed a draft Syrian-Israeli disengagement. Kissinger suggested, and Assad accepted, that the Syrians and the Israelis should come to Washington for separate talks. On 2 March the US announced that Kissinger would hold independent talks with Israel and Syria, aimed at achieving a "separation of troops" agreement for the Golan Heights.[2]

Kissinger arrived in Riyadh the same day to discuss the lifting of the oil embargo with Faisal. According to the Saudi newspaper *Ukaz*, he acknowledged Faisal's disappointment with the US but appealed for cooperation, assuring the monarch of Nixon's commitment to an Israeli withdrawal and his personal confidence that a settlement was now possible. Faisal, however, refused the appeal and insisted on keeping the embargo until Israel withdrew from Jerusalem. Faisal's refusal was based on the following reasons:

1. Kissinger had not obtained a clear-cut position from the Israeli side;
2. Israel had not accepted the Syrian draft proposal for disengagement;
3. Kissinger had failed to exert pressure on the Israelis to withdraw;
4. The Arabs rejected Kissinger's suggestion that the embargo be lifted in stages;
5. The lifting of the embargo was a collective Arab decision.[3]

The disparity in the positions of Faisal and Saqqaf can be attributed to the king's caution in wishing to reserve the right to withdraw in case US promises were not fulfilled. Otherwise, Saqqaf would not have been so adamant and explicit in informing the US president of the decision to lift the embargo.

Faisal was aware that the embargo and the rapid increase in oil prices had catastrophic effects on the ability of Western Europe and the US to counter the Soviet Union; Western economic chaos certainly did not serve the Kingdom's interest. Saudi Arabia could afford friction with the US on regional issues such

---

1. NSA, The White House, Memorandum of conversation between Saqqaf and Kissinger, 2 March 1974.
2. Stein, *Heroic Diplomacy*, p. 156.
3. *Ukaz*, 4 March 1974.

as the Arab-Israeli conflict, but not when the overall strategic perspective was taken into account. Yamani said on 17 March that Saudi Arabia had changed its position on the embargo because "the US had changed its political position ... the Israeli occupation of the Golan Heights must be terminated."[1]

On 18 March, in Vienna, five months after the embargo began, most of the Arab states announced their decision to end it. Yamani did warn, however, that it might be reinstated "if the US stopped its efforts to achieve a just peace in the Middle East".[2] The following day President Nixon told the National Association of Broadcasters in Houston: "We seek a permanent peace as an end in itself ... I am confident that the progress we are going to continue to make on the peace front in the Mideast will be very helpful in seeing to it that an oil embargo is not re-imposed."[3]

The war and the embargo essentially served the same purpose: to break the diplomatic stalemate that had existed since 1967. The 1973 war vastly increased Arab financial power and generated unprecedented Arab solidarity in the form of a Cairo-Damascus-Riyadh axis, which had seemed well positioned to extract major changes in the pro-Israeli policy of the US. But Kissinger's masterful intervention in the conflict neutralized this threat.

Moderating OPEC

The war of October 1973 and the changed dynamics of global demand for oil encouraged many members of the Organization of the Petroleum Exporting Countries (OPEC) to adopt policies based on maintaining oil prices at sufficiently high levels to extend the life of known reserves.

On 24 December 1973, during an OPEC meeting in Tehran, the Shah of Iran decided to set a price of US $11.65 per barrel.[4] Realizing that the Iranian-led price increase on top of the oil production cut had worked to the benefit of the USSR and damaged Western European economies, Faisal pressed the US to bring the Shah into more intense discussions in order to ease prices.[5] Arguing that OPEC members had overshot the mark with the huge jump in oil prices in 1973–4, Saudi Arabia publicly proposed that Iran join in a 20–25

1. *Ukaz*, 17 March 1974.
2. *Ukaz*, 20 March 1974.
3. Department of State, Bulletin, 8 April 1974, p. 368.
4. Safran, *Saudi Arabia*, p. 168.
5. Bronson, *Thicker than Oil*, p. 122.

percent reduction in the posted price, from US $11.65 to US $9.00 per barrel, to enable the world to recover and avoid an economic depression.[1] Though it was Iran and Venezuela that had actually led the battle within OPEC to raise prices, the US media blamed Arab producers,[2] and many regarded the price hike as economic belligerence toward the US.

Saudi Arabia participated in OPEC's price increases, but advocated that these should be gradual. In addition, it became a big export market for US products. Moreover, the Saudis opposed communism, pro-Soviet regimes and leftist movements in the Middle East and in the Third World in general. All these factors were cited by US policy-makers as reasons why Saudi Arabia was critical to maintaining US interests in the region.

In the aftermath of the embargo, the US now needed Saudi cooperation with regard to the supply and price of oil and the recycling of petrodollars, while Saudi Arabia needed continued US support for its ultimate security as well as immensely increased technical assistance. Oil served to generate interdependence between Saudi Arabia and the US, and drew the latter into the Middle East to protect its free flow. To create powerful disincentives for future oil embargoes, the US tried to draw key Arab states into its political and economic orbit. Kissinger believed that heavy Saudi investment in the US economy was the only way to neutralize the oil weapon, as any embargo or huge rise in oil prices would hurt the Saudis there. He wanted "the producing nations to become responsible participants in the international economy".[3]

Kissinger had, while visiting Riyadh on 2 March 1974, met Second Deputy and Interior Minister Prince Fahd, who suggested the creation of joint initiatives to develop large projects in Saudi Arabia and the US. "We want such a relationship because our security interests are parallel," Prince Fahd had said. He had also indicated the Saudis' preference for a close relationship with the US over the Europeans, saying that in the economic field "I would like to see Saudi capital invested in the US ... I would also like to see American capital invested here for the same reason."[4]

1. *The New York Times*, 28 January 1974.
2. V. H. Oppenheim, "We Pushed Them", *Foreign Policy* (winter 1976–7), pp. 40–9.
3. Henry Kissinger, *Years of Renewal* (New York: Touchstone/Simon & Schuster, 1999), p. 677.
4. NSA, The White House, Memorandum of Conversation between Fahd and Kissinger, 2 March 1974.

An interdepartmental study was duly begun on 12 March 1974 to look at developing economic, military and scientific/technological cooperation programmes between the two countries, and on 6 June 1974 the US signed a broad cooperative agreement with Saudi Arabia that involved economics, technology, industry and defence. It called for the establishment of a Joint Commission on Economic Cooperation and joint security cooperation, and brought together officials from both governments to devise strategies for the development of the Saudi economy and for defence modernization.[1] The agreement was described by Kissinger as "a milestone in US relations with Saudi Arabia and Arab countries in general",[2] and by Fahd as opening "a new and glorious chapter in the relations between our two countries".[3]

As a result of the agreement, Saudi Arabia publicly announced, in July 1974, an oil auction of approximately 1.5 million barrels per day on the open market, accepting whatever price the conditions of surplus would generate.[4] However, strong reaction by other OPEC members forced Faisal to cancel the auction on 9 September.

The new US-Saudi interdependence was marked by a 1,000 percent increase in trade between the two countries for the period of 1972–6. In 1974 alone, the Kingdom invested more than a quarter of its earnings in the US,[5] and by 1979 it was the largest single holder of US dollars and government securities and bonds.[6] Oil generated a boom in consumption demand in Saudi Arabia, which translated into a massive import dependency. This dependence on oil revenues also made the Kingdom extremely vulnerable to big fluctuations in oil prices and declines in oil revenues.[7] The oil boom created two negative consequences for Saudi Arabia. First, it accelerated Western penetration, generating domestic interests with a stake in relations with the West. Second, it increased security dependency on the West, enhanced by the Iranian Revolution in 1979.[8]

1. *Ukaz*, 10 June 1974.
2. *The New York Times*, 9 June 1974.
3. *Ukaz*, 9 June 1974.
4. *MEES*, 26 July 1974.
5. Juan de Onis, "A Multibillion Purchase of Treasury Issue Due", *The New York Times*, 7 September 1974.
6. Martin Tolchin, "Foreigners' Political Roles in US Grow by Investing", *The New York Times*, 30 December 1985.
7. Abbas Alnasrawi, *Arab Nationalism, Oil, and the Political Economy of Dependency* (New York: Greenwood Press, 1991), pp. 164–77.
8. Vassiliev, *History of Saudi Arabia*, pp. 398–404.

The 1973 war and the associated oil boom also fuelled Arab interdependence, stimulated by significant transfers of oil wealth to non-oil-producing Arab states and the importation from them of their excess labour by the oil states.

As the December 1974 OPEC meeting approached, the Saudi government sought a compromise between the demands of consumer governments for price relief and those of its OPEC partners for revenue maintenance.[1] Following a Saudi initiative, OPEC established an oil price of US $10.12 per barrel for nine months – far less than the reduction sought by the US.

Saudi production fell during January and February 1975 to a level that was 24 percent lower than that of 1974, in keeping with shrinkage in total OPEC exports. According to Safran, Saudi Arabia's oil strategy was based on the Shah's declaration that he would consider as a hostile act any action to bring the price down, and on the fact that the other Arab oil producers would not be provoked. It also recognized that the world had absorbed the shock of the price increase; that the US attitude towards Tehran's price was ambiguous; and that the US demand was incomprehensible and incredible.[2] Yamani later insisted that the US had to pressure Iran if it wanted Saudi Arabia to use its production capacity on behalf of moderation.[3]

In 1975, the world economy was at the bottom of a recession, with industrial activity at -3 percent from the 1973 level. The US position was that an oil price increase would jeopardize global economic recovery. On 14 September 1975, Yamani said: "We understand that we must work to avoid any action which would be damaging for the world economy."[4] When OPEC decided to increase the oil price by 10 percent at the end of September 1975, Prince Saud was reported in *Ukaz* as saying: "The time was not proper for such a decision." He also said that Saudi Arabia had accepted the decision reluctantly.[5]

Saudi Arabia's position, then, was that in the interests of both OPEC and the consuming countries, moderation had to be a key goal (as it had always been for the Kingdom). Saudi Arabia would always be guided by long-term principles that took world stability as a prime objective, and it continued to play the much-needed role of price moderator and swing producer. Rustow sums

1. *The New York Times*, 10 September 1974.
2. Safran, *Saudi Arabia*, pp. 170–1.
3. Theodore H. Moran, "Modeling OPEC Behavior: Economic and Political Alternatives", *International Organization*, vol. 35, no. 2 (spring 1981), p. 256.
4. *Ukaz*, 15 September 1975.
5. *Ukaz*, 29 September 1975.

up Saudi oil policy from 1974 accordingly: the Kingdom had opposed pressure from OPEC's price hawks for price increases in excess of global inflation; its excess capacity had guaranteed it the all-important role of regulator of OPEC; and to prevent excessive prices, it threatened to increase production.[1]

Saudi Arabia's long-term policy was guided by supply and demand for oil, together with the cost of oil alternatives. In pricing, it was influenced by two basic principles. First, the country did not intend to deprive future generations by rapid exhaustion of its wealth. Second, it did not want to eliminate oil as a major source of energy before it had completely industrialized its economy to provide future income sources other than oil.[2] As a result, it found itself at odds with both Western and OPEC nations, as was apparent at the OPEC meeting in Vienna in September 1975: the Saudis favoured a freeze, or at best a small price increase to assist the emerging signs of world economic recovery, while the OPEC majority favoured a price increase. The meeting produced a deadlock, with the Saudis offering 5 percent and the Iranians demanding 15 percent. The result was a compromise at 10 percent.[3]

For several years following the embargo, Saudi Arabia continued to make financial sacrifices by producing oil above its development needs.[4] During this period the US followed a counterproductive policy of keeping domestic prices artificially low, thereby encouraging consumers to continue their excessive dependence on oil. This also discouraged the search for alternative energy.[5] As a consequence, strong demand in the US created an upward pressure on market prices, but because of the Kingdom's policy, domestic prices did not rise in real terms.

The Peace Process

Saudi Arabia has always seen the resolution of the Arab-Israeli conflict as essential, insofar as continuing hostility with Israel carries with it the potential of endangering Saudi relations with the US. It also strengthens radical forces

---

1. Dankwart A. Rustow, "US-Saudi Relations and the Oil Crisis of the 1980's", *Foreign Affairs* 55 (April 1977), pp. 503–5.
2. Suliman S. Olayan, "Saudi Arabia: The Burden of Moderation", *The Washington Quarterly* 4 (autumn 1983).
3. *The Oil and Gas Journal*, 6 October 1975.
4. Ian Seymour, *OPEC: Instrument of Change* (London: Macmillan, 1980), p. 176.
5. Yergin, *The Prize*, pp. 659–60.

in the region. Kissinger had, from the outset of the 1973 war, sought to bring about a role for the US as a peace broker. With the ceasefire in place he began his famous "shuttle diplomacy" to achieve a separation of forces agreement and promoted a peace conference in Geneva, making stopovers in Riyadh to report on the progress to Faisal. Despite Kissinger's repeated denials, the Saudi embargo and its consequences did affect the pace of his mediation activities, if not their substance. The oil embargo and the ability of the Arabs to inflict high costs on Israel forced US intervention on behalf of a negotiated settlement. The October war had shown that the Arabs could not hope to defeat Israel militarily, but the costs and risks of another war now led the US to take a more active role. Sadat was convinced that the US held the key to Israeli concessions, and most important of all that Kissinger was willing to use its leverage to obtain them. As Sadat recounted in his memoirs, his first meeting with Kissinger seemed to offer new perspectives: "The first hour made me feel I was dealing with an entirely new mentality, a new political method."[1]

The process started with Kissinger stopping in Riyadh on 8 November 1973, having settled the problem of supplying the Egyptian Third Army. He argued the logic of a step-by-step approach and appealed to Faisal for help opening channels of communication with the Syrians. Faisal stated: "There will be no stability and peace unless Israel withdraws from the occupied territories and the Palestinians go back to their own homes." Kissinger affirmed: "The President has now decided to make a major effort to bring about a settlement."[2] Later that day, Kissinger met Prince Fahd, who expressed his hope that the matters that had come between the two countries were "transitory and not permanent in nature". Fahd appreciated that things could not be accomplished overnight, but insisted on using the most expeditious methods possible.[3]

Kissinger stopped again in Riyadh on 14 December to inform Faisal of his progress in promoting Egyptian-Israeli disengagement, along with his intention of discussing a similar scheme for the Golan Heights with Assad. He also told Faisal about his efforts to convene a peace conference in Geneva one week hence, indicating that Israel had some objections to certain procedural points that he would attempt to overcome when he met the Israelis two days later.

1. El-Sadat, *In Search of Identity*, p. 291.
2. NSA, The White House, Memorandum of Conversation between Faisal and Kissinger, 8 November 1973.
3. NSA, State Dept. Records, (POL 7 US/KISSINGER), Memorandum of Conversation between Fahd and Kissinger, 8 November 1973.

Faisal was of the view that Israel, in concert with the USSR, appeared "not to have an interest in having this problem resolved", and told Kissinger: "If Israel is not subjected to some firm pressure, she will continue in the path of arrogance."[1] On 17 January 1974, Egypt and Israel signed a disengagement agreement, which also established a step-by-step approach to peace.[2] Kissinger mediated a settlement of preliminary issues between Syria and Israel on 27 February, thereby opening the way to negotiation on the separation of forces.[3]

In pursuing an Arab-Israeli settlement, Saudi Arabia cultivated its US connections. Faisal would not risk being publicly identified with US policies, but was prepared to facilitate them by means of subtle Saudi diplomacy. Kissinger regularly briefed Faisal and outlined any problems, though without requesting Saudi assistance. However, he reported, he would often later discover a Saudi footprint helping the negotiations along and removing obstacles. At his last meeting with Kissinger on 14 February 1975, Faisal warned him against brokering a separate agreement and urged him to use his best judgement to proceed toward peace.[4]

Kissinger's shuttle diplomacy in February and March 1975 was aimed at bringing about a second limited agreement between Egypt and Israel on the question of Sinai. The Syrians, who objected to this, accused Sadat of seeking a separate political agreement and tried to enlist Saudi support for their position. Sadat stated in reply that he envisaged a purely military agreement, and that he would insist on any Egyptian-Israeli agreement being linked to a similar one between Syria and Israel. Faisal tried without success to arrange for Sadat, Assad, King Hussein and Palestine Liberation Organization chairman Yasser Arafat to meet to coordinate policies, while assuring the Syrians that he would continue to try as far as possible to influence Sadat to limit the scope of any agreement with Israel.[5] However, on 22 March Israel rejected the proposed agreement, which forced Kissinger to announce that the US was prepared to begin a reassessment of its relations with Israel.[6]

---

1. NSA, State Dept. Records (POL 27 ARAB-ISR), Memorandum of Conversation between Faisal and Kissinger, 14 December 1973.
2. Kissinger, *Years of Upheaval*, pp. 958–62.
3. Ibid.
4. Kissinger, *Years of Renewal*, p. 397.
5. Safran, *Saudi Arabia*, pp. 240–1.
6. Quandt, *Decade of Decision*, p. 266.

At Faisal's funeral[1] King Khalid, his successor, arranged a meeting between Sadat and Assad to repair the damage; the two leaders met Khalid in Riyadh on 21 April. The Syrians, who suspected the US of trying to lure the Egyptians out of the confrontation and then forcing them to accept whatever terms Israel could be made to offer, argued that the Arabs should go to Geneva together or not at all. Sadat, on the other hand, believed the Arabs would have little to gain from another military confrontation with Israel and feared that the subsequent deadlock would recreate a solid US-Israel front. In his view, the Arabs should agree on no surrender of territory, no separate agreements and no final arrangements without the Palestinians, while allowing for ample flexibility in method and tactics. The Saudi government, too, was disturbed about the consequences of a stalemate, renewal of military conflict with Israel and the prospect of a political confrontation with the US.[2]

The joint statement at the end of the meeting declared that a more consolidated cooperation had been agreed between Egypt and Syria and that any political move should be part of a comprehensive movement in confronting Israel. They also expressed willingness to achieve a permanent and lasting peace, and their determination not to return to the "no-war no-peace" position.[3] Two days later Prince Saud declared: "Saudi Arabia doesn't object to the reconvening of the Geneva conference." He emphasized that "the Palestinian issue is the cause of the conflict in the Middle East, and it should be dealt with".[4]

Gerald Ford, the new US president, met Sadat in Salzburg, Austria on 21 June. Sadat proposed that Umm Khisheiba, an early-warning-system and surveillance station in the Sinai upon which the Israelis had insisted, should be operated by US civilians rather than by Israelis.[5] During a visit to Washington later that month, Israeli Prime Minister Yitzhak Rabin agreed to a new, deeper Israeli withdrawal line, and Ford presented the idea of US civilian technicians in the buffer zone as a US concept.[6] Thus a new round of shuttle diplomacy got underway on 21 August.

1. Faisal was assassinated in his office on 25 March 1975 by his nephew Faisal bin Musa'id, who had just returned from the US after studying there for many years. Many Saudis accuse the US of masterminding the murder in retaliation for Faisal's role in uniting the Arabs and imposing an oil embargo in 1973.
2. Safran, *Saudi Arabia*, pp. 241–2.
3. *Ukaz*, 24 April 1975.
4. Saudi Press Agency, 26 April 1975.
5. Quandt, *Decade of Decision*, p. 271.
6. Yitzhak Rabin, *The Rabin Memoirs* (Boston: Little, Brown and Company, 1979),

On 1 September 1975, Kissinger concluded a ten-day shuttle with the signing of an Egyptian-Israeli accord, known as "Sinai II", that required Israel to withdraw from the Abu Rudeis oilfields and the Gidi and Mitla passes in Sinai. The two sides also agreed to buffer zones, UN forces and a US civilian presence to supervise the intelligence-gathering station; they also agreed not to use force or the threat of force in resolving their conflict. In addition, Egypt publicly consented to non-military cargo passing to and from Israel through the reopened Suez Canal.[1] Saudi Arabia, which had been consulted throughout the negotiations, endorsed the agreement on 2 September in Riyadh; Prince Saud described it as "a step toward a final settlement". According to Safran, the Kingdom supported the agreement for three reasons. First, it believed the alternative was problematic from its own point of view. Second, it had sufficient leverage with Syria to keep the lines of cooperation open and, third, with the US, which would enable it to repair Egyptian-Syrian cooperation – something both sides needed.[2]

Egypt gradually abandoned the Soviet Union for an alignment with the US, tied closely to the latter's dominant role in the peace process. Convinced that he could not beat Israel, Sadat decided to negate the Israeli threat through cooperative diplomacy. Egypt's realignment was thus a decision to bandwagon, in response to the following:

1. Egypt's economic vulnerability and military and diplomatic weaknesses;
2. The failure of Egypt's other allies to help correct these problems;
3. Sadat's belief that he could reverse the US position.[3]

Sadat sacrificed all other options to appease the US.

Prince Saud met President Ford in Washington on 18 September. Ford assured him that the Sinai agreement was the first step, and that the US would keep working for additional progress. Saud said: "We considered the agreement

---

p. 261.
1. Edward R. F. Sheehan, *The Arabs, Israelis, and Kissinger: A Secret History of American Diplomacy in the Middle East* (New York: Reader's Digest Press, 1976), pp. 190, 245–7.
2. Safran, *Saudi Arabia*, p. 244.
3. Walt, *The Origins of Alliance*, pp. 177–8.

a positive step. We continue to hold that view, but we need assurance that Israel looks at it that way." He also mentioned that Prince Fahd wanted him to raise the matter of the recognition of Palestinians rights, and the possibility of the US making contact with the Palestinians.[1] Saud also said, on 26 September: "It's not logical to conduct the coming negotiations without the Palestinians; ignoring the rights of the Palestinians does not serve peace."[2]

At the end of that month Saud addressed the UN General Assembly, saying that any agreement that did not contemplate the return of Jerusalem to the Palestinians "will not be acceptable". The issue was not one of refugees, but rather of people ejected from land that was legally theirs, and "if the case was not perceived in that perspective, it will be hard to come to a just solution."[3] Saud also spoke to the Foreign Relations Committee of the US Senate on 1 October, pointing out that there would be no real stability in the Middle East unless the Arab lands occupied in 1967 were returned and recognition given to "the right of the Palestinians for a homeland and self-determination". On bilateral relations, he noted that "we share wide mutual interests", but also that these "were in danger because of the instability of the Middle East".[4]

US diplomatic activity during much of 1976 was confined to managing the crisis in Lebanon, as that country erupted into civil war. While the Israelis worried that they might soon face Syrian forces on their northern border as well as on the Golan Heights, Kissinger sought to prevent a clash between the two countries. On 6 October 1976, Saud met Kissinger in New York. Kissinger declared that the US would make a major effort in 1977, and was urged by Saud to make progress on the Palestinian issue. Kissinger replied: "We can't settle the issue without Palestinian participation on the Palestinian question." Saud pointed out that "recognition by the US is what's important to them"; Kissinger was uncertain, asking: "... If we promised them recognition, would they be then prepared to accept [Resolution] 242?" Saud then suggested the desirability of a meeting between a US representative and the Palestinians, adding: "They want recognition of a Palestinian entity." Kissinger replied, in turn: "A Palestinian entity is something else, other than recognition of the

---

1. NSA, The White House, Memorandum of Conversation between Saud and Ford, 18 September 1975.
2. Saudi Press Agency, 27 September 1975.
3. *Ukaz*, 30 September 1975.
4. *Ukaz*, 3 October 1975.

PLO. Does this mean a Palestinian state?" When Saud affirmed this, Kissinger stated: "We can't exclude the PLO from a settlement."[1]

By the next presidential election, shuttle diplomacy had run its course and a comprehensive peace settlement appeared to be the next US move. On taking office, newly elected President Jimmy Carter's approach was that Israel, for the following reasons, should return to within 1967 borders: the Arab states were ready for peace; the Palestinians deserved a homeland; and a smaller Israel would ensure Middle East stability.

Basic to this approach was the conviction that Israel could not have both territory and peace. Many observers identified a December 1975 report from the Brookings Institution as the basis of Carter's policy. Although it was vague, this report broke significant new ground by taking a comprehensive approach, stressing the importance of phased territorial withdrawals.[2] President Carter sought a return to the Geneva conference. Cyrus Vance, US Secretary of State, went to the Middle East in mid-February 1977, and in the spring Carter met Rabin, Sadat, Hussein and Assad to present publicly and privately his administration's plans for Middle East diplomacy.

Crown Prince Fahd and Carter met in Washington on 24 May. The president emphasized the central role of Saudi Arabia in meeting the needs of the US. Their discussions dealt with oil supply as well as the Arab-Israeli conflict, and Fahd agreed to assist the US in building up a strategic petroleum reserve while making it clear that the Saudi government expected the US to do its utmost to bring about a just and lasting solution to the Arab-Israeli conflict.[3] During a private meeting after the state dinner Fahd argued in favour of a Palestinian state.

Fahd had also obtained a written commitment from Carter stating that if the PLO accepted Resolutions 242 and 338 without any reservations, Carter would pressure the Israelis to grant the Palestinians their rights for a homeland. Saudi Prince Bandar bin Sultan took a copy of the letter to Arafat, who was pleased with the content and promised to give a favourable answer in person to Fahd within few days; however, pressure from radical elements

---

1. NSA, The White House, Memorandum of Conversation between Saud and Kissinger, 6 October 1976.
2. Brookings Institution, *Toward Peace in the Middle East: Report of a Study Group* (Washington, DC: Brookings Institution, 1975).
3. *MEES*, 30 May 1977.

in the PLO, Syria, and elsewhere prevented Arafat from taking advantage of Carter's commitment.[1]

In mid-July, Carter met Menachem Begin, the new Israeli prime minister, and confirmed his desire for a Geneva conference as soon as possible: Begin presented a paper outlining his government's positions on procedures for convening the conference and defining Israel's borders.[2] When Vance went back to the Middle East in early August to try to resolve procedural problems for the conference, he tackled the problem of devising a formula that would include Palestinian representation. The Saudi government hinted that the PLO could moderate its policy if properly encouraged, and attempted to get the organization to tone down its position so that it could join the peace process. The Saudis believed that if it could be persuaded to give at least a qualified recognition of Resolution 242, this would be sufficient to enable the US to begin official talks with the PLO.[3]

Carter and Vance both made statements to encourage the PLO to accept Resolution 242, making it clear that if it did so, they would deal with the organization directly. Carter declared on 8 August: "If the Palestinians should say 'we recognize 242 in its entirety but we think the Palestinians have additional status other than just refugees', that would suit us okay."[4] Carter spoke again on 10 August about finding "some solution to the question of the enormous numbers of Palestinian refugees who have been forced out of their homes and who want to have some fair treatment".[5] Vance declared: "PLO acceptance of Resolution 242 would mean that they were recognizing the right of Israel to exist in a state of peace within secure and recognized boundaries".[6]

On 28 August, the Palestinian National Council (PNC), under pressure from the Syrians (who were more concerned about the Saudis' detachment of the PLO from their control than about facilitating the representation of the PLO as such), rejected these overtures.[7] The Saudi government was

---

1. Prince Bandar bin Sultan, interview with the author, October 2006.
2. Jimmy Carter, *Keeping Faith: Memoirs of a President* (New York: Bantam, 1982), pp. 290–1.
3. Cyrus Vance, *Hard Choices: Critical Years in America's Foreign Policy* (New York: Simon & Schuster, 1983), pp. 188–9.
4. PPP, Jimmy Carter, 1977, pp. 1, 460.
5. Ibid., pp. 1, 470.
6. Department of State, Bulletin, 12 September 1977, p. 340.
7. Zbigniew Brzezinski, *Power and Principle: Memoirs of the National Security Adviser, 1977–81* (New York: Farrar, Straus and Giroux, 1983), p. 105.

frustrated and embarrassed by this, and for some time refrained from putting itself forward again.

Meanwhile, a Geneva format acceptable to Israel, the Arabs and the USSR simply could not be found, and by late September it seemed all but impossible to get Arabs and Israelis to agree even on how to talk about peace. Meanwhile, Vance and Andrei Gromyko, the Soviet foreign minister, concluded discussions held on the margins of the UN General Assembly; on 1 October they issued a joint statement in which the US, for the first time, accepted the phrase "legitimate right of the Palestinians people". Their statement also advocated "normal peaceful relations on the basis of mutual recognition of the principles of sovereignty, territorial integrity, and political independence".[1]

Although the PLO was not mentioned by name, one of the main purposes of the exercise was to clear the way for its participation. The administration's objective for the joint statement was the hope that a US-Soviet agreement would lead to Soviet cooperation in persuading Syria to drop its insistence on a veto over every decision at Geneva.[2]

Faced with negative domestic reaction to the reintroduction of the Soviet Union into the peace diplomacy process, as well as Israeli criticism of the statement, the administration tried to smooth over the controversy. Carter asked on 4 October for a meeting with Israeli Foreign Minister Moshe Dayan, the outcome of which was an Israeli-US paper for a Geneva conference format agreeing that Arab representation would be by a unified delegation to include Palestinian Arabs not identified as PLO; that the working groups in which peace treaties would be negotiated would be bilateral; and that the basis for negotiation would be Resolutions 242 and 338.[3] Sadat was disposed to accept the paper, but the Syrians and the PLO opposed it. The Saudis inclined toward the Egyptian position. Carter's Geneva diplomacy seemed stalemated.

In mid-November, Sadat launched the initiative that took him to Jerusalem. Safran sees this as a bold act, rooted in a pragmatic understanding of the relevant politico-strategic realities and the three politico-strategic premises on which it was based. First, the Arabs did not have the option of achieving their minimal objectives through war, and the prolonged stalemate and continuing

---

1. *Ukaz*, 2 October 1977.
2. Carter, *Keeping Faith*, p. 293.
3. Moshe Dayan, *Breakthrough: A Personal Account of the Egypt-Israel Peace Negotiations* (London: Weidenfeld & Nicolson, 1981), pp. 70–1.

disagreements were highly problematic and dangerous. Second, Egypt's economy was in ruins, and Arab assistance would have meant mortgaging Egypt's national decision-making potential; in addition, Israel was likely to pre-empt the Arabs before they had built up their military capabilities. Third, with the US beginning to regard an Arab-Israel settlement as linked with its national interests, achieving Arab objectives through peaceful means seemed to be a highly promising strategy.[1]

Sadat was disenchanted with his fellow Arabs, especially the Syrians, and when the desperate Carter wrote on 21 October requesting his help and reminding him of "your promise to me that, at a crucial moment, I could count on your support when obstacles arose in our common search for peace",[2] Sadat was ready – although the nature of the help Carter sought is not clear.

Egyptian Deputy Prime Minister Hassan Tuhami and Dayan had met in Rabat, Morocco on 19 September to discuss peace possibilities. Tuhami reported to Sadat that Dayan had told him Israel was prepared to return all of the Sinai for a peace treaty.[3] According to Safran, Sadat believed that if Israel and Egypt signed a peace accord, it could be used to advance others through linkage and through US pressures and inducements applied to Israel.[4] The actual period of negotiations went through three phases, culminating in the September 1978 Camp David Accords.

Saudi Arabia wanted, at first, to avoid paying the price of supporting the initiative, and to make the point that it had not been party to Sadat's initiative. On 18 November, it issued a statement expressing surprise and stating that any Arab Middle East peace initiative "must emanate from a unified Arab stand".[5] The initiative had, in fact, shattered the Arab consensus so painfully built up by the Saudis; but, with US support, it seemed likely to lead to a breakthrough toward settlement. The Saudi position was to allow it to take its course without making any obvious contribution to it. For this reason Saudi Arabia did not attend an Arab summit held in Tripoli, Libya on 2 December 1977 to mobilize opposition to Sadat's initiative.

1. Safran, *Saudi Arabia*, p. 256.
2. Jimmy Carter Library and Museum, "The Camp David Accord after Twenty-Five Years", Letter from Carter to Sadat, 21 October 1977.
3. Dayan, *Breakthrough*, pp. 51–2.
4. Safran, *Saudi Arabia*, p. 257.
5. *Ukaz*, 19 November 1977.

Vance visited Saudi Arabia on 15 December, and again the Saudi government did not explicitly reject the Sadat initiative. Prince Saud issued a statement expressing appreciation for US efforts to advance a settlement and voiced the hope that these would result in achieving a "just and lasting solution in the area".[1]

On 30 July 1978, Fahd visited Egypt and was informed by Sadat of his firm intention not to conclude a separate peace agreement and not to neglect Arab rights to regain occupied territory and the Palestinians' right to self-determination.[2] Fahd then met Carter's envoy Alfred Atherton on 10 August, and was told by him of the president's invitation to a summit to be held on 5 September at Camp David, the US presidential country retreat. Fahd appreciated the president's effort, describing it as "a brave step which indicated the good intention of His Excellency [Carter] ... to achieve a permanent and just solution".[3] Fahd also declared on 24 August that the summit was the last chance: "either the matter will be decided in favor of peace or the gate will be finally closed."[4]

The success of the Camp David summit caused an awkward problem for Saudi Arabia. While the Egyptian share of the agreement represented a major historical gain, the Palestinian share was disappointing: it seemed very probable that the parties concerned would reject it. The Saudi government therefore tried to prevent a hostile Arab coalition forming against Egypt.[5]

On 19 September, two days after the signing of the Camp David Accord, Saudi Arabia issued a statement explaining that, while the Kingdom appreciated US efforts before and during Camp David, its response was the following:

> First, [what had been agreed was] an unacceptable formula for a definitive peace, because the Accord did not convincingly set forth Israel's intentions to withdraw from Arab occupied territory including Jerusalem, did not express the Palestinians' right to self-determination and to establish their government, and did ignore the PLO's role. Second, the Saudi government ... does not give itself the right to intervene in the internal affairs of any Arab country, let alone debate its right to recover its occupied land. Third, the Saudi government believes that the current

---

1. Saudi Press Agency, 15 December 1977.
2. Saudi Press Agency, 8 August 1978.
3. Saudi Press Agency, 11 August 1978.
4. *Ukaz*, 24 August 1978.
5. Safran, *Saudi Arabia*, pp. 261–2.

critical circumstances in the Arab world demand a collective unified attitude and a collective Arab stand.[1]

What had emerged from Camp David was closer to a separate peace than to Carter's goal of a comprehensive solution. Carter had tried, unsuccessfully, to gain Saudi support for Camp David, and blamed Saudi refusal to back the Accord on Begin's broken promise.[2] He had been convinced that the Saudi government would support the Accord, and had assured Sadat of this.

Vance went to Riyadh on 22 September to seek a favourable response from the Saudis and to request a public statement from them that they viewed the Accord as an initial step toward peace;[3] but he was told of the Saudi government's surprise that the Accord had not mention Jerusalem. Vance insisted that an agreement on that issue had been unattainable, and that the US would express its position on the matter independently. The Saudi stand derived from "its constant belief that long-term peace in the region will never be sorted out unless it is formulated on a collective base and full equality".[4] Sadat vilified Hermann Eilts, the US ambassador to Egypt, over the failure of the US to obtain Saudi support for the Accord. "You promised to deliver the Saudis," he complained. "Now, we're really in trouble."[5]

By the time of the Arab League's summit in Baghdad on 1 November 1978, a military union had been agreed (on 26 October) between Iraq and Syria as the beginning of a full union between the two countries. Also, the Shah of Iran was facing revolutionary forces that threatened to overthrow his regime. The Saudi government was, therefore, under pressure at the summit from the anti-Camp David forces, but to limit the immediate damage it insisted on rejecting sanctions against Egypt and condemnation of the US. On 28 October, following several consultations and communications with most of the Arab countries, Prince Saud had summed up the Saudi position as based on "the necessity to protect the united Arab stance and support its steadfastness and to bring together the Arab forces to demonstrate our issue on a substantive base". He said the goal of the forthcoming summit was not to isolate Egypt,

1. *Al-Bilad*, 20 September 1978.
2. Emory University, The Carter Center, "Comments by Carter", *Middle East Consultation*, Atlanta, GA, 6–9 November 1983.
3. Saudi Press Agency, 25 September 1978.
4. *Ukaz*, 25 September 1978.
5. Spiegel, *The Other Arab-Israeli Conflict*, p. 363.

as "isolating Egypt and the Egyptian people from the community of the Arab nation is an unimaginable matter".[1]

During the summit, Saudi Arabia called upon the Arabs to clarify their stand toward the Camp David Accord and to support all efforts made by the US or any others to solve the question of the Middle East peacefully, on the condition that these efforts met the Arab position.[2]

On 7 November, Fahd asserted that the outcome of the Accord had neglected the question of Jerusalem. Consequently, he said, "Saudi Arabia does not agree to relinquish or turn down a momentous Islamic issue such as that of Jerusalem with which all Muslims' hearts are connected." As for peace, he added: "The Arab nation wanted, and is still wanting, calling for, working for, peace, and seeks to achieve it through a just and comprehensive solution."[3] The summit resolved not to endorse Camp David or cooperate with its results, and to appeal to Sadat to renounce his signature.

The Saudi position forced Sadat to insist on a much tighter linkage between the Palestinian question and the peace treaty in order to appease his Arab critics. Out of desperation, Carter decided that in this tense atmosphere a presidential trip might turn stalemate into success.[4] He arrived in Egypt on 8 March 1979, and in Jerusalem on 11 March. Having risked his personal prestige by taking the trip, Carter now used that investment to pressure the Israelis. An agreement on a treaty and framework for the West Bank and Gaza was wrapped up on 13 March, and the treaty was signed during a ceremony in Washington, DC on 26 March.

A second Baghdad summit was convened on 27 March, at which Saudi Arabia and other Arab states resolved to apply sanctions against Egypt.[5] At the summit Saud declared: "The rift in Arab ranks, after signing the Egyptian-Israeli treaty, has become a very serious issue that needs to be addressed quickly, so as not to give the opportunity for foreign interference in the region." He also underlined the need to abide by the decisions of the summit.[6] This second summit, which Saudi Arabia had reluctantly abided, forced Egypt into greater

---

1. *Al-Riyadh*, 29 October 1978.
2. *Ukaz*, 4 November 1978.
3. Saudi Press Agency, 7 November 1978.
4. Carter, *Keeping the Faith*, p. 416.
5. Saudi Press Agency, 4 March 1978.
6. Saudi Press Agency, 29 March 1978.

dependence on the US – allowing the virtual neutralization of a core Arab state by a superpower deeply biased in favour of Israel.[1]

The US had overestimated not only what the Saudis *could* do, but also what they would do. The Saudis, as Arabs, were no less opposed to the Accord than their more radical fellow Arabs; they were never inclined to support it directly. As participants in the Arab consensus they were willing to tone down, but not oppose, Arab condemnation of Camp David.

---

1. Charles D. Smith, *Palestine and the Arab-Israeli Conflict* (New York: St. Martin's Press, 1996), pp. 256–8.

CHAPTER TWO

The First Fahd Era (1979–90): From Reserved Cooperation to Far-Reaching Dependence

The period from 1979 to 1990 was characterized by regional instability, countered – at least initially – by weak US resolve. The Soviet threat forced Saudi Arabia and the US into closer cooperation on various strategic areas from Afghanistan to Latin America; by the end of the 1980s the two countries had become interconnected, to the advantage of both.

Throughout 1978 the Saudi government had tried to join up minimally with US policy except when supported by Arab consensus. It avoided making any fundamental choices, therefore; but by the end of that year the pressure to do so had become too intense. Mounting troubles with the Shah's regime, and the unsettled conditions in Yemen, made strategic connection with the US more important than ever.

By then the Saudi government had begun to look to the US to protect it against the likely consequences of the Shah's downfall. Following a visit to Riyadh on 4 December 1978 as President Carter's special envoy, Senator Robert Byrd reported that the Saudi government wanted the US to protect the Gulf. Meanwhile, as Iranian oil production tumbled, the Kingdom's output increased from 7.2 million barrels per day (mbd) in August to 10.3 mbd in November and 10.4 mbd in December.[1] Some Arab states felt the increases indicated too

---

1. Colin Legum et al., eds., *Middle East Contemporary Survey* (*MECS*), vol. III (1978–79) (New York: Holmes and Meier, 1978–1982), p. 785.

close an identification with the US at a time when the Arab states were at odds with it over the Camp David Accord.

On 1 January 1979 the US ambassador to the Kingdom, John C. West, met Prince Saud, who expressed his concerns about events in Iran. The foreign minister stated his belief that if the Shah fell, all the symbols of unity in Iran would disappear, and that there was no real alternative to the Shah.

With the end of the Shah's regime, the Saudis turned to the US for reassurance. The US response was to announce, on 10 January, that it would send unarmed F-15s to Saudi Arabia. When the Shah finally departed Iran on 16 January, Saudi suspicions that the US was more interested in securing the flow of oil than protecting friendly regimes were reinforced.[1]

Under these circumstances, Saudi Arabia was confronted with the necessity of defining its position. On 17 January, Fahd declared that the achievement of peace ought to contain two fundamental conditions: reclamation by the Palestinians of all their legitimate rights and Israeli withdrawal from all occupied territories including Jerusalem. This was the Saudi view of the "endorsement of Camp David negotiations, which aimed at achieving peace, but whose results ... were not acceptable to the Palestinian side". He also referred to the events in Iran, saying: "Current events in Iran prevent the achievement of peace and stability, which are necessary for international peace, unless a new climate exists inside Iran."[2] Four days later the Saudis cut their oil production for the first quarter of 1979 to 9.8 mbd.[3]

At the same time, London-based sources within ARAMCO privately informed officials at the US embassy in London that Saudi Arabia was making all its current excess crude oil available to ARAMCO. It was thought at the embassy that the Saudi decision had something to do with softening the impact on the US of the Iranian shortfall. The former move signalled to the US the Saudi government's displeasure with its policies, but avoided outright confrontation at a time when its help was needed. Saudi Arabia hoped its actions could make the US more responsive to their needs.

The Kingdom was now faced with Iran as a potentially serious danger. During a visit to Riyadh on 10 February, US Secretary of Defense Harold Brown presented proposals for security cooperation on the basis of the situation

---

1. Safran, *Saudi Arabia*, p. 301.
2. Saudi Press Agency, 17 January 1979.
3. William Quandt, *Saudi Arabia's Oil Policy* (Washington, DC: Brookings Institution Press, 1982), p. 16.

in the region, pledging support for the Kingdom against external threats and proposing to base US forces in Saudi Arabia to assist in its defence. For domestic as well as inter-Arab reasons, the Saudis, who had only wanted an "over-the-horizon" presence, promptly declined to accept.[1]

A new crisis between the two Yemens erupted into open warfare on 12 February. The US, on 8 March, agreed to a request by the Saudis to station two Airborne Warning and Control System (AWACS) aircraft in Saudi Arabia to help monitor and defend Saudi airspace.

On 23 February, Fahd cancelled a scheduled March visit to the US in order to dissociate himself from the US peacemaking effort. When the US claimed, in an official explanation, that the cancellation was for health reasons, the Saudi government issued an official denial.[2]

According to Safran, US protection was used to encourage Saudi support for the Egyptian-Israeli peace treaty; Saudi association with the US in opposing the new revolutionary regime in Iran; and Saudi support for the YAR in the showdown with the People's Democratic Republic of Yemen (the newly renamed PRSY).[3] On 17 March, National Security Adviser Zbigniew Brzezinski visited Riyadh to seek Saudi support for the Egypt-Israel treaty and promised to extend US help to meet any danger coming from Arab rejectionists or the Iranians.[4] *Ukaz* reported the declaration of the Saudi Council of Ministers, convened on 19 March, that "security, stability and peace will not be accomplished without a complete withdrawal from all occupied Arab territories".[5] Fahd was also reported as saying: "The Kingdom has special relations with the US, therefore it encounters special problems, but that does not mean a re-evaluation of the relationship."[6] At the same time, Secretary of State Vance declared in Washington that the US would use force to defend vital Saudi oilfields.[7]

Safran also notes that during this period, a disagreement developed within the Saudi ruling establishment, expressed in terms of two alternative approaches – one advanced by Fahd and his supporters, the other by Khalid and his circle.

---

1. *The Washington Post*, 5 May 1979.
2. Saudi Press Agency, 24 February 1979.
3. Safran, *Saudi Arabia*, p. 304.
4. *The New York Times*, 20 March 1979.
5. *Ukaz*, 20 March 1979.
6. *Al-Madina*, 24 March 1979.
7. *The Washington Post*, 19 March 1979.

Fahd favoured US orientation and believed appeasing the revolutionary regime in Iran was a futile exercise. He also thought the Iraqi-Syrian union posed a future danger to the Kingdom's independence. Khalid by contrast favoured Arab orientation, pointing out that the US could not help the Kingdom if Saudi Arabia defied the Arab bloc. Moreover, after the present crisis passed, the Kingdom could, for reasons of self-interest, repair its relations with the US. Following the decision to adopt an orientation toward the Arab bloc, Fahd signalled his dissent by leaving the Kingdom on 22 March for an indefinite holiday in Spain.[1] When asked in an interview on 15 May about the disagreement, he said it was "a baseless imagination of the enemies of Saudi Arabia".[2] In another interview on 18 May he said: "I heard and I read about it, and I do not know how to answer it. Should we bring all the Saudi princes to the US and Europe to say that we are not divided?"[3] Similarly, on 1 July, Khalid said: "What they [the media] discuss is an alleged division and an imagination in the heads of the Kingdom's enemies."[4]

With regard to the alleged differences, it should be noted that it was very unusual for Crown Prince Fahd to have remained outside the Kingdom between March and May when such important developments were occurring. Moreover, if there had in fact been a difference of opinion on the issue in question, it could surely be seen to the credit of the Saudi ruling establishment that it showed concern for preserving solidarity with other Arab countries. The Saudi government was not concerned solely with advancing the Kingdom's own interests, including the relationship with the US.

The Saudi government simply did not believe that Camp David met Arab and Palestinian requirements and, moreover, given their perception of the US record, were unimpressed by the US offer of protection. Thus its rejection of the proposal offered by Secretary of Defense Brown plunged the relationship between the two countries to its lowest point since the embargo. Even so, when asked about the deterioration in relations between his country and the US, Fahd said: "In taking our position on peace, we have not intended to take a hostile position toward the US, or damage its interests."[5]

The Saudis believed their security interests were best served by preserving

---

1. Safran, *Saudi Arabia*, pp. 305–6.
2. *Ukaz*, 16 May 1979.
3. *Al-Hawadith*, 18 May 1979.
4. *Ukaz*, 1 July 1979.
5. *Ukaz*, 16 May 1979.

the US connection as well as by accommodating the Arab bloc opposing the peace treaty. The Saudi newspaper *Al-Riyadh* reported Fahd as saying: "We take our decisions according to the interests of our nation and our national causes, and we will not refrain from granting the necessary assistance to close the rift [in the Arab world] and to restore the unity of the Arab nation so that it can be victorious."[1]

On 27 March, Arab foreign ministers assembled in Baghdad to discuss the application of sanctions as planned. The Saudi foreign minister successfully resisted suggestions to penalize the US, but the conference was brought to a crisis point when he tried to resist a proposal to break off diplomatic relations with Egypt. On 31 March all participants, including the Saudi foreign minister, voted for the break as well as for economic sanctions,[2] and on 23 April the Saudi government severed diplomatic relations with Egypt.[3]

To resist Soviet encroachment, ensure that maritime routes remained open and preserve a source of emergency assistance, the US connection remained essential for the Kingdom despite recent disappointments. But the US resented the Saudis for having partially yielded to pressure, and some elements in the government sought to penalize the Kingdom by restricting cooperation with it. Fahd claimed in response: "These voices are not for the benefit of US-Arab relations."[4]

The US had agreed with Saudi suggestions that their differences regarding the peace treaty should be kept separate from other aspects of their mutual relations. In an interview on 15 May 1979, Fahd asserted that Saudi Arabia wanted to maintain good relations with the US and urged the US to open talks with the PLO.[5] The US responded by saying that the two countries had agreed to keep their sharp differences over the peace treaty from interfering with their close relations in other fields.[6] On 21 June Fahd used similar words when he again urged the US to start an immediate dialogue with the PLO.[7] He maintained that dialogue could lead the PLO to accept Resolution 242, and thus open the way to peace. Fahd added that if the Israelis withdrew to

---

1. *Al-Riyadh*, 25 April 1979.
2. Safran, *Saudi Arabia*, p. 307.
3. *Ukaz*, 24 April 1979.
4. *Al-Madina*, 17 January 1979.
5. *Le Monde*, 15 May 1979.
6. *The New York Times*, 16 May 1979.
7. *The New York Times*, 22 June 1979.

the pre-1967 borders, Saudi Arabia itself would be ready to make peace with Israel.[1]

In July the Saudi government announced that oil production would be increased from 8.8 mbd (at which level it had been since April) to 9.8 mbd.[2] Following the Saudi announcement the US developed indirect contacts with the PLO. The resignation on 15 August of US representative to the UN Andrew Young as a result of the uproar over his direct talks with a PLO representative contributed to Washington's renunciation of its effort.[3]

As a consequence of Egypt's relative decline, several Arab states began to compete among themselves for Arab world leadership, but no new hegemon emerged. The resulting fragmentation unleashed a set of powerful reactions on the peripheries of the Arab world, further upsetting the regional power balance. Some elements in the new regime in Tehran spoke of exporting the Iranian revolution and protecting the rights of Shi'is in neighbouring countries. The Saudi government was deeply disturbed when it learned that the US was still trying to cooperate with Iran's new regime. They took the view that the Americans were driven only by interest in oil, and that they would work with any regime serving that interest.[4] On 27 June, leaders of the Gulf countries and North Yemen (but not Iraq) were invited to attend military manoeuvres being held at Khamis Mushait, near the border with North Yemen. The participants agreed that the US could be relied upon to look after its own interests, but could not be expected to protect the established order or to maintain a ruling house in power.[5]

On 2 October, Fahd met Ambassador West. According to a cable from the US embassy in Jeddah to the State Department, Fahd told the ambassador that the US seemed indifferent to, or impotent over, developments in Iran: "Instead of pressuring the Shah into bringing his thoughts and actions up to date so as to pull the rug from under the communist agitators, you let him go." Fahd also stated that Iran's revolutionary Supreme Leader Ayatollah Ruhollah Khomeini "is a tool, although he may not know it or admit it. The communists are pursuing their designs methodically." He predicted that Khomeini would not last more than a few months, and that Iran would become "another

---

1. *Al-Anouar*, 23 June 1979.
2. Quandt, *Saudi Arabia's Oil Policy*, p. 14.
3. Quandt, *Peace Process*, pp. 238–9.
4. Safran, *Saudi Arabia*, p. 354.
5. *Ukaz*, 29 June 1979 and 1 July 1979.

Ethiopia, ruled by the communists placed there by Moscow". He regretted that the US was not confronting the Soviet threat to the region. Fahd also noted that the US had not reassured its friends in the area and around the world by warning the Iranians against threatening the Gulf states, sending a message to the effect of: "Stop, enough is enough. We and all decent people in the world cannot sit idly by and watch the law of the jungle prevail."[1]

Three events in November and December 1979 made an impact on the Saudi government and set off a series of chain reactions that affected its position and the policies it had tried to promote in the early part of the year. On 4 November Iranian militants stormed the US embassy in Tehran and held US diplomats hostage. This act converted US policy toward Iran into open hostility and confrontation with the new regime. The event also added to the region's instability, which was not in the Kingdom's interest. Then, on 20 November, a group of armed Muslim extremists seized the Grand Mosque of Mecca, which was liberated only after extensive fighting. The third event was the Soviet invasion of Afghanistan on 27 December; the invasion alarmed the US and deepened its involvement in Gulf security.

The seizure of the hostages led the US to dispatch a carrier task force to the Gulf and to impose sanctions against Iran. Thus the confrontation created a shared tactical interest between the US and Iraq that held the prospect of greater Iraqi tolerance towards the Saudis' own security relationship with the US. Certainly, the Saudi government welcomed the reversal of Washington's position. The Soviet invasion of Afghanistan also produced a convergence of objective interests between the US and the Kingdom, as well as a certain convergence of practical policies.[2]

The Soviet Invasion of Afghanistan

Throughout the 1960s and 1970s relations between Moscow and Kabul grew stronger, with the Soviet Union becoming one of Afghanistan's largest sources of foreign aid. In the early 1970s Afghanistan was among the most underdeveloped countries in the world, and these funds helped alleviate its economic woes. However, foreign aid alone could not resolve Afghanistan's emerging political conflicts. The US was aware that political discontent was on the rise

1. NSA, State Dept. Records, US Embassy, Jeddah, to State, "Meeting with Crown Prince Fahd – October 2", October 1979.
2. Safran, *Saudi Arabia*, pp. 357–60.

in the country; the US embassy in Kabul had reported in 1971 that leftist activity had increased, and attributed this rise to increasing disillusionment with prevailing social and economic conditions.

The most organized of the country's leftist groups was the People's Democratic Party of Afghanistan (PDPA). The PDPA had been founded in 1965, with a political orientation towards Marxism. During its early years, it was splintered by quarrels and plots between its two leaders, Nur Mohammad Taraki and Babrak Karmal. In 1967 Karmal formed his own faction, usually identified by the name of its newspaper, which was called *Parcham* ("Banner"). Taraki's rival Khalq ("The People") faction was also named after its newspaper. Both (predominantly Pashtun) offshoots competed for power.[1] Karmal's faction operated as part of the government, Taraki's as the opposition.

By the early 1970s, the Parcham faction had begun holding secret meetings with members of a growing cadre of Soviet-trained military officers, some of whom had begun to congregate around the progressive Royal Prime Minister Mohammed Daoud Khan. Daoud, seen as a strong nationalist leader, collaborated with the Parcham group to lead a coup in 1973, overturning the monarchy of his cousin Zahir Shah and declaring a republic. In July 1973, he became Afghanistan's first president.[2] Daoud sought greater economic independence from the Soviets by exploring closer ties with Iran and the US, but was nevertheless careful not to shun the USSR. As the CIA noted, Daoud "was happiest when he could light his American cigarettes with Soviet matches".[3] The republic's formation helped expanded Soviet power in the region, and generated shared concerns in Washington, Tehran and Islamabad. Iran took the lead in a joint effort to use generous economic and technical assistance to wean Daoud away from dependence on Moscow, and to persuade him to shed the Soviet-backed elements in his government.[4]

As President, Daoud's commitment to reform proved short-lived. In his pursuit of a personal and more independent foreign policy, he managed

---

1. Barnett Rubin, *The Fragmentation of Afghanistan: State Formation and Collapse in the International System* (New Haven: Yale University Press, 1995), p. 93.
2. Raja Anwar, *The Tragedy of Afghanistan: A First-Hand Account* (London: Verso, 1988), p. 76.
3. Central Intelligence Agency (CIA), "Mohammad Daud: President of Afghanistan", 13 August 1973.
4. Diego Cordovez and Selig Harrison, *Out of Afghanistan: The Inside Story of the Soviet Withdrawal* (New York: Oxford University Press, 1995), pp. 15–6.

to alienate Afghan socialists, moderates and religious fundamentalists alike. Some of these fundamentalists, such as Burhanuddin Rabbani, Sibghatullah Mojaddedi and Abdul Rabb-ur-Rasul Sayyaf, wanted to integrate modernization and Islam to counter the disruptive influence of both capitalism and communism. Meanwhile, the conflict between Afghanistan and Pakistan over the status of ethnic Pashtuns in Pakistan's border regions hindered US aid to Afghanistan and contributed to Daoud's turn toward the Soviets.[1] Afghan antagonism toward Pakistan also impeded Iran's offer of aid. In early 1974, an armed revolt was underway in the Baluchistan region of Pakistan, bordering Afghanistan and Iran. Daoud allowed resistance fighters to set up bases in Afghanistan, and provided sanctuary to Pashtun dissidents threatened with arrest in Pakistan. In retaliation, Pakistan provided funds and weapons to Muslim fundamentalists and other anti-Daoud Afghan extremists, who were conducting raids and sabotage inside Afghanistan.[2]

Because of its own sizeable Baluchi community, Iran had its own motives for seeing the armed revolt in Baluchistan quelled and provided Pakistan with US helicopters for use in this effort.[3] During Kissinger's visit to Kabul in November 1974, he pressed for the conflict with Pakistan to be resolved if Daoud hoped to sustain significant economic aid from the US and its allies.[4] By the beginning of 1975, Daoud had agreed with Pakistan to begin talks. In April, he visited Iran and came away with a credit extension of US $2 billion. Shortly after his return, he announced that Afghanistan would not tolerate imported ideology; a few months later, he removed three communists from ministerial positions, including the minister of the interior. By the end of December there were no Parcham members left in Daoud's cabinet.[5]

Meanwhile, Daoud banned the opposition and strengthened ties with Iran and with the US, which welcomed and encouraged Daoud's new foreign policy moves. In 1977 the State Department commented that he had "made significant contributions to the improvement of regional stability".[6] Despite US approval,

---

1. Abdul Samad Ghaus, *The Fall of Afghanistan: An Insider's Account* (Washington, DC: Pergamon-Brassey, 1988), p. 142.
2. Raja Anwar, *The Tragedy of Afghanistan*, pp. 78–81.
3. Cordovez and Harrison, *Out of Afghanistan*, p. 16.
4. Ibid., pp. 19–20.
5. Ghaus, *The Fall of Afghanistan*, pp. 190–4.
6. Department of State, Afghanistan in 1977: An External Assessment, 30 January 1978.

Daoud's authoritarian rule had alienated too many at home. By 1977, Khalq and Parcham, having formally agreed to bury their differences, reunited as a single PDPA under Soviet pressure to do so.[1] Nine months later, the PDPA seized control of the government. The precipitating event was the assassination on 17 April 1978 of PDPA member and vocal critic of the regime Mir Akbar Khaibar, possibly by Daoud's interior minister. Thousands of mourners turned Khaibar's funeral into an anti-government rally, which prompted Daoud to clamp down further on the PDPA. His response provoked party supporters in the army to take action, and in collaboration with the PDPA Daoud was overthrown on 27 April, and killed. The republican government was replaced with a socialist one.[2]

That the Soviets were first to formally recognize the new government reinforced Washington's suspicions that Moscow had engineered the takeover, but US intelligence assessments asserted that there was no evidence of Soviet involvement in launching the coup, that the USSR had probably seen the events as an opportunity to develop another communist regime on its borders. New evidence from numerous and diverse sources, however, indicates that the Soviets had indeed been advised by the PDPA of the impending coup.[3]

With the PDPA's rise to power, the US found itself facing a policy dilemma. A secret memorandum to Vance expressed the need "to avoid driving the regime into a closer embrace with the Soviet Union than it might wish". But it also pointed out various factors favouring a hard-line approach to the new government: "Anti-regime elements in Afghanistan will be watching us carefully to see if we acquiesce [to] or accept the communist takeover ... Pakistan, Iran, Saudi Arabia and others of our friends in the area will see the situation clearly as a Soviet coup. On the domestic front, many Americans will see this as an extension of Soviet power and draw the parallel with Angola, Ethiopia, etc."[4]

According to another memorandum, Pakistan and Iran had long been

1. Anthony Arnold, *The Fateful Pebble: Afghanistan's Role in the Fall of the Soviet Empire* (Novato, CA: Presidio Press, 1993), p. 53.
2. Cordovez and Harrison, *Out of Afghanistan*, pp. 22–8.
3. Henry Bradsher, *Afghanistan and the Soviet Union*, 2nd ed. (Durham, SC: Duke University Press, 1985), pp. 76–81; see also Raymond Garthoff, *Détente and Confrontation: American-Soviet Relations from Nixon to Reagan*, rev. ed. (Washington, DC: Brookings Institution Press, 1994), pp. 985–7.
4. NSA, State Dept. Records, Briefing Memorandum from Harold Sanders to Vance, "Situation in Afghanistan", 30 April 1978.

worried that the radical parties in Afghanistan might take over if Daoud left the scene. The Shah described the April coup as part of Moscow's "grand design" for encircling Iran. Pakistan had worked for many years to break the links between Afghan communists and Pashtun nationalists in its tribal areas, and according to the report it was particularly apprehensive that the new regime might embark on an irredentist course. The memorandum also pointed out that the Chinese, who shared a common border with Afghanistan, would not be happy about the takeover.[1] Yet another US document suggested that the Saudi government interpreted the coup as part of a Soviet-directed campaign to encircle the Gulf and the Arabian Peninsula with radical regimes in preparation for the subversion of the Gulf states. The Saudi ambassador to Pakistan was reported to have said, in May 1978, that the coup had been instigated by the Soviets in order to develop a base from which to subvert Iran and Pakistan.

The Khalq faction's main leaders, Taraki and Hafizullah Amin, rapidly consolidated power, imprisoned a number of their Parcham rivals and sent others off to foreign diplomatic posts, including Karmal, who was initially Deputy Prime Minister. They then moved quickly to implement radical secular reforms.

Ambassador to Afghanistan Aleksandr M. Puzanov of the USSR informed Soviet Foreign Minister Andrei Gromyko that Taraki had said, in a conversation on 29 April: "Afghanistan, following Marxism-Leninism, will set off on the path of building Socialism and will belong to the socialist camp." Puzanov urged further strengthening of the new government by encouraging PDPA unity.[2]

The new reforms served to ignite strong opposition from most of the deeply traditional Islamic population. Many either took up arms against the government or left the country. Some of the fleeing Afghans joined Islamic Afghan dissidents (such as Rabbani, Gulbuddin Hekmatyar, Mojaddedi, Pir Sayyid Ahmad Gailani, Mohammad Nabi Mohammadi and Yunus Khales) in Pakistan. These leaders, who joined Abdul Rabb-ur-Rasul Sayyaf in 1980 and formed their own parties, would eventually unite to form the Sunni Islamic

---

1. NSA, State Dept. Records, Briefing Memorandum from William Bowdler to Warren Christopher, "The Coup in Afghanistan", 1 May 1978.
2. *Tsentr khraneniia sovremennoi dokumentatsii* (TsKhSD/The Centre for the Storage of Contemporary Documentation), Moscow, fond "f." 5, opis "op." 75 delo, "d" 1179, listy "ll." 2-17, notes taken by Odd Arne Westad, Letter from Soviet Ambassador to Afghanistan to Soviet Foreign Minister, 31 May 1978 (Communist Party Archives).

Afghan rebel alliance, later becoming collectively known as the "Peshawar Seven". These party leaders called for a *jihad*, so-called "holy war", against the PDPA. Shi'i Afghans also played an important role as insurgents in the western half of Afghanistan.

Views among US officials were divided. Vance had hopes that Soviet influence could be contained, and believed that by sustaining its limited economic assistance the US could maintain a measure of influence.[1] Brzezinski favoured cutting off US relations with Afghanistan and mounting covert operations to counter Soviet aspirations in the region.[2] Washington duly recognized the new regime officially, and continued modest economic aid. Under-Secretary of State David Newsom made an official visit to Kabul on 13 July and met Taraki, to whom he expressed his government's concern about the one-sided orientation in Afghanistan's foreign policy and the chill in relations.

A month later, the Afghan defence minister Abdul Qadir and two other senior military officers associated with the Parcham faction were arrested on charges of plotting to overthrow the new government.[3] Amin used the plot as grounds for purging the remaining Parcham members from the government. This action substantially narrowed the regime's political base and diminished the reliability of the army.

At the same time, PDPA efforts to impose socialist reform throughout the countryside were meeting with violent backlash. Many people were arrested, and many others ejected from their positions. Provincial administration in much of the countryside was placed under the central control of the Communist Party. Armed opposition erupted. In November 1978, US intelligence reports revealed that fighting in the provinces was escalating, that insurgents appeared to have taken control of large areas of north and east Afghanistan and that Soviet military advisors had been assigned to Afghan units directly engaged in combating insurgents.

A diverse range of rebels was actively engaged in this insurrection, with varying goals. But many of them had shared convictions, such as the universally held perception that they were defending Islam and that the PDPA comprised godless infidels who had sold out Afghanistan to Soviet imperialism. The PDPA,

---

1. Vance, *Hard Choices*, p. 384.
2. Brzezinski, *Power and Principle*, pp. 426–8.
3. Anwar, *The Tragedy of Afghanistan*, pp. 119–23.

for its part, referred to the rebels as the *Ikhwan-i-Shayatin* ("Brotherhood of Satan").[1]

In early December 1978, Taraki and Amin went to Moscow to seek increased assistance for battling the insurrection. On 5 December the two governments signed a twenty-year cooperation and friendship treaty, which Washington perceived as the Soviets' response to the fact that Kabul's authority outside the major cities had collapsed. On 7 January 1979, the Soviets instructed their ambassador in Kabul to inform the Afghan government that its request would be granted for deliveries of goods for the general use of the armed forces and a dispatch of specialists to work with the Afghan armed forces, with favourable conditions.

The US grew increasingly uncomfortable with the new government. To make matters worse, on 14 February the US ambassador, Adolph Dubs, was taken hostage by anti-government elements demanding the release of a political prisoner. He was killed when Afghan police stormed the hotel in which he was being held.

In March, Afghans in the western city of Herat massacred hundreds of Afghan officials and Soviet advisors. Taraki summoned the Soviet chief military advisor, Lieutenant General L. N. Gorelov, as well as the Soviet *chargé d'affaires*, and appealed for help in the form of military equipment, ammunition and rations. He also emphasized the need for ground and air support. During prolonged deliberations in the Central Committee Politburo of the Communist Party of the Soviet Union between 17–19 March, a final decision was taken that it was not the right time to become entangled in a conflict in Afghanistan. Premier Leonid Brezhnev signed documents authorizing the delivery of additional supplies of military materials, armaments, etc, adding: "We must explain to Comrade Taraki and our other Afghan Comrades, that we can help them with everything that is necessary for the conduct of all activities in the country. But the involvement of our forces in Afghanistan would harm not only us, but first of all them."[2]

In Washington, Brzezinski warned President Carter that the Soviets had territorial designs on Afghanistan and possibly the whole South Asia region, arguing that if the new regime in Afghanistan was able to consolidate power

---

1. NSA, State Dept. Records, US Embassy, Kabul, to State, June 1979.
2. TsKhSD, f. 89, per. 25 dok. 1, ll.1, 12-25, document provided by M. Kramer (Harvard University), translation by Carter-Brezhnev Project, Transcript of CPSC CC Politburo Discussions on Afghanistan, 17–19 March 1979..

then the Soviets might turn the country into a launching pad for aggression across the region. Brzezinski pushed a decision through the NSC's Special Coordination Committee (SCC) that required them to be, as he put it, "more sympathetic to those Afghans who were determined to preserve their country's independence".[1] Brzezinski also called for moderate covert support for Afghan dissident groups that had set up headquarters in Pakistan. From April, following the SCC decision, the US had begun quietly meeting rebel representatives. This led, six months before the Soviet invasion, to Carter signing the first directive on 3 July for secret aid to opponents of the pro-Soviet regime in Kabul – an action that actually increased the likelihood of Soviet intervention in Afghanistan. The logic behind this action was to draw the Soviets into a trap in Afghanistan, which presented the US with the opportunity of luring the Soviet Union into its own "Vietnam war".[2]

The conflict in Herat showed that the Soviet client regime in Kabul was steadily losing ground to the insurgency. Soviet officials thought the Khalqi leadership was moving too fast with its reform, and urged the leaders to moderate the pace of change and broaden their political base by including non-communists in the government. However, the regime had little use for Soviet counsel. It responded to the growing opposition with increasing brutality, and the PDPA's base continued to narrow.

On 17 August a top-level Soviet military delegation arrived in Kabul, headed by Deputy Defence Minister General Ivan Pavlovskii. Its mission was to conduct a close-up examination of the military situation and operational conditions in the aftermath of the rebellion.[3] The delegation's rank and composition led to intelligence suggestions that Moscow was contemplating a major decision about the extent and the form of field-level military support it was willing to give to the Taraki regime.

A memorandum on 14 September from CIA director Stansfield Turner to the Carter administration warned: "The Soviet leaders may be on the threshold of a decision to commit their own forces to prevent the collapse of the regime and to protect their sizeable stakes in Afghanistan." The memorandum also

1. Brzezinski, *Power and Principle*, p. 427.
2. *Le Nouvel Observateur*, "Interview with Zbigniew Brzezinski, President Jimmy Carter's National Security Adviser," 15–21 January 1998.
3. Archives of the General Staff of the USSR Armed Forces, *Znamya*, no. 4, 1991, Report from Soviet Deputy Defence Minister Army Gen. Ivan Pavlovskii during visit to Afghanistan, 25 August 1979.

acknowledged that the Soviets would risk amplifying their stake in the ultimate outcome, which would make it harder to resist further increasing their military commitment if their initial steps did not produce the results they sought.[1]

Returning home in early September from a Non-Aligned Movement conference in Cuba, Taraki stopped in Moscow. There he reportedly discussed Amin's future with Soviet officials. Amin, the deputy prime minister, obtained knowledge of the discussion and mounted a counter-plot. Upon his return Taraki was given an ultimatum by Amin, who demanded the dismissal and punishment of officials closest to Taraki on the pretext that they were involved in an imperialist conspiracy against him (Amin). Radio Kabul announced the dismissals on the evening of 14 September, commenting that they had been initiated on Amin's recommendation with Taraki's approval.

Two days later, Radio Kabul announced that Taraki had "requested that he be relieved of his party and government leadership positions due to health reasons and physical incapacity". The announcement specified that Amin had been appointed as the new Party general secretary. Taraki was removed from power and killed shortly afterward.[2]

On 19 September, Brzezinski informed Carter that he believed a Soviet invasion was becoming more probable[3] and asked the CIA director to prepare an intelligence appraisal of Soviet involvement in Afghanistan. An Interagency Intelligence Memorandum circulated on 28 September stated: "Moscow probably views the situations as even more unstable ... and may fear that this coup will fragment the Afghan Army and lead to a breakdown of control in Kabul." It asserted that "the threat raised by the Muslim insurgency to the survival of the Marxist government in Afghanistan appears to be more serious now than at any time since the government assumed power in April, 1978",[4] and predicted that the Soviets had only one military option – to commit massive numbers of ground forces to a potentially open-ended operation. Concluding that Moscow would not believe that saving the Kabul regime was worth this price, the memorandum then listed examples of situations in which Moscow

---

1. NSA, IIM, *The Soviet Invasion of Afghanistan*, p. 21.
2. A. A. Liakhovskii, *The Tragedy and Valour of the Afghani* (Moscow: GPI "Iskon", 1995), p.102 (a report from Gromyko, Andropov, Ustinov and B. Ponomarev to CPSU CC, 29 October 1979).
3. Brzezinski, *Power and Principle*, p. 428.
4. NSA, IIM, *Soviet Options in Afghanistan*, Key Judgement, pp. 1–2 and text p. 4.

would be willing to pay the price, including the prospect of the rise of an anti-Soviet regime, foreign military intervention and prolonged political chaos.

Thus, when Crown Prince Fahd met Ambassador West on 2 October 1979 to discuss the situation in Iran and the communist threat, he also mentioned Afghanistan and expressed a fear that Pakistan might be next for the Soviets. Fahd said Saudi Arabia had seen the "communist fire" approaching for a long time and had alerted the US: "Saudi Arabia's warning and appeals seem, however, to have fallen on deaf ears." He also added that the Soviet presence was threatening to choke the vital interests of the US and the Kingdom and deserved a firm, unequivocal stand. He wanted the ambassador to remind Washington of the Arab saying: "To count the lashes is one thing, but to feel them is something else."[1]

In October, the US embassy in Kabul reported to the State Department that there had been signs of some coolness between the Soviets and Afghan now-President Amin; this had been a hot subject of discussion among the foreign diplomatic corps. On 10 October, Radio Kabul announced that Taraki had died, of "illness"; a week later, an army garrison at Riskhor, about nine miles southwest of Kabul, rebelled and launched an attack on Kabul. It was several days before the rebellion was put down.

A CIA analysis concluded that Saudi Arabia was providing financial and material support to the tribal dissidents in Afghanistan, and emphasized that the Saudi government was motivated by its long and fairly good ties with Afghanistan. Afghan dissident leaders had been travelling regularly to Saudi Arabia by early 1979 to seek support for their cause, and had been told by the Saudis that close cooperation among them was necessary if aid from the Kingdom was to increase. The analysis suggested that Saudi Arabia's satisfaction with the military successes of the rebels would doubtless encourage them to keep up the good fight in the name of God, and predicted that Saudi government support was likely to continue.

During a meeting on 23 October between Director of Arab Affairs in the Saudi foreign ministry Ismail Al-Shura and the political officer at the US embassy, Al-Shura reiterated Saudi concern over developments in Afghanistan and noted that the Saudi government had initially withheld financial assistance to the Afghan rebels in the hope that they could thereby be pushed into

---

1. NSA, State Dept. Records, US Embassy, Jeddah, to State, "Meeting with Crown Prince Fahd – October 2", October 1979.

some kind of common front arrangement. Recently, he said, the Saudis had decided that the resistance effort had to be supported even if the rebels could not come to terms.

By now, the progressive weakness of the Afghan army was becoming increasingly apparent. At the same time, insurgent attacks were growing in size and frequency. On 26 October a DIA assessment claimed: "Without Soviet support the Afghan Army would have collapsed a long time ago."[1] General Pavlovskii and his delegation returned to Moscow on 22 October, and on 5 November presented the Politburo with a grim picture of the situation below the Soviet border. Simultaneously, the Soviets received information about Amin's secret activities, forewarning a possible political shift to the West.

In an interview with several foreign journalists on 6 September 1979, Amin had said: "We do not accuse the US and China ourselves [of directly supporting the insurgents]. We want to have friendly relations with China and the US."[2] At a meeting on 27 September between Amin and J. Bruce Amstutz, the US *chargé d'affaires*, the Afghan president made a pitch for better relations with the US. At another meeting with a US official on 27 October, Amin expressed his acceptance, for the time being, of a polite and limited relationship that both countries would refrain from worsening by word or action. When the US official expressed his concern about the growing Soviet involvement in Afghanistan, Amin replied that it was necessary, as Afghanistan could not maintain itself against foreign interference without Soviet aid.

In addition, the USSR had been receiving reports about further contact with a US agent who was apparently making promises to tribal leaders to shift away from the Soviets and adopt a policy of neutrality while keeping this secret from Soviet officials. All these factors had, on the one hand, created the danger of losing the gains made by the April 1978 revolution, while on the other hand the threat to the Soviet position in Afghanistan risked an increase in anti-Soviet sentiment among the population. The Soviets therefore devised a plan for opposing Amin and creating a new party and state organs.[3]

---

1. NSA, IIM, *The Soviet Invasion of Afghanistan*, p. 22.
2. NSA, State Dept. Records, US Embassy, Kabul, to State, "Prime Minister Amin Reiterates That He Wants Friendly Relations with the US", September 1979.
3. Cold War International History Project (CWIHP), APRF, from notes taken by A. F. Dobrynin and provided to Norwegian Nobel Institute by Odd Arne Westad, Director of Research, Nobel Institute, trans. Daniel Rozas, Personal Memorandum, Andreopov to Brezhnev, n.d. [early December 1979].

On 29 November and for several days thereafter, Soviet military transport aircraft were detected flying into Kabul.[1] Soviet forces were being moved to the USSR-Afghan border, and Warsaw Pact forces were also placed on an advanced state of alert.

The Afghan situation was taken up at a meeting of senior national security officials on 17 December. CIA director Turner reported that the recent movement of new units into Afghanistan had raised the number of Soviet military personnel from 3,500 to an estimated 5,300 and stated: "We believe ... the Soviets have made a political decision to keep a pro-Soviet regime in power and to use military force to that end if necessary."[2] It was decided at this meeting that the US, with Pakistan and the UK, would explore the possibility of providing additional funds, weapons and communications to the Afghan rebels. On 19 December, Turner issued an Alert Memorandum on the Soviet deployment, indicating that reinforcements were also possibly on their way. According to the memorandum, introducing augmented forces would enable the Soviets to hold other key points, engage insurgents and free Afghan army units for operations elsewhere. On 21 December the administration began to publicize extensive details of the expanded Soviet military force in Afghanistan and the build-up north of the Afghan border.[3] On 22 December the National Security Agency director, Vice-Admiral Bobby Ray Inman, informed Brzezinski and Secretary of Defense Brown that the Soviets would begin a major military intervention in Afghanistan within the next seventy-two hours.[4] On 25 December, waves of military aircraft surged into Afghanistan in an airlift that continued at a high level until the evening of 27 December, when it began to tail off.

On 27 December, Soviet troops carried out an assault on Amin's residence that resulted in his death. In a broadcast purporting to be from Radio Kabul, Babrak Karmal of the PDPA announced that Amin had been ousted by the Party and the Revolutionary Council of the Democratic Republic of

---

1. Bradsher, *Afghanistan and the Soviet Union*, p. 176.
2. NSA, Nobel-Compendium, "Record of the Meeting of the Special Coordination Committee", 17 December 1979.
3. *The New York Times*, "Soviet Build-up Seen at Afghan Border", 22 December 1979.
4. Robert Gates, *From the Shadows: The Ultimate Insider's Story of Five Presidents and How They Won the Cold War* (New York: Simon & Schuster, 1996), p. 133.

Afghanistan.[1] By 28 December, the Soviet forces near the border were moving into Afghanistan, and the new regime announced in a broadcast that Moscow had accepted its request for military assistance.

After confirmation from the US embassy in Kabul that the invasion had begun, Brzezinski sent a memorandum to President Carter recommending that more aid be sent to the Afghan rebels. He wrote: "To make the above [aid] possible we must both reassure Pakistan and encourage it to help the rebels ... we should encourage the Chinese to help the rebels also. We should act in concert with Islamic countries both in a propaganda campaign and in a covert action campaign to help the rebels."[2] Shortly afterward, a DIA report expressed the view that "the key motivation that propelled Moscow's move was to bring its long-standing strategic goals closer within reach. Control of Afghanistan would be a major step toward overland access to the Indian Ocean and to domination of the Asian sub-continent."[3]

The Soviet invasion sparked major differences among top US officials regarding the motives underlying the invasion. To Brzezinski, the invasion indicated Soviet assertiveness, which in turn was part of the historical long-term Soviet drive with military power toward the Gulf.[4] Vance, on the other hand, believed the Soviets had badly miscalculated the extent of US and international reaction as well as the resistance thrown up by the Afghan people against the Soviet occupation.[5] The administration contended that the military occupation of Afghanistan had drastically altered the strategic balance in the entire Southwest Asian region, opening it to direct or indirect Soviet penetration. A Soviet position in Afghanistan, according to Brown, would enable Moscow "to put pressure, be it military, political, or internal insurgent, on Iran and Pakistan and the littoral states of the Persian Gulf and the Arabian Sea".[6]

On 4 January 1980, in his address to the nation, President Carter said: "A

---

1. FBIS, Middle East Edition, 28 December 1979, p. S1. See also *The New York Times*, "Afghan President Ousted and Executed in Kabul Coup with Soviet Help", 28 December 1979.
2. CWIHP, Memorandum from Brzezinski to Carter, "Reflections on Soviet Intervention in Afghanistan", 26 December 1979.
3. US Defense Intelligence Agency, Intelligence Commentary, 7 January 1980.
4. Brzezinski, *Power and Principle*, p. 427.
5. Vance, *Hard Choices*, pp. 388–9.
6. US Congress, House of Representatives, Committee on Foreign Affairs, *Foreign Assistance Legislation, Fiscal Year 1981*, Part 1, pp. 202–3.

Soviet occupied Afghanistan threatens both Iran and Pakistan and is a stepping stone to their possible control over much of the world's oil supplies." He pledged military equipment, food and other assistance to help Pakistan. On 6 January Saudi Director for Eastern Affairs Abbas Ghazzawi informed the political counsellor of the US embassy that Saudi Arabia had put forward a proposal for a special session of the Islamic Conference of Foreign Ministers (part of the Organization of the Islamic Conference) to deal with Afghanistan.

The US responded to the crisis with economic sanctions and diplomatic efforts at the UN, along with increased naval deployment to demonstrate resolve to friends and enemies alike. On 23 January Carter also warned the Soviets: "An attempt by any outside force to gain control of the Persian Gulf region will be regarded as an assault on the vital interests of the US, and such an assault will be repelled by any means necessary, including military force." This statement became known as the "Carter Doctrine".[1]

Additional security commitments and arms sales to Saudi Arabia and the Gulf states accompanied the Carter Doctrine.[2] Ronald Reagan, who took over as president in January 1981, reinforced the US security commitment to contain the Soviet Union and declared in a speech: "Maintenance of our alliance partnership is a key to our foreign policy."[3] During this period, Saudi Arabia became more important to the US through its role in projecting American military power. US alliances followed a pattern of extending deterrence capabilities to ward off threats to its ally: that is, the establishment of a military presence in a region creates a deterrent to the expansion of another party. The major criticism of US security assistance, however, is that it has not taken changing regional requirements into account. Despite the developing of systemic, regional and domestic considerations, little modification has taken place in the modalities of US support for its allies.[4]

The invasion represented a threat to both US and Saudi interests, and should, therefore, have provided a perfect occasion for strategic cooperation between the two countries. But Washington's inability to mount a forceful

---

1. Department of State, Bulletin, February 1980.
2. Franklin B. Weinstein, "The Concept of a Commitment in International Relations", *Journal of Conflict Resolution*, vol. 13, no.1 (March 1969), pp. 113–5.
3. *The Washington Post*, 23 February 1983.
4. Philip C. Rusciolelli, *Can America Remain Committed? U.S. Security Horizons in the 1990s*, (Boulder, CO: Westview Press, 1992), pp. 237.

The First Fahd Era (1979-90)

response to the Soviet invasion forced the Saudi government to go its own way.

Within weeks of the invasion Pakistani President Muhammad Zia ul-Haq sent the director of the Pakistan Inter-Services Intelligence (ISI), Akhtar Abdur Rahman, to Saudi Arabia with a warning that the Kingdom faced danger if the Soviet incursion was not checked. Akhtar Abdur Rahman met Prince Turki Al-Faisal, the director of the Saudi General Intelligence Department (GID), and Ahmed Badeeb, the GID's chief of staff. Turki believed that, for the Soviet Union, the occupation of Afghanistan was a step toward increasing its power in the region. He believed it was essential to help the Afghan rebels, and that geographically Pakistan offered the most suitable partner.[1] Soon afterward, Turki dispatched Badeeb to Pakistan to meet Zia and to inform him that the Kingdom had decided to supply cash to the ISI in order to provide military supplies to the Afghan rebels.[2]

When the Islamic Conference of Foreign Ministers was held in Islamabad on 26 January, Fahd expressed his wish that it "achieve unanimity among the Muslims for their wellbeing and strengthen their solidarity".[3] Prince Saud delivered the Kingdom's speech at the Conference, in which he stated that "the Soviet invasion had aroused worry and fear in the nations of the region" and that it had created "a threat to the security and the stability of the area". He added: "The world community until now [had not taken] a decisive action to stop the armed aggression against Afghanistan." He noted, as well: "The Soviet Union's support for the rights of the Palestinians does not extend to it the right to deprive the Afghans of their rights, and its call for Israel to withdraw from Arab occupied lands does not justify its occupation of Islamic land."[4]

During the conference the Saudi government led the denunciation of the Soviet attack on a Muslim country and called for sanctions against Moscow and "a boycott of the puppet Afghan regime".[5] According to Safran, the Saudi government had promoted the conference partly to recover some of its lost prestige following the Mecca incident of the previous year. By demonstrating

---

1. Steve Coll, *Ghost Wars: The Secret History of the CIA, Afghanistan, and bin Laden from the Soviet Invasion to September 10, 2001* (New York: Penguin Group, 2005), p. 81.
2. Ibid., p. 72.
3. *Al-Bilad*, 26 January 1980.
4. *Ukaz*, 28 January 1980.
5. *Ukaz*, 30 January 1980.

its concern for the fate of a Muslim country, Saudi Arabia reinforced its Islamic credentials. But the Saudis also "wanted precisely to destroy its [Soviet Union's] image of a selfless friend of Arab and Muslim peoples and at least put those who would cooperate with it in no better position than those who cooperated with the US".[1] The US viewed the Saudi effort as a welcome indication of shared Saudi-US strategic interests, and sought to build upon it.

Brzezinski claimed that during his visit on 4 February, he had reached an understanding with the Saudi government about greater Saudi-US military cooperation "on a quiet basis". The Kingdom desired closer military ties and better intelligence about Soviet activity in the region, and expressed particular concern about South Yemen.[2] It genuinely feared that the Soviet invasion constituted an increased threat to the Gulf. But its desire to avoid provoking Iran and antagonizing Iraq, both of whom had denounced the Carter Doctrine, led it to look elsewhere for additional security support. The Saudis were also reacting against US indiscretion in discussing the matter openly. According to *Ukaz*, Fahd commented: "Our political basis is that we do not believe in the politics of pacts, defensive belts and axis zones, and we do not accept their return."[3] Prince Saud also reaffirmed the Saudi refusal to allow foreign military bases or facilities in Saudi Arabia, stating: "The Kingdom will not make any agreement with the Americans or anybody else involving any type of facilities."[4]

A few days later, on 25 February, Fahd said: "The flagrant military intervention in Afghanistan is an infringement by the Moscow government of international public law and all international legislation." He declared that "Saudi Arabia agrees with those who feel there is a need for the US to take an urgent and brave attitude to forbid and stop the communist penetration from pushing deep into Afghanistan". Hence, he added, "we monitor with extreme caution this Soviet role and its dubious activities against this region, and at the same time we accurately monitor the reaction of the US to this strategic Soviet activity."[5]

Saudi Defence Minister Sultan bin Abdul 'Aziz said, on 23 March: "Saudi Arabia is willing and is acting to keep the Gulf countries away from foreign

---

1. Safran, *Saudi Arabia*, p. 320.
2. Brzezinski, *Power and Principle*, pp. 449–50.
3. *Ukaz*, 4 February 1980.
4. *Ukaz*, 10 February 1980.
5. *Ukaz*, 25 February 1980.

influence, whether Soviet or American." He added: "The Kingdom will take all necessary action to ensure that the Soviet invasion of Afghanistan will not continue or extend to other areas."[1] In addition, the Saudi Press Agency reported Sultan as saying that "whenever the Kingdom and the Gulf states are exposed to aggression from a bigger and stronger state, then friendly assistance from outside is important".[2] Clearly, Prince Sultan was indicating that in the case of a Soviet threat Saudi Arabia would, in practice, have to seek US assistance.

Furthermore, the disastrous failure of the American attempt to rescue the US embassy hostages in Iran on 24 April, plus a tacit Saudi understanding with the South Yemeni regime, strengthened the Saudis' changed cooperative disposition.[3] Simultaneously, a variety of incidents disturbed relations between the two countries. In late January, a CIA study concluded that the Saudi regime might collapse within two years,[4] and Fahd expressed disappointment that the US seemed incapable of taking urgent and bold action to stop the Soviet thrust. In addition, the Saudi government rebuffed US requests during February and March 1980 to buy oil to fill the Strategic Petroleum Reserve. In May and June, the US denied the Saudi request for a prompt agreement to sell them F-15 enhancement equipment and AWACS aircraft. On 12 May, Fahd said: "The Soviet intimidation directed against this area must be examined with great caution to realize its dimensions and how to overcome it."[5]

Meanwhile, US officials were supporting covert aid to the Afghan rebels. The State Department believed the rebels could tie up some 85,000 or more Soviet troops, but that they were fragmented, lacked effective national leadership and certainly could not force a Soviet withdrawal.

Since 1978, Pakistan had played host to thousands of Afghan refugees and rebels. Pakistan's cooperation was therefore vital for the success of this covert aid provision. Assistant Secretary of State Warren Christopher was sent to placate and reassure Pakistan about its indispensable cooperation and collaboration.[6] Carter also dispatched Brzezinski, first to Egypt and then to Pakistan, where he sought to enlist support for the Afghan resistance. Brown

---

1. *Ukaz*, 23 March 1980.
2. Saudi Press Agency, 26 March 1980.
3. Safran, *Saudi Arabia*, p. 360.
4. *Newsweek*, 3 March 1980.
5. *Ukaz*, 12 May 1980.
6. Brzezinski, *Power and Principle*, pp. 471–3.

was sent to China, seen as another potential ally.[1] Sadat had, meanwhile, authorized US cargo planes to fly from Egyptian bases to deliver arms and supplies to the *mujahideen* in Pakistan.[2] There the CIA turned them over to the Pakistanis to be passed on to the seven main groups of Muslim zealots for training in the arts of guerrilla warfare and urban terrorism.[3]

During Brzezinski's first meeting with Zia in late January 1980, the guiding rule of the alliance – that all arms supplies, finance and training of the fighters must be provided through Pakistan and not directly from the CIA – was dictated by the Pakistani president and agreed to by Brzezinski. Zia imposed three conditions for allowing arms shipments through Pakistan to the *mujahideen*. The donor countries were to maintain absolute silence about the shipments; arms and other war supplies were to be shipped by the fastest possible means to Pakistan; and shipments by air were to be limited to two planeloads a week.[4] In February, Brzezinski was again able to travel to Pakistan, after having secured pledges of financial support from Saudi Arabia, which would eventually match the US total, dollar for dollar. In fact, during the first month of official aid, Saudi Arabia was already providing more funding than the CIA.[5]

The GID funnelled money and equipment to certain Afghan rebel leaders who were outside ISI or CIA control. According to Coll, Badeeb managed to plant Saudi spies through Saudi charities operating in Peshawar, Pakistan. Interviewed by Coll, Badeeb recollected: "We insist[ed] that the Americans [would] not get involved – especially in the beginning."[6]

The US administration was attempting to formulate a response to the Soviet Union invasion of Afghanistan. According to a State Department document, permanent Soviet domination of Afghanistan was seen as likely to enhance Soviet capabilities in supporting subversion and other forms of pressure on governments in the region. The US response to this possibility was to develop an approach to the complex issues of the area, based on a solid

---

1. John K. Cooley, *Unholy Wars: Afghanistan, America and International Terrorism* (London: Pluto Press, 2000), p. 31.
2. Ibid., p. 32.
3. Ibid., p. 35.
4. Ibid., p. 55.
5. Bob Woodward, *Veil: The Secret Wars of the CIA 1981–87* (London: Headline Books, 1987), p.79.
6. Coll, *Ghost Wars*, p. 86.

strategic foundation that related to it in its entirety (including the wider Middle East), and consisted of the following elements:

1. A strong US economy, less dependent on foreign oil;
2. A vital Western alliance, capable of effective cooperation with the Gulf states;
3. An increased US military capability of projecting US strength into the region;
4. A national will to press for resolution of the conflict between Israel and the Arabs;
5. A willingness to commit resources to promote the survival and independence of the governments and peoples of the region.[1]

Two White House meetings were held in the third week of June, attended by the president and all top foreign policy and defence officials. Their deliberations led to the approval of this approach.[2]

Meanwhile, in a press conference during his visit to Paris, Soviet Foreign Minister Gromyko warned Pakistan and said any talk about Soviet withdrawal would be "a mirage, time wasted, and energy lost".[3]

However, the power struggle inside Afghanistan was escalating. According to a State Department report in June 1980, the Soviets were confronted with a dilemma because of intensified infighting between the Khalq and Parcham factions of the PDPA. According to the report, this continuing feud was paralyzing government operations and strengthening the resistance; but if the Soviets were to espouse the cause of one faction to the exclusion of the other, they could further undermine their own base of support.

To raise the costs of the Soviet intervention in Afghanistan, and to deter the Soviet Union from undertaking other Third World invasions, the CIA started shipping weapons secretly to the *mujahideen*, with the CIA's Afghan

---

1. NSA, State Dept., Bureau of Public Affairs, Policy No. 152, "Persian Gulf, Southwest Asia, Indian Ocean: Developing a Cooperative Security Framework", 24 March 1980.
2. Brzezinski, *Power and Principle*, p. 447.
3. NSA, State Dept. Records, US Embassy, Paris, to State, "Gromyko Press Conference in Paris", April 1980.

programme liaising with the ISI.[1] By July, weapons were in the hands of the *mujahideen*, who were already attacking the Soviets with hit-and-run tactics. To give US officials a plausible basis for denial if the Soviets complained, the CIA was purchasing Soviet-made arms from the Egyptians for the resistance.

Newly elected President Reagan favoured a distinctly hard-line policy toward Afghanistan. William Casey, the CIA director, therefore began to redevelop covert operations capability in early 1981,[2] and in mid-February asked the president for a radical restructuring of the covert operations consultation process. The new arrangement placed an absolute premium on secrecy. Casey also managed to lure Henry Rowen, former president of the RAND Corporation, to take over the National Intelligence Council and brought in Herb Meyer, an editor with *Fortune* magazine, as his special assistant. Both were experts on the Soviet economy, which was one of the most important areas of study for Casey.[3]

Believing the Soviets were in trouble, Casey asked Meyer to come up with his own assessment. According to Schweizer, Meyer concluded in his report that Moscow was "terribly vulnerable economically … It should be a matter of high national policy to play to these vulnerabilities."[4] Casey requested a more thorough study to be carried out, and at a meeting of the National Security Planning Group (NSPG) in March, he emphasized that there were new insurgencies developing in the Third World and that the US needed to back these movements with money and political muscle.[5]

Saudi Arabia, from its position as an Islamic state, had decided to break diplomatic relations with the current regime in Afghanistan, and announced its decision on 7 April: "The Kingdom of Saudi Arabia, in a spirit stemming from its Islamic stance and with profound anxiety and deep concern [has] decided to sever diplomatic relations with the ruling regime in Kabul until right is restored."[6]

Casey was in Saudi Arabia early in April to discuss raising the stakes in

---

1. *The Washington Post*, 19 and 20 July 1992.
2. Peter Schweizer, *Victory: The Reagan Administration's Secret Strategy That Hastened the Collapse of the Soviet Union* (New York: The Atlantic Monthly Press, 1994), p. 14.
3. Ibid., pp. 19–20.
4. Ibid., pp. 21.
5. Ibid., pp. 22–3.
6. *Ukaz*, 8 April 1981.

Afghanistan. In his view, Saudi concerns about Soviet intentions presented an opportunity to make the Kingdom a powerful US ally. According to Schweizer, Casey informed Prince Turki about US plans to extend substantial aid to Pakistan, and his intention of pushing for increased aid to the *mujahideen*. Turki agreed that Saudi Arabia would continue to match the US contribution, and revealed that the Saudi government was intending to boost its religious and anti-communist radio broadcasts into Afghanistan and Soviet Central Asia.

Schweizer claims that Casey presented Turki with copies of top-secret CIA reports on Soviet oil production, suggesting that Moscow was financing its world empire through oil exports. Every time the oil price went up by one dollar per barrel, it meant US $1 billion a year in hard currency for Moscow. The US wanted the Saudis to help reduce the price of oil. Casey was assured by Turki, Schweizer alleges, that Saudi Arabia would resist any pressure to cut production and increase prices.[1] During an interview in 2005, Prince Turki said this topic had never been discussed with him, and when asked whether it was discussed with Fahd, his answer was ambiguous: "Not in my presence."[2] It would not be surprising if Schweizer's account was accurate, as this was precisely the sort of policy that the Saudi government had always tried to apply in deflecting/confronting the communist threat.

A CIA study in early June 1981 held that the Soviets had a promising energy sector, but were in great need of technical input from the West. The report noted that maintaining output and exploiting new reserves would require Western technology, and that the US had a near-monopoly on many of the oil-drilling technologies.[3] The declaration of martial law in Poland on 12 December solidified support behind an offensive strategy to roll back Soviet power, as the Soviets were, after all, the catalysts for and sponsors of Polish martial law. On 29 December Reagan announced an embargo that would prohibit US involvement in the gas pipeline project between Europe and the Soviet Union. The US embargo was seen in Europe as a declaration of economic war on the Soviet Union.

Meanwhile, a State Department assessment emphasized that while the *mujahideen* did not have the power to force a Soviet retreat, their record for 1981 appeared to have caused the USSR considerable concern. Among the *mujahideen*'s most impressive achievements that year were successful defensive

---

1. Schweizer, *Victory*, pp. 24–32.
2. Prince Turki Al-Faisal, interview with the author, November 2005.
3. Schweizer, *Victory*, pp. 49–50.

operations against major Soviet offensives. The assessment maintained that the pre-eminent source of strength for the resistance movement was the support it received from the Afghan people, and also indicated that the supply of arms during the spring and summer of 1981 had been adequate. It further pointed out that the most debilitating weakness of the resistance was its lack of unity, which the Soviets were trying to exploit by appealing to regional, ethnic, tribal and religious aspirations in order to gain support for the regime.

On 15 March 1982, as part of the new economic strategy, Under-Secretary of State James Buckley and a team of financial experts began a swing through European capitals to tighten the noose on credits going to the Soviet Union.[1]

Schweizer notes that in May 1982, Casey and Fahd discussed various topics, including Afghanistan and US sanctions. Casey talked about the latest Soviet decision to reduce oil exports to Eastern Europe by 10 percent, a cutback that would allow Moscow to sell more oil to the West and enable the Soviets to generate hard currency, while simultaneously threatening to squeeze Saudi Arabia out of certain markets. Casey also told Fahd that the administration would do its best to curb Soviet energy programmes, but in return it wanted a reduction in oil prices as lower energy prices would boost the US economy, end the rush for alternative energy sources and incapacitate the enemies of Saudi Arabia.[2]

In spring 1982, too, the long-awaited "vulnerability assessments" report was finally completed. The report noted that the Soviet economic system was both rigid and inflexible, and that an infusion of Western technology was a compelling requirement for alleviating bottlenecks and maintaining production levels. It also pointed out that the Soviet system was "peculiarly ill-suited to promoting efficiency and technological progress", and that "the USSR's ability to earn the hard currency it needs to pay for its Western imports is ... already under pressure and may well diminish in the future." The conclusion was that the Soviet energy sector was an area to be exploited.[3]

In Afghanistan, the resistance was now better equipped, and there was deeper cooperation between the different factions; but while the *mujahideen* knew the terrain, they lacked arms and a coherent strategy, which led to a stalemate. A DIA analysis indicated that the resistance lacked "the heavier

---

[1]. Schweizer, *Victory*, p. 79.
[2]. Ibid., pp. 96–9.
[3]. Ibid., pp. 102–5.

weaponry needed to turn the military situation in their favor", and declared: "We believe the Soviets would have to double their strength to break the current stalemate."[1] Even so, the resistance was somewhat of a low-level effort, and the US wanted to increase the costs of the occupation exponentially. Stepping up activity in the northern provinces would threaten Soviet supply lines and preclude the Soviets from bringing more troops into the country. The CIA would also provide satellite intelligence to the resistance.[2]

Early in 1983, the Treasury Department concluded a study of international oil pricing, as world oil prices were an important determinant of both US and Soviet economic health. The report argued that the optimum oil price for the US economy was approximately US $20 a barrel. A lower price would occur either with a drop in demand or through a dramatic increase in production. If Saudi Arabia stepped up production in order to cause the world price to fall, the drop in price would thus have a devastating effect on the Soviet economy. Moscow was already producing at maximum capacity.[3]

In February 1984, Casey met Fahd (who had been king since June 1982) and Turki to inform them that the Afghan strategy was running smoothly, and to brief them on the decision reached with Zia to take the war into Soviet Central Asia. According to Schweizer, Casey wished to bring the Saudi government in on the deal, and wanted to convince Turki to commit his resources in the region to a joint operation.[4] In his interview with the author, Turki said that the Kingdom was against taking the war into Soviet Central Asia for fear of Soviet reprisals against Pakistan. Therefore, according to Turki, the Kingdom refused to participate.[5]

With their overwhelming superiority on the battlefield, the Soviets began carpet-bombing the Panjsher Valley on 20 April 1984, while columns of tanks and armoured personnel carriers on the ground captured much of the valley territory. This large-scale campaign was repeated throughout the summer, putting tremendous strains on the resistance movement, as the massive bombardment was thinning out the civilian population that constituted much

---

1. Defense Intelligence Agency, Directorate for Research, "Afghan Resistance", 5 November 1982.
2. Schweizer, *Victory*, pp. 116–9.
3. Ibid., pp. 140–2.
4. Ibid., pp. 179–81.
5. Author's interview with Prince Turki.

of the *mujahideen*'s support base.[1] ISI director General Abdur Rahman asked that the *mujahideen* be supplied with the necessary material support to give them the possibility of winning the war. Sympathetic members of the US Congress enabled the Reagan administration to double aid to the *mujahideen* in the hope that these new resources would raise the stakes for Moscow.[2]

By 1984, several congressmen wanted the CIA to do more for the Afghan rebels. Casey, therefore, made deals that saw CIA and GID spending on the Afghan *mujahideen* double by year's end. At the same time, Congress tripled the administration's request for fiscal year 1985 to US $250 million. These contributions, in addition to those by Saudi Arabia and others, represented extraordinary infusions of cash and arms that empowered the *mujahideen* to pursue their struggle.[3] On 28 July 1984 Casey wrote to John McMahon, the CIA deputy director, instructing him to conduct "a thorough review and re-evaluation of the Afghan program".[4]

In January 1985, a CIA source on the Soviet General Staff provided detailed information about the USSR's plans for a dramatic escalation of the war. A meeting of the NSPG was convened, and National Security Advisor Robert McFarlane was asked to develop a new strategy. In March, Reagan signed a directive setting out, for the first time, specific strategic objectives in the context of the Afghan war. The new strategy contained a number of elements, including the more effective supply and distribution of weapons to the *mujahideen*; an order to the US intelligence community requiring that more resources be put into collecting intelligence on the Soviet Union; and a heightening of the international political costs of the war. The aim was the outright defeat of the Soviet armed forces in Afghanistan.[5]

During late spring 1985, the US expressed concern about Soviet efforts to cut the *mujahideen* supply lines from Pakistan. Soviet attacks were becoming more sophisticated, causing heavy *mujahideen* casualties. Furthermore, domestic political opposition against the Zia regime in Pakistan was increasing. As it was critical to the success of the resistance that Zia be kept in power, Washington

1. Schweizer, *Victory*, p. 206.
2. Ibid., pp. 206–7.
3. Angelo Rasanayagam, *Afghanistan: A Modern History* (New York: I. B. Tauris, 2005), p. 136.
4. Gates, *From the Shadows*, pp. 37–8.
5. Schweizer, *Victory*, pp. 212–4.

began putting together an assistance package.[1] To solve the resistance's logistical problems, the US would supply more sophisticated equipment – including Stinger missiles, as the *mujahideen* lacked an effective response to Soviet air attacks. However, the Defense Department did not want the Stingers to be used in case they fell into Soviet hands and thus compromised US technology, or were sold to Third World terrorists for use against US targets. Some State Department officials worried that any US weapons system that could turn the tide would so antagonize the Soviet Union that it would sour overall efforts to improve relations.[2]

In May, a CIA review of the five years since the Soviet invasion showed that "the overall insurgency has gradually increased. In 1983 and 1984, insurgents increased attacks on airfields, garrisons, and other military targets." The review estimated Soviet losses to be greater than those of the rebels, and also estimated the "direct Soviet military costs of the conflict from 1980 through 1984 at some US $16 billion."[3]

By the late summer, the US and Saudi Arabia had put into practice two important economic policies. First, the US devalued the dollar, which cut the value of Soviet exports by one quarter. Second, Saudi Arabia decided to increase oil production, now accepting for a variety of reasons what the US had been recommending for some time.[4] By late autumn 1985, production would be increased to reach almost nine million barrels a day. In November the oil price was US $30 a barrel; five months later it had dropped to US $12 per barrel. For Moscow, this represented a loss of US $10 billion,[5] and as a consequence Soviet arms sales dropped 20 percent in 1986 – another loss of US $2 billion.

In early 1986, a letter signed by members of the Politburo was sent to King Fahd, warning him against pushing prices any lower and proposing a secret meeting in Geneva to stabilize prices.[6] It had been necessary to cancel dozens of large Soviet industrial projects for lack of funds.

---

1. Ibid., pp. 228–9.
2. George P. Shultz, *Turmoil and Triumph: Diplomacy, Power and the Victory of the American Ideal* (New York: Charles Scribner's Sons, 1993), p. 692.
3. CIA, Directorate of Intelligence, "The Soviet Invasion of Afghanistan: Five Years After", May 1985.
4. Schweizer, *Victory*, pp. 236–7.
5. Ibid., pp. 242–3.
6. Ibid., p. 255.

The CIA provided the *mujahideen* with Stinger missiles, which improved the rebels' battlefield performance. One Pentagon report claimed that the Stingers had forced "more tactical and air support changes in the last quarter of 1986 and the first quarter of 1987 than in the previous seven years of the conflict".[1] Another undated Joint Chiefs of Staff report claimed that the Stinger missile had changed the course of the war: Soviet helicopter gunships and bombers were no longer able to operate as they had formerly done.

Afghanistan was being converted from a low-grade infection into a haemorrhage. A CIA study stated that "since the invasion of Afghanistan in 1979, the war has become increasingly costly to the Soviets. Over the past seven years they have depleted their weapons inventories, experienced greater aircraft and equipment losses, and sharply increased their use of ammunition." It concluded that they would probably not influence Soviet decisions about their larger objectives.

According to Simpson, the US wanted to offer the Soviets a way out of Afghanistan, but because of the US position on the deployment of Pershing missiles into Europe, it was decided that Saudi Arabia would make the move. Prince Bandar, now Saudi ambassador to the US, then flew to Moscow in February 1988 to meet the Soviet leadership. During the meeting, Soviet Premier Mikhail Gorbachev accused the Kingdom of interfering in the internal affairs of Afghanistan and predicted that the US would let the Saudis down. Bandar emphasized that he had come to find a way for the Soviet Union to make an honourable withdrawal from Afghanistan. Gorbachev again went on the attack, saying: "I know everything you are doing there. You are spending 200 million dollars a year in Afghanistan." Bandar replied: "You are losing people, we are losing money ... but we can always print more, we can always sell more oil." At this point in the discussion Gorbachev asked to see Bandar alone and told him: "If we are not pushed or humiliated or taken advantage of, we will leave. You can tell King Fahd that by next March we will be out of Afghanistan."[2] What was not known to Bandar at the time was that the decision to withdraw had been taken by the Soviet leadership as early as November 1986.

The rising human toll, the costly losses caused by the introduction of the

---

1. US Army, "Impact of the Stinger Missile on Soviet and Resistance Tactics in Afghanistan", March 1989.
2. William Simpson, *The Prince: The Secret Story of the World's Most Intriguing Royal, Prince Bandar bin Sultan* (New York: HarperCollins, 2006), pp. 169–73.

Stingers and the operations on Soviet territory had forced the Soviet retreat. At a Politburo meeting on 13 November 1986, Gorbachev had decided to end the war within one year or, at a maximum, two. In December, he informed Afghan President Mohammad Najibullah, in Moscow, that the Soviet military commitment to his government was limited. On 14 April 1988, the governments of Pakistan and Afghanistan agreed, with the Soviet Union and the US acting as their co-guarantors, to refrain from any form of interference in each other's territory. For their part, the superpowers pledged to stop interfering in Afghanistan, with the Soviet Union agreeing to withdraw its troops.[1] On 15 May 1988, Soviet troops began their ten-month withdrawal from Afghanistan.

The Iran-Iraq War

The assimilation of the Kurds into Iraq posed one of the major challenges to the conception of the state. Since the Ba'th Party had come to power in 1968 it had, on many occasions, attempted to achieve this aim by force. In 1974, the Iraqi government realized it was fighting more than the Kurds: direct Iranian involvement made forced assimilation militarily impossible in the short term and politically difficult in the long term. Essentially, it was the desire on both sides to avoid open warfare that had led to the Algiers Accord of 1975, at which the two countries settled their border disputes.[2] One result of the agreement was that Iran halted aid to the Kurds, which allowed the Iraqis to crush a Kurdish rebellion. However, the price Iraq paid was the abandonment of its claim to full sovereignty over the whole of the Shatt al-'Arab waterway.

A State Department-CIA-DIA analysis on 1 May 1975 outlined the implications of the Algiers Accord. The study noted the Shah's anxiety over establishing regional hegemony, restricting Iraqi influence and covert activities and eliminating foreign leftist influences at work in Baghdad. The study observed: "The Algiers agreement of early March between Iran and Iraq appears to have achieved the Shah's first goal; whether the Shah's other objectives can be attained seems more doubtful." It viewed Iraq's foreign policy options as having been substantially increased as a result of breaking free of its entanglement in the Kurdish rebellion, and pointed out that "Baghdad, moreover, can now

---

1. Amin Saikal, *Modern Afghanistan: A History of Struggle and Survival* (London: I. B. Tauris, 2004), p. 201.
2. Shahram Chubin and Charles Tripp, *Iran and Iraq at War* (Boulder, CO: Westview Press, 1988), pp. 22–3.

allocate more of its resources to accelerating industrial development, and to efforts to subvert Gulf states and Syria".[1]

Although the relationship between Iraq and Iran after 1975 was no longer one of war, it was characterized by watchful tension. From the middle of 1979, after the Shah had been overthrown and the Islamic Republic established, the war of words between Tehran and Baghdad intensified, supplemented by acts of violence of unverifiable provenance along the common border. In June, the Iranian government began publicly to urge the Iraqi population to rise up and overthrow the regime of Saddam Hussein.[2]

The 1979 seizure of the US embassy in Tehran and the Soviet invasion of Afghanistan a month later rocked the US, threatening to undermine its grip on the region and raising the possibility of its Soviet rivals being handed a major geopolitical gain. Its greatest fear was a Soviet takeover of Iran. By April 1980, according to *Le Monde*, there was some evidence that the Soviets had engineered the hostage crisis. The USSR, with its Iranian supporters, was hoping to push the Iranians over the radical brink so that the pro-Soviet *mullahs* could block the normalization of relations with the US.[3]

By mid-1980, Brzezinski began to look more favourably toward Iraq as a potential counterweight to Iran, and as a force to contain Soviet expansionism in the region. On 14 April, he signalled US willingness to work with Iraq, asserting: "We see no fundamental incompatibility of interests between the US and Iraq ... We do not feel that American-Iraqi relations need to be frozen in antagonisms."[4] *The New York Times* reported that during a visit to Jordan in the first week of July that year, Brzezinski met Iraqi officials in Amman with the aim of coordinating activities to oppose Iran's reckless policies. Gary Sick, a former Brzezinski aide, would later remark in an interview that when it came to Iran, "there was no doubt where Brzezinski's heart lay." The Islamic Revolution was a threat to US interests in the region, and a strong Iraq would check Iran's expansionist desires. Sick said: "Brzezinski was letting Saddam

---

1. NSA, Director of Central Intelligence–National Intelligence Officer, "NIO"/ Middle East DCI/NIO 1039-75, "The Implications of the Iran-Iraq Agreement", 1 May 1975.
2. BBC Summary, ME/6144/A5, 8 June 1979, ME/6145/A7, 9 June 1979.
3. Eric Rouleau, "Interview with Nourridine Kianouri, Secretary General of Iran's Pro-Soviet Communist 'Tudah' Party", *Le Monde*, 18 April 1980.
4. Amatzia Baram and Barry Rubin, *Iraq's Road to War* (New York: St. Martin's Press, 1993), p. 256.

assume there was a US green light for his invasion of Iran, because there was no explicit red light."[1]

A Department of Defense report predicted a 50 percent chance that Iraq would attack Iran, and also stated that Iraq felt Iran was militarily weak and could easily be defeated. It was expected that provocation would continue until such time as Iranian leaders reacted and provided Iraqi forces with an excuse to invade.

Brzezinski's discussion in Jordan provided the first hint that the US was looking for new partners in the region that would be able to police the Gulf, and that Baghdad was clearly the best choice. The suggestion that the US attitude towards Iraq might change was warmly welcomed in Baghdad.[2]

To Washington, the revolutionary regime in Iran brought about two important changes to the security of the region. First, the presence of an activist Islamist revolutionary regime was likely to turn the area towards Islamic fundamentalism. Second, the explicit call by the Iranian regime for the overthrow of traditional, pro-Western regimes in the Gulf increased the threat of regional instability.[3]

The US responded by creating the Rapid Deployment Joint Task Force (RDJTF), the overall responsibility of which was to plan, jointly train, exercise and be prepared to deploy and employ designated forces in response to contingencies threatening US vital interests.[4] The political support of important states was viewed by Washington as an indispensable adjunct to its military strategy, particularly in view of the need for access to regional military installations.

Concluding, from US plans for the region, that Washington either thought their regimes were faltering, or doubted their loyalty and was preparing to replace them with more reliable candidates, Saudi Arabia and the other Gulf states took certain steps toward tightening their security. First, they had to find ways of talking to the new regime in Tehran. Two lines of approach were decided upon: Kuwait's foreign minister Sheikh Sabah Al Ahmad Al Jaber

---

1. Quoted in Kenneth R. Timmerman, *The Death Lobby: How the West Armed Iraq* (London: Fourth Estate, 1992), p. 76.
2. Timmerman, *The Death Lobby*, p. 77.
3. Adam Tarock, *The Superpowers' Involvement in the Iran-Iraq War* (New York: Nova Science Publishers, Inc., 1998), p. 51.
4. Headquarters Rapid Deployment Joint Task Force (RDJTF), Fact Sheet, 1981, p. 1.

Al Sabah would pay an official visit to Tehran, and Bahraini Foreign Minister Sheikh Muhammad Mubarak Al Khalifa would contact Ibrahim Yazdi, Deputy Prime Minister and Minister for Revolutionary Affairs of Iran, while they were both in New York attending a meeting of the UN General Assembly.[1] The two meetings did not, however, lead to any halt in the deterioration of relations.

The second step was to find a replacement for US protection. Following on from the above-mentioned joint exercises in 1979 at Khamis Mushait, Saudi Arabia and the other Gulf states had quietly attempted to work out a common policy on such matters as foreign relations and oil, and meetings of specialist ministers for security, information and so on were regularly held.

In May 1980, the Saudis held onto a faint hope that the impending elections in Iran might still produce a coherent and reasonable leadership, as expressed by Crown Prince Fahd on 11 May: "We will just have to wait and see what will happen after the formation of the anticipated parliament."[2]

According to Safran, the Saudis abandoned their appeasement policy toward Iran when they received Saddam on 5 August in the city of Taif for a major visit to coordinate the policies of their respective countries on a range of issues.[3] This view, however, is not in keeping with Prince Bandar's explanation to the author that Saddam had come to Taif to inform Fahd about his intention of attacking Iran. According to Bandar, Fahd advised against the attack and told Saddam that although the Iranians were divided, "once you attacked them they would close ranks and Iraq would find itself fighting a more formidable enemy." Fahd also told Saddam that while the decision to start a war was his, the decision to end it was not. Bandar claimed Saddam returned to Saudi Arabia six months later to tell Fahd that he wished to end the war but was unable to do so, and regretted not having listened to Fahd's advice.[4]

Despite differences in their domestic systems, Iraq and Saudi Arabia had in effect established a tacit alliance. For Iraq, the move provided insurance against revolutionary Iran, additional pressure on Sadat and furtherance of its aim to supplant Egypt as the leading Arab state. For Saudi Arabia, the intention was to counter Iran and find a way to temper Arab condemnation of Sadat in the hope of bringing Egypt back into the Arab fold.

1. Mohamed Heikal, *Iran: The Untold Story* (New York: Pantheon Books, 1982), pp. 199–200.
2. FBIS, 12 May 1980.
3. Safran, *Saudi Arabia*, pp. 361–2.
4. Prince Bandar bin Sultan, interview with the author, October 2006.

The First Fahd Era (1979–90)

Faced with Iran's subversive activities, protracted and escalating border fighting and possibly with US encouragement if not actual complicity, Saddam concluded that he had no alternative but to contain the Iranian threat by resorting to force. He came to believe that the only way to do this was to exploit Iran's temporary weakness following the revolution and to raise the stakes for both sides. On 9 September 1980, Iraqi forces moved to liberate the territories that had been conceded to Iran in the Algiers Accord. On 17 September, in a speech before the Iraqi National Assembly, Saddam formally abrogated the Accord, asserted complete sovereignty over the Shatt al-ʿArab and demanded the return of the islands of Abu Musa and the Tunbs. Five days later, he ordered his armies to cross the border into Iran.

The Iraqis' intention was to impress the Iranian leaders with the quality and resolve of their military strength in order to present them with the choice of escalation or concession. The initial Iraqi onslaught therefore consisted of a land attack across the Iranian border at four points, and a poorly executed pre-emptive air strike against the Iranian air force. The war was largely regarded in Baghdad not as a fight to the death, but more as a means of compelling the Iranian leadership to give official recognition to Iraq's strength.[1] Indeed, Saddam believed the war would end in a matter of days with a crushing Iraqi victory and perhaps even the demise of the Islamic regime in Tehran. But instead of toppling the regime, the Iraqi invasion shored it up. Even pro-monarchists in the Iranian air force closed ranks in defence of their homeland.[2]

At the outset of the hostilities, Radio Baghdad announced on 25 September that King Khalid, in a telephone call, had "affirmed Saudi Arabia's support for Iraq",[3] but the announcement was corrected the following day by the Saudi government, which stated that the king had expressed only "his interest and good fraternal feelings".[4]

The Soviet Union's response was to urge both sides to exercise restraint while accusing the US of having instigated the hostilities. According to the Soviets, the US objective was to increase tension in the area as a prelude to possible seizure of the oil resources of both countries. The Soviets did not want to be forced to choose between their alliance with Iraq and their improving relationship with Iran. One immediate consequence of the invasion was the suspension of

---

1. Chubin and Tripp, *Iran and Iraq at War*, pp. 54–5.
2. Timmerman, *The Death Lobby*, p. 82.
3. FBIS, 30 September 1980.
4. Saudi Press Agency, 26 September 1980.

arms supplies to Iraq from the Soviets. The USSR had been working for many years to penetrate Iran's clerics. When the revolutionary regime took power in 1979 and threw the US out of Iran, the Soviets stood to gain more than they had ever believed possible. Even the pro-Soviet Communist (Tudeh) Party was now invited to join the Tehran government. The Soviet embargo would show the Iranians that the Soviet Union was on their side.[1]

According to a Congressional report, the war threatened US allies in the Gulf with a spillover of the conflict. Washington's room for manoeuvring was restricted by a fear that any help it might extend to one of the sides could backfire dangerously by pushing the other toward Moscow. The US also feared that a clear victory for either side would jeopardize its interests even further. An Iraqi victory would lead to the disintegration of Iran and invite Soviet intervention in that country. In addition, whichever country emerged as a clear winner would find itself well placed to extend its domination over the Gulf and force its own brand of radical anti-Westernism on the existing pro-Western regimes.

Therefore, according to a State Department bulletin, US policy toward the war had four basic objectives:

1. To seek a dynamic balance of power between the warring sides so that neither side achieved victory;
2. To prevent any Soviet exploitation of the conflict to gain a dominant position in either country;
3. To prevent any risk posed by the war to the survival of the Gulf states;
4. To ensure the continuing flow of oil from the Gulf.[2]

The Carter administration's first reaction was to declare neutrality and non-involvement. Thus, when Secretary of State Edmund Muskie met his Soviet counterpart Gromyko in New York, he reportedly received a pledge of neutrality in the war from Moscow in return.[3]

Iraq's war plans had ignored the far superior Iranian navy. The failure to take this into account led not only to Iran's effective blockade of Iraq's port

---
1. Timmerman, *The Death Lobby*, pp. 83–4.
2. Department of State, Bulletin, December 1980, pp. 2–3.
3. Brzezinski, *Power and Principle*, p. 452.

at the head of the Gulf, but also left Iran in a position to interfere with Gulf shipping.

The Saudi government felt compelled to seek US assistance in meeting these threats. According to Safran, the US wanted its backing for Saudi Arabia to be visible yet non-challenging to the Iranians, in order to prevent harm to the US hostages still being held. The Saudis were even more anxious to avoid provoking Iran, and wanted US help to be even less apparent.[1] According to Simpson, Bandar told Chairman of the Joint Chiefs of Staff General David Jones on 28 September: "We want AWACS immediately. We want AWACS for twenty-four-hour surveillance of the Gulf. We can't protect the Kingdom without it. Can you get it for us?"[2]

On 30 September the Saudi government announced that it had requested AWACS "in order to consolidate the Kingdom's air defence capabilities".[3] The US approved immediate deployment to Saudi Arabia of four AWACS aircraft, accompanied by 300 US Air Force crew and ground support personnel.[4] Apart from serving as a powerful symbol of US commitment to Saudi security, the AWACS deployment was a considerable boost to Saudi Arabia's air defence. On 7 October, an unnamed Saudi official informed the Saudi Press Agency: "We have no objection to relying on some friendly nations to supply us with our military needs to defend our country and the Arab nation."[5]

Syria and Libya objected to the deployment, according to Safran, regarding it as US collusion in Iraq's war against Iran and a reflection of the inclination of the Saudi government to join the overall US strategic design for the Middle East. In order to isolate them, the Saudis pushed to convene an Arab summit in Amman in November and to place the Iran-Iraq War on its agenda despite Syrian objections and threats of boycott.[6]

Saudi Arabia felt extremely vulnerable after the Soviet invasion of Afghanistan. This vulnerability was deepened by the perception of Soviet encirclement of the Arabian Peninsula, combined with the Iranian threat. The Arab world was polarized into two rival coalitions. One was a moderate, 'pro-Western' coalition that came to include Egypt, Iraq, Saudi Arabia and the

---

1. Safran, *Saudi Arabia*, p. 367.
2. Simpson, *The Prince*, p. 64.
3. Saudi Press Agency, 30 September 1980.
4. *The New York Times*, 1 October 1980.
5. *Ukaz*, 7 October 1980.
6. Safran, *Saudi Arabia*, pp. 413–4.

Gulf states which moved the bulk of its strategic support and resources from the Israeli front in order to aid Iraq's war against Iran. The US was allowed to expand its presence and influence in the Gulf. The other was the so-called "Steadfastness Front" of Libya, South Yemen, Algeria and Syria. Iran, moreover, had joined Syria in a defensive counter-alliance, bringing it directly into the heart of inter-Arab politics. This translated into a search for security through arms races and militarization.[1] The collapse of Arab solidarity made it easier for hostile external states to exploit Arab division.

While assisting with the provision of Gulf states air defence, the US also threatened to use military force to keep the Strait of Hormuz and the Gulf open to shipping. Carter declared: "It is imperative that there be no infringement of the freedom of ships to and from the Persian Gulf region."[2] At the same time, the US discouraged Saudi Arabia and other Gulf states from allowing Iraqi use of military bases in these states, and requested the Gulf states to stay neutral.

The first public response from the Saudi government was delivered by Prince Saud on the US television programme *Face The Nation*, on 6 October 1980. He stated that "the conflict between Iraq and Iran is dangerous because it is between two Muslim countries", and called for the fighting to cease, adding: "The Kingdom strives to improve relations between Iraq and Iran by stopping the war first, then beginning negotiations."[3]

Instead of the lightning victory that Saddam had expected, Iraqi troops found themselves trapped at the border towns. The invasion had aroused Iranian nationalistic feelings that cut across political lines, and the Iranians had resisted much more fiercely than anyone had anticipated.[4]

According to Safran, the US commitment to confronting the threats raised by the failure of the Iraqi war plan reassured the Saudis, who felt that the ensuing stalemate was potentially much more advantageous to the Kingdom than an Iraqi victory would have been. The longer the deadlock in the battlefield, the greater the chances that the conflict would eventually be

---

1. Hinnebusch and Ehteshami, *The Foreign Policies of Middle East States*, pp. 46–8.
2. Congressional Research Service, "Petroleum Imports from the Persian Gulf: use of US armed forces to ensure supplies, 1981, p. 23.
3. *Ukaz*, 6 October 1980.
4. Timmerman, *The Death Lobby*, p. 91.

settled by negotiations and compromise – thereby leaving the antagonists in a state in which they checked and balanced each other indefinitely.[1]

Saudi Arabia had contemplated the possibility of attempting mediation through the Islamic Conference, but was awaiting the appropriate moment. However, by December, it felt that conditions were finally ripe for calling a formal conference, and it was held on 24 January 1981. The Iranians refused to attend in person because of the presence of Iraqi representatives, but did not object to the conference in principle and accepted its results. In its final declaration, the conference expressed deep concern over the continuation of the war, called on both parties to accept an Islamic mediation and appealed for a ceasefire.[2] On 16 February Iran sent a delegation to Riyadh to discuss mediation with the Saudi government.[3] *Ukaz* reported that upon its arrival, Deputy Chairman of the Iranian Parliament Hussein Haggani stated: "Iran welcomes the Islamic mediation commission aimed at reaching a solution to stop the fighting between Iran and Iraq."[4]

On 1 March the mediation commission presented a plan dealing with the principles for a settlement and specific proposals for ceasefire, withdrawal and negotiations; but the Iranians rejected the plan five days later. *Ukaz* reported that both sides were rigid on the subject of sovereignty over the Shatt Al-'Arab,[5] and that the first secretary in the Iranian embassy in Jeddah had declared: "The position of the Iranian Defence Supreme Council is to reject the cease-fire before an Iraqi withdrawal ... Iran has made some changes to the commission proposals, and has prepared a set of conditions to accept negotiations with Iraq."[6] On 13 March, *Ukaz* further reported that Iraqi Defence Minister Adnan Khairallah had stressed Iraq's willingness "to withdraw from Iranian territory, whenever Iran acknowledges Iraq's land and river navigation rights in accordance with international conventions".[7]

By mid-March, it was clear that the Iranian government would reject a ceasefire unless it was linked to Iraqi withdrawal. *Ukaz* reported the announcement by Iranian President Abolhassan Banisadr in a speech at Tehran

1. Safran, *Saudi Arabia*, p. 368.
2. Saudi Press Agency, 24 January 1981.
3. *Ukaz*, 17 February 1981.
4. *Ukaz*, 20 February 1981.
5. *Ukaz*, 9 March 1981.
6. *Ukaz*, 12 March 1981.
7. *Ukaz*, 13 March 1981.

University that "the cease-fire and the Iraqi withdrawal should be achieved at the same time".[1] On the other hand, there were proponents of stern views similar to those of Grand Ayatollah Hossein-Ali Montazeri, who claimed in a letter to the Iranian Supreme Defence Council that the mediation proposals had not met Iranian wishes, and demanded international arbitration.[2]

Ukaz also reported that the Iraqi newspaper *Al-Thawrah* had called for ample guarantees for an Iraqi withdrawal, and had stressed that "a solid foundation based on a final settlement of rights between Iran and Iraq and the Arab nation is needed for the war to end ... for the benefit of Iran and its neighbours, the Iranian threat to the security of the Gulf should end, Iran should end its claims against Arab lands, and [should] acknowledge Iraqi sovereignty on the Shatt al-'Arab."[3]

Fahd met the Islamic mediation committee on 28 March and declared "the Kingdom's endeavour to end the bloody haemorrhage between Iran and Iraq, and achieve peace".[4] On 30 March Saddam insisted, in a speech, on his country's refusal to withdraw "if Iran [does] not acknowledge Iraq's complete national rights".[5] On the Iranian side, Ali Khamene'i, spokesman for the Supreme Defence Council, declared: "If Iraq does not acknowledge that it is the aggressor, the position will not progress."[6]

The commission submitted a modified proposal on 31 March to meet some of Iran's objections. During the next two months the political struggle in Iran intensified, with clashes over the proposals between President Banisadr and Supreme Leader Ayatollah Khomeini, who took a harder line and dismissed Banisadr in June. Banisadr's downfall ended any hopes the Saudis had entertained of advancing a settlement without victory or defeat for either side through the Islamic Conference's mediation.

However, according to Safran, the endeavour itself was rewarding for the Saudis in other respects. First, it helped justify their semi-neutral position towards the belligerents; second, the involvement of Pakistan as well as Saudi Arabia in the mediation facilitated the advancement of the strategic defence connection between those two countries. (Safran and others have claimed that

---

1. *Ukaz*, 6 March 1981.
2. Ibid.
3. Ibid.
4. *Ukaz*, 29 March 1981.
5. *Ukaz*, 30 March 1981.
6. Ibid.

the Saudi and Pakistani governments signed an agreement whereby Pakistan would station troops in the Kingdom for its protection; *Ukaz*, however, reported that when asked about these claims, Saud categorically denied them.)[1] Third, the Kingdom was encouraged to advance the long-sought project of a collective Gulf security organization under its own auspices. On 4 February 1981, the foreign ministers of the Gulf States had assembled for a conference in Riyadh, at which a Saudi proposal for a Gulf Cooperation Council (GCC) was endorsed. The organization was formally launched on 25 May when the Supreme Council of the GCC, comprising the heads of state of the member countries, held its first meeting in Abu Dhabi.[2] Finally, the stalemate and the attempts at mediation gave the Saudis an opportunity to distance themselves from the US. By doing so they placed themselves in a position to pursue any further US assistance without sacrificing their own "room for manoeuvre".[3]

The Saudis had been engaged in a delicate balancing act between Iran and Iraq. They sought initially to appease Iran while reinforcing ties with Iraq, notwithstanding the contradictory nature of this policy. Despite Baghdad's newfound moderation, the Saudis were understandably worried about their long-term ambitions, and therefore sought to exclude Baghdad from direct security arrangements with the smaller Gulf states. When Iran proved impossible to appease, however, the Saudis embraced the lesser of two threats and began to overtly support Baghdad. There were some claims that Saudi Arabia was providing Iraq with arms. On 5 February 1981, *Ukaz* reported Prince Sultan saying: "Iraq has not requested the Kingdom to provide weapons ... the Kingdom, as it announced earlier, has not endeavoured to widen the war nor to bring about its continuation. The Kingdom has made every effort possible to spare Muslim blood, and to solve the dispute between the two Muslim countries peacefully."[4]

On taking office, the Reagan administration had reaffirmed the Carter principle that its neutrality in the conflict did not mean indifference to its outcome. Secretary of State Alexander Haig announced that the US was determined to protect "its friends and interests that are endangered by the continuation of hostilities in the Gulf".

On 16 February, Haig instructed US officials in the area to "continue to

---

1. *Ukaz*, 10 March 1981.
2. Saudi Press Agency, 27 May 1981.
3. Safran, *Saudi Arabia*, pp. 372–3.
4. *Ukaz*, 5 February 1981.

deny all requests for US government approval to transfer to either Iran or Iraq defence articles", and also specified that "the US position has been to avoid taking sides in an effort to prevent widening the conflict, bring an end to the fighting and restore stability to the area."[1]

The one objective that the new administration had in mind was to reassure its friends in the region that the US was once again a reliable friend and ally. It regarded the Soviets as responsible for the problems of the US around the world; it was, therefore, more prepared than the previous administration to use conventional force to thwart Soviet aims as it perceived them. In the Middle East, it sought to subsume Arab-Israeli issues into an overall strategy for containing Soviet expansion that involved providing incentives to both the Israelis and the Arabs to block Soviet expansion in the area. Reagan would offer the Israelis unprecedented cooperation and increased military assistance, while the Arabs – especially Saudi Arabia – would be fortified with arms in order to contribute to the effort. As Spiegel remarks, a problem with this approach was that little consideration was given to the possibility that the Arabs and Israelis might not accept the deals being offered.[2]

On 17 March the Reagan administration announced its decision to sell AWACS to Saudi Arabia,[3] and on 19 March Haig addressed the House Committee on Foreign Affairs, explaining that the objective behind the administration's decision was "protection of the region in total from any threat, and consolidation of regional security in the Gulf area ... it is important that the Kingdom sees the US as a friend that can be relied on".[4] The US proposed that Saudi Arabia use the relationship as a basis for regional strategic alignment, dubbed "strategic consensus". However, the Saudis were totally unreceptive.[5] When Haig visited Saudi Arabia on 8 April and tried to elicit an endorsement of this concept, the Saudi government resisted him strongly in private and even more strongly in public.[6]

While Reagan and Haig's concept of strategic consensus included an

---

1. Department of State Declassified Documents, State Dept. Records, Haig to All Near Eastern and South Asian Diplomatic Posts, "Military Equipment for Iran and Iraq", 16 February 1981.
2. Spiegel, *The Other Arab-Israeli Conflict*, pp. 399–401.
3. *Ukaz*, 18 March 1981.
4. *Ukaz*, 20 March 1981.
5. Safran, *Saudi Arabia*, p. 412.
6. Ibid., p. 375.

important role for Israel in the continuing conflict with the Soviet Union, Secretary of Defense Caspar Weinberger's approach did not. In September 1981 *The New York Times* reported Weinberger's assertion that Saudi Arabia could make an important contribution to the security of all nations in the area. He argued that the US should strengthen its relations with Saudi Arabia to discourage further Soviet intervention, following recent Western setbacks in Iran and Afghanistan.[1]

Overall, the Reagan administration's policy toward the war meant an increased commitment to Saudi Arabia's security and a strengthening of Saudi-US military cooperation. The centrepiece of this development was providing Saudi Arabia with equipment it had requested from the Carter administration to enhance the capabilities of sixty-two F-15 fighters, as well as selling it AWACS. The US Air Force had undertaken a study of the Kingdom's defence needs, on the basis of which the Pentagon had decided that Saudi Arabia needed AWACS.[2]

An earlier exchange on AWACS throws further light on the attitude of the US side. On 28 February 1981, *Ukaz* reported that Senator Charles Peircy, Chairman of the Senate Foreign Relations Committee, and James Buckley, Under-Secretary of State, had both said that the deal was essential because of the situation in the Middle East.[3] Ambassador West also stated: "The Reagan administration recognized the strategic importance of the Kingdom and the necessity to supply Saudi Arabia with the appropriate equipment to defend itself."[4]

The administration's efforts to convince a sceptical Congress of the wisdom of the sale forced months of national debate. On 24 September, Senator Howard Baker informed the administration that in order for the AWACS deal to pass, a compromise had to be reached. Senator John Glenn had been attempting to work out just such a compromise, in which the Saudis would be supplied with upgraded electronic equipment, identical to that used by the US Air Force, in planes that would be manned by mixed Saudi and US crews. Soon afterward, during a visit by Weinberger to Riyadh, the Saudi government accepted conditions that would satisfy the Senate. According to Haig, the

---

1. *The New York Times*, 29 September 1981.
2. Alexander M. Haig Jr., *Caveat: Realism, Reagan, and Foreign Policy* (New York: Macmillan, 1984), pp. 174–5.
3. *Ukaz*, 28 February 1981.
4. *Saudi Gazette*, edition 1,492, 7 March 1981.

Saudis agreed to a US role in the development of its air defence and to the complete and continuous sharing of information, with no data to be provided to third parties without US consent. In addition, Saudi Arabia agreed to US crews on board the aircraft well into the 1990s, and that the aircraft would not be flown outside Saudi airspace. An arrangement to protect the secret equipment had also been worked out between the two countries.[1]

On 1 October, during intensive personal lobbying to secure Congressional approval for the sale, Reagan declared: "Saudi Arabia we won't permit to be an Iran." Weinberger elaborated on this: "We would not stand by in the event of Saudi requests, as we did before with Iran, and allow a government that has been totally unfriendly to the US and to the Free World to take over."[2] On 29 October, the Senate approved the sale by a vote of fifty-two to forty-eight.

The strengthened Saudi-US alignment was initiated out of perceived strategic interests on the part of US decision-makers. During the 1980s the military component of this alliance became predominant. The Saudis valued the growth of a military relationship with the US, not for the transfer of the technology itself but for the implicit guarantee that came with it. For the US, as Kissinger argued, the sale of advanced weapons to Saudi Arabia was desirable in order to create an interdependent relationship that the US could exploit to increase its leverage.[3]

Additionally, the US expanded military assistance to the Kingdom to bolster Saudi Arabia's position in the Arab world, and to recognise the Saudi role in OPEC and in international finance. US arms sales provided indirect support to the Gulf states, and served as a deterrent to the extension of the Iran-Iraq war.

Meanwhile, at the front, due to difficult climatic conditions and suicide attacks by Iranian militias, the Iraqi army was witnessing a growing number of troop defections as well as many troops being taken as prisoners of war. Combatants even abandoned their weapons and fled. Iran had carried out its first major counteroffensive of the war in January 1981, and in spring and

---

1. Haig, *Caveat*, pp. 188–9.
2. Congressional Research Service, "Arms Sales to Saudi Arabia: AWACS and the F-15 Enhancements", 1982, p. 27.
3. Andrew J. Pierre, *The Global Politics of Arms Sales* (Princeton, NJ: Princeton University Press, 1982), p. 182.

autumn of that year a series of further successful Iranian counterattacks dislodged the Iraqis from many Iranian territories.[1]

Iraq's fortunes in the war took a dramatic turn for the worse on 17 March 1982, when Iran finally succeeded in rallying its forces, throwing the Iraqis into total disarray.[2] Saddam decided to bow to the inevitable, withdraw from Iranian territory and to deploy a static defence along the international border. On 20 June, he announced that his troops had begun the withdrawal from Iran and would complete it within ten days.[3]

With the final collapse of the Iraqi regime appearing imminent, the Saudis tried to enlist Egyptian military intervention to save Iraq and to check Iran; but on 17 May, Field Marshal Talal Abu Ghazala, the Egyptian defence minister, announced his government's decision not to send troops to Iraq. Saudi Arabia now looked to the US. The State Department viewed the dramatic events on the battlefield with alarm. The first step was taken in February 1982, when it removed Iraq from its list of countries suspected of supporting international terrorism – if the US was to aid Baghdad, it had to start by lifting this stigma. Weinberger stated on 21 May that an Iranian military victory over Iraq was not in the interests of the US,[4] and confirmed on 26 May that the US would play a more active role in the coming weeks in trying to end the war. He implicitly warned Iran that if it spread the conflict into the Gulf, the US would protect its vital interests in the area.[5] The US statements forced Ali Akbar Hashemi Rafsanjani, Speaker of the Iranian parliament, to declare that Iran would not seek to cut the flow of oil in the Gulf.[6]

On 8 June, a US special national intelligence estimate predicted that Iraq had essentially lost the war with Iran, and that Baghdad's main concern now was to prevent an Iranian invasion. There was little the Iraqis could do, alone or in combination with other Arabs, to reverse the military situation. A major problem for the US in responding to the current situation would be the search for ways to mitigate Iran's efforts to export its revolution and prevent Tehran from drifting toward the Soviets. The intelligence report emphasized that

1. Ifraim Karsh and Inari Rautsi, *Saddam Hussein: A Political Biography* (London: Brassey's), p. 155.
2. Timmerman, *The Death Lobby*, p. 112.
3. Karsh and Rautsi, *Saddam Hussein*, p. 156.
4. *The New York Times*, 22 May 1982.
5. Ibid., 27 May 1982.
6. Ibid., 29 May 1982.

the Iranian regime could be expected after the war to turn its attention to the Gulf in order to assert its dominance there, claiming: "Tehran is likely to rely on conventional diplomacy (backed by veiled threats) and subversion rather than military force in the pursuit of its objectives."

The report also explored the implications for Saudi Arabia and other Gulf states: "if Iran stops its advance at the border and initiates either a war of attrition or protracted negotiations designed to undermine Saddam, the Gulf states will continue to provide logistic and financial support to prevent Iraq's position from deteriorating further. They will also encourage Jordan and probably Egypt to help bolster Baghdad in whatever way they can."

As far as the implications for US interests were concerned, the report went on to state: "US interests generally would be adversely affected by Iran's carrying the fight to Iraqi territory. Tehran's success in the war would threaten the stability of the Gulf regimes, the US would continue to be criticized by Arab moderates for not doing more to restrain Iran, and the war could easily escalate, particularly if the moderate Arabs intervened on the side of Iraq." However, it was felt that "a protracted, small-scale, border conflict, even accompanied by Iranian subversion attempts, could advance some US interests provided that the conflict remained limited and did not escalate." The document concluded that an effort by Iran to export its own brand of Islamic fundamentalism by force would run up against a potentially more powerful movement in Arab nationalism. While the future emergence of a charismatic, Pan-Islamic leader might prove to be an irresistible trend in the region, Khomeini – despite his appeal in many countries – "was too Shia, too Persian, and too reactionary to forge an effective regional revolution against Sunni establishment and Western influence".[1]

On 13 July, a large-scale offensive was launched in the direction of Basra, Iraq's second-most-important city. But once Iraqi troops were no longer fighting on foreign territory but defending their homeland, they regained their spirit; public morale became buoyant. The failure of the Iranian offensive led to another long period of attrition.

Saddam successfully portrayed the war as a heroic defence of the nation and, by extension, of the Arab world, against a bigoted and aggressive enemy that persistently sabotaged efforts for peace – and that should it fail to contain

---

1. NSA, Director of Central Intelligence "DCI", SNIE 34/36 2-82, "Implication of Iran's Victory over Iraq", 8 June 1982.

the Iranians at the gates of the Arab world, it would not be the only casualty of the Iranian Revolution but the entire Gulf would be devoured by the fundamentalist Persians.[1] By alarming his neighbours and the world at large with this apocalyptic vision of a belligerent, fundamentalist Middle East, Saddam managed to drive some of his allies to ensure that Iraq did not lose the war.

The Soviet Union continued its arms embargo for eighteen months, but by June 1982 the situation in the Middle East had changed – and not to the advantage of the USSR. The Iranians had seized the initiative on the ground; Israel had invaded Lebanon and defeated the Syrian air force; and some Iranians were publicly calling for support for the rebels in Afghanistan. The Soviet Union could afford to teach Saddam a lesson, but not to lose yet another war; failure to honour a long-standing commitment, however, would have fatally damaged its credibility in the Third World.[2] By November 1982, some 1,200 Soviet advisors had returned to Iraq, and the provision of weaponry to Iraq resumed.

Meanwhile, fear of the fall of the Ba'thist regime in Iraq and a subsequent Iranian victory led to a perceptible change in US policy. The shift included:

1. "Operation Staunch", an active US diplomatic effort to identify and halt arms shipments to Iran;

2. The provision of Commodity Credit Corporation credits to Iraq for purchases in the US;

3. Vocal condemnation of Iran at the UN and elsewhere;

4. The provision of military intelligence to Iraq.[3]

In August 1982, the CIA established a direct, top-secret link with Iraq to provide intelligence from US satellites, and Casey met senior Iraqis to encourage more attacks on Iran – especially against economic targets.[4] Saddam's call for a

---

1. Fuad Matar, *Saddam Hussein: The Man, the Cause and the Future* (London: Third World Centre, 1981), pp. 141–2.
2. Shahram Chubin, *Soviet Policy Towards Iran and the Gulf*, Adelphi Papers, no. 157 (London: International Institute for Strategic Studies, 1984), pp. 26–27.
3. US Congress, Senate, Committee on Foreign Relations, "War in the Persian Gulf: The US Takes Sides", Senate Staff Report, S PRT 100-60, November 1987, pp. 21–2.
4. Woodward, *Veil*, p. 480.

negotiated settlement to the war and his retreat had removed a major obstacle to better relations between the US and Iraq, and intensified the former's policy tilt toward the latter. "The US has undertaken a number of steps to shore up Iraq and to forestall an Iranian victory," declared a staff report by the Senate Foreign Relations Committee.[1]

Reagan continued the build-up of the RDJTF, and established the new Central Command (CENTCOM) on 1 January 1983. He then expanded the Carter Doctrine to include as a US interest a threat of any kind to the Saudi regime as, in addition to somewhat indefinable internal unrest, the threat of Iranian air attacks against oil facilities and of political terrorist bombings had become a realistic cause of concern. There was also a willingness to keep the Straits of Hormuz open should the Iranians attempt to stop shipping through that waterway.[2]

On 18 April 1983, Iranian-backed Hizbullah bombers managed to wipe out some of the CIA's best Middle East experts, who were meeting at the US embassy in Beirut. Iranian-backed terrorists would now launch a series of attacks against the US and its allies throughout the Middle East.[3] These events dramatically altered US perceptions of the Middle East, and provided a final incentive for the tilt toward Iraq. When new Secretary of State George Shultz met Foreign Minister Tariq Aziz of Iraq in Paris on 10 May 1983, he expressed the US's wish for an ending to the war, adding: "We consider it debilitating for both countries [and] dangerous to the others in the area." Shultz mentioned US neutrality in the conflict, but observed that Aziz knew "we had been helpful to Iraq in various ways".[4]

Frustrated by Iran's refusal to come to any kind of ceasefire agreement, the Iraqis decided to change tactics, attacking Iranian oil terminals in the Gulf and tankers carrying deliveries of crude from Iranian ports. To carry out these

---

1. US Senate, "War in the Gulf: A Staff Report Prepared for the Committee on Foreign Relations", August 1984.
2. Harold H. Saunders, "The Iran-Iraq War: Implications for US Policy", in Thomas Naff, ed., *Gulf Security and the Iran-Iraq War* (Washington, DC: National Defense University Press, 1985), pp. 64–5.
3. John Prados, *Presidents' Secret Wars: CIA and Pentagon Covert Operations from World War II Through the Persian Gulf* (Chicago: Ivan R. Dee, Publisher, 1986), pp. 378–9.
4. Declassified Documents, State Dept., Sec. of State George P. Shultz, Cable to the State Dept., "Sec.'s May 10th Meeting with Iraq Foreign Minister Tariq Aziz", 11 May 1983.

attacks, the Iraqis requested Super-Etendard attack planes capable of launching Exocet anti-ship missles from France.

Aziz went to New York in October for another meeting with Shultz, this time at the UN, seeking approval for Security Council Resolution 540, which condemned Iran for continuing the war. News had by now leaked out that Iraq was trying to acquire the five Super-Étendard planes, and tensions were mounting around the world as Iran threatened to blockade the Straits of Hormuz. Aziz argued that Iraqi attacks on Iranian shipping could shorten the war as, without the money to purchase arms, Iran would soon be forced to cease fighting. On 17 October the Saudi newspaper *Al-Jazirah* claimed that the US had finally agreed to France's sale of the planes to Iraq, and that Shultz had informed the French government the previous month that the US would drop its opposition to the sale.[1] By the end of 1983, Iraqi pilots had begun picking off tankers at Iran's only oil terminal at Kharg Island. It was the start of the tanker war, aimed at crippling Iran's oil exports.[2]

A State Department memorandum on 7 October discussed the Iranian strategy of bringing about the Iraqi regime's political collapse through military attrition coupled with financial strangulation, and pointed out that if the Iranians kept up this pressure they could, in the course of the coming year, bring about this objective: "It is in this context that a possible tilt toward Iraq should be considered," the memorandum added. This tilt would include financial, diplomatic and military support. Financially, the US would aid Iraq in exporting more oil through Turkey, Saudi Arabia and Syria; diplomatically, it would promote an initiative in the UN to discourage further attacks on oil-related facilities in the Gulf, so as to establish an area of tacit agreement between the parties upon which an eventual ceasefire could be built. Militarily, it was thought desirable to discourage the supply of critical equipment to Iran, to permit US-controlled equipment to reach Iraq through third parties and, if Iran were to attack Iraqi oil installations in the Gulf again, to help Iraq defend its oil export operations in conjunction with its friends and allies. The memorandum stated: "The US willingness to take firm action would reassure the Gulf states of our support for their security ... we assume that other actions ... such as providing tactical intelligence, would continue as necessary." It concluded: "Further tilt toward Iraq would, we believe, have the following

---

1. *Al-Jazirah*, 17 October 1983.
2. Timmerman, *The Death Lobby*, pp. 135–8.

effects in the region: further improve our bilateral relations with Iraq and encourage its non-alignment, [and] support our objective of avoiding Iraq's collapse before revolutionary Iran without going so far as to alarm Israel."[1] The tilt toward Iraq clearly resulted from US balance-of-power policies, intended to co-opt Iraq into the pro-US regional system and to punish Iran.

When Donald Rumsfeld, Reagan's special envoy to the Middle East, met Saddam on 20 December 1983, he carried a handwritten letter for the Iraqi leader proposing that the US and Iraq renew diplomatic relations. Rumsfeld told Saddam that the US and Iraq had shared interests in preventing Iranian and Syrian expansion. Saddam informed him that the Iraqi leadership had examined the circumstances surrounding the severance of relations and their possible resumption, and had noted the need to consider the careful timing of any decision. The war had intervened, and an added complication was that the US and others might misunderstand the resumption and attach the wrong reasons to it. Saddam understood that the West had legitimate interests in the Arab region, but that they sometimes behaved on the basis of incomplete or faulty analysis. What, he wondered, would have happened to the Gulf states and the Arabian Peninsula if Iraq had not stood fast? However, Iraq had now overcome the dangerous stage of the military situation and now it was a question of time.

Rumsfeld, in turn, noted the need to address more fundamental problems such as security in the Gulf and the circumstances of the Palestinian people. In the opinion of the US, it would be advantageous for Egypt and Iraq to play their natural roles in the region so that the ambitions of others were not inflated. Regarding the war with Iran, the US agreed it was not in the interests of either the region or the West for the conflict to create greater instability, or for the outcome to be one that weakened Iraq's role or enhanced the interests and ambitions of Iran. Rumsfeld also mentioned the risk of escalation in the Gulf and the possible closing of the Straits of Hormuz. On the issue of escalation, Saddam said that Iraq's patience should not be misunderstood: "It was not for Iraq to look after the world's interests before its own."[2] The US embassy in Jeddah informed the State Department that an unnamed Saudi

---

1. Declassified Documents, State Dept., Bureau of Near Eastern and South Asian Affairs Information, Memorandum from Jonathan T. Howe to Lawrence S. Eagleburger, "Iran-Iraq War: Analysis of Possible US Shift from Position of Strict Neutrality", 7 October 1983.
2. Declassified Documents, State Dept., US Embassy in UK to State Dept.,

official had described Rumsfeld's visit to Iraq as a "very good development" from the Saudi perspective.¹

After three years of war, Saddam had demonstrated that Iraq could weather a Soviet arms embargo and Iranian "human wave" attacks without collapsing. Rumsfeld's visit convinced US policy-makers that it was necessary to launch a major effort to block arms supplies from reaching Iran. As Iran needed American spare parts and weapons to continue the war, it turned to the black market. The Iranians also turned to Israel, Turkey and others to purchase materials from national stockpiles through various intermediaries.

"Operation Staunch" set out to convince these US allies to stop such sales. A State Department document described it as a series of steps designed to persuade Iran to end hostilities and to ensure that Iraq understood that escalation of the war in the Gulf threatened the world's oil-importing countries. The document was to be widely circulated to the highest officials in foreign governments. The US believed it was in the interests of the West to discourage the emergence of either side as dominant in the region, and recent events had demonstrated Iran's intention to use violence to spread its revolution throughout the region. The plan would not permit the transfer of US-controlled arms to either combatant, and would continue to urge restraint upon both sides. Every government would be asked to consider desisting from any traffic in military equipment (whatever its origin) between itself and Iran, at least until a ceasefire was in place. As long as the war did not disrupt oil supplies, the US was content simply to contain it, arguably pleased that these two potential candidates for Gulf hegemony checked and weakened each other to the benefit of US allies in the Gulf.

China had sold Iraq US $3.6 billion worth of weapons by 1983; by 1985 it was also selling weapons to Iran. According to Simpson, when Prince Bandar was informed of the new US policy, he approached Shultz to obtain his agreement on making an offer to the Chinese: "We will buy all the weapons they are going to sell to Iran and give them to Iraq." Shultz endorsed the idea. Bandar also approached China to acquire intermediate-range ballistic missiles for Saudi Arabia itself, in addition to the weapons that were to be sold on to Iran. After several clandestine meetings in Washington, Pakistan and Beijing, a deal was reached with the Chinese in 1988. Bandar informed Shultz about

---

"Rumsfeld Mission: December 20 Meeting with Iraqi President Saddam Hussein", 21 December 1983.
1. NSA, State Dept. Records, US Embassy, Jeddah, to State, "Saudi Official Commands, US/Iraqi Contacts", 7 December 1983.

the agreement with China to buy the weapons destined for Iran – but omitted any mention of the missiles.

Bandar had to bring the missiles into the Kingdom without the knowledge of the US. Silos also needed to be built to house them. Bandar contrived a clever ploy, telling the US that Fahd had decided to move the Saudi armament depot as far as possible from Riyadh to prevent it from falling into the wrong hands in the event of a military coup. The US accepted and supported the notion. Bandar then added that to give the Chinese a strong incentive not to renege on their promise, the Kingdom would ask them to build the new depot. The US again had no objection.

When satellite images eventually revealed the missiles, the US initially believed they carried nuclear warheads. US law stipulates that the White House must report the discovery that another country has acquired a nuclear capability to Congress within forty-eight hours. On 7 March 1988, Bandar met with Reagan, who said: "We understand that you people have acquired nuclear missiles. That is not acceptable to us … I would like an official answer on this issue." Bandar explained that the acquisition of the missiles was purely a deterrent move, adding: "I can assure you categorically that the Kingdom does not have nuclear missiles."

Bandar went back to Saudi Arabia and returned to Washington with a letter that emphatically denied any nuclear weapons purchase but confirmed the purchase of missiles as a result of the US's refusal to sell short-range Lance missiles to the Kingdom in 1985. It also gave assurances that the missiles were not intended for offensive purposes, but that if attacked, the Kingdom could defend itself.[1] Saudi Arabia believed the purchase of these missiles would be a major demonstration of its independence. They constituted a low-level deterrent as well as a symbol of Saudi willingness to retaliate against any potential strikes.

A 1984 State Department document on the Iran-Iraq war discussed possible Iranian escalation scenarios and advised that should the Gulf states even request US intervention "it might not be in our interests to intervene". A major interruption of Iranian oil exports might force the Iranians to take more extreme retaliatory measures, which could include attacks against critical oil installations and other important economic targets in Saudi Arabia or the other Gulf states, as well as the possible prevention of Gulf oil shipping.

---

1. Simpson, *The Prince*, pp. 152–61.

The First Fahd Era (1979–90)

However, Iran was likely to avoid any military action that would prompt US military involvement. The State Department document also noted that such Iranian actions would be designed to demonstrate the inability of the US to protect its interests and defend the Gulf states. It urged the US to continue to work through third parties to urge restraint and to promote a negotiated settlement, strengthen ties with the Gulf states and seek combined military planning and deployment with other US allies. It also warned that the Gulf states would see an Iranian victory as a defeat for the US: "They might question our commitments and our reliability as a friend and security partner." It suggested a number of deterrent actions to take against Iran.[1]

On 5 April 1984, a National Security Decision Directive outlined measures that needed to be taken to improve the capacity of the US to deter an expansion of the conflict in the Gulf and to defend US interests. Certain actions were agreed, along the following lines:

1. Political-military missions were to undertake consultations with key Gulf states;
2. US intelligence gathering in the region was to be improved;
3. The defensibility of area facilities would be enhanced in cooperation with regional states to reduce the vulnerability of US personnel and facilities in the Gulf;
4. US military activities and facilities in the Gulf would enhance anti-terrorist capabilities;

---

1. NSA, State Dept. Records, "Iran-Iraq War: US Responses to Escalation, Scenarios and Threats to Persian Gulf States", 24 March 1984. The document described several deterrent options available to the US. It could direct assistance towards Iraq, which would symbolize US support against Iran since Iraq was not in need of armaments. It could offer assistance to third parties to enable support for Iraq, and encourage countries with deployable forces to go to Iraq's aid, and allow them to use weapons of American origin towards this effort (but this would not include the transfer to Iraq of equipment originating in the US). Third-party assistance to Iraq was to be promoted, including continued financial support from the Gulf states to Iraq, and France and other Western arms suppliers were to be encouraged to support Iraq more vigorously. Increased US support for the Gulf states' defence would include arms transfers and force deployments designed to shore up Gulf defences and would reassure the Gulf states that the US would work with them to avoid further Iranian military expansion or subversion.

5. A plan of action to avert Iraqi collapse would be prepared.[1]

Early in 1984, Saddam had launched the so-called "Tanker War" to shift from stalemate on the battlefield to a new and potentially more rewarding arena. In March, an Iraqi Super-Étendard fired an Exocet missile at a Greek tanker south of Kharg Island. Iran reciprocated in April, launching its first attack against civilian commercial shipping by shelling an Indian freighter. In 1984, there were thirty-seven Iraqi and seven Iranian attacks. According to Karsh, Iraq was aiming to tempt Iran into trying to close the Straits of Hormuz, which would interrupt the West's supply of oil and precipitate Western action to end the war. It was also trying to limit Tehran's oil exports and thus its ability to finance its war effort.[2]

Iraq's tanker attacks did significantly affect Iran's exports, and weakened its economy. Iran was forced to adopt a shuttle service of small tankers to trans-ship the oil to less vulnerable loading points farther down the Gulf.[3] However, it refused to be provoked into extensive retaliation, and the Tanker War died down.

Although the eruption of the Tanker War increased US anxiety and reportedly led to a review of Gulf contingency plans, it was not followed by any concrete action. But US support for Iraq was apparently extended into the strategic arena. The US passed satellite photos to Iraq to enable it to detect approaching Iranian warplanes, and to deploy artillery and armour to better effect on the battlefield. In addition, it provided warnings of Iranian air attacks on ships in the Gulf, supplemented by twelve-hourly reports on Iranian military activity on the ground. US satellites, as well as US AWACS in Saudi Arabia, were used to feed valuable information to Iraq about the movement of Iranian forces.[4] According to Simpson, Prince Bandar recalled: "We worked with the Iraqis to give them AWACS information, as they [the Iraqis] were going to hit

---

1. NSA, National Security Decision Directive 139, from Ronald W. Reagan, "Measures to Improve US Posture and Readiness to Respond to Developments in the Iran-Iraq War", 5 April 1984.
2. Efraim Karsh, *The Iran-Iraq War: A Military Analysis*, Adelphi Papers, no. 220 (London: International Institute for Strategic Studies, 1987), p. 29.
3. Ibid., p. 30.
4. *Financial Times*, 19 June 1984.

targets in the southern part of Iran. I remember them landing in Saudi Arabia where we refuelled them so that they could go back home."[1]

On 25 September 1984, a DIA report assessed political, economic and military conditions in Iraq and predicted: "Iraq will most likely continue to escalate its attacks against targets in the Gulf." Saddam believed that increased international condemnation of Iranian retaliatory strikes against third parties, restriction of arms sales to Iran and reduction of Iranian oil sales would all serve his objective and end the war on terms favourable to Iraq. The report suggested that economic conditions would remain tight until Iraq could substantially increase its income, but that "this problem will remain manageable over the next few years". The report attributed Baghdad's ability to manage its economy to "growing international confidence in Iraq's future" and to the fact that the Gulf Arabs "will have little choice but to continue their economic assistance". Iraq perceived that "attacks on selected Gulf targets have affected both the Iranian economy and its war-making potential", and Baghdad confirmed that it was seeking to internationalize the conflict. It did not display any enthusiasm for engaging its armed forces in new adventures, including any future Arab-Israeli conflict.

The report also speculated as to what might happen once the war ended: "Iraq's intransigence in settling territorial claims to two Islands [Bubiyan and Warban] with Kuwait, despite Kuwaiti support during the war, suggests that Baghdad's relationship with the Arab Gulf states will continue to experience strains." It outlined the implications of all this for Iraq-US relations. In the short term, it would hinge on Iraq's perception of Washington's willingness to provide assistance on concessionary terms and to deny the same to Iran. In the longer term, the political relationship between Iraq and the US would centre on Arab-Israeli issues and on the US-Israel relationship.[2]

A National Security Study Directive dated 6 November 1984 suggested that the State Department should chair an inter-agency review to coordinate US strategy and ensure balanced progress in the security relationship with Saudi Arabia. It suggested several measures, including expediting the delivery of approved sales and providing timely responses to Saudi requests; assessing Saudi military capabilities to meet extant threats; and planning to facilitate the

---

1. Simpson, *The Prince*, p. 177.
2. NSA, Defense Intelligence Agency, Intelligence Report, "Defense Estimative Brief: Prospects for Iraq", 25 September 1984.

movement and deployment of US forces that could be sent to the Kingdom in a major emergency.

Saudi Arabia had become the leader of the Arab states in the Gulf, and US military assistance was indirectly protecting these states as well. The Saudis were also trying to weaken and destabilize pro-Soviet regimes, which contributed to and enhanced the image of the country for the US – which benefited, too, from Saudi Arabia's exercise of regional leadership through the GCC. Saudi Arabia had effectively formulated a coherent political and military strategy that involved indirect US influence over the policies of the Gulf states.

On 26 November, Aziz met Shultz and expressed appreciation for Washington's efforts to stop the flow of Western arms to Iran, noting that Iraq's superiority in weaponry ensured its defence. Shultz remarked that superior intelligence was also an important factor in Iraq's defence, and that Iraq was the most secure of any country from Iranian threats in that respect – though he questioned whether the smaller Gulf states could survive such threats. He assured Aziz that the US would continue to work with its allies in dealing with Iran, in particular curbing the transfer of Western arms to Tehran.

In late 1984, the Saudi government asked the US to approve the purchase of forty-two additional F-15 fighters and other military equipment. In February 1985, Reagan informed Fahd and Bandar of his inability to secure Congressional approval for this request. According to Simpson, Reagan told Fahd: "I support it, I agree with it, but the Congress will not go with me. So it's your call. If you want me to go with it, I'll go with it, but we will lose." Fahd immediately replied: "No, no, no ... I don't want you to be humiliated or embarrassed because if you are, I will be embarrassed too. I appreciate your attitude, but you know, Mr. President, I support you. You believe in peace through strength, and I'm like you. The stronger you are, the less chance for war ... If you were me ... what would you do?" The president replied quickly: "If I were you, I would go somewhere else and buy it."[1] Eventually, Saudi Arabia turned to the UK and signed a deal to buy seventy-two Tornado fighter planes, in what became known as the long-running al-Yamamah ("Dove") programme.

Iran's sense of purpose had declined after mid-1982. By then, it was no longer defending its own territory, but fighting on Iraqi soil. Economic dislocation from the war gave rise to great frustration as shortages of basic commodities

---

1. Simpson, *The Prince*, p. 135.

worsened and corruption and the black market flourished.[1] A US National Security Decision Directive dated 11 June 1985 predicted that major changes were possible in Iran as a result of the instability caused by war pressures, economic deterioration and regime infighting. The directive noted: "The Soviet Union is better positioned than the US to exploit and benefit from any power struggle." It emphasized the need for the US to protect its interests in skirmishes among the Iranian leadership over succession.[2]

On 8 December 1985, Ali Akbar Velayati, Iran's foreign minister, visited Saudi Arabia. At the end of the visit Saud said: "We sense no improvement in the Iranian position which would hint at the possibility of a positive move to end this destructive war." Saud added that Iraq had accepted a peaceful solution to the conflict, and hoped "that Iran matches this attitude with a similar stance".[3]

Iran generated widespread surprise when, on 9 February 1986, its army swept across the southern border with Iraq and occupied the Fao Peninsula – within gunshot range of Kuwait. On 13 February, *Ukaz* reported that Saud had urged all Arab states to utilize their capabilities to end the war, and expressed the Kingdom's anxiety and regret over the latest development. He called on Iran "to stop the fighting and respond to the peace initiatives that guarantee the right of both sides, and lead to friendly relations for the peace and the stability of the area".[4] *Ukaz* also reported that on 21 February, during a Security Council session to discuss the Iranian attack, Saudi Minister of State for Foreign Affairs Muhammad Masoud had appealed to the Council to take a prudent position against the latest escalation, and against the attempt to hinder peace efforts. In his speech, he urged Iran to agree to a ceasefire, and expressed his hope that "the international community brings to bear decisive pressure to end the war."[5]

GCC foreign ministers met in Riyadh on 3 March to study, as *Ukaz* reported, the dangerous situation in the region. At the end of the meeting a joint statement maintained: "The Iranian threats have created an atmosphere

---

1. Karsh and Rautsi, *Saddam Hussein*, p. 173.
2. NSA, The White House, NSC, National Security Decision Directive, "US Policy Toward Iran", 11 June 1985.
3. Saudi Press Agency, 11 December 1985.
4. *Ukaz*, 13 February 1986.
5. *Ukaz*, 21 February 1986.

of tension ... the council urges Iran to refrain from threats which upset security and stability of the area."[1]

Over the next few weeks the Iranians reinforced their position on the Fao Peninsula, and there were real concerns in the Gulf and in the West that Iran might be winning the war after all. According to a State Department document, the occupation of the peninsula had heightened concern among Gulf state leaders about the security of their countries and the free flow of oil. Saudi Arabia was actively searching for symbols of its ties with the US to send a message of deterrence to Iran. The document stated that it was primarily for this reason that Fahd had asked the US "to notify arms sales now", and also mentioned that Saudi Arabia had stepped up its assistance to Iraq over the past month. Iran had criticized the Saudi government for this, and complained bitterly about Saudi oil policy. By lowering oil prices, the document surmised, Saudi Arabia "has probably hurt Iran more than have Iraq's attacks on its tankers and oil facilities."[2]

Unable to expel the Iranians, Iraq struck back hard against Iranian oil tankers and export terminals in the Gulf.[3] The assaults on Kharg Island had already forced Iran to use a shuttle service to the Sirri and Larak oil-loading terminals. In August 1986, Iraqi planes succeeded in attacking Sirri Island for the first time. Kharg Island was temporarily closed in October, and in November Iraq extended its attacks to Larak.[4] Iran adopted a number of diplomatic and military actions. It launched missile attacks against Iraq, increased its threats to retaliate against the Gulf states and increased naval inspections of vessels passing through the Straits of Hormuz.[5] In September, Iran had begun to single out Kuwait-flagged vessels for attack, as well as vessels bound to or from Kuwait. The Gulf states, meeting in October, issued strong protests and urged the Arab League to "reconsider its relations with Iran".[6]

These tactics along with Iran's success in the land war increased insecurity

1. *Ukaz*, 4 March 1986.
2. NSA, State Dept. Records, Bureau of Near Eastern and South Asian Affairs, Memorandum, "Issue Paper: Gulf War Update" and "Issue Paper: US Attitude Toward Iran", attached, 27 February 1986.
3. Timmerman, *The Death Lobby*, pp. 228–31.
4. Elizabeth Gamlen and Paul Rogers, "US Reflagging of Kuwaiti Tankers", in Rajaee Farhang, ed., *The Iran-Iraq War: The Politics of Aggression* (Gainesville, FL: Florida: University Press of Florida, 1993), p. 127.
5. Ibid., p. 127.
6. *The Guardian*, 27 October 1987.

among the Gulf states, and Kuwait requested US protection for its ships in September. The US was initially hesitant, but when Kuwait later chartered three tankers from the Soviet Union (which were put under the Soviet flag), the US informed Kuwait in May 1987 that it was willing to escort eleven Kuwaiti tankers through the Gulf, provided they flew the US flag. Secretary of Defense Weinberger explained the reasoning behind the decision, saying that had these measures not been taken "we would be accepting Iran's right to close the international waters of the Gulf"; the Soviet Union, for its part, "would be more than happy to become the sole guarantor of the security of the small Gulf states".[1]

"Operation Earnest Will" was then implemented, involving 18,000 US troops defending shipping in the Gulf. The US limited itself to dispatching army helicopters equipped with special night-vision, which eventually detected and helped capture an Iranian ship that was sowing mines. The Saudis were extremely concerned about a potential Iranian attack combined with a Shi'i uprising, and insisted that the presence of US helicopters in the country not be made public. The helicopters were only permitted to fly after dark, and had to complete their operations before dawn.[2] During 1987 and 1988 "Earnest Will" doubled the US naval presence in the Gulf from six to thirteen warships and authorized nearly 100 escort missions.

Many of the US's allies were reluctant to stand behind it for fear that Washington, under pressure from Congress, the press and the public, would pull back at the first sign of any danger to US forces. Nor had US hopes for land bases been fulfilled. Even Saudi Arabia did not allow US planes to use Saudi airfields as bases for providing air cover for any of the escorted convoys.[3] Instead, the US used aircraft carriers and bases in the other Gulf states.

Eventually, on 29 February 1988, and with US encouragement and support over the following two months, Saddam ordered over 150 missile strikes and numerous air raids against major Iranian population centres. Iran was in no position to challenge Iraq, as US efforts to prevent Iran from acquiring weapons had been effective in limiting Iran's capabilities. All Iran could do was intensify attacks against Gulf shipping – but such a move would involve

1. Caspar W. Weinberger, *Fighting for Peace: Seven Critical Years in the Pentagon* (New York: Warner Books, 1990), pp. 387–9.
2. Roger Cohen and Claudio Gatti, *In the Eye of the Storm: The Life of General H. Norman Schwarzkopf* (London: Bloomsbury, 1991), pp. 193–4.
3. Shultz, *Turmoil and Triumph,* pp. 926–7.

the risk of direct confrontation with the US, which Iran was anxious to avoid. In April, Iraq went on the offensive and, after fierce fighting, recaptured the Fao Peninsula. In May, Iraq drove the Iranians from their positions east of Basra, and a month later dislodged them from the Majnoon Islands. In early July, Iraq drove the remaining Iranian forces out of Kurdistan, and later that month gained a small strip of Iranian territory along the central part of the Iran-Iraq border. On 18 July 1988, Iran, confronted with all these setbacks, accepted Security Council Resolution 598 for a ceasefire.[1]

According to Simpson, the quest for peace had begun late in 1987. Fahd had informed Bandar that Saddam had asked for Bandar's help supporting Tariq Aziz, who was then in New York attempting to close a deal for a ceasefire. At the same time, UN Secretary General Javier Pérez de Cuéllar was also trying to obtain a ceasefire agreement. However, neither side was ready for peace at that particular moment. Having agreed to take the talks to Geneva, away from the media presence, Pérez de Cuéllar and Bandar slowly began to stitch together an agreement. Both delegations carried a draft agreement back to their countries.

A few days later, they all met in New York. Aziz arrived with Saddam's acceptance. The Iranians, however, wanted minor alterations. Aziz refused to change anything, telling Bandar "the reason I cannot change it is because this has been agreed by Saddam. I cannot change it until Saddam agrees." Bandar told Aziz to telephone Saddam "and tell him this is what you recommend", to which Aziz replied: "Are you crazy? I don't care if the war continues for ten years. I don't want to lose my life. Crossing Saddam means death!" Bandar then explained the situation to Fahd, who instructed Bandar to call Saddam himself. When Bandar called Saddam, he informed him: "We are almost done, but I have a complaint. We are stuck on couple of words. They really need changing and your foreign minister will not agree." Saddam replied: "Bandar, you don't just represent Saudi Arabia, you represent Iraq and Saudi Arabia. Anything you agree to, I accept." Bandar said: "But your man is being very stubborn." Saddam replied: "We'll send a word to him." The following day, all parties had signed the agreement; this was the beginning of the eventually successful attempt to obtain a ceasefire that ended in July 1988.[2]

---

1. Karsh and Rautsi, *Saddam Hussein*, pp. 173–4.
2. Simpson, *The Prince*, pp. 180–6.

The First Fahd Era (1979–90)

The 1982 Israeli Invasion of Lebanon

Israel's "Operation Litani", the invasion of southern Lebanon in 1978, had failed in its objectives to rid Lebanon of the Palestine Liberation Organization (PLO) and to isolate the country from the rest of the Arab world through a peace treaty with the politically dominant Christian Maronite class.[1] The Israelis and the Maronites had a mutual enemy in the PLO, as well as a desire to dislodge the Syrians from Lebanon. In December 1980, Bashir Gemayel, son of Pierre Gemayel, leader of the Phalange Party, had cemented an alliance with Israel and promptly began skirmishing with the Syrians in Lebanon's Bekaa Valley,[2] where he had begun building a road to connect the valley's main Christian town of Zahle with the Maronite heartland in the Mount Lebanon region.

As tension began to simmer between the Phalangists and the Syrians in Zahle, new Secretary of State Haig arrived in the Middle East. In Israel, he adopted a tough-minded, trenchant approach that struck the Israelis as a refreshing change from the Carter administration's line. Haig spoke bitingly of Syrian President Assad's regime and left the Israelis with the distinct impression that the US intended to take a hard line toward Syria, the Soviet Union's chief client state in the region. With Haig running the State Department, the Israelis felt they could allow themselves to adopt a militant posture *vis-à-vis* Syria. Israeli Prime Minister Begin held a closed session with Haig in April 1981, at which no minutes were taken; but, according to Schiff and Ya'ari, Begin later let slip a telling remark: "Ben-Gurion used to say that if you're pursuing a policy that may lead to war, it's vital to have a great power behind you."[3]

That same month, *Ukaz* carried an official Saudi statement: "The Kingdom emphasizes that it is necessary for the international community to carry its responsibility and take decisive action to stop the continuing Israeli aggression on Lebanon."[4]

According to Schiff and Ya'ari, the Syrians considered the Zahle road a serious threat to an area they regarded as vital to the defence of Damascus, and for which they would be prepared to take up arms, even against Israel.

---

1. Deborah J. Gerner, *One Land, Two Peoples: The Conflict Over Palestine* (Boulder, CO: Westview Press, 1994), p. 124.
2. Richard B. Parker, *The Politics of Miscalculation in the Middle East* (Indianapolis: Indiana University Press, 1993), pp. 174–5.
3. Ze'ev Schiff and Ehud Ya'ari, *Israel's Lebanon War* (New York: Simon & Schuster, 1984), p. 31.
4. *Ukaz*, 8 April 1981.

On 25 April, they began bringing in troops by helicopter and placing them in positions to block the progress of the road and to confront Bashir Gemayel's militia. On 28 April Israel's air force intervened, and shot down two Syrian helicopters. The following day Syria responded by moving surface-to-air missiles (SAMs) near Zahle for the first time since entering Lebanon in 1976. Begin threatened to destroy the missiles in turn. On 30 April, Samuel Lewis, the US ambassador to Israel, informed the Israelis that Reagan was sending Special Ambassador Philip Habib to discuss the matter with the Syrians.[1]

Habib arrived in Riyadh on 16 May. Saudi Assistant Foreign Minister 'Abdul Rahman Mansouri told *Ukaz* that discussions with Habib had centred on the latest developments in Lebanon, and that "the Kingdom's endeavours to achieve peace in the area never wavered and from the nature of the Kingdom's role ... discussions centred on the prevention of explosion in the area".[2] On 18 May the Saudi Press Agency carried an official government statement to the effect that "the Kingdom monitors with great anxiety and disapproval the continuous Israeli aggression on Lebanon", and that in the face of this serious aggression "the Kingdom stresses again its stand with Lebanon and its desire to back and support the legitimate Lebanese authority ... in addition, we are determined to stand with Syria to confront any aggression that will threaten its sovereignty, independence, and territory." King Khalid dispatched the Deputy Commander of the National Guard 'Abdul 'Aziz Al-Twajri to Assad with a letter,[3] and Crown Prince Fahd said the Kingdom would support Syria in the face of the Israeli action: "If Israel attacks Syria, all the Arabs will fight with and beside Syria."[4]

Before the SAMs complication, the Saudis had tried to persuade the Syrians to halt their campaign; when they resisted, the Saudis suspended financial support for Syrian forces in Lebanon.[5] When asked about the suspension, Prince Saud denied that it had occurred.[6]

1. Schiff and Ya'ari, *Israel's Lebanon War*, pp. 33–5.
2. *Ukaz*, 17 May 1981.
3. Saudi Press Agency, 18 May 1981. The contents of the letter are unknown, but there is speculation that this was in fact a communiqué from the US to Assad containing some kind of proposal to have Syrian missiles removed from the Bekaa Valley.
4. Saudi Press Agency, 21 May 1981.
5. William Quandt, *Saudi Arabia in the 1980s* (Washington, DC: Brookings Institution Press, 1981), p. 9.
6. *Ukaz*, 24 May 1981.

The Saudi government then sought collective Arab cover for further action, both in collaboration with Habib and independently. It arranged for a meeting of Arab foreign ministers in Tunis on 26 May, which in turn appointed a follow-up committee composed of Saudis, Syrians, Lebanese and Kuwaitis to promote a settlement of the escalating crisis. According to *Ukaz*, the ministers spoke about "supporting the PLO with every possible means to continue its responsibilities" and also called on the US "to stop all types of support for Israel", putting it on notice: "The continuation of the support will lead to serious confrontation between the Arab nation and the US."[1]

On 28 May, Israel renewed its bombing of PLO concentrations in South Lebanon. The immediate purpose of the attacks was to effect a controlled escalation of tension and ultimately to trigger a war. The PLO held back for fear that a vigorous reaction would only provoke a crushing ground assault. Israel stepped up its bombing of PLO positions on 10 July, but this time the action touched off a fierce reaction when the PLO finally responded with an unprecedented two-week barrage. Firing off twenty field guns and a number of advanced Katyusha rockets, this "War of the Katyushas" paralyzed the entire sector of northern Israel. For ten days the Israelis tried and failed to establish a military solution to counter the PLO's artillery challenge.[2]

Meanwhile, under an accord arranged by the Arab committee, the Syrians agreed on 30 June to end the siege of Zahle and allow a Lebanese police force to replace the Phalangists there. *Ukaz* reported that the Saudi ambassador to Lebanon, 'Ali Al-Shaer, had expressed the hope that "this step will be followed by other steps on the road to complete resolution of the Lebanon crisis."[3] The Saudis also worked with Habib in trying to defuse the state of affairs. A Saudi statement on 20 July observed that by escalating the situation, Israel was providing proof "of its determination to ruin all the positive outcomes that had been achieved by the Arab committee".[4] On 24 July Habib, working through the Saudis, had secured a ceasefire agreement from the PLO. Israel agreed to end its attacks, and doing so effectively constituted the first agreement ever achieved between it and the PLO. There was no formal, signed document; the PLO and the Israelis simply agreed separately with Habib as to what

---

1. Ibid.
2. Schiff and Ya'ari, *Israel's Lebanon War*, pp. 35–6.
3. *Ukaz*, 1 July 1981.
4. *Ukaz*, 20 July 1981.

would and would not happen.[1] On 25 July, *Ukaz* reported that Al-Shaer had delivered a message from Fahd to Lebanese President Elias Sarkis. After the meeting Al-Shaer said that "the letter explained all the efforts expended to reach a ceasefire", adding that he had discussed "the necessary steps to be taken to ensure the ceasefire, therefore creating an atmosphere to allow us to find new steps to resolve the whole crisis".[2]

Begin had agreed to such unpromising terms because he was convinced that, whatever the agreement, a war against the PLO was inevitable. As early as October 1981, Begin informed Haig that Israel intended to move militarily into Lebanon but hoped to avoid Syrian involvement. All that was required was an appropriate excuse.[3] Begin resented the widespread interpretation that he had tacitly recognized the PLO by concluding a ceasefire agreement with it.[4]

As the winter and spring of 1982 proceeded, Israeli Defence Minister Ariel Sharon waited for the PLO to hand him his pretext, though Habib noted that since 24 July 1981 "there had not been a single incident on the Israeli-Lebanese border".[5] By March 1982, operational plans for a war were advanced and detailed. On 21 April, Israel broke the ceasefire with the PLO by bombing targets in South Lebanon, and massed its forces along the northern borders. The pretext was the death of an Israeli soldier, whose vehicle had hit a mine in a zone controlled by Saad Haddad of the breakaway South Lebanon Army.[6]

The PLO response was restrained: Arafat wanted to prove he was a strong leader and could maintain the ceasefire. He also recognized that Israel was trying to provoke the PLO into retaliation, which would then provide the necessary justification for an attack.[7] The pretext the Israelis were waiting for arrived on 3 June when Shlomo Argov, the Israeli ambassador to Great Britain, was shot and critically wounded. The Israelis' response was to bomb over twenty-five sites around Beirut and elsewhere in Lebanon. The Palestinians responded with a twenty-four-hour rocket barrage targeting northern Israel.[8] Reagan urged Begin not to widen the attack, and Saudi Arabia informed the

1. Parker, *The Politics of Miscalculation in the Middle East*, p. 181.
2. *Ukaz*, 25 July 1981.
3. Haig, *Caveat*, pp. 326–7.
4. Safran, *Saudi Arabia*, p. 341.
5. John Boykin, *Cursed Is the Peacemaker: The American Diplomat Versus the Israeli General, Beirut 1982* (Belmont, CA: Applegate Press, 2002), p. 53.
6. Schiff and Ya'ari, *Israel's Lebanon War*, pp. 53–5.
7. Gerner, *One Land, Two Peoples*, p. 125.
8. Boykin, *Cursed Is the Peacemaker*, p. 59.

US that Arafat was willing to suspend cross-border shelling; but by that time it was too late, and Begin had been fully engaged.[1]

On 5 June, the Israeli cabinet approved a large-scale invasion of Lebanon, "Operation Peace for Galilee". Begin informed the US that the objective was to drive the PLO back 40 km from the Israeli border. Israel asked the US to tell Syria that its forces would not attack Syrian military units unless they attacked the Israelis first.[2]

On 6 June, Israeli armour and infantry columns crossed the border into Lebanon, supported by extensive air strikes and sea landings. On 7 June, Saudi Arabia condemned the Israeli attack. Fahd "called upon the Arab and Muslim leaders to relinquish their differences and rise to the level of responsibility to confront their enemies".[3] For the next three days, Syrian forces did not intervene, nor were they attacked by the Israeli air force. However, on 9 June, when Israeli advances began to threaten their lines, the Syrians reacted. In two days the Israeli air force destroyed all Syria's SAMs and shot down eighty-three Syrian fighter aircraft without suffering a single loss. As a result, Syria agreed to a ceasefire on 11 June, independently of the PLO.[4] On 13 June, Israel closed the ring around Beirut. Sharon's objectives had now been achieved: the PLO was trapped in Beirut, Israeli forces had linked up with the Phalangists and the Syrians had been badly defeated in the air and in the Bekaa Valley.

The Saudis were outraged at this new episode of Israeli aggression. Their specific concern centred on the fear-induced pressure on them, from within and without, to take action that would be damaging to their vital interests.[5] On 10 June 1982, Fahd stated: "What is happening in Lebanon is as unprecedented as it is unreasonable to leave defenceless people to face all these deadly weapons."[6] But the Saudis also realized that they could not antagonize the US when the Iranians were launching a successful offensive against Iraq. AWACS with US personnel were protecting their country, and the US Navy was securing shipping in the Gulf. On 10 June Saud met Reagan in Bonn and warned the US

---

1. Haig, *Caveat*, p. 336.
2. Ibid., p. 337.
3. *Ukaz*, 8 June 1982.
4. Safran, *Saudi Arabia*, pp. 341–2.
5. Galia Golan, *The Soviet Union and the Israeli War in Lebanon*, Research Paper 46 (Jerusalem: Soviet and East European Research Centre, 1982), p. 13.
6. *Ukaz*, 11 June 1982.

of harsh consequences if it did not intervene,[1] commenting after the meeting: "The Kingdom expects a clear stand from the US regarding Lebanon to achieve an Israeli withdrawal from Lebanese territory." Saud's perception was that the Reagan administration shared "the same anxiety in assessing the dangerous situation", and hoped that "this anxiety and assessment may translate into a clear US position to achieve a complete Israeli withdrawal." President Reagan's advisor Edwin Meese mentioned that Reagan had sent a resolute letter to Begin urging him to initiate a ceasefire and an immediate withdrawal.[2]

After Israeli forces had allied with the Phalangists and surrounded West Beirut, their objective changed to disarming and removing the PLO from the city rather than insisting on the organization's destruction or surrender. To accomplish this, Israel attempted a strategy of siege and attrition. The US sought to end the siege by mediating, through Habib, the removal of the PLO from the city, as part of the wider objective of seeking the removal of all foreign forces from Lebanon.[3] On 13 June Saudi Arabia expressed concern that the Israelis might storm Beirut.

On 16 June, the White House delegated Vice President George Bush and Weinberger to offer official condolences from the US on the death of King Khalid. During the visit, now-King Fahd told Bush that US non-intervention would have a negative effect on Saudi-US relations in one form or another.[4] Saud also met Bush, and discussed the UN calls for a ceasefire and Israeli pullout. During the meeting Saud made it clear to Bush that "attaching the Israeli withdrawal to the withdrawal of all non-Lebanese forces from Lebanon was a subject which should be left for the Lebanese government", and expressed his hope that "the US [would] intervene effectively to curb Israeli defiance ... US non-intervention will have a negative effect in one way or another on Arab-US relations."[5]

According to *Ukaz*, the Saudi government warned Israel on 19 June not to invade Beirut, declaring: "The invasion of an independent Arab capital will nullify Arab political efforts in all fields and the Arabs will face their historical responsibilities, and defend their territories with all their means, and Saudi

---

1. Arabic & World Selected News Agency, Beirut, [Lebanon's Invasion (*Ijtiyah Lubnan*)] undated, p. 296.
2. *Ukaz*, 11 June 1982.
3. Safran, *Saudi Arabia*, p. 345.
4. Arabic & World Selected News Agency, Beirut, p. 347.
5. *Ukaz*, 17 June 1982.

Arabia, by declaring this, consolidates her stand with other Arab countries in her complete solidarity with the Lebanese and Palestinian people, and ... will be the first to answer the call of duty."[1]

Secretary of State Haig claimed that Habib was informed of Arafat's readiness to begin negotiations on the day of the meeting between the US delegation and the Saudis. The PLO asked for a forty-eight-hour ceasefire to work out the details, to which the Israelis agreed. Haig said that on the following day the PLO, on advice from the Saudis, had hardened its position, and he was of the view that after the meeting with Bush the Saudis had advised the PLO to play for a better outcome.[2] Haig's claim cannot be verified by other sources. In any case, if it is accurate, the Saudis had acted from a sense of duty and obligation toward the Palestinian people.

According to Haig's own account, he informed Reagan on 24 June that Fahd supported the US position on West Beirut: that the PLO must lay down its arms and depart. The French also agreed that the PLO must disarm. Both would convey this view to the PLO.[3]

On 25 June, after Israel had mounted its biggest artillery barrage against Beirut, Fahd informed Reagan of the Kingdom's "extreme discontent at the Israeli persistence in executing its hostile designs against Lebanon". He insisted that the US should assume "its full responsibility toward events in Lebanon".[4] White House aides rushed to reassure the Saudis. Haig, whose soft stance on Israel was not popular with everyone in the Reagan administration, tendered his resignation, which Reagan accepted. Two days later, the US warned Israel against new attacks on Beirut. According to Safran, the Saudis viewed Haig's resignation and the US warning as a sign of change in US policy.[5]

The Arab League's foreign ministers met again in Tunis on 27 June. The Saudis managed to convince the delegates to create a second, small committee to follow developments and explore options. Its membership included representatives from Lebanon, Syria and the PLO, plus Saudi Arabia, Kuwait and Algeria.[6] The committee met in Taif, Saudi Arabia, on 29 June, and considered a PLO withdrawal – including the scope, modalities and places to

1. *Ukaz*, 20 June 1982.
2. Haig, *Caveat*, pp. 343–4.
3. Ibid., pp. 345–6.
4. *Ukaz*, 26 June 1982.
5. Safran, *Saudi Arabia*, p. 347.
6. *Ukaz*, 28 June 1982.

which it might withdraw. At the conclusion of the meeting, Saud announced that the group had discussed "ways to execute the Arab decision related to removal of the Israeli aggression from Lebanon and the feasible actions for the Arabs toward this aggression".[1] A course of action had been worked out with three objectives:

1. To avoid a massacre in Beirut;
2. To retain a PLO existence in Lebanon, in possession of a reasonable force;
3. To guarantee an Israeli withdrawal.

Habib reported on 28 June that the PLO was demanding a symbolic military presence in Lebanon and a political presence in Beirut. According to *Ukaz*, the breakthrough came on 2 July when Habib passed on information that the Lebanese, after talks with the PLO and the Saudi government, were united on a plan. As soon as a country had been found to accept them, the PLO would withdraw, leaving a small political office and a token residual force of about 600 men in the northern city of Tripoli. Following the departure of the PLO a phased withdrawal of all foreign forces would begin, with the adjustment of the Israeli lines. The Lebanese government demanded an international peacekeeping force – but not under the auspices of the UN – in Beirut, and requested the US to contribute troops. *Ukaz* noted that the US accepted the plan in principle, while Israel totally rejected any plan that left the PLO in Beirut. Israeli Labour Party leader Shimon Peres, however, believed that "there was an even chance that Habib would succeed in negotiating a peaceful withdrawal of the PLO."[2]

On 4 July Haig asked the Saudis to deal with the Arabs in finding a country or countries to accept the PLO and in exploring a Syrian withdrawal.[3] The Saudis informed him that after talks with Fahd, Assad had agreed to receive the PLO – both the leadership and the rank-and-file – in Syria. Moreover, Assad

---

1. *Ukaz*, 30 June 1982
2. *Ukaz*, 5 July 1982.
3. Haig was still in his post (his successor, George Shultz, having not yet been confirmed) but left at the president's request on 5 July 1982; see James Chace, "The Turbulent Tenure of Alexander Haig", *The New York Times*, 22 April 1984.

gave assurances that Syria would withdraw its military forces from Lebanon once that country's government requested it to do so.[1]

Reagan indicated on 6 July that the US was willing to participate in a multinational force to facilitate the withdrawal process.[2] Fahd welcomed this decision and agreed to send Saud, together with Syrian Foreign Minister Abdel Halim Khaddam, to Washington to meet with Reagan and now-Secretary of State George Shultz.[3] On 20 July Saud and Khaddam told Shultz they had come on a mission from the Arab League. Saud declared: "The Arab delegation's mission is to conduct discussions with the US regarding the execution of UN resolutions related to Lebanon, and the necessity for Israeli forces to withdraw." He expressed his wish that the discussions "establish peace and stability in Lebanon".[4] Both Saudi Arabia and Syria feared that if the PLO evacuated Beirut, the families they left behind would be slaughtered; they also believed Israel intended to stay in Lebanon, creating a "North Bank".[5]

The Arab League committee convened again on 28 July in Saudi Arabia, endorsing a plan the following day for a complete PLO withdrawal, stipulating guaranteed safe passage for PLO members out of Beirut and assured future security for Palestinians remaining in Lebanon.[6] On 29 July, Arafat sent Habib a document outlining steps for a PLO departure, which signalled an unequivocal and firm decision on the part of the PLO to depart.[7] However, two days later the Israelis mounted the fiercest bombardment of Beirut since hostilities had begun, and advanced into parts of West Beirut. According to Shultz, Bandar phoned him on 4 August and reported that Fahd had called the Israeli attack "the beginning of the disaster. The US must do something. US prestige is on the line, and so is Saudi Arabia's." The king had requested that "the President intervene immediately so that drastic steps are not necessary".[8]

According to Shultz, Habib believed that this Israeli advance undermined the plan for PLO departure and thought that, with this new development, an Israeli withdrawal would have to be achieved before the PLO agreed to

---

1. Haig, *Caveat*, pp. 349–50.
2. Ibid., p. 351.
3. Shultz, *Turmoil and Triumph*, p. 48.
4. *Ukaz*, 20 July 1982.
5. Shultz, *Turmoil and Triumph*, pp. 50–1.
6. *Ukaz*, 30 July 1982.
7. Shultz, *Turmoil and Triumph*, p. 52.
8. Ibid., p. 58.

leave. Habib urged the US to impose sanctions on Israel unless it ceased fire, withdrew and restored electricity and water supplies to the city.[1] In a private message to Begin, President Reagan insisted that a ceasefire be in place until the PLO had left Beirut, saying sharply: "The relationship between our two nations is at stake."[2]

Fahd contacted Reagan again on 5 August to ask him to prevent an all-out attack in Beirut, especially as resolution of the crisis was achievable and close.[3] Reagan therefore sent another message to Begin, saying Habib's negotiations must continue and a ceasefire must be established according to the lines of 1 August, not the lines that had resulted from the escalated fighting on 3 August.[4]

Bandar reported to Shultz on 5 August that Fahd had declared: "Wherever the PLO elects to go, we will work to assure it is accepted."[5] On 6 August the PLO accepted all the main points of a withdrawal plan negotiated by Habib.[6]

Despite the aversion of some Arab leaders to the PLO, they could not be seen to be obstructing any solution. As the US would be committing ground troops to supervise a PLO evacuation, the Arab states would have been put in a bad light had they prevented an evacuation from taking place. They realized they might face uprisings from their own PLO sympathizers if they let the PLO fighters be slaughtered in Beirut. The Arab leaders also had a hard time resisting Saudi pressure and promises of economic assistance.[7] After Tunisia announced on 10 August that it would agree to harbour the PLO headquarters and some fighters, it became much easier for other Arab states to come forward.

Before leaving Beirut, Arafat made one last demand: a US/international guarantee for the safety of Palestinian civilians left behind. To accommodate this demand, Habib asked for and received Israeli assurances that they would not enter West Beirut or take any reprisals against the remaining Palestinians. On 5 August, Habib also received Bashir Gemayel's confirmation of the same

---

1. Ibid., p. 59.
2. Ibid., p. 60.
3. *The New York Times*, 6 August 1982.
4. Shultz, *Turmoil and Triumph*, p. 60.
5. Ibid., p. 62.
6. Safran, *Saudi Arabia*, p. 350.
7. *Newsweek*, "The End Game in Beirut", 23 August 1982.

assurances on behalf of the Phalange Party. Habib also gave, both verbally and in writing, US assurances of the safety of the civilians.[1]

A deal was finally made whereby Israeli attacks on Beirut would end, the Palestinian fighters would leave Lebanon and redeploy in several Arab countries and a multinational peacekeeping force would assure the security of Palestinian civilians in Lebanon. Prior to departure from Beirut, Arafat sent a telegram to King Fahd in which he acknowledged the Saudi role in facilitating a peaceful end to the crisis: "Your productive and good natured efforts and contacts with President Reagan have saved many lives of your Palestinians and Lebanese sons," he wrote, adding: "Our people will never forget King Fahd for his candid patriotic and nationalist stands."[2]

The PLO evacuation began on 21 August, and the last of the PLO fighters left Beirut on 1 September. Ten days later, the US withdrew its forces.[3] Gemayel was elected President on 23 August and assassinated on 14 September; in response to this event, Israeli forces defied the agreement and returned to Beirut the next day. According to Shultz, Fahd sent a message insisting that his honour, name and credibility were at stake should Israel remain in Beirut, and emphasized that the situation made it difficult for Saudi Arabia to extend any assistance to the US.[4]

On 16 September, Phalangist militiamen received clearance from the Israeli Defence Force to enter the Sabra and Shatila refugee camps, in Israeli-controlled territory. Over the next forty hours, they proceeded to murder as many as 1,000 people, the majority of whom were Palestinian women, children and elderly men. The Palestinians and other Arabs blamed the US, which had guaranteed the safety of the Palestinian civilians left unprotected when the PLO evacuated Beirut.

Covert Operations

This section on covert action by the US is based on secondary sources; American primary sources remain classified, and Saudi sources implicitly unwilling.[5]

---

1. Shultz, *Turmoil and Triumph*, p. 105.
2. *Ukaz*, 16 August 1982.
3. Gerner, *One Land, Two Peoples*, p. 126.
4. Shultz, *Turmoil and Triumph*, p. 104.
5. As mentioned in the introduction to this book, attempts to facilitate Saudi cooperation by the author were initially promising; but Saudi sources later

Since the Watergate scandal that saw the resignation of President Nixon, the CIA had encountered enormous problems organizing operations requiring total secrecy. Carter, who felt it was important to wipe out the stigma of a rogue CIA that, as he put it, "had a role in plotting murder and other crimes",[1] adopted a means of avoiding direct CIA involvement in covert operations that could go wrong and backfire on the US. This method, refined and applied with skill by Kissinger, involved getting others to do what you want done while avoiding the responsibility or blame if the operation fails.[2]

During Fahd's visit to the US in May 1977, Carter stated: "When we saw a particular problem, either in our country or around the world, and as soon as this need became known by the leaders of that great country [Saudi Arabia], the need was met in a quiet but very effective and friendly way."[3]

Deep concerns about Soviet and Cuban military intervention in Ethiopia and Angola respectively, and about Marxist liberation movements elsewhere in Africa and in Latin America, compelled some allies of the US to conduct informal covert operations, that were, for a time, highly effective. A new anti-communist alliance was beginning to take shape, the members of which were determined to be their own masters and not agents of the US. Thus the Safari Club came into being.[4]

The idea that states with an interest in curbing the spread of communism in Africa should combine to take action came from Comte Claude Alexander de Marenches, head of French external intelligence, the Service de Documentation Extérieure et de Contre-Espionnage (SDECE). Five governments were persuaded by his arguments: France, Iran, Saudi Arabia, Egypt and Morocco.[5] The aims of the Soviets in Africa were considered by the Club to comprise control over the continent's raw materials and over the sea routes round Africa, plus the manipulation of client states.[6] A founding agreement was signed on 1 September 1976, and an operational centre was established in Cairo, although

---

declined to engage further to present their own analysis of the cooperation between the two countries.
1. Carter, *Keeping Faith*, p. 143.
2. Cooley, *Unholy Wars*, p. 24.
3. PPP, Jimmy Carter, 1977, p. 1,006.
4. Heikal, *Iran*, p. 113.
5. Ibid.
6. Ibid., pp. 113–4.

The First Fahd Era (1979–90)

several meetings of the Safari Club took place in Saudi Arabia and France as well.[1]

The Club's first successful operation was in Zaire in 1977, when a dissident general threatened to seize the mineral-rich province of Katanga. President Mobutu Sese Seko appealed to the Club for assistance, which came from Moroccan and Egyptian forces.[2] The US was supportive of the Club; according to *The New York Times*, Assistant Secretary of State Alfred Atherton recalled that the US had approached the Saudi government implicitly: "It sure would be helpful if [Morocco's] King Hassan had a way to get his troops to Zaire."[3]

A much bigger target presented itself the same year in Somalia. Somali President Siad Barre set out to claim the disputed Ethiopian province of Ogaden for Greater Somalia with Soviet aid, which alarmed the US and the members of the Club. However, Ethiopia had undergone a Marxist revolution in 1974; as that country was obviously a much more attractive prize for the USSR than Somalia, the Soviets began rushing military and economic aid to the Ethiopian regime. US military installations were subsequently ousted from Ethiopia, a huge victory for the Soviets: for control of both South Yemen and Ethiopia meant control of the strategic Strait of Bab El-Mandeb at the mouth of the Red Sea. As Brzezinski pointed out: "If Ethiopia and South Yemen become Soviet associates ... there will be a serious and direct political threat to Saudi Arabia. This is something we simply cannot ignore."[4]

Thus Barre found himself deserted by his Soviet backers, but the Safari Club was prepared to step in. "Get rid of the Soviets and we would supply you with arms," it informed Barre, who duly expelled the Soviets. Egypt sold Somalia Soviet arms worth US $75 million, paid for by Saudi Arabia.[5] In the end, Barre was caught in a superpower deal whereby the Soviets refrained from meddling in Rhodesia in return for the US ceasing support for the Somali campaign in Ogaden.

In the mid-1970s, Saudi Arabia began paying the bills for the Chadian army to repel Libyan incursions into Chad's northern border area, and to curb Soviet influence. Saudi Arabia viewed the Libyan adventure as a means of

---

1. Cooley, *Unholy Wars*, p. 26.
2. Heikal, *Iran*, p. 114.
3. *The New York Times*, 21 June 1987.
4. Brzezinski, *Power and Principle*, p. 181.
5. Heikal, *The Road to Ramadan*, p. 126.

extending influence into sub-Saharan Africa and putting pressure on Sudan.[1] Between 1975–76 Saudi aid to Sudan increased from US $25 million to US $164 million. A CIA report acknowledged that Saudi aid had helped the Sudanese government survive leftist efforts to bring it down. Atherton claimed: "We encouraged the Saudis to help [Sudan's President Gaafar al-Nimeiry]."[2] Prince Turki said, in a speech: "There was total rejection of Marxist ideas by the Kingdom, and for that reason we supported US policies against Communism."[3] Furthermore, according to Simpson, whenever Bandar was asked if the Kingdom was engaged in these activities against the communists at the request of the US, his reply was along the lines of: "Saudi Arabia does not have a relationship with the Soviet Union, not because of America but because they are atheists."[4]

The detachment between Saudi Arabia and Egypt after Camp David, the fall of the Shah, the retirement of de Marenches and, finally, the adoption by the US of a policy of rolling back leftist governments all over the world eventually spelled the dissolution of the Safari Club.

The Reagan administration's top foreign-policy priority was the undermining of the Sandinista government in Nicaragua. In 1979, long-time President General Anastasio Somoza Debayle was overthrown, and control of the country passed to the leftist Sandinistas. At first the US was ambivalent about the Sandinistas. Carter gave the new government US $39 million in emergency food aid; though it accepted the money, Nicaragua's ties to Cuba and the Soviets grew stronger, and its support of Marxist rebels in El Salvador increased. Carter suspended the aid, and Reagan vowed that Nicaragua would receive no more until it was fully democratic.[5]

The US began to consider ways to assist opponents of the Sandinista regime, who came to be known as the Contras. Initial support for the Nicaraguan resistance came from Argentina, which in early 1981 organized and supplied paramilitary forces. However, by 1981 the Contras were looking to the US

1. *The New York Times, Report of the Congressional Committee's Investigation: The Iran-Contra Affair, with the Minority View* (New York: Times Books, 1994), pp. 37–8.
2. *The New York Times*, 21 June 1987.
3. Prince Turki Al-Faisal, Speech at Georgetown University, Washington, DC, 26 February 1975.
4. Simpson, *The Prince*, p. 112.
5. *The New York Times, Report of the Congressional Committee's Investigation*, pp. 37–8.

The First Fahd Era (1979–90)

for support, and Reagan committed vast diplomatic, economic and military resources to reverse what he saw as Soviet gains in the region through Cuba and Nicaragua. In December 1981, he authorized a covert CIA action programme to support the Contras – but these activities did not remain hidden for long. When its policy was questioned during a Congressional debate, the administration replied that it had no intention of overthrowing the Sandinista government.[1]

In early 1982, disillusioned Sandinista Comandante Edén Pastora defected from the ruling junta, organized the Sandino Revolutionary Front (FRS) and declared war on the Sandinista government.[2] By autumn 1982, the American press was reporting on the growing US involvement in Nicaragua. The administration again stated that it was not seeking to bring down the Nicaraguan government, but was simply preventing it from exporting revolution to El Salvador. Out of this emerged an amendment to the Defense Appropriations bill for fiscal year 1983, introduced by Representative Edward P. Boland and later known as "Boland I". This first Boland Amendment prohibited the CIA from using funds for the purpose of overthrowing the government of Nicaragua,[3] and questions concerning the level of compliance with the Boland Amendment increased throughout 1983.

In October 1983, the US House of Representatives voted to halt all aid to the paramilitary groups fighting the Nicaragua government. However, the Senate wanted aid to continue, and in early December the House and Senate agreed to a compromise: a cap of US $24 million would be placed on Contra funding, and the CIA would be barred from using its contingency reserves to make up any shortfall.[4]

The administration then decided to intensify the CIA's covert activities while funding still remained. A special inter-agency working group concluded: "Given the distinct possibility that we may be unable to obtain additional funding in FY [Fiscal Year]-84 or FY-85, our objective should be to bring the Nicaragua situation to a head in 1984." In the autumn, speedboats carried out attacks against the Sandinistas' patrol craft and fuel tankers, and at the end of December, Sandino Harbour was mined by the CIA. By March 1984, plans

1. Ibid., p. 40.
2. Ibid., p. 41–2.
3. Ibid., p. 42.
4. Ibid., p. 45.

had been made to support an attack by Pastora on the town of San Juan del Norte.[1]

By February 1984 the US $24 million that had been earmarked by Congress for the Contras was being rapidly depleted. CIA director Casey wrote a memorandum to National Security Advisor Robert C. McFarlane on 27 March, stating: "In view of possible difficulties in obtaining supplemented appropriations to carry out the Nicaragua covert action project through the remainder of this year, I am in full agreement that you should explore funding alternative with the Saudis."[2]

Chuck Cogan, chief of the CIA's Near East division, had a back-channel relationship with Bandar. In spring 1984, he raised the issue of obtaining funds for the Contras with him. According to Woodward, Bandar checked with Riyadh and received a negative reply based on the following: the US did not offer anything in return; the policies of the two countries in Central America were at odds; and there was no guarantee that the whole issue would remain secret. According to Simpson, McFarlane met Bandar again in May to request help. When Bandar asked if Reagan had acknowledged the request, McFarlane said; "He did, and you can check with him yourself, but you can't talk to anybody else. I will take you there to see him and he will say 'Thank you'."[3] The Saudis agreed to contribute US $8–$10 million to the Contras at the rate of US $1 million a month, and funnelled US $8 million to the Contras over the next eight months.[4]

NSC staff member Colonel Oliver North was given responsibility by McFarlane for arranging the transfer of funds. In summer 1984, CIA covert assistance to the Contras began to wane as funds diminished. Meanwhile, further legislation that would bar the CIA from future support for the Contras – the second Boland Amendment – had been passed by the House in early August. While Boland II cut off funding for the Contras, it did hold out some hope for renewing Contra aid in the future by allowing the White House to seek a US $14 million appropriation on an expedited basis after 28 February 1985.[5]

Boland II did not cause any immediate crisis for the Contras, as steps taken

---

1. Ibid., pp. 45–6.
2. Woodward, *Veil*, p. 350.
3. Simpson, *The Prince*, p. 120.
4. Woodward, *Veil*, p. 351–5.
5. *The New York Times, Report of the Congressional Committee's Investigation*, p. 51.

months earlier ensured their survival: the US $1 million-a-month pledged by the Saudis in June bridged the gap until December. However, with the Contras running out of funds, McFarlane turned to Bandar once more. In early February 1985, Saudi Arabia agreed to contribute an additional US $24 million, which meant that its contributions between June 1984 and March 1985 totalled US $32 million.[1] The Saudi contribution was made in the spirit of advancing relations and cooperation with the US in defence against communism, and it opened the door for other third parties to contribute money in support of the Contras. According to Simpson, Bandar explained the Saudi acceptance of support for the Contras: "We had no problem with that ... it was a sovereign operation outside the USA and so we were not breaking any laws."[2]

---

1. Ibid., pp. 54–5.
2. Simpson, *The Prince*, p. 118.

CHAPTER THREE

The Later Fahd Legacy (1990–2001): From Reliance to Mutual Liability

A change came about in the relationship between the US and Saudi Arabia during the period from 1990 to 2001, as a result of two significant developments: the end of the Cold War (with the subsequent disintegration of the Soviet Union) and the 1991 Gulf War. This chapter examines how the US planned its response to the threatened stability of the Gulf, and analyses the effect of the US military presence in Saudi Arabia on the relationship between the two countries. Finally, we shall look at the threat of terrorism as it relates to both Saudi Arabia and the US.

The Soviet invasion of Afghanistan and the Iran-Iraq war raised concerns over regime stability in the Gulf. The US expressed concern regarding the possibility of outside-influenced coups and subversion, and declared that it would work to prevent such occurrences. To protect its interests, the US negotiated both formal and informal access arrangements with several countries in East Africa and Southwest Asia. It signed formal agreements with Kenya and Somalia that allowed for naval support and sea control activities, while Djibouti agreed to the use of its port and airfield by US forces. An unwritten understanding with Egypt and a strategic cooperation agreement with Israel linked these countries into the CENTCOM access network.

Turkey and Pakistan responded somewhat ambiguously to the US request for bases in these countries to be used for US military operations in the Gulf. Turkey insisted that its base agreements were subject to formal endorsement by the North Atlantic Treaty Organization (NATO) if they were to be used by US military forces for Gulf action. Pakistan rejected a formal access agreement with the US but agreed to informal cooperation that included provision of rations to the US military by Pakistani supply ships and the use by the US of Pakistani airfields for maritime surveillance operations.[1]

In the Gulf, only Oman permitted the US to use some of its airfields and ports. The desire of Saudi Arabia and the other Gulf states for strategic cooperation with the US was offset by doubt and suspicion regarding US objectives, its support for Israel and, more importantly, the fear of provoking radical, anti-Western forces domestically and in the region.

Despite US pressure, the Saudis refused even to grant it access to the Kingdom's base facilities. Nevertheless, the US built several Saudi bases to NATO specifications, and also supervised the pre-positioning of combat equipment delivered from the US. In some cases the equipment and base facilities were in excess of Saudi Arabia's own defence requirements. As CENTCOM commander General P. X. Kelly testified before the Senate Armed Services Committee: "It is our view that if the government of Saudi Arabia perceived a serious threat to the Kingdom, the Government of the US would be invited into Saudi Arabia ... In this scenario, the Saudis would make available for our use any spare parts, bases, munitions, facilities and support equipments."[2]

Saudi Arabia and the other Gulf states looked for an "over-the-horizon" US military role. Though politically ideal, it was a poor way to signal military commitment on the part of the US towards regional adversaries.

US support for Israel was responsible for its failure to elicit greater cooperation from Saudi Arabia and the Gulf states, despite the threat from Iran to the latter. The historical importance of the Palestinian issue in Arab politics had too important a bearing on the desire of these states to cooperate with the US. As Fahd put it: "If we want to contain Communism and alien influences, we should solve the Palestinian question justly and comprehensively, so that no one will find himself compelled to seek assistance from those [the

---

1. Jamal Rashid, "Pakistan and the Central Command", *Middle East Report* (July-August 1986), pp. 28–34.
2. US Congress, Senate, Committee on Armed Services, "Military and Technical Implications of the Proposed Sale to Saudi Arabia of Airborne Warning and Control System (AWACS) and F-15 Enhancements, 1981", 97th Cong., 1st sess., 1981, p. 84.

Soviets] whom we fear may influence our principles."[1] Saudi Arabia and the Gulf states also had their doubts as to whether the US would come to their rescue in a time of crisis, given US treatment of the Shah of Iran.[2]

Additionally, because of the threat of possible seizure by the US of oilfields during the embargo crisis, US Gulf strategy was seen in the region as a new tool to enable the US to carry out such threats whenever needed.[3] The Kuwaiti daily *Al-Siyasah* reported: "The Pentagon has begun to implement part of a plan prepared by military experts for invading Arab oilfields."[4]

The dilemma facing Saudi policy-makers at this time stemmed from the fact that the current strategy was ostensibly one of self-reliance in defence and security, yet both inadequate and politically troublesome for the Kingdom – for a policy of self-reliance required the mobilization of citizen manpower into the armed forces. The Saudi social contract, as it had developed since the early 1970s, rested on the provision of benefits to citizens, not on the extraction of resources from them. Instituting a national service requirement would upset the implicit deal between state and society. Other factors were that women and minorities were excluded from joining the armed forces.

The political and demographic barriers to full utilization of the Kingdom's military manpower resources, combined with the number of potential military threats in the region, meant that the Saudi government had to seek external allies. Yet close ties with the US left it open to attacks by domestic and regional enemies alike. Military security rationale required the link with the US, but domestic security imperatives required that link to be as unobtrusive as possible. For the Saudi government, the ideal situation continued to be represented by the aforementioned "over-the-horizon" US presence – i.e. close enough to come to the Kingdom's aid but sufficiently distant to avoid the political problems associated with the relationship.[5]

---

1. Saudi Press Agency, 23 February 1980.
2. Abdul Kasim Mansur, "The American Threat to Saudi Arabia", *Survival* (January-February 1981), pp. 37–8.
3. Anthony H. Cordesman, *The Gulf and the Search for Strategic Stability: Saudi Arabia, the Military Balance in the Gulf, and Trends in the Arab-Israeli Military Balance* (Boulder, CO: Westview, 1984), p. 259.
4. *Al-Siyasah* (Kuwait), 13 November 1979.
5. F. Gregory Gause III, "From Over the Horizon to into the Backyard: The US-Saudi Relationship and the Gulf War", in David W. Lesch, ed., *The Middle East and the United States: A Historical and Political Reassessment* (Boulder, CO: Westview Press, 2003), pp. 357–63.

US military planners, for their part, recognized the need to plan for a wide variety of threats. Contingency planning took into account the possibility of a Soviet invasion of the Gulf as well as other non-Soviet threats. Testifying to Congress, Under-Secretary of Defense (under Carter) Robert Komer did not rule out US involvement if the Iraqis invaded Saudi Arabia, or if South Yemen tried to invade the Kingdom. Accordingly, US military operational planning for CENTCOM envisaged the need to deter and defeat the worst-case feasible threat, which was defined as an all-out Soviet invasion of Iran. Although it was viewed as the least likely scenario to threaten US interests in the Gulf, records suggest that American military planners factored it in: "If we have the capability of posing a credible deterrent to the worst case, then we believe that we have the capability of meeting lesser contingencies."[1]

Consequently, when Iraq came under serious military pressure from Iran at the beginning of 1983, the US and Saudi Arabia cooperated closely in establishing the "Fahd Line", an air defence identification zone and forward air defence system for the Saudi coast.[2]

Later, when an Iraqi missile hit the navy frigate USS *Stark* on 17 May 1987, "Operation Earnest Will" was mounted to defend shipping in the Gulf. During 1987 and 1988 the Saudis and the US military worked hard to improve communication and command, complete with secure telephone lines. The US constructed and equipped a special command bunker for the Saudi air force beneath the Saudi Ministry of Defence. All these works would prove important to the future success of the Gulf War operation.[3]

Following the 1988 ceasefire between Iran and Iraq, the US could not afford to adopt a "hands-off" policy with regard to Iraq; the latter was too powerful. If left to its own devices, Iraq's capacity to destabilize the whole region was enormous. A National Security Directive (NSD-26) was, therefore, signed by George Bush (now President) on 2 October 1989, emphasizing the need to intensify cooperation with Iraq. It also warned, however, that Iraqi meddling in the affairs of foreign countries could lead to economic sanctions.

---

1. US Congress, House of Representatives, Committee on Armed Services, Subcommittee on Military Installations and Facilities, "Hearings on H.R. 1816 (H.R. 2972) to Authorize Certain Construction at Military Installations for FY 1984", 98th Cong., 1st sess., 1983, p. 987.
2. Anthony H. Cordesman, *Saudi Arabia: Guarding the Desert Kingdom* (Boulder, CO: Westview Press, 1997), p. 191.
3. Cohen and Gatti, *In the Eye of the Storm*, pp. 193–4.

As a result of the Soviet military retreat from Afghanistan, CENTCOM was able to develop an operating plan to cope with regional conflicts in the Gulf. Although a year had passed since the ceasefire with Iran, Saddam had not reduced the size of his military; Iraq had too weak an economy to absorb its now million-man army back into civilian life.[1] CENTCOM Commander-in-Chief General H. Norman Schwarzkopf, Jr, who had been appointed in July 1988, had made three trips to the Gulf by the spring of 1989. As he relates in his autobiography, he was amazed to find that the Saudi government was concerned about Iran, not Iraq. Saudi thinking was that as soon as Iran had rearmed, it would once again be fighting Iraq and menacing the Gulf states. The Saudis, meanwhile, downplayed the idea of a possible threat from Iraq.[2]

Similarly, in November 1989, the Kuwaiti newspaper *Al-Qabas* reported a difference of perception regarding Iraq: that of Richard Clarke, US Assistant Secretary of State, who had given the "Iraqi threat" as the justification for acceding to a Saudi request to obtain certain US tanks. The newspaper carried an official Saudi denial of such a probability: "We stress, in unequivocally denying such suspicions, the profound fraternal connections and the deeply rooted close kinship relationship that exists between Saudi Arabia and Iraq."[3]

In January 1990, Schwarzkopf ordered a computerized command post exercise; this was an annual war game codenamed "Internal Look", and was to be scheduled for August 1990 in order to explore possible responses to an Iraqi invasion of the Arabian Peninsula. The game involved eight exhausting twenty-hour days during which CENTCOM's staff, as well as components of the US Army, Navy, Air Force and Marine Corps, would practise running a war by using computer programs instead of actual forces in the field. Based on a pre-existing Pentagon plan known as Plan 1002, which had been designed to counter any threats to the vast oil reserves of the Arabian Peninsula, the exercise was duly codenamed "1002-90". Schwarzkopf ordered that the focus for Plan 1002-90 and "Internal Look" be shifted to Iraq as an aggressor.[4]

---

1. H. Norman Schwarzkopf, with Peter Petre, *It Doesn't Take a Hero: The Autobiography: General H. Norman Schwarzkopf* (London: Bantam Press, 1992), pp. 278–86.
2. Ibid., p. 278.
3. *Al-Qabas*, 16 November 1989.
4. *US News and World Report, Triumph Without Victory: The Unreported History of the Persian Gulf War* (New York: Times Books, 1992), pp. 29–30.

The Later Fahd Legacy (1990–2001)

The Invasion of Kuwait

On 15 February 1990, the Voice of America (VOA) broadcast an editorial predicting the end of police states all over the world, including Iraq.[1] The Iraqis demanded clarification; the US officially apologized and sacked whoever had been responsible for this prediction. Even so, the US failed to approve some loan credits to Iraq under an agricultural programme organized by the Commodity Credit Cooperation, despite this arrangement having existed for many years between the two countries.[2]

During March, relations between Washington and Baghdad soured further on account of the execution of a British journalist accused of spying and the discovery of an Iraqi network for smuggling munitions-list, nuclear-related capacitors out of the US through Britain to Iraq.[3] Saddam interpreted the US reactions as an all-encompassing conspiracy against Iraq. Within the Iraqi leadership there was an overwhelming belief that US foreign policy towards the Arab world, and Iraq in particular, had always been based on a set of intended conspiracies. Following the execution of the British journalist, according to Tariq Aziz, the Iraqis started to fear a conspiracy[4] and therefore concluded that they could expect little from the US in return for good behaviour. In a speech delivered at an Arab Cooperation Council summit, Saddam accused the US, with its naval presence in the Gulf, of trying to control the Gulf and its oil: "If the Gulf people, along with all Arabs, are not careful, the Arabian Gulf will be governed by the US."[5]

On 1 April, Saddam issued his thunderous threat to Israel: "The West will be deluded if they imagine that they can give Israel the cover to come and strike ... By God, we will make the fire eat half of Israel if it tries to do anything against Iraq."[6] US anger at the threats against Israel convinced the Iraqis that

1. Voice of America, Washington, DC, Transcript of the Editorial, 15 February 1990.
2. Amatzia Baram, "U.S. Input into Iraqi Decision-making, 1988–1990", in David W. Lesch, ed., *The Middle East and the US: A Historical and Political Assessment* (Boulder CO: Westview Press, 1996), pp. 338–39.
3. Ibid., p. 340.
4. *US News and World Report, Triumph Without Victory*, pp. 15–6.
5. Reported in *The New Yorker*, 24 June 1991, pp. 64–7. The Arab Cooperation Council was founded in February 1989 by North Yemen, Iraq, Jordan and Egypt.
6. Bob Woodward, *The Commanders* (New York: Simon & Schuster, 1991), p. 201.

any attempt to lead an Arab political front against the peace process would meet with opposition from the US.

Despite his exaggerated rhetoric, Saddam asked King Fahd to resolve any possible misunderstanding with the US. If Fahd would send an emissary to Baghdad, Saddam would send a message to President Bush. The king duly dispatched Prince Bandar, who arrived on 5 April in Baghdad. According to Woodward, Saddam told Bandar that his words had been misunderstood to mean he intended an offensive strike against Israel. Saddam said: "I want to assure President Bush and His Majesty King Fahd that I will not attack Israel." In return, he wanted the US to assure him that Israel would not attack Iraq. During the meeting Saddam cautioned against a theory being circulated by imperialist-Zionist forces that he had designs on his neighbours, insisting this was not the case. He justified the verbal assault on Israel by saying that it had been two years since the ceasefire and that his people were becoming relaxed: "I must whip them into a sort of frenzy or emotional mobilization so they will be ready for whatever may happen."[1]

Bandar delivered Saddam's message to Bush and reminded Bush of the 1981 Israeli attack on Iraq's Osiraq nuclear reactor. Woodward reports that Bandar expressed Saddam's eagerness to assure him of his intentions, stating: "... They would like to have an assurance that Israel will not attack them, because they are getting nervous." Having received a commitment by Israel that it would not attack Iraq if it was, in turn, not attacked by Iraq, the White House duly passed its assurances directly to Saddam.[2]

All this changed in Baghdad during an extraordinary Arab Summit meeting on 28 May, which witnessed a major offensive on the part of Iraq and its Arab supporters against Israel, Soviet-Jewish immigration, the US and, by implication, Arab moderates.[3] During the closed session Saddam also accused some "Arab brothers" of flooding the world oil market and bringing down prices, and warned that his country regarded this as an all-out war against Iraq. According to Saudi General Prince Khalid bin Sultan, Saddam behaved

1. Ibid., p. 202.
2. Ibid., pp. 203–4.
3. Baram, "US Input into Iraqi Decision-making, 1988–1990", pp. 341–2.; Fouad Matar, ed., *Gulf War Panorama: A Factual Documented Account* (Beirut: Arab Institute for Research & Publishing, and London: Fouad Matar Consultancy for Media, Documentation and Research, 1994), pp. 514–8.

The Later Fahd Legacy (1990–2001)

during the summit like a "man with a strong sense of being wronged who was no doubt preparing to take by force what he considered his due".[1]

Following the summit, Saddam instructed Iraq's media to launch a campaign against Kuwait and the United Arab Emirates (UAE). He also sent Deputy Prime Minister Dr Sa'dun Hammadi on a tour of the Gulf to demand financial assistance and an agreement on oil production in order to boost the price of oil. The Saudi newspaper *Al-Sharq al-Awsat* reported Hammadi's comments to the effect that as two Arab countries had "violated the latest OPEC quota, and one of them had exercised the violation for many years", he had therefore adopted "the open dialogue method with the brothers, not for the intention of exposure but rather to search for solutions to protect the interests of all".[2]

On 8 July Fahd sent the Saudi oil minister, Hisham Nazer, to inform Saddam of the efforts by the Saudi government, along with Kuwait and the UAE, to bring stability to the oil market. Nazer also told Saddam that the Saudi government had called a meeting of the GCC oil ministers in Jeddah on 10 July.[3] It was announced that, following a Saudi initiative, it had been decided that "the production ceiling should not be increased except if all thirteen members of the organization, including UAE, agreed."[4]

On 17 July, Saddam delivered a blistering speech, charging that "some of the greediest Gulf Arabs" had conspired with the imperialists, and that artificially low prices were a "poisoned dagger" thrust into Iraq's back.[5] At the same time, a note was delivered to the Secretary General of the Arab League by Aziz, which accused Kuwait of stealing oil from the Rumeilah oilfield – a disputed territory claimed by Iraq. The oil policies of Kuwait and the UAE were considered by Iraq to be part of a Zionist and imperialist plot against the Arabs.[6]

During the third week of July, Chairman of the Joint Chiefs of Staff Colin Powell was given satellite photos showing an Iraqi deployment of three divisions near Kuwait's border, about 35,000 strong. Some units were identified as part of the Republican Guard, Saddam's elite troops.[7] Joint

---

1. HRH General Khaled bin Sultan, with Patrick Seale, *Desert Warrior: A Personal View of the Gulf War by the Joint Forces Commander* (London: HarperCollins, 1995), p. 157.
2. *Al-Sharq al-Awsat*, 27 June 1990.
3. Ibid., 9 July 1990.
4. *Ukaz*, 11 July 1990.
5. *US News and World Report, Triumph Without Victory*, pp. 20–1.
6. *Al-Hayat*, 25 July 1990.
7. Colin L. Powell, with Joseph E. Persico, *My American Journey* (New York:

Chiefs analysts believed Saddam might seize a single Kuwaiti oilfield or take two small islands in the Gulf as a lever in the ongoing negotiations.[1] Powell, however, instructed CENTCOM to prepare a two-tiered plan for possible US involvement. The first tier was designed to retaliate against Iraq, while the second was designed to defend against any Iraqi move.[2] According to National Security Advisor Brent Scowcroft, the Saudis put their own forces on alert on 23 July; Saudi Arabia declared to the US that the matter was best resolved by the Arabs themselves.[3]

King Fahd and President Hosni Mubarak of Egypt assured the US that Saddam would not invade, and advised it to avoid inflammatory words and actions.[4] The pan-Arab daily *Al-Hayat* reported on 25 July that the Saudi Council of Ministers had discussed "existing endeavours to encompass any conflict between brothers and to encourage the handling of matters in a brotherly spirit and with an amicable manner".[5] Nevertheless, the Saudi government was concerned about the course of events, and on 21 July Fahd dispatched Saud to Baghdad with a personal message for Saddam urging restraint. According to Simpson, Saud told Saddam: "You are mobilizing your forces and you have a hundred thousand troops on the Kuwaiti border." Saddam replied: "Prince Saud, if I need to invade Kuwait, I don't need a hundred thousand; twenty thousand would be enough. This is just our annual exercise, don't worry about it."[6] Saddam assured the Saudis he had no military intentions. (After the war, Iraq would claim this statement had been conditional on the negotiations making progress, ignoring the fact that it takes two to negotiate.)

On 24 July, Fahd sent Bandar to the UK to meet with British Prime Minister Margaret Thatcher and compare thoughts on Saddam's real intentions. Bandar conveyed Fahd's intentions to stand by Kuwait whatever happened, as doing so was in the direct interests of Saudi Arabia's own security as well.[7]

Random House, 1995), p. 460.
1. Woodward, *The Commanders*, pp. 207–8.
2. Ibid., p. 209.
3. George H. W. Bush and Brent Scowcroft, *A World Transformed: The Collapse of the Soviet Empire, the Unification of Germany, Tiananmen Square, the Gulf War* (New York: Alfred A. Knopf, 1998), p. 309.
4. *The New York Times*, 23 September 1990.
5. *Al-Hayat*, 25 July 1990.
6. Simpson, *The Prince*, p. 191.
7. Alan Munro, *Arab Storm: Politics and Diplomacy Behind the Gulf War* (London: I. B. Tauris, 2006), pp. 22–3.

At the same time, Mubarak went to Baghdad and Kuwait to try to mediate the dispute, and was informed by Saddam that the troop movement was merely designed to scare the Kuwaitis. Mubarak suggested that both sides send delegations to Saudi Arabia to try to resolve their differences without violence, and Saddam accepted this proposal.[1] According to *Al-Hayat* Mubarak said he hoped his efforts would lead to a resolution of the conflict, uniting the Arabs, and also related ideas that had been put forward for the settlement of the dispute. These included:

1. Stopping the media campaigns and threats of war;
2. Containing the conflict in Arab hands;
3. Arranging a meeting between the two sides, with Egypt and Saudi Arabia present;
4. Postponing discussion of the border dispute.[2]

According to Scowcroft, Bandar informed Bush that his government and the Arab states were pleased with Mubarak's mission, and that Saudi Arabia found the US handling of the situation satisfactory.[3]

Earlier, on 24 July, State Department spokeswoman Margaret Tutwiler had stated: "We do not have any defense treaties with Kuwait, and there are no special defense or security commitments to Kuwait."[4] April Glaspie, the US ambassador to Iraq, met with Saddam the following day. She did not warn him about the concentration of his troops at the Kuwaiti border, but on the contrary informed him that the US did not have an opinion on the dispute between Iraq and Kuwait, and that it did not have a defence treaty with any of the Gulf states.[5] According to Prince Khalid, Saddam had asked Glaspie to deliver a message to Bush. Khalid claimed the message ran something to the effect of: "As you know, I have successfully fought off Iran. But instead of rewarding me, the British and the Kuwaitis are driving me into a corner. Please note that my record on oil is absolutely clean. I have never acted irresponsibly

---

1. *US News and World Report, Triumph Without Victory*, pp. 22–3.
2. *Al-Hayat*, 26 July 1990.
3. Bush and Scowcroft, *A World Transformed*, p. 310.
4. James Ridgeway, *The March to War* (New York: Four Walls Eight Windows, 1991), p. 30.
5. Woodward, *The Commanders*, pp. 211–2.

over oil, and never will. I want our dialogue to continue. I am the man with whom you should do business in this region."[1]

There has been speculation, especially in the Middle East, that the US deliberately led Saddam into a trap, and that these statements were part of that design. It has been said that the US motive was to destroy Saddam's military capabilities and force Saudi Arabia and other Gulf states to accept a US military presence in their territories out of fear of Saddam. Scowcroft defends the pre-invasion US position, explaining that the US had warned against belligerent behaviour and had also stated that it would stand by its friends in the region. He argues that if the US had been more aggressive, and if Saddam had invaded, then the US would have been accused of provocation; he also claims that Washington had made no threats to intervene because its friends in the region had advised it not to do so; in addition, it required regional support for whatever action it might have chosen to take.[2]

After the Kuwaitis had declared themselves ready to attend the meeting in Saudi Arabia, Fahd sent Saud to Baghdad on 28 July. Saud secured Iraq's agreement to attend. According to Simpson, Saud asked Saddam about his intentions. This offended Saddam, who took Saud to task: "Prince Saud, if you were not from Saudi Arabia, I would not receive you. How can you doubt my word? I gave my word of honour to King Fahd not to make a military move to scare the Kuwaitis. So don't even think about it."[3] As Munro notes, Saud indicated that Kuwait was prepared to come up with some sort of financial offer, and that the Saudis were also ready to help, as the Kingdom's priority was to ease Iraq's aggressive mood.[4]

Meanwhile, Kuwaiti Crown Prince Sheikh Sa'd Al Sabah stated that Kuwait would not bow to "intimidation, threat, and extortion".[5] *Al-Hayat* also reported an Iraqi official as saying that the meeting would be a "preparatory and protocol meeting", adding: "It is essential for the Kuwaiti Crown Prince to know that whoever comes to meet with Iraq should be prepared to remove the harm and aggression that has been inflicted on Iraq, and be responsive to Iraq's legitimate rights."[6]

1. Sultan, *Desert Warrior*, p. 162.
2. Bush and Scowcroft, *A World Transformed*, p. 313.
3. Simpson, *The Prince*, pp. 194–5.
4. Munro, *Arab Storm*, pp. 29–31.
5. *Al-Hayat*, 26 July 1990.
6. Ibid., 28–29 July 1990.

Evidently, Iraq was bidding for pan-Arab leadership, believing that its power potential entitled it to this status. Kuwait, apparently with US encouragement, seemed to provoke rather than conciliate its powerful neighbour.

On the day of the meeting, the Iraqi government newspaper *Al-Jumhuriyah* had reported: "Iraq is attending the Jeddah meeting to regain its rights, not to listen to brotherhood and solidarity talk." *Al-Hayat* reported on 1 August that US Assistant Secretary of State for Near Eastern Affairs John Kelly had declared: "The US intends to offer all it can to assist its friends in the Gulf when they are confronting threats, and the US is determined to preserve stability there."[1] The US was able to use the region's economic failures and conflicts to contain attempts to challenge its hegemony. It could be said that Washington only needed the collapse of Soviet power to restore many features of the imperialist age.

The meeting having been postponed for a day, the two delegations arrived in Jeddah on 31 July. The Kuwaiti side was headed by Crown Prince Al Sabah, and the Iraqi side by Izzat Ibrahim al-Douri, Vice-Chairman of the Revolutionary Command Council. In effect, the meeting failed before it had even started; al-Douri termed it a protocol meeting, and continued to insist that the Iraqi demands be accepted without debate. He also claimed to be suffering from a headache, and proposed a second meeting to be held in Baghdad on 6 August.

At this point Saudi Arabia took the unusual step of issuing a disclaimer concerning the Kingdom's role in the meeting: "The government of Saudi Arabia ... would like to clarify that the role undertaken by the Kingdom of Saudi Arabia in the meeting of brothers has been confined to providing a cordial atmosphere between the two sides, without any participation in the closed-door bilateral meeting between the representatives of the two countries."[2]

At the Pentagon on 1 August, Schwarzkopf delivered his scheduled biannual briefing to the Joint Chiefs. It focused on the disposition of the Iraqi military and presented satellite photos that were only a day or so old. In updating Plan 1002-90, Schwarzkopf's strategists had prepared a comprehensive response to Iraqi troop movements, and had come up with four immediate options to deter Saddam. The first was to redeploy the USS *Independence* carrier-battle group in the Gulf; the second was to move more B-52 bombers into the

---

1. Ibid., 1 August 1990.
2. Saudi Press Agency, *The Echoes of the Saudi Position During the Events of the Arab Gulf, 1990–1991* (Riyadh, KSA), pp. 12–5.

strategic US base at Diego Garcia in the Indian Ocean; the third, to move five of the maritime pre-positioning ships into a holding pattern off Oman or even into the Gulf. The fourth option was to move a wing of F-15 fighters over to Saudi Arabia.[1]

On the eve of Iraq's invasion of Kuwait on 2 August, according to Secretary of State James Baker, Iranian President Hashemi Rafsanjani received a personal message from Saddam expressing Iraq's intention to live in peace with Iran on "our 840-kilometre seacoast". This new Iraqi frontier being described extended to the UAE, and included Saudi Arabia's Gulf coast.[2]

The early hours of 2 August witnessed the army of an Arab country invading an Arab neighbour. The decision to invade was bold, dramatic and decisive. There was no ambiguity about it, except as to how far it would go. It represented a strategically consequential move on the part of Iraq that presented Arab and Western states with stark and serious choices. According to General Khalid, the Saudis, in evaluating potential threats to its Eastern Province, had never anticipated a land attack from its northern Arab neighbour. As it took into account only the possible threats of air and naval attacks that might come from Iran across the Gulf, the northern border remained but lightly defended.[3]

When news of the invasion reached Fahd, he did not believe it at first. He tried to telephone Saddam, but was told the Iraqi leader could not be reached. According to *Al-Sharq al-Awsat*, Saddam's assistants told the king: "The President is not in his office." The newspaper reported over a decade later that Saddam had admitted a year or so afterwards to having, in fact, been available – but he had not answered Fahd's call because he knew the king would have asked him to withdraw from Kuwait, "and this was what I didn't want to hear."[4] Finally, after many attempts, Fahd managed to speak with Saddam, who assured the king that there was nothing to worry about, and that he was sending al-Douri to explain the situation.

Al-Douri went to Jeddah on the afternoon of 3 August. He insisted that the status of Kuwait had now been rectified, and that he wished only to assure the king about the safety of Saudi Arabia. However, al-Douri's visit,

---

1. *US News and World Report, Triumph Without Victory*, pp. 33–4.
2. James A. Baker III, with Thomas M. De Frank, *The Politics of Diplomacy: Revolution, War and Peace, 1989–1992* (New York: G. P. Putnam's Sons, 1995), p. 300, note.
3. Sultan, *Desert Warrior*, pp. 8–9.
4. *Al-Sharq al-Awsat*, 30 July 2004.

along with two days of telephoning and consultations with Arab and foreign leaders, convinced King Fahd that Saddam meant to stay in Kuwait, and that no Arab force could expel him.[1]

Meanwhile, Bush issued a statement condemning the invasion and called for "the immediate and unconditional withdrawal of all Iraqi forces".[2] During an NSC meeting on 2 August, CIA director William H. Webster informed Bush that the Iraqi forces in Kuwait were being resupplied and reorganized, and that they could continue their march to Saudi Arabia with ease. Addressing the meeting, Schwarzkopf pointed out that the US had only two possible responses. The first involved retaliatory air strikes, which would be limited and punitive; the second involved the execution of Plan 1002-90 for the defence of Saudi Arabia. This would require between 100,000 and 200,000 military personnel, and would take months to execute; it also meant that Saudi Arabia would need to allow the US to establish a series of bases.[3] During the meeting, Defense Secretary Richard Cheney warned: "Saudi Arabia and others will cut and run if we are weak." Powell wondered if the US should declare Saudi Arabia a vital interest.[4] However, no decisions were taken just then, as the president needed time to consult with other world leaders.

In the early hours of the invasion, the Kuwaiti government requested US military assistance through the US embassy in Kuwait – even though the request was by now more than a little late.[5] Bush wanted the UN Security Council to denounce Iraq as soon as possible. He and Baker were convinced that UN action would send a strong and unambiguous message. The UN duly issued Resolution 660, which declared that, under Articles 39 and 40 of the UN Charter, the Security Council:

1. Denounced the Iraqi invasion of Kuwait;
2. Demanded that Iraq pull back its forces entirely and without any conditions to the locations from which they had been deployed on 1 August 1990;

---

1. Sultan, *Desert Warrior*, pp. 17–8.
2. Woodward, *The Commanders*, p. 223.
3. Ibid., pp. 224–8.
4. Bush and Scowcroft, *A World Transformed*, p. 317.
5. *US News and World Report, Triumph Without Victory*, p. 36.

3. Called on Iraq and Kuwait immediately to begin intensive negotiation.[1]

There were fourteen votes for the resolution, no votes against and one abstention (Yemen).[2]

Bush telephoned Mubarak and King Hussein, both of whom told the US president that they were working to find an Arab solution. Later, Bush talked to an agitated Fahd, who explained how Saddam had assured him that he "had no interest in attacking Kuwait". This, Fahd maintained, was "because he [Saddam] is conceited. He doesn't realize that the implications of his actions are upsetting the world order ... He is following Hitler in creating world problems – with a difference: one was conceited and one is both conceited and crazy. I believe nothing will work with Saddam but the use of force." Fahd also told Bush of his telephone conversation with Saddam: "I asked him to withdraw from Kuwait now, and that we would not consider any [imposed] regime to be representative of Kuwaiti public opinion." He further urged, to Bush: "Mr President, this is a matter that is extremely serious and grave. It involves a principle that can't be approved or condoned by any reasonable principle or moral." The king concluded the call by saying: "I hope these matters can be resolved peacefully ... if not, Saddam must be taught a lesson he will not forget for the rest of his life – if he remains alive."[3]

Bush told Prince Bandar he feared the Saudis' request for US assistance would come too late, and that the US would not be able to help. When Bandar alluded to the unarmed F-15s sent by the Carter administration in the last days of the Shah's regime in 1979, Bush was offended: "I give my word of honor," he told Bandar. "I will see this through with you."[4] For the Saudis, the prospect of the US stirring up local opposition and then "cutting and running", as had happened in 1984 with Reagan's withdrawal under fire from Lebanon, was a distinct possibility.[5] To convince the Kingdom that the US could be a reliable partner, Bush wanted Bandar to view top-secret satellite photos and the US defence plans. Bandar duly went to the Pentagon and was shown the

---

1. United Nations Security Council Resolution 660, 1990.
2. Saudi Press Agency, *The Echoes of the Saudi Position During the Events of the Arab Gulf, 1990–1991*, p. 20.
3. Bush and Scowcroft, *A World Transformed*, pp. 320–1.
4. Woodward, *The Commanders*, pp. 240–1.
5. Sultan, *Desert Warrior*, p. 26.

The Later Fahd Legacy (1990-2001)

latest images, which showed that the Iraqis were on Saudi Arabia's doorstep. When Cheney expressed US willingness to help, Bandar asked, again: "Like Jimmy Carter did?"

Powell and Cheney reassured him that this time the US meant business. Bandar then enquired about the size of US assistance. "All told," Powell replied, "about one hundred thousand troops, for starters."[1] If this kind of force were in place, Bandar said, the Kingdom would be able to take such aggressive action as shutting down the Iraqi oil pipeline. He affirmed that there had been three serious border incursions by the Iraqis on 4 and 5 August, and that after the third incursion the Saudis had been unable to reach any Iraqi authority on the telephone hotline that had been set up between the two countries.[2]

Bush saw the invasion as a challenge to US post-Cold War leadership, and was clear in his intention that it would not be allowed to stand. The overriding reason was Washington's belief that Saddam's intentions went far beyond taking over Kuwait. According to Scowcroft, Deputy Secretary of State Lawrence Eagleburger asserted during an NSC meeting on 3 August that Saudi Arabia would be the next target for Saddam. Cheney argued: "If he [Saddam] does not take it [Saudi Arabia] physically, with his new wealth he will still have an impact and will be able to acquire new weapons. The problem will get worse, not better."[3] With an attack on Saudi Arabia, Saddam would thus have gained control over a tremendous amount of the world's oil supply.

The question now was whether the Saudis would accept a sizeable US military presence, such as that called for by Plan 1002-90. When Bush telephoned Fahd on 4 August and was asked by the king for a technical team to brief him, Bush promised to send such a team immediately.[4] *Al-Hayat* reported on 5 August that Bush had said: "The safety and freedom of Saudi Arabia is very important to the US, and I made this clear to King Fahd in my long conversation with him ... If Saudi Arabia asks for assistance from the US, I will respond with any possible means. The matter is as grave as that."[5]

On 6 August, the five permanent members of the Security Council agreed to support draft Resolution 661, which spelled out the terms of economic and

---

1. Powell, *My American Journey*, p. 465.
2. Woodward, *The Commanders*, p. 244.
3. Bush and Scowcroft, *A World Transformed*, p. 321-4.
4. *US News and World Report, Triumph Without Victory*, pp. 72-4.
5. *Al-Hayat*, 5 August 1990.

military embargo. The entire Council vote was near-unanimous, with only Yemen and Cuba abstaining.[1]

US officials now decided to send Fahd an offer he could not refuse. At the same time, it worried about the consequences if the technical team failed. If that happened, it would effectively be sending Saddam an open invitation to invade.

In Saudi Arabia, Fahd ordered scouts into Kuwait to see whether they could locate the Iraqi forces said to be massed on the Saudi border. According to Woodward, the scouts reported on their return that there were no Iraqi troops close to the border. Bandar argued that the fact of there being some doubt in itself created a strong reason to receive the US team and to listen to their presentation, with which Fahd agreed.[2] Woodward's account, however, is inconsistent with that given by General Khalid, who claimed that a two-star Saudi general who had spent three days inside Kuwait and had even travelled right up to Safwan, in southern Iraq, had reported that Saddam had far more troops than he needed and was steadily reinforcing his army.[3]

On 6 August, Fahd met the US team, led by Cheney, who emphasized the two-pronged strategy of sanctions plus a defensive force for Saudi Arabia. Fahd was keen to see the satellite photos, and was impressed by the images and by the size of the Iraqi forces. "If this invasion of Kuwait is not countered," Cheney told the king, "the consequences for the Kingdom of Saudi Arabia will be grave." He pointed out that if US forces were going to arrive, they would have to begin doing so immediately, and concluded by saying that once the threat had vanished, the US forces would leave. An animated conversation then broke out in Arabic between the Saudis. Crown Prince 'Abdullah bin 'Abdul 'Aziz was concerned that no internal consensus had been built among key tribal and religious leaders that could sustain such a controversial decision, and wanted more time to consider an appropriate response from Saudi Arabia.

However, with Iraqi troops at his doorstep, Fahd did not have the luxury of time to build such a consensus.[4] He therefore approved the US deployment but demanded that it would not constitute a permanent presence, and that

1. *US News and World Report, Triumph Without Victory*, pp. 81–2.
2. Woodward, *The Commanders*, pp. 258–9.
3. Sultan, *Desert Warrior*, p. 11.
4. Association for Diplomatic Studies and Training (ADST), *Frontline Diplomacy: The US Foreign Affairs Oral History* (Arlington, VA: ADST, 2000) (specifically the oral history of former US Ambassador to Saudi Arabia Chas Freeman).

sensitivity would be shown toward the customs of the country. Cheney offered repeated assurances that the US forces would leave when asked, and that they would maintain a discreet presence.[1] The US was the only country with sufficient power projection capability to deter Iraq and provide Saudi Arabia with security.

According to Khalid, the decision of the king to request the US presence was the result of a long-term consensus among the royal family that if the security of the Kingdom was threatened, and if Saudi forces were not capable of defending it, then they would not hesitate to request assistance from any friendly nation – including the US.[2] Moreover, even if the king did not expect Iraq to invade his country, he needed to prepare for the worst-case scenario. A powerful Iraq, encompassing an occupied Kuwait, would dominate the Gulf; over the long term Saddam would then be in a position to intimidate Saudi Arabia.[3]

The purpose for the US in deploying troops was to retain control of Gulf oil reserves central to Western economies. As Under-Secretary of Defense Paul Wolfowitz stated in his testimony to Congress: "The main reason American forces are in the Persian Gulf region is to make sure that no hostile power, and particularly not this brutal Iraqi dictatorship, is allowed to dominate the energy supplies that are the lifeblood of the world economy."[4]

Furthermore, within the wider context of Washington's global strategy, the Iraqi invasion was a challenge to the world order that the US sought to reshape and defend. The US required an opportunity to show the world that its military power was still viable and indeed essential, and to demonstrate its resolve to protect its regional clients. Finally, the US military-industrial complex needed a new mission to justify continued spending. The invasion also constituted a perfect opportunity to banish the "Vietnam syndrome".[5]

---

1. Cohen and Gatti, *In the Eye of the Storm*, p. 190.
2. Sultan, *Desert Warrior*, p. 24.
3. Raymond Hinnebusch, *The International Politics of the Middle East* (Manchester, UK: Manchester University Press, 2003), pp. 212–3.
4. US Congress, House of Representatives, Committee on Foreign Affairs, Subcommittees on Arms Control, International Security and Science, and on Europe and the Middle East, "Proposed Sales to Saudi Arabia in Association with the Conduct of Operation Desert Storm", 101st Cong., 2nd sess., 31 October 1990, p. 32.
5. Hinnebusch, *The International Politics of the Middle East*, pp. 215–7.

There are several rationales sometimes given for the invasion. First, in the words of Hinnebusch:

> [After the rise of the Ba'thists to power] an ideological thrust was given to the notion that the arena of political competition was not within a single state, but was a contest for pan-Arab leadership; once they consolidated the state at home, they started to act on these ambitions in the region.[1]

Second, according to Frankel, was the British attempt to limit Iraq's access and power projection into the Gulf, which had forced Iraq to accept unfair demarcation of its southern and southeastern borders with Iran and Kuwait. This British action was contested by successive Iraqi rulers.[2] Third, by the end of the Iran-Iraq war, Iraq was militarily strong enough to pursue an activist foreign policy against its weaker neighbours. Fourth concerns Iraq's massive build-up of military power which, being in excess of its own substantial economic base, had bankrupted the country. Saddam hoped, therefore, to slash Iraq's foreign debt by adding Kuwait's wealth, and to launch the ambitious reconstruction programme he had promised.[3] Fifth, the decision to invade Kuwait might have been based on the assumption that the major Arab states – Egypt, Syria and especially Saudi Arabia – were more likely to prefer working out a coordinated Arab response, thus forestalling decisive action and giving Saddam a better chance of either getting away with his Kuwaiti land grab or installing a puppet regime.[4] Finally, Saddam might have perceived the US approach as encouragement: Washington's double-edged, confused policy gave Saddam no hint that any decisive action would be taken if Iraq invaded Kuwait.[5]

On 2 and 9 August, Bush signed executive orders freezing Kuwaiti and Iraqi assets in the US and prohibiting transactions with Iraq and Kuwait.

On 9 August Fahd gave a speech in which he underlined the grave situation facing the Arab nation, and explained his decision to invite Arab and other

---

1. Ibid., pp. 208–9.
2. Glenn Frankel, "Lines in the Sand", in Micah Sifry and Christopher Cerf, eds, *The Gulf War Reader* (New York: Times Books, 1991), pp. 17–8.
3. Karsh and Rautsi, *Saddam Hussein*, p. 213.
4. Michael Barnett, "Institutions, Roles, and Disorder: The Case of the Arab state", *International Studies Quarterly* 37 (1993), pp. 271–96.
5. Janice G. Stein, "Deterrence and Compellence in the Gulf, 1990–91: A Failed or Impossible Task?" *International Security*, vol. 71, no. 2 (1992), p. 149.

The Later Fahd Legacy (1990–2001)

friendly forces into the Kingdom. He declared: "Following this sorrowful incident, Iraq massed a big force on the Kingdom's border ... The Kingdom expressed its welcome to the participation of the brotherly Arab and friendly forces. In response to this, the US, Britain and other countries sent air and land forces to support the Kingdom's armed forces."[1] On the same day, Bush notified Congress of his decision to deploy US forces in response to the Saudi request.

Al-Ahram reported on 11 August that King Fahd had drawn attention to the fact that Iraq had invaded Kuwait, despite having denied any intention of doing so. Saddam, the king said, "had informed President Mubarak, and informed us through Prince Saud Al-Faisal that they were not thinking of any aggressive act against Kuwait". He added: "An attempt was organized to return things to their natural place, and to communicate to find a just solution, but we were unable to achieve it."[2] According to *Al-Sharq al-Awsat*, Bandar blamed Saddam for the deterioration of the situation: "What Saddam has done is disgraceful and does not stem from Arabism or Islam." He indicated that "the brotherly and friendly forces" were placed "at Saudi Arabia's disposal and will leave at the Kingdom's request".[3]

On 12 August, Bandar stated: "We cannot risk our sacred shrines, our independence and our people's dignity by falling victim to such aggression." He pointed out that while Saddam was now criticizing the Kingdom for the support it was receiving from the US and others to protect its territory, "he had asked the Kingdom to support him and to facilitate US assistance every time he had a problem during the Iran-Iraq war, and considered this a patriotic act."[4]

Al-Sharq al-Awsat also reported Fahd's statement on 14 August: "We are a country that will not initiate aggression, but we will make it impossible to attack us ... how can we believe that Saddam has no intention of attacking the Kingdom, when he has broken his promise and betrayed his pledge?"[5]

On 16 August Princes Saud and Bandar met President Bush. According to the president, Saud made it clear that the Kingdom wanted the US to use

---

1. Saudi Press Agency, 9 August 1990.
2. *Al-Ahram*, 11 August 1990.
3. *Al-Sharq al-Awsat*, 11 August 1990.
4. *Ukaz*, 12 August 1990.
5. *Al-Sharq al-Awsat*, 14 August 1990.

force as early as possible.[1] On 19 August Saud said: "The wound is profound, and the disaster so great." He pointed out that Arabs had called on the world to help the dispossessed Palestinians, and that now Arabs had been attacked by fellow Arabs. He added: "Iraq wants an Arab solution but will not apply the Arab League Charter that stands clearly against any Arab aggression toward another Arab country."[2] *Al-Sharq al-Awsat* also reported Saud as saying that Saudi Arabia's shortfall in military readiness to confront Iraq by itself stemmed from the fact that the Kingdom had provided so much help to Iraq in its war against Iran.[3]

On 20 August, Bush signed National Security Directive 45, outlining US interests in the Gulf. These included access to oil and the security and stability of key friendly states in the region. The directive set out four demands that would guide US policy during the crisis:

1. The immediate, complete and unconditional withdrawal of all Iraqi forces from Kuwait;
2. The restoration of the legitimate government of Kuwait;
3. A commitment to protect Saudi Arabia and the other Gulf states;
4. Protection for US citizens abroad.

By mid-August, the US-Saudi Joint Directorate of Planning had been briefed on the US's unilateral plan to defend Saudi Arabia. The Saudis wanted US forces to enter the country through ports much further north (Ras Mishab and Al Khafji), and to establish defences along the northern Saudi border – sparking disagreement between Washington and Riyadh as a result of divergent military objectives. The US focused on the critical ports and oil facilities, whereas Saudi Arabia wanted to protect all territory and population centres in the Kingdom. Schwarzkopf met with Saudi military leaders on several occasions to ensure that coalition decision-makers understood the risk of a stationary defence along the border was unnecessary and unacceptable, particularly at a time when force ratios favoured Iraq so dramatically.

Command and control of coalition forces were eventually established with

---

1. Bush and Scowcroft, *A World Transformed*, p. 349.
2. *Ukaz*, 19 August 1990.
3. *Al-Sharq al-Awsat*, 19 August 1990.

separate but parallel lines of authority, with US and Saudi forces remaining under their respective national command authorities. Earlier, on 9 August, Fahd had appointed Khalid as Joint Forces Commander. According to Khalid, the US initially offered to deploy its forces, and Saudi Arabia simply agreed. No formal instruments were exchanged, nor were any detailed guidelines laid down. A few days later Khalid met the CENTCOM Army commander, Lieutenant General John Yeosock, and they invented a body known as the C3IC (Coalition Coordination Communications and Integration Cell). It became responsible for resolving all problems related to logistics, intelligence sharing, training, allocation of firing ranges and so on. Eventually it was split into ground, air, naval, logistics, special operations and intelligence sections.[1]

Later, after Schwarzkopf arrived in Saudi Arabia on 26 August, an arrangement was established for parallel lines of authority. This structure defined the relations between Khalid and Schwarzkopf. Khalid's powers were restricted to the area of responsibility under the Joint Forces Command inside Saudi Arabia. As agreed, the Saudi lieutenant general became the principal contact between incoming Arab and other friendly forces and the Saudi authorities. He claimed that a mutual agreement on the concept of the operation, the employment of forces, responsibilities of the various national contingents, rules of engagement, training schedules and various other things needed to be obtained.[2]

On 28 August Prince Sultan met Schwarzkopf, who reassured him, promising him: "He [Saddam] will suffer the greatest losses in the history of warfare." Sultan told Schwarzkopf: "That is not what I want to see. I have no wish to damage Iraq." He went on to say that, if Saddam persisted in his position, "then we will do everything in our power to stop him." According to Khalid, this outlook reflected the Saudis' dilemma: they needed the US to confront Saddam, but regretted having to take up arms against an Arab state.[3]

By the first week of September the initial surge of deployment had ended, and Schwarzkopf's minimum deterrent force of 40,000 soldiers was in place. Plan 1002-90 was becoming a reality in the sands of the Saudi desert.[4] Bush was therefore able to proclaim, in an address before the US Congress on 11

---

1. Sultan, *Desert Warrior*, pp. 28–35.
2. Ibid., pp. 194–5.
3. Ibid., pp. 189–90.
4. *US News and World Report, Triumph Without Victory*, p. 147.

September: "Iraq will not be permitted to annex Kuwait. That's not a threat, that's not a boast, it's just the way it's going to be."[1]

During the next few weeks, diplomatic efforts by Bush and Baker brought several European and Arab countries into a rapidly expanding coalition against Iraq. In time, this coalition would come to incorporate thirty-three countries.[2]

By now, most of Bush's close advisors were beginning to argue that even if the US and its allies succeeded in defending Saudi Arabia and forcing Iraq out of Kuwait by employing economic sanctions, Saddam would be left in Baghdad with a million-man army and with chemical and biological weapons intact. They maintained that the administration's objective should be altered to encompass the eradication of Saddam's military machine, and especially his weapons of mass destruction.[3] King Fahd, speaking on 29 September, called on Saddam to resolve the issue peacefully: "President Saddam Hussein must override the obstacles just as he did with Iran."[4]

By 1 October, Saddam's forces in Kuwait numbered over 430,000, an indication of his intention to stay. Schwarzkopf saw a very narrow window within which an offensive operation could be conducted in January and February 1991, and a political decision had to be made by the end of October.[5]

During a meeting on 30 October attended by Bush, Cheney, Baker, Powell and Scowcroft, the president decided to double the number of US forces in Saudi Arabia to over 400,000 and to begin the diplomatic drive to obtain the passage of Security Council Resolution No. 678. The resolution, achieved on 29 November, gave Saddam an ultimatum to leave Kuwait by 15 January 1991 or face eviction. US policy had moved away from simply defending Saudi Arabia to actively liberating Kuwait by military means, and was thus clearly based on preventing Iraq from emerging as a regional hegemon and to maintaining its own hegemony in the Gulf and in the wider Middle East. Ground forces doubled, the number of tanks tripled, air power was boosted by 30 percent and the naval force also doubled.[6]

According to Schwarzkopf, Baker met Fahd in Saudi Arabia to explain

---

1. Bush and Scowcroft, *A World Transformed*, p. 371.
2. Cohen and Gatti, *In the Eye of the Storm*, p. 207.
3. *US News and World Report, Triumph Without Victory*, p. 140.
4. *Ukaz*, 30 September 1990.
5. Cohen and Gatti, *In the Eye of the Storm*, pp. 229–30.
6. Schwarzkopf, *It Doesn't Take a Hero*, p. 376.

the US decision to prepare an offensive that would be launched from the Kingdom. Fahd replied: "While we all still want peace, if we must go to war, Saudi Arabia's armed forces will fight side by side with yours." During this meeting, Baker mentioned that Israeli involvement might occur as the result of an Iraqi attack. Fahd advised against this, but indicated that if Israel was attacked and decided to defend itself, Saudi armed forces would continue to fight by the side of the US.[1]

On 10 November Schwarzkopf briefed his commanders on the offensive plan known as "Operation Desert Storm". The concept for "Desert Storm" was based on a four-phased operation aimed at the destruction of Iraq's centres of gravity: leadership; chemical, biological and other weapons; ballistic missiles; and the Republican Guard. Phase I would include extensive air attacks against Iraq from coalition forces, with the objective being to destroy Iraq's ability to command and control, eliminate its chemical and biological capabilities and neutralize other strategic targets. In Phase II, the air campaign would progressively shift to the Kuwaiti theatre of operation (KTO) to establish air supremacy there and to isolate the battlefield by cutting supply lines and blocking escape routes. In Phase III, the battlefield would be prepared by air and artillery attacks, focused on reducing the effectiveness of Iraqi defences in the KTO. In Phase IV, multi-axis ground, naval and air attacks would be initiated.

In late November and early December, Schwarzkopf personally briefed the military and civilian leadership of Saudi Arabia about "Operation Desert Storm".

On 29 November, the day the UN passed SC Resolution 678, Bush announced his readiness to receive Aziz in Washington as well as Baker's willingness to go to Baghdad to meet with Saddam at a mutually convenient time between 15 December and 15 January. This was a necessary step to prove to Congress and to the American public that Bush was willing to exhaust all diplomatic alternatives before declaring war. According to Woodward, the Saudis were displeased that the US had failed to consult the Kingdom regarding this decision, and believed the contacts would send the wrong message to Saddam.[2] Simpson noted that both Fahd and Bandar were afraid that Saddam would accept the UN resolution and withdraw his forces from Kuwait and

---

1. Ibid., pp. 372–3.
2. Woodward, *The Commanders*, pp. 335–6.

claimed that, in Bandar's view, Saddam might well wait at the Kuwaiti border to attack again once the coalition forces had left.[1]

According to the US's Middle East envoy, Dennis Ross, Bandar was very nervous about the president's initiative. He told Ross, before the US delegation had left for Geneva to meet Aziz: "Jimmy Baker is too good at producing deals; don't let him do one that we will all regret."[2] However, on 3 December, *Al-Riyadh* reported an official Saudi statement: "The Kingdom expresses its satisfaction at President Bush's announcement, which is seen as a positive step if a peaceful solution to this dangerous crisis is to be achieved."[3]

On 4 January 1991, a statement by the Iraqis announced that Aziz had agreed to meet Baker, and proposed that the meeting should take place on 9 January in Geneva. This meeting was a complete failure, with Aziz refusing to accept a letter for Saddam from Bush[4] in which Bush declared: "What is at issue here is not the future of Kuwait – it will be free, its government will be restored – but rather the future of Iraq. This choice is yours to make."[5]

On 15 January, Bush signed National Security Directive 54. It envisaged military actions, authorized by various UN resolutions, to enforce Iraq's withdrawal from Kuwait. The directive also noted that the economic sanctions imposed on Iraq had had "a measurable impact upon Iraq's economy but have not accomplished the intended objective of ending Iraq's occupation of Kuwait".[6]

On 17 January, coalition aircraft attacked Iraqi units in Iraq and Kuwait, initiating the air campaign of "Operation Desert Storm". On 24 February, after thirty-nine days of the most lethal and intensive air attack in the history of warfare, the ground offensive was initiated. On 28 February, only 100 hours after the campaign had begun, Bush determined that "Operation Desert Storm"'s objectives had been met and ordered a cessation of hostilities, bringing military operations to an official close.

Legitimate military and political factors prevented the pursuit of a policy

---

1. Simpson, *The Prince*, p. 236.
2. Dennis Ross, *The Missing Peace: The Inside Story of the Fight for Middle East Peace* (New York: Farrar, Straus and Giroux, 2004), p. 74.
3. *Al-Riyadh*, 3 December 1990.
4. Cohen and Gatti, *In the Eye of the Storm*, p. 253.
5. PPP, George Bush, 1991, Book I, 1 January–30 June 1991 (Washington, DC: US Government Printing Office, 1992), pp. 36–7.
6. NSA, George Bush, National Security Directive 54, "Responding to Iraqi Aggression in the Gulf", 15 January 1991.

aimed at dislodging Saddam from his control over Iraq. The US did not want to defeat Iraq absolutely and risk the fragmentation of the state to the benefit of Iran. Moreover, if the war had been taken deeper into Iraq, the coalition might have fractured. Finally, the US feared the risk of greater American casualties by shifting fighting from the desert to the cities.[1]

The war ended with the liberation of Kuwait, but the coalition did not seek an unconditional surrender. Nor were there any war-crime trials, the significance of which Prince Khalid emphasized, contending that it meant there was no comprehensive settlement because no document of any sort had been signed by the Iraqis.[2] He noted that the coalition's victory did not banish all regional threats, nor did it guarantee the long-term security of the Gulf. According to Simpson, Bandar also claimed that the humanitarian ceasefire had resulted in something less than a satisfactory victory, arguing that even though the war was won, Saddam was still in power. He was also unhappy about the timing of the ceasefire, later stating: "I believe that, militarily, we stopped too soon, and I believe politically that we did the right thing. Although, now, two years later, I think even politically it would have paid off had we continued that war."[3]

The disagreement over how the war ended reflects the difference in objectives between the two sides. Saudi Arabia was primarily motivated by its desire to eliminate Saddam's threat to the Kingdom, while the US was worried about Iran's gains from the total destruction of Iraq's military capabilities and also needed Saddam's ever-present threat to justify its military presence in the area.

Most puzzling is the question of why Saddam failed to take advantage of the peace efforts that had provided him with a means to extricate Iraq from the onset of war. He could have used negotiation to achieve one of his purposes – namely to split the coalition.

The Gulf War demonstrated the value of pre-positioning military equipment as well as building up the facilities of friendly countries in the event of regional military contingency. However, it opened the region up to much greater penetration from outside, and shifted regional balance of power to the advantage of the non-Arab peripheries. In the view of some structuralists, the Gulf War was used to demonstrate the continuing indispensability of US

---

1. *The Washington Post,* 12 January 1992.
2. Sultan, *Desert Warrior,* p. 437.
3. Simpson, *The Prince,* p. 233.

hegemony for protecting the control of oil by the world capitalist core against Third World challenges, and to restore the US protectorate over global oil resources.

The Madrid Peace Conference

The end of the Gulf War strengthened Saudi Arabia and other moderate Arabs. The war had also brought the Soviet Union, long a force for trouble in the area, into partnership with the US in seeking peace in the Middle East. It therefore created an unprecedented opportunity to pursue the possibility of peace between Israel and the Arabs. As US envoy Ross observed: "We've just seen an earthquake. We have to move before the earth resettles, because it will, and it never takes long."[1]

During the Kuwait crisis Saddam had linked his invasion of Kuwait with the Arab-Israel conflict. In order to repel Saddam, Baker had repeatedly pledged that as soon as the crisis had been resolved the US would address the Middle East problem.[2] Simpson reported Scowcroft's statement that the US had quietly said to Fahd: "You stick with us here – let's focus on this, after this is over ... We'll give you our private word that we'll move after this is over."[3] In his speech to the UN General Assembly on 1 October 1990, Bush stated that after the unconditional Iraqi withdrawal from Kuwait, there might be an opportunity for "all the states and peoples of the region to settle the conflicts that divide the Arabs from Israel".[4]

In the aftermath of the Gulf War a sense of urgency prevailed. All major governments now emphasized that there was a window of opportunity for peace in the Middle East and elsewhere. The end of the Cold War and the Gulf War had both created a new strategic environment that offered opportunities for greater stability in the region. The end of the Cold War had also averted the need to prevent the Soviets from extending and using their influence in the region to the disadvantage of the US position and the interests of Israel and pro-Western Arab states.

The emerging political conditions of the New World Order – the post-Cold War vision outlined by Bush in his 11 September 1990 speech to Congress

---

1. Baker, *The Politics of Diplomacy*, p. 412.
2. Ibid., p. 414.
3. Simpson, *The Prince*, p. 244.
4. *The New York Times*, 2 October 1990.

– made the resolution of the Palestine-Israel conflict even more imperative. But with Iraq defeated, the PLO and Jordan discredited for having sided with Iraq during the war and Syria struggling to adjust to the loss of Soviet support and to US dominance, Israel emerged with an unusually favourable balance *vis-à-vis* the Arab states. For Israel, peace, if it was to come, had to be essentially on its terms.[1]

The Gulf War had effectively demolished the official Arab consensus on Palestine, eroded Arab solidarity and exposed regime insecurity in the Gulf region. In addition, Arab solidarity against Israel had broken down, thereby eliminating an important source of pressure for Israeli concessions.[2]

As early as autumn 1990 – before the US went to war – Ross had met and held separate discussions with Sergei Tarasenko, Soviet Foreign Minister Eduard A. Shevardnadze's closest advisor, and Eytan Bentsur, Director General of the Israeli foreign ministry. Both urged the US to broaden the scope of its peace efforts beyond creating a dialogue between the Israelis and Palestinians from the Occupied Territories.

The US developed a two-track approach to negotiations: parallel sets of talks between the Israelis and Palestinians from the territories on the one hand, and between Israel and neighbouring Arab states on the other.[3] In order for Israel to agree to negotiations, it had to impose its own diplomatic framework, and duly set a number of conditions that were accepted by Baker, including the following:

1. Israel would only discuss an interim settlement for self-government with the Palestinians; final status talks would begin three years later;
2. The US opening statement at any future peace conference would refrain from delineating any plan for settlement;
3. Participation in negotiations would be limited to Palestinians living in the West Bank and Gaza only.

---

1. Alexander L. George, "The Gulf War's Impact on the International System", in Stanley A. Renshon, ed., *The Political Psychology of the Gulf War: Leaders, Publics, and the Process of Conflict* (Pittsburgh: University of Pittsburgh Press, 1993), pp. 309–12.
2. Yahya Sadowski, "Revolution, Reform or Regression? Arab Political Options in the 1990 Gulf Crisis", *Brookings Review*, vol. 9, no. 1 (winter 1990–91), pp. 17–21.
3. Ross, *The Missing Peace*, pp. 65–6.

Furthermore, Israel wanted the conference to lead immediately to direct negotiations along the two tracks.[1]

The US believed that the Gulf War opened a window of opportunity to end the Middle East conflict, and on 6 March 1991 Bush addressed a joint session of Congress on the cessation of the Gulf War, declaring: "We must do all that we can to close the gap between Israel and the Arab states and between Israelis and Palestinians ... the time has come to put an end to the Arab-Israeli conflict."[2] In order for this opportunity to become reality, the Arabs would have to suspend their economic boycott of Israel and the Israelis would have to freeze Jewish settlement in the Occupied Territories.[3]

With solid backing from the Saudis, Baker sought to start negotiations, taking advantage of the war's outcome – which had so enhanced the position of moderate and conciliatory elements within the Arab world. Bush was prepared to put pressure on Israel by linking financial guarantees for US loans (needed to help the settlement of Soviet Jews in Israel) to the progress of the peace negotiations. The PLO leadership, faced with new realities, yielded to the idea of a team from within the Occupied Territories participating in the negotiations. According to Simpson, Prince Bandar spoke with several renowned Palestinian academics at US universities about the proposed talks, telling them: "Listen, things are going to move in the Middle East, whether you like it or not ... We might talk with Arafat later on, but for the moment he can't be there."[4] At the same time, Saudi Arabia was ready to help mobilize moderate Arab governments and move things forward while the climate for negotiations was favourable.[5]

On 8 March, Baker arrived in Riyadh, where he met King Fahd and put forward the concept of a two-track approach to the negotiations. He also asked whether the Saudis would be prepared to take confidence-building steps, either unilaterally or collectively. According to his own account, Baker

1. Naseer H. Aruri, *Dishonest Broker: The U.S. Role in Israel and Palestine* (Cambridge, MA: South End Press, 2003), pp. 73–4.
2. PPP, George Bush, 1991, pp. 218–19.
3. Glenn Frankel, *Beyond the Promised Land: Jews and Arabs on the Hard Road to a New Israel* (New York: Simon & Schuster, 1994), pp. 288–9.
4. Simpson, *The Prince*, p. 245. These academics were the late Edward Said (professor of history at Columbia University, New York), Walid Khalidi (professor of politics at Harvard University), and the late Professor Hisham Sharabi (from the Contemporary Arab Studies programme at Georgetown University).
5. Munro, *Arab Storm*, pp. 345–6.

assured Fahd that any concession on the king's part would be held in the strictest confidence: "You must trust me enough to tell me what you can do ... and know I won't put it on the table publicly without knowing what you get in return from Israel." Fahd, according to Baker, seemed prepared to adopt a leadership position in the peace process. He informed Baker of his readiness to approve full economic and diplomatic relations with Israel, provided that a homeland was established for the Palestinians, and stated: "I want once and for all to reach a settlement of the Arab-Israeli problem ... Allah might well have desired Saddam's crisis to serve as a springboard from which to solve this greater problem."[1]

It is important to note, however, that the opening of relations with Israel was not unconditional – it depended on what was offered in return. An official statement by the Saudi government on 9 April formally denied reports from Israel that Saudi Arabia was planning to recognize the Jewish state. It said: "Western media agencies have today broadcast a report from Israeli radio alleging that the Kingdom is examining the announcement of its recognition of Israel, and that Prince Saud Al-Faisal the Foreign Minister will arrive in Cairo today to conduct discussions with President Mubarak about the matter." The statement denied the report: "All that is in the report is fabricated and unfounded."[2]

On 10 March, Bandar informed Baker of Fahd's support in principle for the two-track approach, and that the king would consider specific steps, depending on Israel's reaction. Baker cabled Bush to inform him of Fahd's approval, and added: "American standing has never been higher, and the Arabs are impressed enough with the US's ability to deliver on its word to grant us some room to move forward."[3] Fahd sent Bandar to gain the support of Mubarak and Assad for the process. Bandar also informed Ross that he would work with the Palestinians in the territories to come up with possible partners for the negotiations. During his March tour of the Middle East, Baker received the same message from all the other principal leaders in the area: that it was time for a US initiative to solve the Middle East conflict. In Israel he informed Israeli Prime Minister Yitzhak Shamir of the Arabs' readiness for negotiations with Israel, if Israel would negotiate with the Palestinians. He also reported the Arabs' willingness to take confidence-building steps. At the

---

1. Baker, *The Politics of Diplomacy*, pp. 418–9.
2. *Ukaz*, 10 April 1991.
3. Baker, *The Politics of Diplomacy*, p. 420.

same time, Ross met with some leading members of the ruling Likud Party, informing them of the Saudi position.[1]

Shamir did not share Baker's optimism about Arab moderation. He was also worried that, with the Cold War over, the US might shift its position from being Israel's patron and ally to a more neutral stance of honest broker between Arabs and Israelis.[2] The secretary of state returned again to the region in April. After considerable effort on Baker's part, Shamir reluctantly accepted the US initiative, but *Ukaz* reported on 12 April 1991 that Israel had insisted on the exclusion of the PLO from the peace process. Shamir also claimed that Israeli settlements were not linked to the peace negotiations, and pledged to continue building them.[3] Baker used Shamir's acceptance to demonstrate to Fahd and Mubarak the prime minister's readiness to launch the two-track negotiations; both leaders agreed to press Assad. But Assad imposed four conditions, of which the most unacceptable for the US was that the conference be continuous as well as held under the aegis of the UN.[4]

The US tried to forge a compromise between Assad and Shamir, but neither was prepared to budge. To make things worse, Fahd informed Baker during the latter's visit to Saudi Arabia on 21 April that the Saudis would not attend any peace conference. According to Baker, he asked the king for a mild statement in support of peace that he could use to put Shamir on the defensive; but Fahd refused, alleging it would inflame Arab public opinion. Baker reminded the king: "We were there for you. We need you to be there for us. How can we be partners in war but not in peace?" Fahd finally promised to study the matter further and inform Baker. A few days later, according to Baker, the Saudis did issue a bland statement supporting the peace conference. Baker attributed Fahd's reluctance to the absence of Prince Bandar, who at that time was in Megève, France, recuperating from a back injury.[5]

Shamir argued that it showed the Arabs were not prepared to negotiate directly with Israel.[6] In response, Baker came up with a proposal during a ten-hour meeting with Assad in Damascus that the US would guarantee the border between Israel and Syria in both directions after peace. Assad assured

1. Ross, *The Missing Peace*, pp. 68–9.
2. Frankel, *Beyond the Promised Land*, p. 289.
3. *Ukaz*, 12 April 1991.
4. Ross, *The Missing Peace*, p. 71; see also *Ukaz*, 13 April 1991.
5. Baker, *The Politics of Diplomacy*, pp. 452–3.
6. Ross, *The Missing Peace*, p. 72.

Baker that he would consult with the Syrian leadership and come back to the secretary. On 3 May Assad conveyed his acceptance.[1]

To reduce Shamir's options for escape, Ross then went to see Bandar and warned him of the danger that the moment for pursuing Arab-Israeli peace could be lost; nor would anyone be able to understand why Saudi Arabia was now doing nothing for peace. During this meeting, Ross submitted a twofold proposal. The GCC, represented by its Secretary General, would attend the peace talks – not as a participant, but as an observer. Following the conference, which would initiate bilateral negotiations, it would attend subsequent multilateral talks as a participant. Bandar liked this idea and assured Ross he would work on it. To ensure that Baker had an edge over Shamir when they met, Ross also asked for the announcement to be made on the eve of their next trip to the region.[2]

Bandar met Bush and Baker on 7 May. According to Baker, the US president asked the prince to pass Washington's request on to King Fahd, and also requested that Saudi Arabia announce its participation in multilateral working groups on regional issues. Bush also wanted Fahd to state publicly that Saudi Arabia would suspend the state of belligerence against Israel in exchange for Israel's halting of settlement activity. The president told Bandar: "We've got to get Saudi Arabia leaning forward." When Bandar consulted the king, however, he agreed only to the announcement and to participation in multilateral talks.[3] On 12 May, *Al-Hayat* reported a statement by the chairman of the GCC: "If invited, the GCC is willing to participate as an observer in the proposed peace conference."[4]

However, Assad retreated from the commitment that had been conveyed on 3 May to the US. Meeting Shamir without any Syrian commitment took away any little leverage with him, and he refused to modify his position. Bush then sent a letter to all the leaders in the region, detailing US ideas for launching negotiations and asking each leader if he would be prepared to attend a conference based on these points.[5] On 14 July, Assad accepted, stating that the plan was "an acceptable basis for achieving a comprehensive solution".[6]

1. Ibid., p. 73.
2. Ibid., pp. 74–5.
3. Baker, *The Politics of Diplomacy*, pp. 459–60.
4. *Al-Hayat*, 12 May 1991.
5. Ross, *The Missing Peace*, pp. 75–6.
6. Aruri, *Dishonest Broker*, p. 75.

Having gained Assad's acceptance, Baker needed a reciprocal gesture from both the Arabs and Israelis, and took up a suggestion by Bandar that Mubarak issue a statement linking Arab willingness to suspend the boycott to an Israeli suspension of settlement activities. Bandar argued that it would be easier for Fahd to ratify what Mubarak had proposed, rather than the other way round. Baker and Mubarak met on 18 July, and at the press conference that followed, Mubarak issued the statement.

On 19 July Baker met Fahd and told the king: "I can't leave Saudi Arabia with no result." Fahd agreed to issue a statement supporting Mubarak's initiative. He declared that "the Middle East has changed", and that "if we're going to go for peace, boycotting companies from friendly countries does not make sense." Baker also wanted the king's help to press the Jordanians and Palestinians to form a joint delegation, and to keep the PLO invisible. Fahd agreed to help.[1]

On 21 July, *Ukaz* carried an official Saudi statement: "The Kingdom follows with great care the positive stand taken by President Assad to participate in the proposed peace conference and the statement by President Mubarak in which he mentions that Israel should suspend building settlements in return for the Arabs suspending the boycott." The statement added that, on these grounds, "the Kingdom supports Mubarak's statement", and that "Saudi Arabia believes that the will for peace shall be given precedence over all other issues."[2]

On 21 July Baker arrived in Israel, where Shamir told him he needed time to give his full acceptance to the US plan.[3] Following a Bush-Gorbachev summit in Moscow from 30 July – 1 August, Shamir agreed to the US's terms.

On 18 October, a letter of invitation, signed by the US and the Soviet Union and accompanied by a letter of assurances, was sent to the intended participants. The main principles espoused in the letter of invitation were that peace would be based on Security Council resolutions 242 and 338, on the principle of territory for peace and that the negotiations would involve a regional conference. After four days, this would lead on to bilateral negotiations; but the conference would have no power to enforce the outcomes. The negotiations would be conducted in phases, beginning with talks on interim self-government, and reiterated in the accompanying letter of assurances to the Palestinians. This letter added several other specific points, namely that the Israeli occupation would come to an end, but that this could be accomplished only through negotiations. The

---

1. Baker, *The Politics of Diplomacy*, p. 490.
2. *Ukaz*, 21 July 1991.
3. Aruri, *Dishonest Broker*, p. 75.

The Later Fahd Legacy (1990–2001)

UN would be represented by an observer, and the Palestinians could choose their own delegation (however, the US stipulated that its members be residents of the Occupied Territories). Last but not least, Jerusalem would never again be divided, and its final status would be decided in negotiations.[1]

On 20 October, Baker and the new Soviet foreign minister, Boris Pankin, made a joint announcement in Jerusalem that the conference would be convened in ten days' time in Madrid and would last from 30 October – 2 November.[2] *Ukaz* reported on 28 October that the GCC foreign ministers had issued a statement welcoming the convening of the Madrid conference, expressing the GCC's "deep satisfaction with the existing Arab coordination in these circumstances and hopes for its continuation, not only before the conference but during its different stages".[3]

The Madrid Conference duly opened on 30 October. Fahd told *Ukaz* on that day: "The rigid Israeli stance will not distract us from exerting more effort and total cooperation to carry forward the will for peace and justice." He added: "It is unnatural that the world inclines toward security, peace, stability and cooperation under the new world order, while our area remains a centre of continuous tension."[4]

Bush and Gorbachev were the conveners of the conference, and the rest of the participants were represented at the foreign-minister level – except for Shamir, who chose to lead the Israeli delegation himself.[5] In his speech to the conference, Bush spoke of the need for territorial compromise; the Syrians interpreted this as a change in the ground rules of the conference, and said that unless Bush's statement was corrected they could not sit with the Israelis. Again, Ross turned to Bandar, who managed to receive assurances that the Syrians would indeed sit with the Israelis.[6]

Ukaz reported on 2 November that Baker had remarked on how "King Fahd proved with words and deeds that there are new chances for peace between the Arabs and Israel after the Gulf War." The king, said Baker, had "demonstrated his commitment to relying on a new method in the Arab world".[7]

---

1. Ibid., pp. 76–7.
2. Ross, *The Missing Peace*, p. 80.
3. *Ukaz*, 28 October 1991.
4. *Ukaz*, 30 October 1991.
5. Ross, *The Missing Peace*, p. 80.
6. Ibid., pp. 80–1.
7. *Ukaz*, 2 October 1991.

Although the Madrid Conference and the subsequent rounds of negotiation did not constitute a complete failure, nor could they be judged a great success. Rhetoric and political posturing rather than serious discussion dominated the conference; key definitional disputes and procedural issues remained important even after the negotiations had begun; and the most difficult substantive issues – such as Jerusalem and Israeli settlements – were completely ignored. The lack of rapid results illustrated yet again the complexity of the problem and the inability of any outside actor, even the US as the world's superpower, to impose a solution upon the conflicting parties.

Changing Dynamics: The End of the Cold War, US Military Presence and the Rise of Islamism

Throughout the Cold War, there had been many reasons for Saudi Arabia and the US to work together. In addition to oil, the Kingdom's geographic location and ideological leanings underpinned the special relationship. All of Saudi Arabia's kings had sought ties with the US, and during the Cold War a set of mutually shared global interests had been defined. However, the communist threat was eliminated with the collapse of the Soviet empire, and the end of the Gulf War enabled the US to penetrate the region in a way it had not been able to do before. Shared interests were now crumbling.

In the Middle East, US power was applied so systematically against states that the US was now widely perceived as a malign hegemon. Many countries in the region sought to use, evade or appease US power but, given the weaknesses of these states, it was perhaps inevitable that actual resistance would chiefly take a non-state form. The Saudi government now had to take account of Islamist activism in the Kingdom. Saudi Arabia had served as the base from which Kuwait was liberated; Islamist opposition then grew after the Gulf War, with the Islamists using the war to illustrate their general discontent.

With the invasion of Kuwait, the Saudis had reversed their previous aversion to an open US military presence in their country. The religious establishment, through the Council of Senior *Ulama*, issued a *fatwa* (religious judgment) permitting the arrival of non-Muslim troops in Saudi Arabia.[1]

While a large segment of the Saudi population accepted the necessity of US military support, a substantial minority regarded it as a violation of

---

1. Saudi Press Agency, *The Echoes of the Saudi Position During the Events of the Arab Gulf, 1990–1991*, pp. 40–2.

Islamic principles. When around forty-five women drove cars in Riyadh on 6 November 1990, Saudi Islamists perceived this bold move as having been reinforced by the US military presence – and they felt it would further erode Islamic authority in the country.[1] In practice, Western penetration into the region stimulated a resurgence of cultural and religious resistance. The West was resented because it was seen to be pursuing an agenda targeting the Muslim and Arab worlds.

On 21 November 1990, Fahd denied that Saudi Arabia had made any agreements permitting foreign forces to be stationed permanently in the country, pointing out that friendly forces "have been deployed here at the Kingdom's request and will return to their countries when we ask them to do so".[2] The US military presence, in fact, caused significant difficulty for the Saudi government. The monarchy was now exposed as hypocritical for being highly dependent on the "infidel" US. The strongest criticism came from young religious scholars. In September 1990, Dr Safar al-Hawali, an Islamic scholar and Dean of the Islamic College at Umm al-Qara University in Mecca, circulated taped sermons criticizing the presence of foreign forces. Al-Hawali believed that, for the West, the Gulf had become the most important region in the world because of its oil resources, and had therefore devised strategies to occupy it. This conception was central to the way Islamists viewed the US role in the region.[3] Many Arabs and Muslims perceived that, far from being relegated to mere history, the struggle with imperialism was continuing in new forms.

According to al-Hawali, the New World Order was nothing but a cover for the West's domination of the world. He believed the invasion of Kuwait was orchestrated by the West to gain a foothold for its troops, and that the purpose of the war was not oil, but was the humiliation of Islam.[4] Similarly, another Islamic scholar, Salman al-'Awdah, a faculty member at Imam Muhammad Ibn Saud University in Riyadh, warned that the US had come to assume

---

1. Mamoun Fandy, *Saudi Arabia and the Politics of Dissent* (New York: St. Martin's Press, 1999), p. 49.
2. Saudi Press Agency, *The Echoes of the Saudi Position During the Events of the Arab Gulf, 1990–1991*, p. 329.
3. Safar Al-Hawali, *Haqaiq hawl azmat al-khalij* [*Realities Behind the Gulf Crisis*] (Cairo: Dar Makka al-Mukarama, 1991), pp. 25-27.
4. Ibid., pp. 83–7.

responsibility for the failing Saudi state.[1] This new generation of Islamists was referred to as the *sahwa*, or "awakening sheikhs".

The Saudi regime retains its legitimacy from its status as the protector of Islam; the stronger its legitimacy, the greater the autonomy it is likely to receive from society in pursuit of foreign policy. Thus, when US troops remained in Saudi Arabia, the radical opposition viewed them as a prop for what had become an illegitimate government.

In May 1991 the "Letter of Demands", signed by a group of about 400 Islamists, was submitted to the king. Among other things, it called for an Islamic foreign policy that would avoid alliances in violation of Islamic law, and argued for a supervisory role for the religious establishment. This letter was distributed inside the Kingdom along with anti-Western sermons.[2] In June the Council of Senior *Ulama* published a statement asserting that "advice to Muslim rulers should be given in private", and which also disapproved of the method used in publishing and distributing the letter. "This method does not serve the welfare of the people," it stated.[3]

The letter was followed a year later by a "Memorandum of Advice" that, among other things, demanded a more rigorous application of religious norms and the building up of a strong army that would guarantee Saudi Arabia's independence and its championing of Muslim causes. It also condemned the US as the embodiment of evil and the spearhead of the Western Christian war on Islam.[4] Once again, the Council of Senior *Ulama* examined the memorandum and issued a statement on 18 September 1992, denouncing it and its contents and declaring it "in violation of the religious advice methodology". The Council cautioned against "injustice, unfairness and highlighting the 'cons' while overlooking the 'pros'". It also warned against "all kinds of perverted intellectual linkages and commitment to principles of foreign groups and parties".[5] The Islamists had clearly benefited from the Saudi government's support for Islamic activities in spreading their own Islamic appeal.

1. Joshua Teitelbaum, *Holier Than Thou: Saudi Arabia's Islamic Opposition* (Washington, DC: Washington Institute for Near East Policy, 2000), pp. 20–32.
2. R. Hrair Dekmejian, "The Rise of Political Islamism in Saudi Arabia", *Middle East Journal* (autumn 1994), pp. 635–8.
3. *Ukaz*, 4 June 1991.
4. Daryl Champion, *The Paradoxical Kingdom: Saudi Arabia and the Momentum of Reform* (London: Hurst & Co., 2003), pp. 219–29.
5. *Ukaz*, 18 September 1992.

Faced with this situation, the monarchy mobilized its resources to deal with the new challenge – one that had come from an Islamic environment that the Saudi regime had itself created, shaped and maintained. In March 1992, in an attempt to pacify and contain the opposition, King Fahd announced three important administrative reforms.[1] This move was intended to show that the regime was open to some degree of change, without really addressing the issues raised by the opposition (members of which were, at the same time, appointed to a consultative council).

Oil Issues: The Kingdom's Diminishing Significance

Following World War II, the US can be seen as having promoted a project for a hegemonic world order, which envisioned a global economy governed by free trade. Oil was indispensable to the energy-intensive form of capitalism. US strategists explicitly envisioned a symbiotic relationship between the vital, robust capitalist Free World and globally projected US military power. Protecting the Free World was used to justify US interventions. It sought to establish predominance in the Gulf region, considering the control of the Middle East and its oil resources in part as a means to maintain geopolitical and geo-economic leverage over Europe and Japan and thereby securing a unipolar position for the US.

Oil interest was the motive behind the US's defence of Saudi Arabia and its liberation of Kuwait. Had Saddam been allowed to dominate the Gulf, he could have manipulated the oil supply to achieve any price he desired. The US political leadership decided, after the Gulf War ended, that the best method of protecting US interests was to diversify oil supplies.

This issue must be placed within the overall framework of US energy policy at this time. With the end of the Cold War, resource issues resumed their central role in US military planning. The current focus on resources reflects the growing importance of industrial power and the economic dimensions of security. In the past, the defining parameters of power and influence resided in the possession of a mighty arsenal and the maintenance of extended alliance systems; nowadays, however, they are associated with economic dynamism and the cultivation of technological innovation.

---

1. Madawi Al-Rasheed, *A History of Saudi Arabia* (Cambridge: Cambridge University Press, 2002), p. 172. The reforms were: the Basic Law of Government, the Law of Consultative Council and the Law of the Provinces.

Bill Clinton was first to articulate this perspective during the 1992 US presidential campaign (which he would go on to win). In December 1991 he told students at Georgetown University: "Our economic strength must become a central defining element of our security ... We must organize to compete and win in the global economy."[1] Clinton also suggested: "Prosperity at home depends on stability in key regions with which we trade or from which we import critical commodities, such as oil and natural gas."[2]

After the Gulf War, US leaders continued to emphasize the importance of unhindered oil supply to the health and stability of the global economy. At the same time, the US sought to diversify oil sources, importing from Africa to the North Sea to Canada. According to US calculations, not only would doing so cushion the US – "albeit temporarily" – from any possible disruption in the Gulf; just as importantly, it would reduce OPEC's market share and thereby weaken that organization's influence on oil supplies and prices.[3]

Eager to lessen its dependence on Gulf oil, the US started to place heavy emphasis on development of Caspian Sea energy resources. In 1997, the State Department told Congress that the Caspian basin held 200 billion barrels of oil – about ten times the amount found in the North Sea and a third of the Gulf's total reserves. Stuart Eizenstat, Under-Secretary of Energy, told a Senate committee: "The Caspian Sea is potentially one of the world's most important new energy-producing regions."[4] At a meeting in August 1997, Clinton told Heydar Aliyev, President of Azerbaijan: "In a world of growing energy demand, our nation cannot afford to rely on any single region for our energy supply." By working closely with Azerbaijan to develop its resources, "... not only do we help Azerbaijan to prosper, we also help diversify our energy supply and strengthen our nation's security."[5]

---

1. *Harvard International Review*, "A New Covenant for American Security" (summer 1992), pp. 26–7.
2. National Security Council, *A National Security Strategy for a New Century* (Washington, DC: December 1999), p. 21.
3. Saman Sepehri, "The Geopolitics of Oil", *International Socialist Review* 26 (November-December 2002), pp. 10–11.
4. US Congress, Senate, Committee on Foreign Relations, Subcommittee on International Economic Policy, Export and Trade Promotion, "U.S. Economic and Strategic Interests in the Caspian Sea Region: Policies and Implications", 105th Cong., 1st sess., 23 October 1997, p. 13.
5. White House, Press Office, "Visit of President Heydar Aliyev of Azerbaijan", 1 August 1997.

However, tension among the five countries bordering the Caspian over how to divide the sea, and disagreement over the best transport route, hampered the development of Caspian oil and gas.

By 1995, Saudi Arabia had taken second place to Venezuela on the list of top foreign suppliers of oil to the US. In 1995, 17.0 percent of US oil imports and 7.6 percent of total US oil consumption came from Saudi Arabia; the corresponding figures for Venezuela were 18.7 percent and 8.4 percent respectively.

As a result of fluctuating Venezuelan production, decreased global demand and increased OPEC quotas, from late 1997 to early 1999 the oil industry experienced its worst price collapse in fifty years. It was blamed on a perceived massive oil glut then flooding the world market.[1] Lower oil prices and decreasing oil income, coupled with a rising population, had serious consequences for Saudi Arabia. These economic difficulties were also behind the increasing degree of cooperation between Saudi Arabia and Iran. This displeased the US, but improved relations between the two energy producers allowed OPEC members to tighten quotas and reverse the decline in prices. At the same time, the Saudi government decided not to increase its production capacity, despite the forecasts of growing global demand.[2] As prices rose during 1999 and 2000, the US urged the Saudis toward a more flexible oil policy, which prompted proposals in Congress to increase domestic production and restrict trade with oil producers unless they agreed to increase production. Yet Saudi Arabia was concerned with the Kingdom's economic recovery rather than with underwriting a Saudi-US partnership.

The Peace Process and Declining Saudi Influence

Saudi Arabia had always shown a commitment to the Palestinian struggle, from the 1945 meeting between Ibn Saud and Roosevelt at Great Bitter Lake to the convening of the Madrid Conference. The Saudi insistence on resolving the plight of the Palestinians, in most cases, even went against the Kingdom's own interests. After Madrid, the monarchy was confronted with three major changes affecting its role in the Middle East peace process. The importance

---

1. Mathew R. Simmons, *Twilight in the Desert: The Coming Saudi Oil Shock and the World Economy* (New Jersey: John Wiley & Sons, Inc., 2005), pp. 82–3.
2. Bronson, *Thicker Than Oil*, p. 228.

of these changes meant that Saudi Arabia was frozen out of the process; the Kingdom was, as a result, less willing or able to play a role in promoting it.

The First Post-Madrid Change in US-Saudi Relations

The Madrid conference inaugurated a series of bilateral and multilateral talks that made real progress in settling differences between Israel and the Arab states. According to Simpson, Bandar said: "After the Madrid conference, a lot of taboos were broken."[1] This momentum generated an environment of hope and expectation that did not require any Saudi involvement; the Saudi role was thus less significant than it had been previously.

On 13 September 1993, the Israelis and the Palestinians signed the Oslo Accords, which created the Palestinian Authority. *Ukaz* had reported on 11 September that Fahd had received a phone call from Clinton informing him of the agreement. The king saluted "this historical step toward peace", and advanced his hopes for "the continuation of His Excellency's [Clinton's] good deeds."[2] On 30 September 1994, Saudi Arabia joined the other GCC states in ending enforcement of the secondary "indirect" boycotts of Israel.[3] Apart from this, the Kingdom had no direct role in the events that were now unfolding in Palestine.

Given the weakness of a collective Arab stance, the Palestinians had no alternative to the unilateral deal reached at Oslo. The Accords also led to Jordanian and Syrian moves toward their own separate agreements with Israel – though only Jordan achieved such an agreement. The process, therefore, neutralized the prospect that the Arab states would ever again unite against Israel.

The US received an Israeli offer in the summer of 1993 to withdraw fully from the Golan Heights, providing Syria met Israel's demands. Assad responded guardedly. In the end, the US and the Israelis agreed to put the offer on hold, to be revisited when Syria was able to meet Israeli concerns.

From 18–21 July 1994, Secretary of State Warren Christopher shuttled between Israel and Syria, clarifying the territorial matter known as "the June 4 line". (On 4 June 1967, the Syrian border had been positioned at the waterline of the Sea of Galilee, whereas the international border was around ten yards

---

1. Simpson, *The Prince*, p. 254.
2. *Ukaz*, 11 September 1993.
3. *Al-Hayat*, 2 October 1994.

back from the waterline. This posed problems for Israel, as it touched on the northeast quadrant of the sea and might, therefore, be seen as conveying to Syria riparian rights to the water itself.) From all appearances, an Israel-Syria deal was now in the cards.[1] Israel and the US saw an advantage in keeping Assad and Arafat in negotiations at the same time, with both countries thinking that neither leader would want to be last in line, thereby considerably increasing the pressure on each. (On 26 October that same year, Israel and Jordan signed a peace treaty.[2])

It seemed, in the first part of 1995, that progress was being made on all fronts. But on 24 July, when a Palestinian suicide bomber detonated a bomb in Tel Aviv that killed five Israelis, Israel suspended negotiations and sealed the border.[3] The Israelis and Palestinians, however, had managed to finalize a complex agreement that came to be known as Oslo II, granting self-rule to 450 Palestinian towns and villages, and was signed on 28 September. Saud commented on the agreement: "Without a doubt it is a positive step toward a just and lasting peace ... [but] peace cannot be partitioned. Without achieving an agreement on the Lebanese-Syrian track, the peace will be a fragmentary peace."[4]

At the end of October Israeli Prime Minister Rabin was assassinated. In February and March 1996, more terrorist attacks took place, and around fifty Israelis were killed. The effect on public opinion was dramatic. Led by the Likud Party, the right wing won the next Israeli elections. The defeat of the left-wing Labour Party had a devastating effect on the peace process, which was brought to a halt and became set into a spiral of actions and reactions that hampered any chance of expanding on all the gains achieved from the bilateral negotiations that had followed Madrid.

The US kept Saudi Arabia at arm's length from the peace negotiations partly as a function of design and from the belief that peace could be achieved through bilateral discussion. The Saudis continued to maintain their distance. In Jordan in 1999, during the funeral of King Hussein, Clinton reportedly approached Crown Prince 'Abdullah and asked if he would like to meet the Israeli leaders in attendance; 'Abdullah replied: "I believe, Your Excellency Mr

---

1. Quandt, *Peace Process*, pp. 331–2.
2. Ibid., p. 333.
3. Ibid., p. 336.
4. *Ukaz*, 30 September 1995.

President, that there are limits to friendship."[1] (The crown prince had taken on a greater role in leading Saudi Arabia after King Fahd was incapacitated by a major stroke early in 1996.)

The peace process delivered significant benefits to both the Palestinians and the Israelis, but the terms of the process were only ever supposed to be interim. The entire process was undermined by the absence of a final settlement, which had been projected for 1994–2000. A key moment of failure came during the talks, held under US auspices at Camp David, in July and August 2000. When the Israelis and Palestinians were unable to reach a final-status agreement, Clinton tried to persuade Saudi Arabia to make some gesture that would make it easier for Arafat to complete a deal on Jerusalem. Frozen out of earlier conversations, the Saudis were now reluctant to become seriously engaged.[2]

When the al-Aqsa *intifada* erupted in September 2000 between the Israelis and the Palestinians, it heightened the already significant anti-US and anti-regime sentiment in Saudi Arabia. A demographic surge, combined with the presence of Arab satellite television and the recent introduction of the Internet into Saudi Arabia, put pressure on the Saudi leadership. Inflamed by constant television broadcasts of Israeli military action against the Palestinians, the Saudi population was also enraged at the US, which was widely perceived as backing the Israelis, and angered by their own government's ties to Washington.[3] Palestinian grievances certainly stirred up internal Saudi public opinion, and there was a widespread sense in the Kingdom that US policies were unjustly biased against the Palestinians.

Unable to handle the situation, the US shifted from one stance to another, seeking alternately to mollify Saudi Arabia and Israel. Early in 2001, after President George W. Bush had taken office, and as a gesture in response to US policies, 'Abdullah refused an invitation to visit the US.[4] On 25 June 2001, he delivered a veiled rebuke to Washington by hinting: "We are a country with high credibility with all parties in the Arab and Islamic worlds. Maybe we are also the one qualified to persuade all concerned to come to the peace

---

1. Josh Pollack, "Saudi Arabia and the U.S., 1931–2002", *Middle East Review of International Affairs*, vol. 6, no.3 (September 2002), p. 86.
2. Bronson, *Thicker Than Oil*, p. 230.
3. Pollack, "Saudi Arabia and the U.S., 1931-2002", p. 88.
4. Ibid.

table. But we cannot play this role ... while Israel continually frustrates every peace initiative."[1]

While maintaining his distance, 'Abdullah repeatedly called on the US to restrain Israel. His discontent became a troubling matter for Washington. *Al-Watan* reported in June 2001 that now-Secretary of State Powell had met the crown prince in Paris, and that 'Abdullah had informed Powell of the desperation and discontent of Arab governments and Arab public opinion as a result of US support for Israel.[2] In mid-July, the former President Bush telephoned 'Abdullah to urge him, without success, to visit the US.[3] *Al-Sharq al-Awsat* reported that 'Abdullah had complained to Bush Senior that the existing US administration was too closely tied to the Israeli government, and made a clear and direct criticism of its handling of the Israeli-Palestinian conflict. He expressed the view that the US should display a better understanding of the Palestinian position and be more forthcoming in its objections to actions taken by Israel. Bush Senior assured 'Abdullah that George W. Bush would "take the correct steps". The aim of the telephone call, according to *Al-Sharq al-Awsat*, was to defuse 'Abdullah's anxieties and prevent Saudi-US tensions over the Palestinian conflict from permanently fracturing the relationship.[4]

In fact, the Bush administration continued to show little interest in brokering a Middle East peace, and increasingly tilted toward Israel as a partner with shared values. 'Abdullah dispatched Prince Bandar with a letter threatening a break in Saudi-US relations. Bandar's *démarche* carried a message that "a time comes when peoples and nations part. We are at a crossroads. It is time for the US and Saudi Arabia to look to their separate interests."[5] According to *Al-Watan*, Bandar's letter indicated that US partiality to Israel was complicating Saudi efforts to adopt the right policies for the mutual benefits of the two sides.[6]

On 2 September 2001, a letter confirming Bush's commitment to the establishment of a Palestinian state was sent to 'Abdullah. The crown prince wrote back, attaching a letter from Arafat that pledged to fulfil Bush's

---

1. *Financial Times*, 25 June 2001.
2. *Al-Watan*, 11 October 2001.
3. *The New York Times*, 15 July 2001
4. *Al-Sharq al-Awsat*, 16 July 2001.
5. *Al-Hayat*, 6 November 2001.
6. *Al-Watan*, 11 October 2001.

requirements for restarting the peace talks.[1] According to *Al-Hayat*, the Saudi government convinced the US of the necessity for Bush to meet Arafat, and a meeting was scheduled for the end of September.[2]

US hegemony proved, in practice, to be counterproductive in terms of establishing a stable order based on negotiated settlement. The collapse of the peace process suggests that order-building may have been more feasible on the basis of symmetry in power rather than hegemony. Massive US aid to Israel enabled it to insist on a peace settlement on its own terms. Because of the sharp power asymmetry between the Palestinians and the Israelis, the former's needs went unsatisfied and the conflict remained unresolved. US sponsorship of the peace process fostered an Israeli regional hegemony.

The Second Post-Madrid Change in Saudi-US Relations

The Clinton administration had viewed a Saudi role in the peace process as no longer instrumental. Whereas Reagan had viewed Saudi Arabia as the key to peace between Israel and the Arab states, Clinton regarded the Kingdom as no more than an important supporting actor in the process. Reagan had written explicitly in his autobiography that Arab-Israeli peace "should come through bilateral agreements just as it did with Egypt ... that's why we want to start with Saudi Arabia."[3]

Bush Senior's defeat in the presidential elections of 1992 was difficult for Prince Bandar and the monarchy as a whole. Bandar had established a workable friendship and understanding with the Bush administration, which had treated him with far more than the accepted level of contact and influence accorded other ambassadors; but, according to Simpson, Bandar was kept at arm's length by the Clinton White House. In Bronson's opinion, Bandar was regarded by Clinton and his aides as a Bush loyalist, and they found it unacceptable that Bandar had been a fixture at the Republican National Convention in 1992. National Security Advisor Tony Lake and his deputy, Samuel "Sandy" R. Berger, indicated that they wanted Bandar to be treated like any other ambassador.[4]

Simpson claims that, five days after Clinton became president, Lake, in his new capacity, summoned Bandar to meet the new chief executive. When the

---

1. *The Washington Post*, 10 February 2002.
2. *Al-Hayat*, 6 November 2001.
3. Ronald W. Reagan, *An American Life: The Autobiography* (New York: Simon & Schuster, 1990), pp. 412–5.
4. Bronson, *Thicker Than Oil*, p. 204.

Saudi ambassador arrived the following day, Clinton's staff kept him waiting. Finally, Clinton walked past the waiting area where Bandar was sitting, took him aside and said: "Look, let's set up another time to meet so that we can discuss a few things."[1] Simpson also reveals other events that shed some light on why the Clinton administration chose to downgrade Bandar's role. In early 1990, the prince had received a request from Clinton, then Governor of Arkansas, to come and see him. Bandar had cancelled the meeting three times. On the third occasion, Clinton had actually arrived at the Saudi embassy. Another story, recounted by Prince Bandar's private secretary Sherry Cooper, concerns the fact that during the presidential primaries Clinton, looking for funding for a library, had shown up at the Saudi embassy without an appointment and asked to meet Bandar. Cooper told Simpson: "Mr. Clinton didn't get his appointment and went on to become President." She added: "I guess he never forgot that."[2]

What is certain is that the relationship between Bandar and Clinton was nowhere as close as that which Bandar had enjoyed with Bush. The ramifications of the changed relationship were that the Saudis shied away from helping with and promoting Arab-Israeli peacemaking, or counselling prudence among the Arab peace partners.

The Third Post-Madrid Change in Saudi-US Relations

The stroke suffered by Bandar's mentor King Fahd meant that more power was given to Crown Prince 'Abdullah. Fahd had been pro-US, regarding the interests of the two countries as overlapping, and Bandar had been his main instrument in conducting foreign policy. Bandar had always tried to probe for areas in which to enhance and strengthen the Saudi-US relationship, whereas 'Abdullah has more of an Arab nationalist orientation. For him, embracing the relationship simply seemed to undermine Saudi domestic stability. A significant shift now began to take place, made more problematic by the fact that Bandar was not very close to 'Abdullah.

Close ties to the US were also becoming unpopular inside the Kingdom. On the domestic scene, King Fahd handed over administrative affairs of state to 'Abdullah on 3 January 1996,[3] although he formally revoked this decision

---

1. Simpson, *The Prince*, p. 272.
2. Ibid., pp. 273–4.
3. *Al-Hayat*, 3 January 1996.

on 23 February.[1] Uncertainty and a great deal of confusion arose as to who was ruling, or should rule, the country.

The Military Relationship

In the wake of the Gulf War, the US presence in the region reached levels comparable to Western penetration in the pre-Nasser age. No state by itself or in concert with others in the region was in a position to establish a Middle Eastern order independent of US influence. At the turn of the millennium, no new security system had emerged, and states continued to rely on US protection.

"Operation Desert Storm" marked the high point in Saudi-US relations, as Saudi Arabia and the US enjoyed an opportunity to forge a new relationship. However, their association became strained by Saddam's survival and his efforts to disrupt regional stability. The US was regularly compelled to mass its forces in the area – something with which the Saudi monarchy, faced with growing domestic problems, was not comfortable. The two sides struggled to develop a consensus on how to deal with the Iraqi threat. The failure to remove Saddam caused the US to expend greater resources to maintain the security and stability of the region, while the continued US military presence threatened to de-legitimize the Saudi government.

On 18 May 1993, the Clinton administration adopted a "dual containment" policy to confront the threat posed in the Gulf by the Iran and Iraq. Outlining the US's approach to the Middle East, Martin Indyk, Director of Middle East Affairs at the NSC, began by noting the ongoing Arab-Israeli peace negotiations, the balance of power in the Gulf and the rise of radical movements that, cloaked in religious garb, challenged governments across the Arab world with their potential for destabilizing the region.[2] Saudi Arabia's dependence on US protection from Iraq and Iran underpinned and abetted the US determination to maintain its enhanced military presence. In practice, Washington's "dual containment" of Iran and Iraq limited Iranian attempts at moderation and hindered the normalization of Iran's role in the region.

Iraq's refusal to implement UN resolutions, and its continuing threat to the

---

1. Ibid., 23 February 1996.
2. Sami G. Hajjar, *U.S. Military Presence in the Gulf: Challenges and Prospects* (Carlisle Barracks, PA: The Strategic Studies Institute, Army War College, March 2002), p. 9.

security and the stability of the Gulf, necessitated that the US maintain forces in the region. Washington therefore signed cooperative defence agreements (also referred to as access agreements) with Saudi Arabia and other Gulf states. However, the Saudis avoided the detailed Defense Cooperative Agreement that had been signed between the US and some of the Gulf states. The US presence in the Kingdom, regarded by the Saudi government as an essential security shield, was based on tacit understanding rather than on legal documents.[1]

As a result, the US military had concluded that the peacetime strategy of UNCENTCOM (so called because CENTCOM was then implementing UN resolutions signed at the end of the Gulf War) relied on the pillars of "presence, security assistance, and combined exercises". In 1995, CENTCOM Commander-in-Chief General J. H. Binford Peay III expanded these strategic pillars, adding "power projection" and "readiness to fight" to theatre strategy.[2] Moreover, senior US officials made it clear that the US was prepared to assume the lead role again or, if required, to act entirely on its own. In 1995, Joseph Nye, Assistant Secretary of Defense, declared that US forces were prepared to defend vital American interests in the region – unilaterally, should it come to that.

Saudi Arabia supported the US presence, but at the same time was very sensitive to it. The monarchy's continuous worry about the public profile of its US military connection stemmed from fears about its domestic consequences. In September 1991, during one of the US confrontations with Iraq, Prince Sultan had even urged the US to spread its deployment out to Kuwait and even to capture an airfield in Iraq itself to use as a base, instead of using Saudi Arabia as a military staging area.[3]

Despite its cordial relations with Washington, Riyadh maintained its views against US strikes against Iraq, and during subsequent Iraq-US confrontations in October 1994 and September 1996 Prince Sultan restated his reluctance to allow the US to use Saudi facilities to stage attacks on Iraq.[4] When Saddam attacked the Kurds in northern Iraq in September 1996, *Ukaz* reported that the Kingdom had not permitted US military action to be launched from its

---

1. Ibid., pp. 37–46.
2. Central Command, Posture Statement, 1995, p. 39.
3. *The New York Times*, 30 September 1991.
4. David W. Lesch, ed., *The Middle East and the United States* (Boulder, CO: Westview Press, 1996), p. 365.

territories.[1] When asked about this denial of access, Sultan said: "It has never been requested, and even if it had been, we would have refused." Sultan also reiterated the Saudi position on US force: "As long as it [US attacks on Iraq] is under the aegis of the UN, we have nothing to do with it."[2]

Further tension occurred during "Operation Desert Fox" in December 1998, officially mounted to punish Saddam for ignoring compliance with UN resolutions: the Saudis refused to allow the US the use of its bases for attacks against Iraq.[3] According to Cordesman, during "Desert Fox" the US unilaterally reinforced its troops in the Kingdom without Saudi Arabia's permission. Similarly, on 16 February 2001, despite an agreement not to strike north of the thirty-second parallel without Saudi permission, the US struck well north of the thirty-third parallel.[4]

Faced with internal problems in justifying the US presence, the Saudi government was unable to reach a political consensus with the US as to how to deal with Iraq. Dual containment offered no solution. Saudi Arabia needed an Iraq that was neither too weak nor too strong: a weak Iraq could represent a threat to regional stability caused by its disintegration, while a strong Iraq represented a military threat to the Gulf states. Meanwhile, the plight of the Iraqi people became daily fodder for local news reports in the Kingdom, and Arab public opinion laid the blame for their suffering on the US. The US failure indicated the beginnings of an erosion of its hegemony. Washington's unilateralism also provoked dissatisfaction and increasing independence of action among its regional allies.

Terrorist/Opposition Threats, 1991–96

Intellectual trends within both US and Saudi societies had damaging implications for relations between the two countries, as they impacted upon government policy and public opinion alike. With the end of the Cold War, the US no longer had a rival for global hegemony. Observers sought new ways of understanding the fault lines and potential sources of conflict in

---

1. *Ukaz*, 4 September 1996.
2. Ibid., 12 September 1996.
3. Daryl Champion, "The Kingdom of Saudi Arabia: Elements of Instability Within Stability", *Middle East Review of International Affairs*, vol. 3, no. 4 (December 1999).
4. Cordesman, *Saudi Arabia Enters the Twenty-first Century*, p. 38.

the post-Cold War world; one of these was the thinking that saw the world divided into fundamentally different and clashing civilizations.[1]

By the time Clinton took office in 1992, anti-Islamist voices had succeeded in promoting the notion of an "Islamic threat". In his article "The Roots of Muslim Rage", then-Professor of History at Princeton University Bernard Lewis traced the conflict between Islam and the West to the classic Islamic division of the world into two opposing forces: the House of Peace (*dar al-islam*) and the House of War (*dar al-harb*). In such a view, according to Lewis, any civilization outside Islam – by the very fact that it is not Islamic – is considered an enemy. The problem posed by Islamic extremists, as implied by Lewis's argument, was not that they grounded their violent ideology in their own interpretation of Islam but that they believed their interpretation was the correct one. Lewis maintained that violent intolerance was thus inscribed within the origins of Islam as the logical result of such reasoning, and that eventually this rage came to be directed primarily against the US. He insisted this had little to do with US support for authoritarian and oppressive regimes in the Muslim world, or for Israel, or imperialism, or indeed for anything else the US had done or was now doing. The main source of "Muslim rage" was simply Muslims' inability to tolerate "the domination of infidels over true believers". Summing up, Lewis stated: "This is no less than a clash of civilizations – the perhaps irrational but surely historic reaction of an ancient rival against our Judeo-Christian heritage, our secular present, and the worldwide expansion of both."[2]

Lewis's assertion is presented as incontestable, but before any claims are made concerning the relationship between religion and violence, the role of sacred texts and sacred models in demanding, motivating and justifying violence must be examined. Christianity's own history of inquisitions, pogroms, conquests, enslavement and genocide offers little support for its assertions that Islam's Prophet or its sacred texts display a propensity for violence that is any greater in degree or different in kind. It is also inaccurate as well as misleading to explain the Muslim struggle simply as a manifestation of the rage about Islam's inferiority to Western civilization.

---

1. Zachary Lockman, *Contending Visions of the Middle East: The History and Politics of Orientalism*, (Cambridge: Cambridge University Press, 2004), p. 233.
2. Bernard Lewis, "The Roots of Muslim Rage", *The Atlantic Monthly*, vol. 266, no. 3, September 1990, pp. 47–60.

Such an explanation simply ignores history, politics and complex local, regional and global contexts in the most reductionist, simplistic way.

Ironically, in making such claims about Islam, Lewis was in agreement with many contemporary Islamic radicals.[1] Other inflammatory and hysterical pieces were published, including *The Muslims Are Coming, the Muslims Are Coming* by the right-wing academic Daniel Pipes.[2] Then, in 1993, Samuel Huntington, Professor of Political Science at Harvard University, contended in an article titled "The Clash of Civilizations" that Islam and the West were engaged in a "quasi-war" that was being waged over fundamental issues of power and differing views of right and wrong. Huntington insisted that the adversary did not comprise only militants: "The underlying problem for the West is not Islamic fundamentalism ... It is Islam, a different civilization whose people are convinced of the superiority of their culture and are obsessed with the inferiority of their power."[3] Lost in the witch-hunt were some fundamental facts:

1. The Muslim world is neither united nor homogeneous;
2. Islamic societies are currently in retreat in the face of an ascendant West;
3. Muslim states are either too impoverished to launch a confrontation against the West or too dependent upon the West to stage such a confrontation.[4]

As US troops arrived by the thousands in Saudi Arabia in September 1990, al-Hawali declared that the Gulf crisis was part of a broader Western plot to dominate Muslims.[5] Al-Hawali's concern was the Saudi state's subordinate position to the US, whose culture he saw as extremely hostile to Islam. His

---

1. Emran Qureshi and Michael A. Sells, *The New Crusades: Constructing the Muslim Enemy* (New York: Columbia University Press, 2003), pp. 4–5.
2. Daniel Pipes, "The Muslims Are Coming, the Muslims Are Coming", *National Review*, 19 November 1990.
3. Samuel P. Huntington, "The Clash of Civilizations?", *Foreign Affairs* 72 (summer 1993), pp. 22–49.
4. Hisham Melhem, *Dual Containment: The Demise of a Fallacy* (Washington, DC: Georgetown University Center for Contemporary Arab Studies, Edmund A. Walsh School of Foreign Service, 1997), p. 9.
5. Fandy, *Saudi Arabia and the Politics of Dissent*, pp. 67–73.

main target was the American Christian right, which he believed was a central rather than a peripheral movement in US politics and that in the future it would play a major role in any conflict with or within the Middle East.[1] Al-Hawali's knowledge of the West was bound to seem impressive to an Arab audience. For one thing, he provided answers about US support for Israel, and about the anti-Muslim and anti-Arab position adopted by the US media. He also supported his ideas by quoting influential US figures who publicly expressed extremely anti-Muslim sentiments.[2]

Al-'Awdah, the other 'awakening sheikh', called for the re-Islamizing of society by purging liberals from government offices, schools and positions in the media. Al-'Awdah reproduced the Wahhabi view that the Saudi-Wahhabi alliance made Saudi Arabia a bulwark for Islam, and that because of the special nature of the Kingdom, it was essential to block the infiltration of foreign cultures and to eliminate the non-Muslim presence.[3]

Although there is a greater appreciation of the complexities of the Muslim world now than a generation ago, most Americans still view radical Islam as a cause for instant alarm; they have been fed a steady diet of books, films and news reports depicting Arabs as demonic anti-Western Others, and Israelis as heroic pro-Western partners.[4] The Muslim world, however, is locked in a vortex of change and economic chaos, but its political systems are abysmal. Rather than offering hope for a better life, these systems offer little but oppression and despair. Enhanced technology for intimidation and repression has further rendered peaceful change in the region a virtual impossibility.

Many inhabitants of Arab and Muslim cultures today relentlessly debate the cause of their malaise, with most placing the blame on the colonialism that swept the Islamic world during the nineteenth and twentieth centuries. The era of independence that followed World War II was simply replaced by a more insidious form of economic and cultural colonialism that threatened to transform the very roots of Arab and Islamic society.[5] Radical Islamists have

---

1. Ibid., p. 62.
2. Ibid., pp. 84–5.
3. Ibid., pp. 98–101.
4. Douglas Little, *American Orientalism: The U.S. and the Middle East Since 1945* (London: I. B. Tauris, 2003), p. 314.
5. Monte Palmer and Princess Palmer, *At the Heart of Terror: Islam, Jihadists, and America's War on Terrorism* (New York: Rowman & Littlefield, 2004), pp. 22–3.

viewed the US as the Muslim world's strongest principal enemy. The roots of Islamist anti-Americanism go deep, long predating the Islamic Revolution in Iran in 1979 or the rise of *jihadist* movements in the 1990s. The sense of confronting a conspiracy is a crucial element in understanding the motives and justifications of contemporary Islamist anti-Americanism, in developing the image of the "American enemy".[1]

It has been argued by Islamists that Muslim societies had declined in relation to the West and become backward, and that the problem was not Islam but Muslims themselves. After all, the first generation of Muslims, the *salaf*, had enjoyed glorious worldly success. But at some point, Muslims had taken a wrong turn along the path of history. Therefore, it was necessary to return to the ways of the Muslim ancestors, the *salaf*, in order to reproduce their worldly success. The idea that Muslims had strayed from the true religion offered an opening for re-examining and re-evaluating the sources, beliefs and practices.[2]

The 1970s were marked by the sudden emergence of militant Islamist movements in most of the world's Muslim nations. During this period, the impact of Saudi Arabia on Muslims throughout the world was less visible than that of Khomeini's Iran; but the effect was deeper and more enduring. The Saudis raised a new standard as a foil for the corrupting influence of the West, while still managing to remain a staunch ally of the US and the West against communism.[3]

The Islamic Revolution, which was followed immediately by the Soviet invasion of Afghanistan, brought the region into the geopolitical spotlight. By destabilizing one of Washington's principal military allies in the world's richest oil-producing region, this revolution made it easier for the Soviets to fill the political void. Thus, the Islamist question became part and parcel of a wider US-Soviet struggle. The obvious step towards solving both problems was a US-sponsored *jihad* against the Soviets in Afghanistan. A Vietnam-style war would be inflicted on the Soviets, Pakistan would be bolstered in its struggle with India and the *jihadists* would be preoccupied in Afghanistan.[4]

1. Reuven Paz, "Islamists and Anti-Americanism", *Middle East Review of International Affairs*, vol. 7, no. 4 (December 2003).
2. David Commins, *The Wahhabi Mission and Saudi Arabia* (London: I. B. Tauris, 2006), pp. 130–2.
3. Gilles Kepel, *Jihad: The Trail of Political Islam* (London: I. B. Tauris, 2004), pp. 61–2.
4. Palmer and Palmer, *At the Heart of Terror*, p. 97.

The Later Fahd Legacy (1990–2001)

The Islamic world had not seen an armed *jihad* for nearly a century. However, in the service of a contemporary political objective, the CIA was now determined to create one. Historically, the tradition of "lesser *jihad*" had comprised two different – and conflicting – notions. The first was that of a just war against occupiers, whether non-believers or believers. The second, conflicting, notion was that of a permanent *jihad* against doctrinal tendencies in Islam that were officially considered to be heretical. This remains a tradition with little historical depth in Islam. To CIA planners, an established armed *jihad* was particularly appealing. The Afghan *jihad*, in reality, was a US *jihad*.[1]

Because the war against the Soviets was to be a religious war, the infrastructure had to be profoundly religious in nature. Many fighters in the conflict came from Arab countries, giving rise to the term "Afghan Arabs" (whether they were Arabs or not). At the outset, *ulama* with recognized credentials issued *fatwas* interpreting the Soviet intervention as an invasion of the territory of Islam by the impious. This made it possible to proclaim a "defensive *jihad*", which, according to the *shari'a*, obliged every individual Muslim to participate.[2] The calls for a *jihad* and its implementation in Afghanistan were not initiated by Muslim states as such, but by trans-national Islamic religious networks.

The blueprint for the Afghan *jihad* was worked out by the CIA, in collaboration with Pakistan's ISI and the GID of Saudi Arabia. In this operation, the CIA remained at more than arm's length. What transpired was a proxy war run through third and fourth parties, which effectively marginalized mainstream traditionalist/nationalist Muslim organizations and elevated highly ideological but exiled Islamist factions. The simple fact was that, whereas traditionalists understood their struggle within a national frame of reference, ideologues found meaning in the struggle as the beginning of an international *jihad*.[3] The result was a lack of coherence in overall US policy. The real damage done by the CIA was not in providing arms and financial support, but in providing information on how to produce and spread violence capable of creating terror.[4] When the Soviet Union withdrew in 1989, reports and complaints about the growing force of militant Islamic volunteers began to reach the CIA. But with the advent of the Soviet pullout and the subsequent

---

1. Mahmood Mamdani, *Good Muslim, Bad Muslim: America, the Cold War, and the Roots of Terror* (New York: Pantheon Books, 2004), pp. 127–8.
2. Kepel, *Jihad*, p. 139.
3. Mamdani, *Good Muslim, Bad Muslim*, p. 155.
4. Cooley, *Unholy Wars*, p. 90.

collapse of the USSR and the demise of the Cold War, the West lost all interest in Afghanistan.[1]

By financing the Afghan *jihad*, Saudi Arabia preserved its credibility with even the most radical of Sunni militants. But Saddam's invasion of Kuwait and the Saudis' request for US assistance ruined the entire edifice it had been erecting so patiently since the 1960s to dominate the Islamic world. The consensus built around a conservative Islam that had attracted allegiances in every quarter thanks to its religious rigour and financial generosity would never be the same again after the Gulf War.[2]

The *jihadists* emerged from the war in Afghanistan with an exhilarating sense of victory and an unshakable faith in their ability to reclaim the Islamic world in the name of God. They had acquired a new sense of legitimacy. The Soviets had been the enemy of the moment, but the *jihadists* saw little difference between the Soviet Union and the US. Both were godless, and both were guilty of usurping Muslim lands.[3] After the Afghan war the *jihadist* movement assumed a trans-national character as veteran *mujahideen* returned to their home countries and dispersed to other sites of Muslim insurgency such as Algeria, Bosnia and Chechnya. It was from this movement that Usama bin Laden and al-Qaʿida emerged to confront Saudi Arabia and the US.

Still, in the general scheme of things, the Afghan Arabs were no more than extras in the Afghan war. It was the lessons they learned from the *jihad*, rather than their contribution to it, that proved significant. They mixed with militants from other countries and were indoctrinated in the most extreme ideas about *jihad*.[4]

Bin Laden had returned in 1989 to Saudi Arabia, where he spoke at countless mosques and private gatherings.[5] According to Prince Turki, when asked about his activities bin Laden said he was "only calling for support for the Afghan people".[6] After the Iraqi invasion of Kuwait, bin Laden proposed to deploy his Afghan fighters to reverse the aggression towards the Saudi government.

1. James Ridgeway, *The Five Unanswered Questions About 9/11: What the 9/11 Commission Failed to Tell Us* (New York: Seven Stories Press, 2005), p. 131.
2. Kepel, *Jihad*, pp. 205–7.
3. Palmer and Palmer, *At the Heart of Terror*, p. 99.
4. Peter L. Bergen, *Holy War, Inc.: Inside the Secret World of Osama bin Laden* (London: Weidenfeld & Nicolson, 2001), pp. 60–1.
5. Yossef Bodansky, *Bin Laden: The Man Who Declared War on America* (Roseville, CA: Prima Publishing, 2001), p. 28.
6. *Al-Sharq al-Awsat*, 7 November 2001.

The Later Fahd Legacy (1990–2001)

He met Prince Sultan and offered him up to 100,000 fighters: "There are no caves in Kuwait," Sultan told bin Laden. "You cannot fight them from the mountains and caves. What will you do when they lob the missiles at you, with chemical and biological weapons?" Bin Laden's answer – "We will fight them with faith" – did not impress Sultan.[1]

The Saudi regime's credibility was weakened in Islamist circles, as Islamists were outraged by the Kingdom's willingness to allow US troops into the Kingdom.[2] Wahhabi doctrine made the Saudi request for US assistance difficult to justify. The Islamists initially condemned Iraq's invasion of Kuwait, but at the same time they opposed Western military intervention because they believed it would bolster Western domination.[3]

The crisis included challenges to senior *ulama* from Islamists and liberal reformers alike inside the Kingdom. Thanks to the expansion of religious schools and universities during the 1980s, the Islamists enjoyed a large and receptive audience. Many of their graduates had encountered and embraced the Islamic revivalist ideas taught by teachers and professors who were Muslim Brothers (among them Dr Muhammad Qutb, brother of the leading figure of the Muslim Brotherhood in the 1950s and 60s, Sayyid Qutb). Thus, by the 1990s, the revivalists had rejected Western influence and were resentful of Western domination. They also condemned their rulers for failing to safeguard Islam and for betraying it for the sake of protecting selfish interests.[4] By the 1990s there was, in addition, a large and steadily increasing population of young men who, lacking any reasonable expectation of suitable or steady employment throughout the Muslim world, were easy targets for radicalization.

With the positioning of US forces in Saudi Arabia, bin Laden applied the Soviet-Afghan analogy of an invading infidel in the Muslim heartland to the US. In early 1992, he issued a *fatwa* calling for *jihad* against the Western "occupation" of Islamic lands, specifically singling out US forces for attack. In the ensuing weeks, he delivered an often-repeated lecture on the need to

---

1. Douglas Jehl, "Holy War Lured Saudis as Rulers Looked Away", *The New York Times*, 21 December 2001.
2. Tim Niblock, *Saudi Arabia: Power, Legitimacy and Survival* (London: Routledge, 2006), p. 153.
3. Commins, *The Wahhabi Mission and Saudi Arabia*, pp. 176–7.
4. James L. Gelvin, *The Modern Middle East: A History* (New York: Oxford University Press, 2004), pp. 291–9.

cut off "the head of the snake". While his allied Islamist groups were focused on local battles, bin Laden concentrated on attacking the US.[1]

Clinton's initial National Security Strategy in July 1994 gave minimal credence to the nascent threat of trans-national terrorism, noting: "The only responsible US strategy is one that seeks to ensure US influence over, and participation in, collective decision-making in a wide and growing range of circumstances." With respect to the use of force, it added: "We must carefully select the means and level of our participation in particular military operations."[2]

On 13 November 1995, an explosion was detonated in the office of the programme manager for the Saudi National Guard in Riyadh, killing seven people (including five US citizens) and injuring sixty others. According to the Saudi magazine *Al-Majallah*, the attack was executed by bin Laden's operatives.[3] Subsequently, on 31 May 1996, four Saudi nationals were executed for their role in the bombing by the Saudi government.[4]

On 25 June 1996 an even more deadly explosion occurred at the Khobar Towers apartment complex housing US Air Force personnel near the Dhahran airbase, killing nineteen US servicemen and injuring many others. This event prompted the relocation of most US military personnel to more remote sites in Saudi Arabia to improve security.[5] Secretary of State Madeleine Albright told Prince Bandar: "The US expects the full assistance of the Saudi government on this matter."[6] *Al-Sharq al-Awsat* reported Bandar's comment on 30 June that "the Kingdom welcomes the US participation in the ongoing investigations", and that "there is no objection to the US investigator's involvement in the

---

1. The New York Times and the National Commission on Terrorist Attacks Upon the United States, *The Complete Investigation: The 9/11 Report* (New York: St. Martin's Press, 2004), pp. 87–8.
2. William J. Clinton, "Advancing Our Interest Through Engagement and Enlargement: A National Security Strategy of Enlargement and Engagement" (White House, July 1994), in Alvin Z. Rubinstein, Albina Shayevich and Boris Zlotnikov, eds, *Clinton Foreign Policy Reader: President Speeches with Commentary* (New York: M. E. Sharpe, Inc., 2000), pp. 28–9.
3. *Al-Majallah*, 4 May 1996.
4. *Ukaz*, 1 June 1996.
5. *Al-Hayat*, 27 June 1996.
6. Thomas Blood, *Madam Secretary: A Biography of Madeleine Albright* (New York: St. Martin's Press, 1997), p. 106.

investigation". Bandar emphasized that "the Khobar attack will not be an excuse to damage the relationship."[1]

The Saudi government allowed the US's Federal Bureau of Investigation (FBI) to deploy a team to the Kingdom. According to Simpson, Bandar explained the rationale for allowing the US to conduct an investigation on Saudi soil: the Saudi government was so angry and offended that the attack had been against its guests; therefore "normal political and legal barriers whereby people would spend weeks negotiating the parameters of the investigations were dropped right there and then."[2] *Al-Hayat* also reported Bandar's assurances that the Saudis were willing to cooperate with the US to uncover the perpetrators. He insisted: "The protection of our guests is our responsibility, and we spare nothing to provide it."[3]

Although the US press criticized Saudi Arabia for its lack of cooperation in the investigation of the attack, Simpson notes the statement by Louis Freeh, the director of the FBI: "The criticism that they [the Saudis] were not cooperative, as I told many people, was not well founded ... the Saudis went well beyond cooperation, they were actually going to support our prosecution." When the investigation revealed some Iranian involvement, the Saudi government, according to Freeh, agreed to Rule 15 – a US legal procedure that provided for testimony and evidence obtained from witnesses in Saudi Arabia to be recorded and taken back to the US and used as evidence in a US trial. Freeh commented: "Despite these extremely sensitive and complex issues, the Saudis put their own interests aside to aid the FBI."[4]

The Saudi government did, however, demand that the US make an official request for evidence. It needed this done in order to protect itself against allegations from Iran that the Kingdom was freely pointing to Iran as the perpetrator. Freeh explained that the Saudis had made it clear that "if you ask for it we will provide it" and, according to him, the Saudis wanted the US "to make a request and be serious about the consequence of getting that information, which ironically would be more adverse to the Saudis than to us". Bandar told Freeh: "By giving you the evidence that will allow you to go after the Iranians ... by not responding and ignoring this threat, you are putting

---

1. *Al-Sharq al-Awsat*, 30 June 1996.
2. Simpson, *The Prince*, p. 277.
3. *Al-Hayat*, 8 July 1996.
4. Simpson, *The Prince*, pp. 279–81.

everybody in jeopardy, not just the Saudis."[1] According to Simpson, Freeh made it clear that the problem was with the US side, not with the Saudi side, noting: "We could not get our leadership, the President or Vice President, to ask for the evidence." Apparently, the Clinton administration remained reluctant to take decisive military action against Iran, and never requested the evidence. (As the Saudi government could not afford to upset Iran without the solid backing of the US, Bandar spoke with National Security Advisor Berger, asking him: "Tell me, what you are going to do with the information if we share it with you?"[2])

Freeh, exasperated by the Clinton administration, then asked former President Bush to intercede with the Saudis – whereupon, according to *The New Yorker*, the crown prince instructed Saudi authorities to make witnesses available to the FBI.[3] *Al-Sharq al-Awsat* duly reported that the US had officially indicted thirteen Saudi nationals, plus a Lebanese national, in connection with the attack. US Attorney General John Ashcroft expressed his gratitude: "This indictment would not been possible without the Saudi effort."[4] Most of those indicted were believed to be in Iran.

From 1996 the issue of bin Laden, who was living at that time in Sudan, began increasingly to impinge on the Saudi-US relationship. To ease foreign pressure, a secret meeting was held in February of that year between Sudanese and Saudi officials. They offered to extradite bin Laden to Saudi Arabia, but asked that he be spared legal prosecution, a request the Saudis were unwilling to grant.[5] On 19 May, bin Laden returned to Afghanistan.

Throughout bin Laden's time in Sudan, he had maintained guesthouses and training camps in Pakistan and Afghanistan. Pakistan had become home to an enormous population of Afghan refugees, and as the badly strained Pakistani education system could not accommodate them, the government increasingly allowed privately funded religious schools to serve as a cost-free alternative. Over time, these schools produced large numbers of half-educated young men with no marketable skills, but with deeply held Islamic views.[6] Pakistan

---

1. Ibid., p. 282.
2. Ibid., p. 284.
3. *The New Yorker*, 14 May 2001.
4. *Al-Sharq al-Awsat*, June 2001.
5. *The New York Times* and The National Commission on Terrorist Attacks Upon the United States, *The Complete Investigation*, p. 93.
6. *The New York Times*, "How the Holy Warriors Learned to Hate", 18 June 2004.

viewed these young Afghans as a source of potential trouble at home but useful abroad, as those who joined the nascent fundamentalist Taliban movement could perhaps restore order in Afghanistan and make it a cooperative ally. Pakistani intelligence officers reportedly introduced bin Laden to Taliban leaders in Kandahar,[1] and when Jalalabad and then Kabul fell to Taliban forces in September 1996, bin Laden cemented his ties with them.[2]

Bin Laden, the Kingdom and the US, 1996–2001

Bin Laden, no longer politically constrained, clearly believed he had new freedom to publish his appeals for *jihad*. In August 1996 he issued his declaration of *jihad*, the goals of which were to drive US forces out of Saudi Arabia, overthrow the Saudi government, liberate Islam's holy sites of Mecca and Medina and support Islamist revolutionary groups around the globe.

The alliance with the Taliban provided al-Qa'ida with a safe haven from which to train and indoctrinate fighters and terrorists, import weapons, forge ties with other *jihadist* groups and leaders and plot and staff terrorist schemes. According to Prince Turki, the Taliban had pledged to prevent bin Laden from threatening the Kingdom's interests – although Turki did state that the Taliban "could not, or would not exercise any authority on him [bin Laden] to prevent him from taking actions to disturb security".[3]

Meanwhile, the US undertook tremendous efforts to arrive at a political solution for Afghanistan, not just for reasons of prospective corporate investment there but also because of other key concerns such as human rights, narcotics and terrorism. During a meeting between Assistant Secretary of State for South and Central Asian Affairs Robin Raphel and Deputy Foreign Minister Albert Chernyshev of Russia, Raphel indicated a growing desire in Washington to resolve the Afghan conflict and proposed an arms embargo.

Following the takeover of Kabul by the Taliban, the State Department instructed the US embassy in Pakistan to gather information about the organization as well as to convey messages to it. Some of these talking points demonstrate the wish to locate bin Laden.

On 8 December 1997, Taliban officials met Assistant Secretary of State

---

1. Ahmed Rashid, *Taliban: Militant Islam, Oil and Fundamentalism in Central Asia* (London: Yale University Press, 2000), p. 139.
2. Ibid., pp. 19–21.
3. *The New York Times*, 18 June 2004.

for South and Central Asian Affairs Karl Inderfurth in Washington. When questioned by Inderfurth about having granted refuge to bin Laden, one of the officials replied that if they expelled bin Laden he would only go to Iran and cause more trouble. Another representative noted that the Taliban had not invited bin Laden to Afghanistan; he had already been inside the country "as a guest of the previous regime when they took over".[1]

In February 1998, bin Laden and Ayman al-Zawahiri, *emir* of the Islamist group Egyptian Islamic Jihad and al-Qaʿida's second in command, published what they termed a *fatwa* issued in the name of the "World Islamic Front". Claiming that the US had declared war against God and his Messenger, they called for the murder of any American anywhere in the world as the "individual duty of every Muslim who can do it in any country in which it is possible to do it".[2] Seizing on symbols of Islam's past greatness, bin Laden promised to restore pride to people who considered themselves the victims of successive foreign masters. In his rhetoric he used cultural and religious allusions to the holy Qur'an and some of its interpreters, and drew selectively from multiple sources – Islam, history and the region's political and economic malaise. This *fatwa* appears to have been a public launch of sorts, heralding a stronger, renewed al-Qaʿida. Bin Laden had maintained or restored many of his links with terrorists elsewhere in the world, and had strengthened ties within his own organization. Having merged with Egyptian Islamic Jihad, al-Qaʿida promised to become the general headquarters for international terrorism.

In spring 1998 Saudi Arabia quietly disrupted an al-Qaʿida cell in the Kingdom that was planning to attack US forces with shoulder-launched missiles. The CIA's director George Tenet took advantage of this opportunity to ask Saudi Arabia for help against bin Laden. ʿAbdullah promised Tenet an all-out secret effort to persuade the Taliban to expel bin Laden so that he could be sent to the US or to another country for trial.

Turki followed this up at a meeting in June with Taliban leader Mullah Omar. Employing possible incentives mixed with threats, he received a commitment that bin Laden would be expelled. Turki reported Omar's statement: "We are ready, and our interests are with you [Saudi Arabia], not

---

1. NSA, State Dept., Cable, "Afghanistan: Meeting with the Taliban", 11 December 1997.
2. *Al-Quds al-ʿArabi*, 23 February 1998.

with an individual." Omar requested the establishment of a joint commission to organize the handover.[1]

Before the move to Afghanistan, al-Qaʿida had concentrated on providing funds, training and weapons for actions carried out by members of allied groups. All this would change in the summer of 1998, after which al-Qaʿida, under the direct supervision of bin Laden and his chief aides, would plan, direct and execute future attacks. On 7 August, bomb-laden trucks drove into two US embassy compounds, roughly five minutes apart – about 10.35 AM in Nairobi, Kenya, and 10.39 AM in Dar es Salaam, Tanzania. Shortly afterwards, *Al-Quds al-ʿArabi*, a London-based Arabic newspaper, received a telephone call proclaiming the formation of "the Islamic Army for the Liberation of the Holy Places" and announcing that the attacks had been carried out by a "company of a battalion of this Islamic Army".[2]

On 14 August, the CIA and the FBI provided Clinton with detailed evidence that the operation had been carried out by al-Qaʿida. During the meeting a CIA report from a source in Afghanistan mentioned that bin Laden and his high-ranking staff were to hold a meeting on 20 August to review the results of their attacks and plan the next wave. According to counter-terrorism advisor Richard A. Clarke, Clinton asked Berger to coordinate all action required for a military response, also to be scheduled for 20 August, saying: "Listen, retaliating for these attacks is all well and good, but we gotta get rid of these guys once and for all."[3]

There was considerable debate as to whether to strike targets outside Afghanistan, including the al-Shifa pharmaceutical plant in Khartoum, which, according to intelligence reports, was manufacturing precursor ingredients for nerve gas with bin Laden's financial support. On 20 August, US Navy vessels in the Arabian Sea fired cruise missiles. Though most of these hit the intended targets – the al-Shifa plant as well as training camps in Afghanistan – neither bin Laden nor any other terrorist leader was killed.[4]

The ways in which Clinton and his advisors chose to handle bin Laden's

---

1. *Al-Sharq al-Awsat*, 4 November 2001.
2. US v. bin Laden, "Closing Statement by Assistant US Attorney Ken Karas", 2 May 2001, pp. 5,426–39.
3. Richard A. Clarke, *Against All Enemies: Inside America's War on Terror* (London: Free Press, 2004), pp. 184–5.
4. *The New York Times* and The National Commission on Terrorist Attacks Upon the United States, *The Complete Investigation*, pp. 170–1.

threats reflected their unwillingness to bear substantial economic, military and political costs in order to achieve grand strategic objectives. While Clinton recognized that terrorism represented a growing danger to the US, he was relatively cautious in confronting al-Qa'ida, instead of retaliating with a more robust military response to attacks such as those on the two embassies.[1]

The Clinton administration's final National Security Strategy in December 1999 promulgated three overarching objectives: to enhance the US's security; to bolster its economic prosperity; and to promote democracy and human rights abroad.[2] As with the 1994 strategy, this one failed to recognize the seriousness of terrorism.

Clinton made two sets of errors with respect to the manner in which he confronted bin Laden. First, he was late in recognizing the severity of the danger posed by al-Qa'ida. Second, after acknowledging the grave threats presented by bin Laden, he remained reluctant to take decisive military action against either al-Qa'ida or those regimes upon which it was suspected of relying for support. As Dick Morris, one of Clinton's top domestic political advisors during his initial term, noted: "On issues of terrorism, defence and foreign affairs, generally, [Clinton] was always too wary of criticism to act decisively."[3] Clinton had, in fact, had two clear opportunities to respond decisively to attacks carried out by al-Qa'ida on US civilian and military targets – the August bombings of the two US embassies and the suicide bombing in October 2000 of the Navy destroyer *USS Cole* in Aden – but unfortunately, the trend continued.

In the wake of the US missile strike, the Taliban hardened its stance on extraditing bin Laden, and its religious leaders issued a *fatwa* requiring Muslims to protect him. On 26 August, the Taliban received a letter from the US providing evidence that bin Laden had engaged in terrorist activities, but this was seen by the Taliban as not specific enough to warrant his extradition. Thus, when Turki returned in September 1998 to seek fulfilment of the earlier promise, Mullah Omar refused to expel bin Laden and denounced Saudi Arabia, which then suspended diplomatic relations with Afghanistan. When

1. Pauly, *US Foreign Policy and the Persian Gulf*, p. 67.
2. John Lewis Gaddis, "A Grand Strategy of Transformation", *Foreign Policy* (November-December 2002), pp. 50–1.
3. Dick Morris, *Off with Their Heads: Traitors, Crooks and Obstructionists in American Politics, Media and Business* (New York: Reagan Books, 2003), pp. 97–8.

'Abdullah visited Washington in late September, he informed Clinton about the Taliban's refusal.[1]

US efforts continued, and on 11 October, the US ambassador to Pakistan William B. Milam met the Taliban Minister of Foreign Affairs Wakil Ahmed, who asked questions regarding the possible treatment in Saudi Arabia of bin Laden should he be turned over to the Saudi authorities. With the diplomatic options seemingly no more promising than the military options, however, Washington issued a formal warning to the Taliban "that the US reserves the right to take military action concerning Bin Laden and will hold the Taliban directly responsible for any terrorist activities Bin Laden engages in."[2]

In November, the Taliban announced that there was insufficient evidence to implicate bin Laden in terrorist activities. In an extensive discussion with the US embassy's Deputy Chief of Mission in Pakistan, Alan W. Eastham Jr, Ahmed claimed: "The Taliban had given the Saudis an authentic proposal for resolving the Bin Laden issue … It was only Saudi pride that stood in the way."[3] Ahmed was referring to two alleged proposals made to Saudi Arabia concerning bin Laden. The first outlined the formation of a joint Saudi/Afghan committee of *ulama* to examine evidence of bin Laden's involvement in terrorism. The second would allow family members of any Saudis killed in the Khobar Towers explosion to bring their cases to Afghan courts. Without Saudi confirmation of these claims, it is difficult to substantiate them. Conceivably, any Saudi hesitation in the first case might have been due to the difficulty that would have ensued in finding a credible Saudi scholar willing to participate in such a committee. Reluctance to entertain the second proposal could have had to do with a lack of confidence in Afghanistan's judicial system.[4]

Saudi Arabia, which had a long and close relationship with Pakistan, was already pressing Pakistani Prime Minister Nawaz Sharif with regard to the Taliban and bin Laden. During his visit to Pakistan in October 1998, 'Abdullah put a tremendous amount of pressure on Sharif. Clinton also invited Sharif to

---

1. *Al-Sharq al-Awsat*, 4 November 2001.
2. NSA, State Dept., US embassy, Islamabad, cable, "Usama bin Laden: Coordinating Our Efforts and Sharpening Our Message on bin Laden", 19 October 1998.
3. NSA, State Dept., cable, "Osama bin Laden: Taliban Spokesman Seeks New Proposal for Resolving bin Laden Problem", 28 November 1998.
4. NSA, State Department, US embassy, Islamabad, cable, "Usama bin Laden: High-Level Taliban Official Gives the Standard Line on bin Laden with a Couple of Nuances in October 11th Meeting with Ambassador", 12 October 1998.

Washington on 2 December, and telephoned him on 18 December to discuss bin Laden.

On 6 July 1999, Clinton issued an executive order effectively declaring the Taliban regime a state sponsor of terrorism. In October, pushed by the US, a UN Security Council Resolution (UNSCR 1267) added both economic and travel sanctions to this action.

Clinton had contacted Sharif again in June to urge him to persuade the Taliban to expel bin Laden. Sharif suggested instead that Pakistani forces might try to capture bin Laden themselves. The two leaders met again in Washington in early July, and Clinton complained about Pakistan's failure to take effective action with respect to the Taliban and bin Laden. Sharif repeated his earlier proposal and won approval for US assistance in training a Pakistani Special Forces team for an operation against bin Laden. However, Sharif was deposed in October by his own military, and the plan was terminated.

Clinton had authorized the CIA to work with several governments to capture the al-Qa'ida leader, and extended the scope of efforts to include bin Laden's principal lieutenants. The CIA discussed different options, including the possibility of putting US personnel on the ground in Afghanistan – perhaps as part of a team joined to a deployment of the CIA's own officers. Doing so would have required a major policy initiative to make a long-term commitment, to establish a durable presence in Afghanistan and acceptance of the associated risks and costs. However, no option was rated as having more than a 15 percent chance of achieving its objective.

Inderfurth met Taliban representative Abdul Mujahid on 25 October, and was presented with two proposals. The first was that the Taliban would confine bin Laden in Afghanistan under the supervision of the Organisation of the Islamic Conference, the Non-Aligned Movement or the UN. Inderfurth rejected this proposal, noting that it did not meet the requirements of UNSCR 1267. The second proposal was for a panel of Islamic scholars to decide bin Laden's future. One scholar would be from Afghanistan, one from Saudi Arabia and one from a third country. Inderfurth remarked that if this process took place, the US hoped it would lead to extradition; however, Washington would not be bound by the panel's decision. But, as was very often the case, the discussions were followed by Taliban declarations that no evidence existed against bin Laden, and that he would not be expelled as the UN resolution demanded.

For bin Laden, there were lessons to be learned from the US retaliation and pressure on the Taliban to extradite him:

1. The US was an impotent superpower;
2. He was becoming a symbol of resistance to the US and to a global order deemed to be unjust;
3. The Taliban had become increasingly dependent on his support. The Saudis had ended their financial support, and Pakistan's military support had also ceased.[1]

For Riyadh, the implications were:

1. That bin Laden's stature had grown among disaffected Saudis, which led to the incitement of young Saudis joining al Qa'ida;
2. That the Saudi government was unable to confront the religious establishment, which was indirectly promoting a favourable view of al Qa'ida. Any consideration of doing so was made difficult, if not impossible, by the climate of public opinion.[2]

Meanwhile, according to Prince Turki, the CIA was told by the GID at the end of 1999 that the Kingdom had put Nawaf al-Hazmi and Khalid al-Mihdhar (who were later accused of being two of the perpetrators of the attacks on New York in September 2001) on its watchlist. Turki later said: "We told them [the CIA] that those persons are on our watchlist because of their connection to al-Qa'ida, the bombing of the two embassies, and smuggling weapons to the Kingdom in 1997."[3]

Although disruptive efforts around the world had achieved some success, the core of bin Laden's organization remained intact. The CIA worked hard with foreign security services to detain, or at least keep an eye on, suspected al-Qa'ida associates, and disruption and arrest operations were mounted against terrorists in eight countries. Through the CIA's Counter-Terrorism Center (CTC) and the State Department's Antiterrorism Assistance Program,

---

1. Niblock, *Saudi Arabia*, p. 161.
2. Ibid., pp. 162–3.
3. *Al-Watan*, 18 October 2003.

the US had enhanced the capabilities of several foreign states to collect intelligence on al-Qaʻida and to thwart its operations. As a result of these partnerships, simultaneous action against over twenty al-Qaʻida cells was carried out in December 1999, to prevent possible attacks during the period of the Millennium celebrations. In mid-December 1999, Clinton signed a Memorandum of Notification giving the CIA broader authority to use foreign proxies to detain bin Laden's lieutenants without having to transfer them to US custody.

Meanwhile, NSC staff advised Berger that the US had only been "nibbling at the edges" of bin Laden's network, and that more terror attacks were forthcoming – that it was not a question of "if" but "when" and "where".[1]

The 12 October 2000 attack on the *USS Cole*, which killed seventeen crew members and wounded at least forty others, galvanized al-Qaʻida's recruitment efforts. In late 2000, CIA and NSC staff began to think about the counter-terrorism policy agenda they would present to the new administration of President George W. Bush. The CTC produced a paper, informally referred to as the "Blue Sky" memo, which was sent on 29 December to Richard Clarke, now National Coordinator for Security, Infrastructure Protection and Counter-Terrorism. The memo proposed:

1. A major effort to support the anti-Taliban Northern Alliance in Afghanistan through intelligence sharing and increased funding;

2. Increased support to the Republic of Uzbekistan to strengthen its ability to fight terrorism and to assist the US in doing so;

3. Assistance to other anti-Taliban groups and proxies that might be encouraged to passively resist the Taliban.

The CIA memo noted that a multifaceted strategy would be needed to produce real change. As the Clinton administration drew to a close, Clarke and his staff developed a policy paper of their own. They proposed a goal to "roll back" al-Qaʻida over a period of three to five years. Over time, the policy would be to try to weaken and eliminate the network's infrastructure.

---

1. NSC, Memorandum from Paul Kurtz, member of the White House counterterrorism team, to Berger, "Roadmap for March 10th Principals Committee (PC) Meeting", 8 March 2000.

"Continued anti-al-Qaeda operations at the current level will prevent some attacks," wrote Clarke's team, "but will not seriously affect the ability to plan and conduct attacks."[1]

---

1. NSA, NSC, "Strategy for Eliminating the Threat from Jihadist Networks of al-Qa'ida: Status and Prospects", December 2000.

CHAPTER FOUR

The 'Abdullah Era (2001–6): Confrontation, Mutual Accusation and Disappointment

The period covered in this chapter has been described as the "The 'Abdullah Era", though Fahd remained *de facto* ruler of the Kingdom until 2005. The disastrous events of 11 September 2001 compelled 'Abdullah, with the acceptance of the Saudi royal establishment, to take full charge of government policy and confront the aftermath of that notorious date.

The attacks on US targets on 11 September 2001 (now known universally as "9/11") drove a wedge between the US and Saudi Arabia. As mutual suspicions and accusations arose publicly, the two countries found themselves for the first time on a collision course. Washington accused Riyadh of failing to help curb extremism and hatred, while Saudi Arabia accused the US of imposing its values and dictating an alien way of thinking without concern for the impact on Saudi society.

Both sides also neglected the roots of the problem, which had started with the war against the Soviets in Afghanistan. At the end of the conflict, the US had lost interest in that now-de-stabilized country and chose to ignore the dangers emanating from it. For its part, the Kingdom ignored Saudi *jihadist* activities in Bosnia and Chechnya, and the implications of such participation for Saudi youth. In addition, toward shared geo-strategic ends, the US had accepted – and at times actively encouraged – Saudi proselytizing, while the Saudi government, in order to maintain control over domestic affairs, pandered to the most radical elements within the Kingdom's religious establishments.

Both countries thus shared the blame for promoting the short-term benefits that led to the catastrophic events of 9/11 as well as the subsequent invasions of Afghanistan and Iraq (in 2001 and 2003, respectively) and their aftermath.

The occupation of Iraq created further problems for the two countries. The failure of the US to reconstruct Iraq post-invasion had devastating implications for the US and for the entire Arab Middle East, and ignited a sectarian conflict the effects of which have severely damaged regional stability. The Iranian penetration of Iraq was another outcome of the occupation, as the ill thought-out policies of the US – which involved the dissolution of the Iraqi army and de-Ba'thification – effectively handed majority-Shi'i Iraq to the Iranians. In advance of the US occupation, the Saudis had warned Washington that it was making a grievous mistake. Saudi Arabia now found itself facing the probability of Iraqi disintegration along with increased Iranian influence in Iraq, and with it the Arab Middle East, with inadvertent new bases now available for al-Qa'ida from which to plan and organize terrorist activities.

9/11 and its Impact

On taking office, George W. Bush and his principal advisers had all been briefed on terrorism and terrorists, including bin Laden. National Security Advisor Condoleezza Rice was generally aware that terrorism had changed since her initial service with the first Bush administration, and therefore paid particular attention to the question of how counterterrorism policy should be coordinated. She asked Philip Zelikow, Professor of History at the University of Virginia, to advise her, with the result that amidst all the changes that accompanied the transition of administrations, there was significant continuity in counterterrorism policy.[1]

Clarke, National Coordinator for Security, Infrastructure Protection and Counterterrorism, tried to get Rice – and Bush – to give very high priority to terrorism and to act on the agenda he had pushed during the last few months of the Clinton administration. Rice did not respond directly to Clarke's memorandum, however, nor was any NSC principal committee meeting on al-Qa'ida held until 4 September 2001.[2] According to the 9/11 Commission

---

1. Final Report of the National Commission on Terrorist Attack Upon the U.S., "The 9/11 Commission Report", New York: W. W. Norton & Co., 2004, pp. 198–200.
2. Ibid, p. 201.

Report, Rice's delayed response can be attributed to two main factors. First, the CIA, while stating that a "strong circumstantial case" could be made against al-Qaʿida, also noted that it continued to lack "conclusive information on external command and control" of the attack. Second, in addition to terrorism the new administration faced many other problems, including the collapse of the Middle East peace process, a crisis with China in April over a US spy plane, and controversy over promoting a new nuclear strategy that allowed anti-missile defence.[1]

At the end of March 2001, the intelligence community disseminated a terrorist threat "advisory" indicating a heightened threat of Sunni extremist terrorist attacks against US facilities, personnel and other interests.[2] The interagency Counterterrorism Security Group reported on 20 April: "Bin Laden is planning multiple operations."[3] Reports similar to these were made available to Bush in his regular morning intelligence briefings with CIA director Tenet. While these briefings discussed general threats to the US and its interests, specific threats were all overseas.[4]

An Arab television station, MBC, reported on 25 June that some al-Qaʿida leaders were saying that the next weeks "[would] witness important surprises", and that US and Israeli interests would be targeted.[5] A briefing for top officials on 30 June stated that bin Laden's operatives expected "near-term attacks" to have "dramatic consequences of catastrophic proportions",[6] and reports in mid-July indicated that although bin Laden's plans had been delayed for as long as two months, they had not been abandoned.[7]

During the spring and summer of 2001, Bush had asked whether any of these threats pointed to the US. The CIA decided, therefore, to write a brief summarizing its understanding of the danger. A written daily briefing to the president on 6 August, titled "Bin Laden Determined to Strike in US", indicated that bin Laden "prepares operations years in advance and is not deterred by

---

1. Ibid., pp. 201–3.
2. CIA Cable, "Intelligence Community Terrorist Threat Advisory", 30 March 2001
3. CIA, Senior Executive Intelligence Brief (SEIB), "Bin Laden Planning Multiple Operations", 20 April 2001.
4. *The 9/11 Commission Report*, p. 256.
5. *Al-Watan*, 25 June 2001.
6. CIA, SEIB, "Bin Laden Planning High-Profile Attacks", 30 June 2001.
7. CIA, SEIB, "Bin Laden Plans Delayed but Not Abandoned", 13 July 2001.

setbacks ... Bin Laden wants to hijack a US aircraft to gain the release of 'Blind Shaykh' 'Umar 'Abd Al-Rahman and other US-held extremists."[1]

On 11 September, the inevitable occurred. Bin Laden's terrorist network hijacked four airliners and attacked the World Trade Center in New York and the Pentagon near Washington DC, leaving a death toll estimated at about 3,000 from both attacks. The events raised two immediate questions for the White House: Who was responsible for the attacks, and how should the US respond? In addressing the nation that evening, Bush stated: "We will make no distinction between the terrorists who committed these acts and those who harbor them."[2] In the ensuing days, evidence implicating al-Qa'ida mounted rapidly.

On 12 September, a Saudi official source stated: "The Kingdom strongly condemns acts which contradict with all religious values and civilized principles."[3] On 13 September 'Abdullah declared: "Any sane man who believes in God and understands the everlasting message of Islam, stands opposed to terrorism as a crime against all humanity. We in the Kingdom of Saudi Arabia are fully prepared to cooperate in every manner to bring about an end to the scourge of terrorism."[4]

Ukaz reported on 14 September that 'Abdullah had appealed for Bush to respond wisely to these horrible circumstances, and had confirmed the Kingdom's willingness "to cooperate in every way that will uncover the identity of the perpetrators". Bandar, too, said that the Kingdom "rejects any person connected to terrorism", adding that Islam itself clearly rejects terrorism and noting: "If it is proven without any doubt that those who committed these acts were people adhering to Islam in name, they represent only themselves."[5] On 20 September Prince Saud met Bush and said after the meeting: "This action, as much as it is directed to the US, is also directed at the Islamic World to drive a wedge between the Islamic World and the rest of civilization." He added that the Kingdom would do its utmost to fight terrorism.[6]

The US built an international "coalition of the willing" to confront al-Qa'ida

---

1. NSA, CIA, Presidential Daily Briefing, 6 August 2001.
2. PPP, George W. Bush, Book I, vol. 2, 2001, pp. 1,099–1,100.
3. *Ukaz*, 12 September 2001.
4. Saudi Embassy, Washington, "Embassy Issues Summary Report on Fight Against Terrorism", 27 August 2002, http://www.saudiembassy.net/2000News/Statements/StateDetail.asp?cIndex=161, last accessed June 2007.
5. *Ukaz*, 14 September 2001.
6. *Ukaz*, 21 September 2001.

and the Taliban, and on 7 October launched "Operation Enduring Freedom". Working with the Afghan Northern Alliance, US forces removed the Taliban from power, thereby reducing al-Qaʻida's ability to organize and direct future terrorist operations on the scale of the 9/11 assaults.[1]

Faced with strong domestic public opinion against the US, Saudi Arabia was unable, at least publicly, to come out in support of the military operation in Afghanistan. Bandar was reported as saying: "The US has not asked the Kingdom to use its military bases."[2] Prince Saud confirmed that: "As to the Kingdom, it has not been asked to provide military assistance." He added: "Each country, in accordance with its capabilities and abilities, has to do what is in its power."[3] Secretary of State Powell expressed his understanding of the difficulties faced by the Kingdom and by Egypt, noting that "... there are people inside the two countries who do not like what we are doing".[4]

Almost immediately after 9/11, US intelligence concluded that fifteen of the nineteen hijackers were of Saudi origin. This reality, which had probably been deliberately orchestrated by bin Laden, made the Kingdom the object of suspicion and criticism in many quarters of the US. The Saudi regime was depicted by some American media as the embodiment of obstinacy and lack of cooperation.[5] One editorial asserted that the Kingdom "is rapidly becoming an obstacle in the campaign against terrorists", and went so far as to state: "Saudi policies have become ... a genuine menace to the US."[6] According to Prince Saud, bin Laden's aim was "to drive a wedge between Saudi Arabia and the US".[7]

On 17 October, an "unnamed Saudi official" denounced the US press attacks on Saudi Arabia: "The mobilization of Western and US public opinion against the Kingdom is a well-known subject in its directions and who's behind

---

1. For an in-depth examination of "Operation Enduring Freedom", see Tom Lansford, *All for One: Terrorism, NATO and the US* (Aldershot, UK: Ashgate Publishing, 2002).
2. *Al-Sharq al-Awsat*, 1 October 2001.
3. *Al-Watan* 2 October 2001.
4. Agence France-Presse (AFP), 21 October 2001.
5. Jane Perlez, "Saudis Uncooperative, White House Aides Say", *International Herald Tribune*, 12 October 2001.
6. "Out of Saudi Arabia", *International Herald Tribune*, 22 January 2002 (editorial reprinted from the original *Washington Post* article, dated 21 January 2001).
7. Saudi Embassy, Washington, "Prince Saud's Address to US-Saudi Arabian Business Council", New York, 26 April 2004, http://www.saudiembassy.net/2004News/Statements/SpeechDetail.asp?cIndex=400, last accessed June 2007.

it."[1] (The source was probably referring to the Israel lobby.) Saudi Interior Minister Prince Naif bin 'Abdul 'Aziz was reported as having said: "This campaign is unjustified and ... the Zionists are behind it"; he was also said to have indicated that the American press was not interested in Saudi society: "Most of the US media is unable to understand us, and we do not see any willingness to understand."[2] Saudi Defence Minister Prince Sultan described the perpetrators of the attack as "criminals and saboteurs", and insisted that his country should not be blamed. He maintained that the Saudi participants were "apart from the Muslim community, and nationalism. They bear their own responsibilities, not us." He also depicted 9/11 as an "accursed day because innocent people were murdered".[3]

The perception in the US was that the Saudi government carried an indirect responsibility for what had happened. In July 2002, Laurent Murawiec, an analyst at the US government-funded RAND Corporation think tank, gave a briefing to the top Pentagon advisory board portraying Saudi Arabia as an enemy of the US. Murawiec described the Kingdom as "the kernel of evil, the prime mover, the most dangerous opponent" in the Middle East, and also proposed targeting its oil resources, financial assets and holy places. The briefing represented a point of view that had growing currency within the Bush administration, as well as among neoconservative writers and thinkers closely allied with administration policy-makers.

When Bandar was asked about the briefing, he said: "I think it is a misguided effort that is shallow, and not honest about the facts ... repeating lies will never make them facts."[4] Prince Saud also dismissed the comments as "mere fantasy", commenting: "Unfortunately there are people who try to stir up doubts and shock the historical relations between the two countries ... We have not changed, but others want to interpret everything as danger, and consider that the Kingdom constitutes a danger to the world just because it is there."[5] Powell promptly telephoned Saud to tell him that Bush did not view the Kingdom as a potential enemy.[6] An NSC spokesman emphasized: "These

---

1. *Ukaz*, 17 October 2001.
2. *Al-Watan*, 7 February 2002.
3. *Al-Hayat*, 11 September 2002.
4. Thomas E. Ricks, "Briefing Depicted Saudis as Enemies", *The Washington Post*, 6 August 2002.
5. *Al-Sharq al-Awsat*, 8 August 2002.
6. *Arab News*, 8 August 2002.

opinions do not reflect the administration's point of view ... President Bush and his administration consider Saudi Arabia a friend and a strong and firm ally."[1] Rumsfeld, now Secretary of Defense, telephoned Prince Sultan to express his and the department's unhappiness about the report and its contents. He said the report "represented the personal point of view of the writer only, and not that of the US Defense Department".[2]

On 12 August, the Saudi Council of Ministers discussed US press reports on the Saudi-US relationship and expressed its "appreciation for the friendly statements emanating from US officials".[3] On 29 August Bush reportedly telephoned 'Abdullah and praised the historical relationship between the two countries, asserting that the frequent press articles were "irresponsible words, [which] don't in any way express the reality of the relationship and do not reflect its established firmness".[4] However, other articles similar in tone to the RAND briefing continued to be published in the US media.

The impact that such attacks were having on Saudi-US relations was in turn reflected in the Saudi press, which reacted strongly to such treatment. *Al-Riyadh* stated: "The obstacles posed by the American media separate the Arabs and America." It outlined the dubious role that the US media, through its bias toward Israel, had played by depicting the Arabs as barbarians, and by showing Arab and Muslim traditions and beliefs as the height of backwardness. The newspaper declared: "At this point the dialogue with the US loses its *raison d'être*."[5] *Al-Riyadh* wrote, in another editorial: "This is a conflict where the strong seek to take possession of the minds of peoples, to use terrorism against other peoples' holy places, and to plunder resources."[6] Daoud Al-Shirian, a Saudi columnist for *Al-Hayat*, explained how Saudi fears of the continued use of the expression "Saudi Arabia's hostility towards the US" were justified, claiming: "this change is likely to affect official policy if it gains the support of pressure groups and centres of influence in the corridors of American policy."[7]

Writing in *Al-Hayat*, Saudi ambassador to the UK Ghazi Algosaibi claimed

1. *Al-Sharq al-Awsat*, 7 August 2002.
2. *Al-Sharq al-Awsat*, 9 August 2002.
3. *Al-Yaum*, 13 August 2002.
4. *Ukaz*, 29 August 2002.
5. *Al-Riyadh*, 27 November 2001.
6. *Al-Riyadh*, 18 December 2001.
7. *Al-Hayat*, 18 August 2002.

that the right-wing Christian alliance, supported by the Zionist lobby, was conducting the campaign against Saudi Arabia. He wrote:

> In the new political reality, Saudi Arabia [is perceived in the US] as closer to [the camp of] enemies than to that of friends. This approach did not emerge suddenly from the Pentagon report ... anyone who has monitored the American media since the September events and tried to read behind the lines realizes that there is an "orchestra" carefully leading and feeding the attack on Saudi Arabia.[1]

The Congressional report on the events of 9/11 was published on 24 July 2003. By order of the US and against the wishes of the Saudi government, twenty-eight pages of this document were kept secret. Allegedly this was to protect Saudi Arabia from public suspicion with regard to having indirectly provided financing for the hijackers. *The Washington Times* reported on 29 July that Senator Pat Roberts, Chairman of the Senate Select Committee on Intelligence, had said that the pages were removed to avoid embarrassing the Saudi government.[2] Bandar, according to *The Guardian*, said: "First we were criticized by 'unnamed sources'. Now we are being criticized with a blank piece of paper ... We can deal with questions in public, but we cannot respond to blank pages."[3] Bush met Saud, who called for the release of the classified section of the report to enable the Kingdom to rebut the allegations contained therein, but Bush refused the request.[4] In September, Saud said: "We are angry when we are accused without being given a chance to defend ourselves."[5] In addition, some relatives of the 9/11 victims mounted a lawsuit against some Saudi top officials.[6]

Suggestions made in the press by right-wing political commentators to

---

1. *Al-Hayat*, 21 August 2002.
2. *The Washington Times*, 29 July 2003
3. *Guardian Unlimited*, 25 July 2003.
4. Alfred B. Prados, "Saudi Arabia: Current Issues and U.S. Relations", Congressional Research Service Report (Washington, DC: Library of Congress), 4 August 2003.
5. Saudi Embassy, Washington, "The Saudis Respond: Foreign Minister Prince Saud Interviewed by Scott Macleod", *Time* exclusive, Paris, 10 September 2003. For further details see: http://www.saudiembassy.net/2003News/Statements/StateDetail.asp?cIndex=215.
6. *The New York Times*, "Sept. 11 Families Join to Sue Saudis, Banks, Charities and Royals Accused of Funding al Qaeda Terrorists", 16 August 2002.

split Saudi Arabia into several smaller states were met in the Kingdom with official outrage and ripostes in the Saudi media, as though a genuine "leak" had suggested this was actually a scenario the US was considering.[1] In any case, strong American reaction had an impact on the Saudi-US relationship. First, it placed it at the forefront of national debate, limiting the White House's freedom of action. Second, the distinction between governmental attitudes and public criticism was not well defined. Both governmental and non-governmental condemnation centred on the political and educational systems in the Kingdom, and on economic reform. There was also continuing criticism of the Saudi government for failing to stop the flow of Saudi human and material resources to al-Qa'ida.[2]

The Saudis' initial failure to acknowledge the citizenship of the 9/11 perpetrators further exacerbated growing anti-Saudi sentiment. For more than a year after 9/11, most Saudis refused to believe that bin Laden had planned, and that fifteen Saudi nationals had carried out, the attacks executed on that day.[3] Prince Naif alleged on 28 November 2002 that the Zionist-controlled US media had manipulated 9/11 events and had turned US public opinion against the Arabs and Islam: "We [must] put big question marks and ask who committed the events of September 11 and who benefited from them. Who benefited? I think they [the Zionists] are behind these events." The interior minister also hinted that a foreign power was involved: "I still cannot believe that nineteen youths, including fifteen Saudis, carried out the attack with the support of bin Laden and his al-Qa'ida. It's impossible."[4] However, according to Simpson, Bandar stated categorically in an interview about 9/11 that "the Zionists were not behind it ... It is an evil work done by evil people who were targeting your country but also targeting the relationship between our two countries."[5]

The fierce US media accusations directed against the Kingdom as a veritable wellspring of terrorists did nothing to endear the US to the Saudis in general. Prince Saud said in a speech to the US-Saudi Arabian Business Council on 26 April 2004: "If Saudi Arabia is guilty for what he [bin Laden] has become,

---

1. Jamie Glazov, "Symposium: The Future of U.S.-Saudi Relations", *FrontPage Magazine*, 11 July 2003.
2. Niblock, *Saudi Arabia*, pp. 164–5.
3. Bronson, *Thicker Than Oil*, pp. 233–5.
4. *Al-Riyadh*, 28 November 2002.
5. Simpson, *The Prince*, p. 318.

the US must surely share the blame."[1] Saud also contended that exaggerated reporting and biased conspiracy allegations hurt both countries and helped the extremists.

Fighting Terrorism

All terrorist groups are formed for a reason. While an act of terrorist violence results in brutal killing and carnage, the motivation that drives the terrorist to commit the atrocity may well be a deep-seated devotion to a noble cause. Terrorists acquire ever-greater power and influence by nurturing and developing fear and anger through the use of violence.[2]

The State Department defines terrorism as "premeditated, politically motivated violence perpetrated against non-combatant targets by sub-national groups or clandestine agents, usually intended to influence an audience".[3] According to Davies, writing in 2003, there were about fifty international terrorist groups currently active around the world, of which almost half were religiously motivated.[4]

It is unsurprising that religion should have become a far more popular motivation for terrorism in the post-Cold War era: leftist ideologies were abandoned, discredited by the collapse of the Soviet Union, while the promises of munificent benefits from the liberal-democratic capitalist states have so far failed to materialize in many countries throughout the world.[5]

Bin Laden deliberately framed al-Qaʻida's struggle in uncompromisingly theological terms, effectively weaving the strands of religious fervour, Muslim piety and a profound sense of grievance into a powerful ideological force. According to Saud, al-Qaʻida was bent on installing its brand of fundamentalism in Saudi Arabia and elsewhere in the Middle East, and increasingly saw the

---

1. Saudi Embassy, Washington, "Prince Saud's Address to U.S.-Saudi Arabian Business Council", New York, 26 April 2004.
2. Barry Davies, *Terrorism: Inside a World Phenomenon* (London: Virgin Books, 2003), pp. 3–4.
3. United States Department of State, Office of the Coordinator for Counterterrorism, "Patterns of Global Terrorism 2003" (Washington, D.C.: State Dept., Publication 11124, April 2004), p. xii.
4. Davies, *Terrorism*, pp. 28–30.
5. Mark Juergensmeyer, "Terror Mandated by God", *Terrorism and Political Violence*, vol. 9, no.2 (summer 1997), p. 20.

US as an obstacle to its goals. To achieve its objective, according to Saud, "it had first to drive a wedge between Saudi Arabia and the US".[1]

The US response to 9/11 was an extended "War on Terror", starkly defined by Bush when he stated: "Either you are with us, or you are with the terrorists."[2] Within days of 11 September, Bush and Ashcroft proposed an omnibus package of "anti-terrorism" measures for approval by Congress. Congressional leaders labelled the package of proposals the USA PATRIOT Act (which stood for "Uniting and Strengthening America by Providing Appropriate Tools Required to Intercept and Obstruct Terrorism"), and the measure was passed overwhelmingly. The Act covers a range of subjects, from surveillance and immigration procedures to money laundering to victim compensation funds. It is, in effect, a jumble of provisions that amends and expands a host of pre-existing federal laws.[3]

According to Palmer and Palmer, the severest threat for the US was considered to be that posed by Islamist terrorism. One stream of Islam does not distinguish politics from religion, thus distorting both. It is further fed by grievances accentuated by bin Laden and widely felt throughout the Muslim world. There is no common ground from which a dialogue can proceed with this stream. It can only be destroyed or utterly isolated.

Resentment toward the security measures put in place by the US following the 9/11 attacks ran deep in Muslim countries, even among leaders, and arose from four widely accepted perceptions of the US:

1. That it was attempting to bring the entire region under its control through manipulation;
2. That it wished to exploit the region;
3. That it sided with Israel;
4. That it had declared war on Islam.[4]

---

1. Saudi Embassy, Washington, Address by Minister of Foreign Affairs HRH Prince Saud Al-Faisal to the Council on Foreign Relations, "The US and Saudi Arabia: A Relationship Threatened By Misconceptions", New York, 27 April 2004.
2. PPP, George W. Bush, Books I and II, 2001, "Address Before a Joint Session of the Congress on the U.S. Response to the Terrorist Attacks of September 11", 20 September 2001, pp. 1,140–4.
3. CATO Handbook for Congress, Washington DC: CATO Institute, pp. 199–201.
4. Palmer and Palmer, *At the Heart of Terror*, pp. 32–5.

The US conception of its terrorist enemy covered both al-Qaʻida and a wider radical ideological movement in the Islamic world. The first enemy had been weakened but continued to pose a grave threat, while the second was gathering its strength and would menace the US long after the destruction of al-Qaʻida.[1]

The US-led war on terror was a significant element in provoking religious and nationalist feelings in the Kingdom. Combined with pre-existing suspicion of US designs and resentment of its behaviour, this war generated a level of anger that seemed likely to have repercussions for many years to come and was itself a source of concern for the Saudi government.[2] At the launch of the 2001 US military campaign in Afghanistan, reports of anti-US resentment and of popular sympathy for bin Laden – even if largely by default – proliferated in the Kingdom. For example, a former member of the Saudi Council of Senior *Ulama*, ʻAbdullah bin Jibrin, issued a *fatwa* calling on Muslims to support the Taliban.[3] Jamal Khashoggi, Deputy Editor of *Arab News*, wrote: "There are very few people in Saudi Arabia who are prepared to criticize bin Laden, especially among the more religious."[4] *The International Herald Tribune* reported that the Saudi intelligence director, Prince Nawaf, had acknowledged that after 9/11 the majority of Saudi youth sympathized with bin Laden. The report also indicated that 95 percent of Saudi nationals aged between twenty-four and forty-one (as surveyed by Saudi intelligence) were found to be supportive of bin Laden's cause.[5]

9/11 created a challenge to the country's ability to address issues ranging from terrorist financing to domestic reform. On the issue of financing terrorism, the Kingdom faced a barrage of US press articles and editorials accusing Saudi Arabia and its people of helping to create and sustain bin Laden and his terrorist organization. One prime example is the editorial in *The New York Times* of 14 October 2001, which focused on the Kingdom's tolerance of and the royal family's passive attitude toward terrorism, and Saudi connections to Islamic fundamentalist terrorism.[6]

Under such pressure, the US perceived a need to send a high-level

---

1. *The 9/11 Commission Report*, p. 363.
2. Champion, *The Paradoxical Kingdom*, pp. 239–40.
3. *Daily Star*, 5 October 2001.
4. Ibid., 23 November 2001.
5. *International Herald Tribune*, 28 January 2002.
6. *The New York Times*, 14 October 2001.

delegation to the Kingdom to discuss the allegations. *Al-Hayat* reported that the delegation, which arrived in Riyadh on 8 December, consisted of Treasury, State Department and NSC officials. Saudi sources said the Kingdom had agreed to receive the delegation in the hope of explaining procedures for monitoring fundraising by Saudi charity organizations that contributed to Muslim causes all over the world.[1] According to Agence France-Presse, a senior White House official described the mission as "a great example of the spirit of cooperation and the dialogue between our two countries".[2]

Saudi Arabia's support for Islamic causes has never meant the support of terrorism or violent Islamic extremism. In the past, the Saudi government has repeatedly taken action to suppress the latter, and through supervising, funding and defining the qualifications of *imams* has therefore succeeded in developing powerful tools to use in restricting the actions of Saudi clerics.[3] Cordesman observes that Riyadh was indeed careless in some of its funding for Islamic causes, providing aid to certain Islamic movements and charities without properly examining their true character; the money was subsequently funnelled by these organizations into extremist causes.[4] It should be noted, however, that most of these funds went through private channels, and that this was beyond the control of the Saudi government. Indeed, the movement of capital and of individuals was almost impossible for Saudi Arabia – as well as other countries – to regulate. Even so, the vast majority of the private donors would appear to have been unaware of a specifically terrorist-oriented end-usage of any particular funds. Moreover, it was equally important for the West to understand that resentment in the Islamic and Arab world would continue to present problems for the West regardless of any actions taken by Saudi Arabia.[5]

Bandar countered US media assumptions by saying: "The idea that the Saudi government funded, organized or even knew about September 11 is malicious and blatantly false."[6] In discussing the challenges facing the Kingdom, he explained: "The priority became: where do we concentrate? Fighting

---

1. *Al-Hayat*, 9 December 2001.
2. AFP, 6 December 2001.
3. Anthony H. Cordesman, *Saudi Security and the War on Terrorism: International Security Operations, Law Enforcements, International Threats, and the Need for Change* (Washington, DC: Center for Strategic and International Studies, March 2002), p. 17.
4. Ibid., p 20.
5. Ibid., pp. 28–9.
6. *Guardian Unlimited*, 25 July 2003.

the terrorists, trying to grab their money, or explaining our position to the American people?"[1]

The Western notion of the separation of civil and religious duty does not exist in Islamic culture. Supporting charitable works is an integral function of governments in the Islamic world, and until 9/11 many Saudis would have perceived Riyadh's oversight of charitable donations as interference in the exercise of their faith.[2] Clearly, Saudi decision-makers were not prepared simply to accede to any US demand except on terms that were deemed balanced, compatible with the conception of their role and in keeping with domestic standing and interests.

Al-Qa'ida has moved its money through smuggling and through bank transfers taking advantage of unsuspected holes in the global financial and the growing Islamic banking systems. It also used the *hawala*,[3] an underground network enabling money transfers with virtually no paper trail.[4] Efficiency, reliable access to remote or undeveloped regions and low costs make the system attractive for the transfer of illicit or terrorist-destined funds. The events of 11 September brought into focus the ease with which informal value transfer systems can be utilized to conceal and move illicit funds.[5]

Paul O'Neill, Secretary of the Treasury, arrived in the Kingdom on 5 March 2002 and held discussions with Saudi Finance Minister Ibrahim Al-Asaf on terrorism financing, transfer transparency and the activities of charitable organizations.[6] According to *Al-Hayat*, O'Neill advised: "The Kingdom has to act more vigorously in identifying suspects involved in terrorism financing." He then explained the US position toward charitable activities: "We support charitable behaviour and its continuation ... but we want to be sure where

---

1. *'Ain al-Yaqeen*, 3 October 2003.
2. *The 9/11 Commission Report*, p. 69.
3. Alternative remittance systems represent informal or unregulated means of transferring value between or among multiple locations. Often these systems are composed of geographic networks and are described by a variety of specific terms depending on the region or community they serve. The term *hawala* is often used to describe alternative remittance systems or services in the Middle East.
4. Clarke, *Against All Enemies*, p. 192.
5. US Congress, Senate, Committee on Finance, "Financial War on Terrorism: New Money Trails Present Fresh Challenges", 107th Cong., 2nd sess., 9 October 2002, p. 35.
6. *Al-Hayat*, 6 March 2002.

the charity organization's funds come from and where they go to, and we want the Saudis to imitate us." He added: "We don't say that all Saudi charity organizations are bad, but there are certain parts of their activities that need to be monitored." In conclusion, he said he had found "great cooperation from the Saudi authorities in many aspects, and an understanding of the US administration's views".[1]

The first joint designation of terrorist supporters was made by the US with Saudi Arabia on 11 March 2002, when the two countries together identified the Al-Haramain Islamic Foundation, a Saudi-based non-governmental organization located in Somalia and Bosnia-Herzegovina, as linked to al-Qa'ida. It was then forwarded to the UN Security Council Sanctions Committee for inclusion under UNSCR 1333/1390, which has a mandate blocking the actions of bin Laden and associates. On 9 September 2002, the US and Saudi Arabia also jointly referred Wa'el Hamza Julaidan, one of bin Laden's associates and a supporter of al-Qa'ida terror, to the Sanctions Committee.[2] Alan Larson, Under-Secretary of State for Economic and Agricultural Affairs, said in his testimony to Congress: "The government of Saudi Arabia sees al-Qa'ida as a threat and ... has been cooperating with efforts to cut off financial flows to al-Qa'ida."[3]

In his testimony before the House Financial Services Committee, FBI director Robert Mueller stated that Saudi authorities were working with the US Treasury on identifying sources of terrorist funding, and that "substantial strides" had been made in that process. Deputy Treasury Secretary Kenneth Dam also testified to the same committee that the Treasury and Saudi Arabia were consulting carefully on the issue, and that the Kingdom should be praised for its efforts.[4]

Furthermore, Saudi Arabia had helped identify a sophisticated network consisting of shell companies and organizations woven through more than twenty-five nations that had been used by bin Laden to move money about. *Al-Riyadh* reported on 13 October that, as a result of the Kingdom's assistance, more than US $70 million of al-Qa'ida funding had been frozen around the

1. *Al-Hayat*, 7 March 2002.
2. US Congress, "Financial War on Terrorism", p. 38.
3. Ibid., p. 50.
4. Saudi Embassy, Washington, "FBI, Treasury Department Praise Saudi Efforts to Stop Terrorist Financing", 20 September 2002, http://www.Saudiembassy.net/2002News/Press/PressDetail.asp?cYear=2002 & cIndex=50.

world.[1] Saudi Arabia and the US maintained a counterterrorism committee comprising intelligence and law enforcement personnel who met regularly. Saudi Arabia also joined the Group of Twenty Finance Ministers and Central Bank Governors to develop an aggressive plan of action directed at rooting out and freezing terrorist assets. The Saudis also took concrete steps to create an institutional framework for combating money laundering. According to Bandar: "No one who has the facts can say that Saudi Arabia has been soft on terrorism."[2]

On 16 October, the influential Council on Foreign Relations (CFR) think tank published a task force report called "Terrorist Financing". It pointed out that al-Qaʻida's financial backbone was constructed on the basis of funds from charities: "For years, individuals and charities based in Saudi Arabia have been the most important source of funds for al-Qaʻida, and for years, Saudi officials have turned a blind eye to this problem."[3] The report claimed that Saudi Arabia had taken two or three steps in cooperation with the US, but insisted that "a hundred more steps and Saudi Arabia may be where it needs to be".[4] It also alleged that by not moving quickly enough, the Saudis "are setting the stage for their own eventual demise",[5] and declared that US efforts to curtail terrorism financing were impeded "by a lack of political will among US allies".

According to the CFR report, the White House, confronted with this situation, had decided not to use the full power of the US "to pressure or compel other governments to combat terrorism financing more effectively".[6] One of the report's key criticisms was that when the US claimed "Saudi Arabia is being cooperative" when in fact it was not, its adversaries would believe that "the US does not place a high priority on this issue."[7] It therefore recommended that significant "source and transit" countries, especially Saudi Arabia, should be made to cooperate fully with US and international requests for law enforcement. This, according to the report, meant "allowing US

1. *Al-Riyadh*, 13 October 2002.
2. Saudi Embassy, Washington, "Saudi Actions to Crack Down on Terrorist Financing", 18 October 2002, http://www.saudiembassy.net/2002News/Press/PressDetail.asp?cYear=2002 cIndex=55.
3. Council on Foreign Relations, Task Force Report, *Terrorist Financing*, 2002, p. 8.
4. Ibid., p. 20.
5. Ibid., pp. 20–1.
6. Ibid., p. 21.
7. Ibid., p. 24.

investigators direct access to individuals or organizations ... suspected of being involved in terrorist financing". It recommended that Saudi Arabia regulate charities under its jurisdiction.[1]

In response to the CFR report, the Saudi embassy in Washington issued a press release on 17 October, stating: "This opinion is based on false and inconclusive information." It emphasized the Bush administration's appreciation of the close cooperation between the two countries in the war on terrorism; it maintained that the Kingdom had implemented new laws and regulations to combat terrorism financing, and that Bandar had stated: "It is unfortunate that the Task Force prepared their report without input from the US or Saudi government ... the Task Force was either unaware of, or chose not to recognize, the many actions we have taken."[2]

Al-Sharq al-Awsat reported on 27 November 2002 that some NSC officials had recommended Bush to urge the Saudis to take punitive measures against individuals assumed to be financers of terrorism within ninety days, or the US would act separately to bring these financers to justice. A senior US official reportedly stated that the Bush administration would tell the Saudis: "We don't care how you solve this problem, just find a solution." *Al-Sharq al-Awsat* also reported that a Saudi official had questioned the wisdom of leaking such outrageous comments to the press, arguing that American bureaucracy had obstructed the close cooperation between the two countries. The Saudi official claimed there was inadequate coordination among different US entities fighting terrorism, pointing out: "During three months, we received four identical requests from different US agencies." The official added: "We both are main targets for terrorism, so what is the logic compelling us to obstruct or suspend the investigations?"[3] The next day, Powell denied that the US was considering such a move. He said: "In our anxiety and desire to protect ourselves, we must not risk breaking relationships with a good friend of the US for many years and a strategic partner."[4]

Saudi Arabia began to review its charities, and established new regulations to prevent charitable funds from being misused by "evildoers". Saudi charities

1. Ibid., p. 30.
2. Saudi Embassy, Washington, "Response to CFR Report", 17 October 2002. For further information see:http://www.saudiembassy.net/2002News/Press/PressDetail:asp?cYear=200& cIndex=54.
3. *Al-Sharq al-Awsat*, 27 November 2002.
4. *Al-Iqtisadiyya*, 28 November 2002.

were also barred from sending any funds abroad. In May 2003, the Saudi government established a task force to fight terrorism. Officials announced in June that all offices belonging to the Al-Haramain Foundation located outside the Kingdom would be closed, acknowledging that Riyadh's lack of economic control was the reason for the closure.[1] In October 2004 the Saudi government dissolved the organization as part of its measures for fighting terrorism.[2]

In August 2003 Saudi Arabia and the US established a joint task force to deal with terrorism financing. This force operated as an integrated unit and brought the resources of both governments to bear. Between 21–25 September, Saudi Arabia hosted a team from the intergovernmental Financial Action Task Force (FATF) to perform a joint evaluation on the procedures the Kingdom had taken to combat money laundering and terror financing.[3]

On 28 February 2004, the Kingdom issued a statement on the creation of a charity commission, declaring that to eliminate any misdeeds that might undermine charitable Saudi operations abroad or distort their reputation, King Fahd had approved the creation of the Saudi National Commission for Relief and Charity Work Abroad. This body would be given exclusive responsibility for all charity work and relief undertaken outside the Kingdom.[4] According to 'Adel Al-Jibeir, Saudi Ambassador to the US: "The National Commission is being established to ensure that all charitable donations abroad reach their intended recipients, and to protect charitable donations from possible abuse."[5]

On 24 March, Deputy Assistant to the US Treasury Juan C. Zarate testified before the House International Relations Committee that the efforts of the Kingdom "fall directly in line with international cooperation and continue to improve in substantively important ways". He stated: "The Kingdom has taken important steps, independently and along with the US, to attack al-Qa'ida's finances." He further explained that the US had, in the short term, engaged the

---

1. *Al-Sharq al-Awsat*, 2 August 2003.
2. Ibid., 6 October 2004.
3. Saudi Embassy, Washington, "Saudi Arabia's Progress on Economic, Education and Political Reforms", 7 November 2003. For further information see: http://www.saudiembassy.net/2003News/Press/PressDetail.asp?cYear=2003 cIndex=163.
4. Saudi Embassy, Washington, "Statement on Creation of a Charity Commission", 28 February 2004, http://www.saudiembassy.net/2004News/Statements/StateDetail.asp?cIndex=320.
5. Saudi Embassy, Washington, Information Office, "Saudi Arabia and the US Take Joint Action Against Terror Financing", 2 June 2004.

Kingdom in eliminating key sources and conduits of terrorist support, and had established direct mechanisms to enable the two countries to work together. Over the long term, the US was working with the Kingdom to enhance the transparency and accountability of formal and informal financial systems. Zarate concluded: "The systemic actions undertaken by the Saudis will take more time to produce results."

According to Zarate, these systemic actions would address aspects that had been exploited by terrorist organizations in the past. The main concern of the US was with the abuse of the charitable sector by terrorist supporters. He stated: "Saudi Arabia has acknowledged this vulnerability and is taking action to safeguard the integrity of the charitable sector." He also pointed out that on 24 May 2003 the Saudis had issued comprehensive new restrictions on the financial activities of the Kingdom's charities. He said: "These restrictions go further than those of any country in the world. We appreciate the effort of the Kingdom to date – they have put the lives of their agents and people on the line to fight this battle."[1]

In its fifteenth annual report, the FATF included an evaluation of Saudi Arabia's laws, regulations and systems to combat money laundering and terrorism financing, according to which, it appeared, Saudi officials had "taken action to increase the requirements for financial institutions on customer due diligence, established systems for tracing and freezing terrorist assets, and tightened the regulation and transparency of charitable organizations".[2]

The Saudi education system had been accused in the US media of contributing to anti-Western sentiments and providing fertile ground for extremism.[3] Such claims of direct links between educational curricula and terrorism resonated well in a world of "with us or without us". Saudi reaction to these accusations involved a gradual move from outright rejection to a hesitant

---

1. Treasury Department, The Office of Public Affairs, JS-1257, "Testimony of Juan C. Zarate, Deputy Assistant Secretary Executive Office for Terrorist Financing and Financial Crimes, Before the House of International Relations, Subcommittee on the Middle East and Central Asia", 24 March 2004.
2. Saudi Embassy, Washington, "FATF Releases Evaluation of Kingdom's Mechanism Against Terrorism Financing and Money Laundry", 2 July 2004, http://www.saudiembassy.net/2004News/Press/PressDetail.asp?cYear=2004 cIndex=234.
3. Neil MacFarquhar, "Aviation Challenged: Education, Anti-Western and Extremist Views Pervade Saudi Schools", *The New York Times*, 19 October 2001.

acknowledgement that the Saudi school curriculum had several defects, and that there was a need for a total re-evaluation of the system.[1]

In a 27 January 2002 *Ukaz* report, Saud explained how people in the West sometimes resorted to extremism, and in some cases adopted mass suicide. In the Middle East, tragic scenes of Palestinian children being killed and of Palestinian homes being destroyed were mobilizing people. However, images of these events were not distributed by Saudi schools. Saud claimed the Palestinian cause had been utilized by terrorists to mislead youth into inciting violence, and that "these young people had not been motivated by our educational curricula or our political policies – which favour peace ... they themselves were misled". According to Saud, a team had surveyed school curricula after 9/11, and had found that 85–90 percent of the content encouraged peace, 10 percent might be questionable, and 5 percent was problematic: "... The problem is not an education problem."[2]

In March 2002, Saudi Minister of Education Ahmed Al-Rasheed stated that the first phase of curriculum revision, which focused on correcting and getting rid of certain material from textbooks, had already been completed. The second phase, which aimed at encouraging creative thinking and self-learning, and at providing students with the skills and materials necessary for modern life, was continuing.[3] Revising curricula had highlighted the divergence and polarization of opinion between conservative religious forces and more liberal voices as to the pace, extent and shape of reform.[4] While there had been efforts to tone down the message and to include teachings about tolerance, previous generations were already indoctrinated by the message propagated over earlier decades.[5]

It was certainly true that young Saudis were ill equipped to face modern challenges. Despite huge investment in the Saudi education system, there was also an increased prospect of unemployment and poverty. An analysis of history textbooks for grades four to twelve undertaken by Professor Reima

1. *Arab News*, "Al-Rasheed Vows to Correct Defects in Education System", 7 January 2003.
2. *Ukaz*, 27 January 2002.
3. *Gulf News*, UAE Newspaper, 7 March 2002.
4. *Al-Hayat*, 24 January 2004.
5. Michaela Provop, "The War of Ideas: Education in Saudi Arabia", in Paul Aarts and Gerd Nonneman, eds, *Saudi Arabia in the Balance: Political Economy, Society, Foreign Affairs* (London: Hurst & Co., 2005), pp. 61–5.

Al-Jarf of King Saud University revealed that 68.5 percent of subjects covered Islamic themes, 30 percent looked at Saudi history and only 1.5 percent was concerned with global developments. Al-Jarf also contended that world history was important in creating global awareness among students, and in making them understand the world as being "different people and nations, interacting with one another". Furthermore, the approach to teaching relied heavily on memorization "… and did not develop independent and critical thinking among students".[1]

In his interview with *Time* on 10 September 2003, Saud proclaimed: "The books have been changed for the new school year. The instructions to the teachers have been changed." He denied that school textbooks constituted a "breeding ground" for terrorists: "The breeding ground for terrorists was Afghanistan, and is the Israeli-Palestinian crisis."[2]

Arab News reported on 13 December 2003 Prince Turki's emphasis that not only was the Kingdom trying to hunt down al-Qa'ida members, it was also "combating the ideas that made them terrorists". The Saudi government was "trying to deny terrorism its tools for attracting citizens", and was doing this, he pointed out, "by educating youth and stressing the moderate nature of Muslims who reject extremism and violence, as well as by providing jobs and addressing economic difficulties".[3]

At the end of December 2003, a former judge, 'Abd al-'Aziz Al-Qassem, prepared a study titled: "Religious Educational Curriculum: Where is the Defect?" His analysis noted that school curricula "encourage violence towards others, and mislead the pupils into believing that in order to safeguard their own religion, they must violently repress and even physically eliminate the 'other'". He recommended "re-examining all education curricula in order to clear out infidelity tendencies, while retaining juristic comprehension toward the 'other' and 'civilizations'".[4]

While there is widespread consensus that the education system has to be reformed to cater more satisfactorily to the demands of the employment market, reform initiatives so far have largely shied away from controversial issues such

---

1. *Arab News*, 23 May 2003.
2. Saudi Embassy, Washington, "The Saudis Respond: Foreign Minister Prince Saud Interviewed by Scott Macleod."
3. *Arab News*, 13 December 2003.
4. *Al-Hayat*, 31 December 2003.

as reducing the overall percentage of religious education.[1] There are certain powerful forces that would prefer a policy of withdrawal and stagnation, and which manifest hostility and rejection to changes considered as imposed from outside as part of a conspiracy against Islam. *Al-Hayat* reported on 3 January 2004 that 156 Saudi religious scholars had issued a statement warning the government against any step toward changing the religious curricula in schools. These scholars indicated that it would be considered as the first step along the road of "thwarting [Islam]", which would call for a "resolute stance".[2]

The US has placed intense pressure on Saudi Arabia to purge its education curricula of material supportive of terrorism and anti-US attitudes. But according to Palmer, tampering with Islamic education deepens the impression that the US has declared war on Islam. It is an extremely sensitive issue redolent of both the Crusades and colonialism. Teachers supportive of terrorists will preach terror and anti-US sentiments regardless of the contents of the government curriculum.[3] *Al-Sharq al-Awsat* reported Saud as saying: "Reform does not rest on educational curricula, but rather on the educational process in its broader form, through concentration on the role of teachers and other procedures."[4]

Within days of the 9/11 events, US neoconservatives were criticizing Arab governments, including allies such as Egypt and Saudi Arabia, for spawning radical groups and stifling moderates. They appealed to Bush to make the democratic transformation of the Middle East a cornerstone of the war on terrorism – an idea that gained the endorsement of the administration and attracted mild bipartisan support in Congress.[5] In a speech in November 2003, Bush announced a new "forward strategy of freedom" for the Middle East. On 12 December the State Department launched the Middle East Partnership Initiative to fund political, economic and educational reform programmes in the Middle East.[6]

On 15 December Powell reportedly said: "The matter is subject to how the

---

1. *Arab News*, 5 December 2003.
2. *Al-Hayat*, 3 January 2004.
3. Palmer and Palmer, *At the Heart of Terror*, p. 182.
4. *Al-Sharq al-Awsat*, 7 January 2004.
5. Amy Hawthorne, *Political Reform in the Arab World: A New Ferment?* Carnegie Endowment for International Peace, Carnegie Papers, no. 52, October 2004, p. 5.
6. Ibid., p. 6.

Saudis decide on how to transform their society." He added that the US was only trying to be of assistance, explaining: "It is not the US's role to dictate change, rather it is to enter into discussion with our friends."[1] On 7 January 2003, Prince Saud had said that the Saudi government "wants to move in every direction", but that this move would not be imposed by a revolution from the top; rather it would depend on "the speed and patience of the existing social fabric". He declared that the Saudi government "does not want to impose matters that people do not want".[2]

The Saudi press also responded to the US call for reform. 'Abd Al-Karim Abu Al-Nasser, a columnist for *Al-Watan*, wrote that the US was actually diverting attention from the fundamental problem: "the Israeli problem – which makes the region insecure and unstable, feeds terrorism and violence, and provides some Arab regimes with justification for repressing their citizens". Al-Nasser added that the Arabs were not convinced about the sincere regard of the US for their interests "when it acquiesces in Israeli atrocities".[3] 'Abd Al-Rahman Al-Rashed, editor of *Al-Sharq al-Awsat* – despite being a supporter of the initiative – wrote that "the problem is with the engineer of the plan, towards whom the general feeling is of a [force] that destroys the Middle East and humiliates its Arab inhabitants. Why, then, should any group agree to cooperate with it?"[4]

On 9 May 2003, Bush proposed the establishment by 2013 of a US-Middle East Free Trade Area, which would involve the US working with the countries of the Middle East in graduated steps to increase trade and investment with the US and with the world economy. It would also assist them with implementing domestic reforms, instituting the rule of law, protecting private property rights (including intellectual property) and creating a foundation for openness, economic growth and prosperity. In July of that year Saudi Arabia signed a Trade and Investment Framework Agreement with the US.[5]

In a speech to the Saudi Consultative Council on 17 May 2003, King Fahd said: "I would like to confirm that we will continue on the path of political and economic reform."[6] On 3 August, 'Abdullah announced the establishment

---

1. *Ukaz*, 15 December 2002.
2. Ibid., 7 January 2003.
3. *Al-Watan*, 15 December 2002.
4. *Al-Sharq al-Awsat*, 21 December 2002.
5. White House, Press Office, "US-Middle East Free Trade Area", 9 May 2003.
6. Saudi Embassy, Washington, "Political and Economic Reform in the Kingdom

of the King 'Abdul 'Aziz Centre for National Dialogue, to promote the public exchange of ideas as an essential part of Saudi life and to bring together leading figures from across Saudi Arabia and the political and social spectrum to discuss important issues facing the Kingdom. The crown prince expressed his hope that the Centre would "establish a channel of responsible expression" that would create "a pure atmosphere where wise stances and enlightened opinions which reject terrorism can be released".[1]

Additional steps were taken by the Saudi government to implement domestic political reform. On 13 October 2003, Fahd had approved plans to introduce elections for half of the members of each municipal council,[2] and on 29 November he approved changes that would enhance the legislative role of the Consultative Council.[3]

On 27 February 2005, Saud announced that the government was serious about reform and was working to ensure that those reforms that were implemented would not break the social fabric of the country: "Reform has to come from inside the countries of the region and must fulfil the requirements of the people."[4]

Saudi Arabia remains, in many ways, a closed society, and there are clear boundaries as to what levels of political activity are permitted and what can and cannot be said. In broad terms, however, the Saudi regime is now more accepting of dissent and media criticism, as long as it is not directed at the overthrow of the regime or lead to violence.[5] For the Saudis, the way in which the US is critical – whether about politicians, public figures or opinion leaders – is cause for concern. The US wants to see reform and change in the Saudi society and public culture. But, as Prince Turki said: "We're not going to change just because you told us to. We are changing and reforming society because it is the right thing to do for the country."[6]

---

of Saudi Arabia", December 2006, p. 1.
1. *Al-Iqtisadiyya*, 4 August 2003.
2. Saudi Embassy, Washington, "Political and Economic Reform in the Kingdom of Saudi Arabia", p. 1.
3. Ibid., p. 2.
4. Saudi Embassy, Washington, Prince Saud Al-Faisal Interview with *Newsweek/The Washington Post*, "Changes in the Kingdom – On Our Timetable", Lally Weymouth, 27 February 2005, http://www.saudiembassy.net/2005News/Statements/StateDetail.asp?cIndex=505.
5. Cordesman, *Saudi Security and the War on Terrorism*, p. 14.
6. Saudi Embassy, Washington, "I Think We Need to Talk", New Saudi Ambassador

Any reluctance on the part of the Kingdom to fight terrorism evaporated when terrorism struck at home. Cooperation had already become significant, it improved even more after foreign corporate housing compounds were bombed in Riyadh on 12 May 2003, killing thirty-five and wounding over 160. Saudi Arabia openly discussed the problem of radicalism, criticized the terrorists as religiously deviant, reduced official support for religious activity outside the country, closed down suspect charitable organizations and publicized arrests. Bandar called for his government to wage a *jihad* of its own against the terrorists: "We must all, as a state and as a people, recognize the truth about these criminals … if we do not declare a general mobilization, we will lose this war on terrorism."[1]

One tends to believe that before the May attack in Riyadh, it would have been difficult for the Saudi government to act so decisively against Islamic extremism given the local political environment. This attack and other attacks in September and November 2003 jolted many Saudis into seeing that Islamic extremism was a far more powerful internal threat than they had realized. This public awareness enabled the regime to tackle the threat much more strongly than it had done previously.

The Occupation of Iraq

The invasion and subsequent occupation of Iraq must be put into a wider context. On 8 March 1992, *The New York Times* published part of the draft of a document prepared by the Pentagon. The "Defense Planning Guidance" (DPG) outlined the political and military strategy of the US after the Cold War. Commissioned by Cheney, then Secretary of Defense, and overseen by then-Under-Secretary of Defense for Policy Paul Wolfowitz, the DPG described a world of danger and power struggles in which the US had to remain the superpower: "Our first objective is to prevent the re-emergence of a new rival," it declared.[2] After the leak, President Bush (Senior) ordered the Pentagon to rewrite the document; when it was released in May, the language about pre-

---

to the US Prince Turki Al-Faisal at the Brookings Institution, Washington, DC, 19 June 2006. For details see http://www.saudiembassy.net/2006News/Statements/SpeechDetail.asp?cIndex=623.
1. *Al-Watan*, 1 June 2004.
2. *The New York Times*, Excerpts from Pentagon's Plan, "Prevent the Re-emergence of a New Rival", 8 March 1992, p. 14.

eminence had gone, and instead it made reassuring noises about cooperation and alliances. The DPG of 1992 accurately foreshadowed Bush the younger's national security strategy of 2002, which itself laid the foundation for what came to be called the Bush Doctrine.

In 1996, the Institute for Advanced Strategic and Political Studies, a Jerusalem-based think tank with an affiliated office in Washington, DC, produced an important study on the Middle East for Israeli Prime Minister Binyamin Netanyahu. Richard Perle, a former Reagan defence official, and Douglas Feith, who had worked under Perle in the Reagan administration and was then Under-Secretary of Defense for Policy, were among the Institute's advisers at that time. The result of their efforts was a working paper called "A Clean Break: A New Strategy for Securing the Realm",[1] and it called for Israel to free itself from both socialist economic policies and the burdens of the peace process. The paper also included plans for Israel to help re-establish the Hashemite throne in Iraq, and advised: "Removing Saddam should be an important Israeli strategic objective in its own right – as a means of foiling Syria's regional ambitions." The monarchy would win over Iraq's Shi'is, which would "help Israel wean the South Lebanese Shiia away from Hizbullah, Iran, and Syria." Then the Palestinians, isolated and alone, would have to accept Israeli demands. That would unlock almost every stubborn problem of the Middle East: the Israeli-Palestinian conflict, terrorism, the resistance of Hizbullah, the reliance of the US on oil from Saudi Arabia and the Saddam regime.[2]

In 1997 Robert Kagan, a speechwriter for former Secretary of State George Shultz, and William Kristol, Chief of Staff for former Vice President Dan Quayle, helped found the Project for the New American Century (PNAC), a neoconservative policy institute and pressure group. The PNAC comprised such "neocon" figures as Rumsfeld, Wolfowitz, Perle and William Bennett, and was created to devise a strategy for US military power in the post-Cold War era.[3] On 26 January 1998, the PNAC presented an open letter to President Clinton urging him toward effecting regime change in Iraq: "The current policy,

---

1. The Institute for Advanced Strategy and Political Studies, "A Clean Break: A New Strategy for Securing the Realm" (Jerusalem, Washington), http://www.israel.economy.org/start1.htm.
2. Ibid., p. 3.
3. George Packer, *The Assassins' Gate: America in Iraq* (London: Faber & Faber, 2005), p. 23.

which depends for its success upon the steadfastness of our coalition partners and upon the cooperation of Saddam Hussein, is dangerously inadequate."[1] Within a few months the Republican Congress had pushed Clinton to sign the Iraq Liberation Act, which appeared to signal more active support for the conservative opposition and made regime change part of official US policy.[2]

The PNAC's 2000 report, "Rebuilding America's Defenses: Strategy, Forces and Resources for a New Century", provided a review of US forces in the Gulf since the end of the first Gulf War and made it clear they should be there to stay. It also recommended a downgrading of the Saudi position in the constellation of US policy, and identified both Iran and Iraq as US adversaries.[3] On 22 May 2002, Kristol appeared before the House of Representatives, where he said: "The Saudi regime is more part of the problem than part of the solution." He also urged the US to develop strategic alternatives to its reliance on Riyadh, and stated that although the Saudi regime still exerted the strongest influence on oil prices, other oil sources could be developed. He emphasized that "removing the regime of Saddam Hussein ... would be a tremendous step toward reducing Saudi leverage. Bringing Iraqi oil fully into world markets would improve energy economics." He reinforced his argument by stating: "From a military and strategic perspective, Iraq is more important than Saudi Arabia. And building a representative government in Baghdad ... would be a useful challenge to the current Saudi regime."[4]

By 2000, Iraq had become the leading cause for neoconservatives, not because Clinton's policies had failed but because they saw Iraq as the test case for their ideas about US power and world leadership. During the 2000 presidential campaign, Kagan and Kristol published a collection of essays called "Present Dangers", contributors to which included many leading hawks among foreign-policy specialists. Following the election, the names of neoconservatives who had known one another from their years in and out of power became

1. The Project for the New American Century (PNAC), "A Letter to Clinton", 26 January 1998, http://www.newamericancentury.org/iraqclintonletter.htm, accessed February 2009.
2. Sarah Brown and Chris Toening, "Why Another War? A Background on the Iraq Crisis", *Middle East Report* (MERIP), December 2002, pp.10-1.
3. PNAC, *Report on Rebuilding America's Defenses: Strategy, Forces and Resources for a New Century* (Washington, D.C.: PNAC, September 2000).
4. William Kristol, "Testimony Before the House Committee on International Relations Subcommittee on Middle East and South Asia", 22 May 2002, http://www.newamericancentury.org/saudi-052302.htm, accessed May 2007.

visible throughout the Bush administration. Many of them had served under Reagan, and retained the sense of victory that the defeat of communism and the emergence of the US as the world's only superpower had given them.[1]

On 10 January 2001, Bush, at Cheney's request, was briefed on Iraq by the Pentagon generals.[2] At the new administration's first national security meeting on 5 February, officials reviewed Iraq policy.[3] In April, at the administration's first meeting on terrorism, Clarke found that Bush's new appointees, especially Deputy Secretary of Defense Wolfowitz, were far more interested in the threat from Iraq than in that from al-Qaʻida. During the meeting Wolfowitz told Clarke: "You give bin Laden too much credit. He could not do all these things like the 1993 attack on New York [the first to target the World Trade Center], not without a state sponsor."[4]

In the spring of 2001, the National Energy Policy Development Group (NEPD), published a report titled: "Reliable, Affordable, and Environmentally Sound Energy for America's Future". It offered an assessment of oil dependency and the need to diversify imports, and identified Saudi Arabia as the "linchpin of supply reliability to world oil markets".[5] It warned that the share of US oil demand met by net imports was projected to jump from 52 percent in 2000 to 64 percent in 2020 barring any shift in policy.[6] The NEPD therefore encouraged the expansion of US oil interests in Africa, Russia and Central Asia.

Speaking to the Los Angeles World Affairs Council on 8 May 2000, Saudi oil minister Ali Al-Naimi stated that some experts were promoting the issue of security and supply, criticizing high dependence on non-domestic sources. If this concept applied generally, no major commodity would be imported from outside. He explicitly declared that the Saudi goal was the stability of the oil market for the benefit of consumers and producers alike.[7]

1. Packer, *The Assassins' Gate*, pp. 36–8.
2. Bob Woodward, *Plan of Attack* (New York: Simon & Schuster, 2004), pp. 9–12.
3. Ibid., pp. 13–4.
4. Clarke, *Against All Enemies*, pp. 231–2.
5. National Energy Policy Development Group (NEPD), *National Energy Policy: Reliable, Affordable, and Environmentally Sound Energy for America's Future*, Report of the NEPD (Washington, DC: US Government Printing Office, 2001), section 8, pp. 3–4.
6. Ibid., section 1, p. 13.
7. Saudi Embassy, Washington, "Looking Ahead: The Oil Market and Its Future", Ali I. Al-Naimi, Saudi Minister of Petroleum and Mineral Resources at the Los

Until 11 September 2001, these ideas had found plenty of disciples among right-wing think tanks in Washington, DC, but had failed to make an impact on the conduct of US foreign policy. The events of 9/11 changed this overnight. Within a week of the attacks, Wolfowitz and I. Lewis Libby, Chief of Staff to the Vice President, urged a military campaign against bin Laden as well as against Iraq and Lebanon.[1] During an NSC meeting on 12 September, Rumsfeld raised the question: "Why shouldn't we go against Iraq, not just al-Qa'ida?"[2] Wolfowitz also argued that Iraq would be easier than Afghanistan.[3] Five days later, Bush said: "I believe Iraq was involved, but I am not going to strike them now. I do not have the evidence at this point."[4]

In late 2001 Rumsfeld summoned senior military leaders to a meeting that had been called to ponder the war plan for another potential adversary. Greg Newbold, Chief Operations Deputy for the Joint Chiefs of Staff, outlined CENTCOM's OPLAN 103–98, the armed forces' contingency plan in the event of a war with Iraq. The plan reflected long-standing military principles about the force levels that were needed to defeat Iraq, to control a population of more than 24 million and to secure a nation the size of California with a porous border.[5]

In a radio address to the nation on 6 October 2001, the rhetoric began to shift. Bush stated: "America is determined to oppose the state sponsors of terror."[6] In November, he linked the war on terrorism to weapons of mass destruction (WMD),[7] and in his State of the Union address on 29 January 2002, Bush named Iraq – along with Iran and North Korea – as part of "an

---

Angeles World Affair Council, 8 May 2000, http://saudiembassy.net/2000News/Statements/SpeechDetail.asp?cIndex=346.

1. Patrick E. Tyler, and E. Sciolino, "Bush Advisers Split on Scope of Retaliation", *The New York Times*, 20 September 2001, p. 1.
2. Bob Woodward, *Bush at War* (New York: Simon and Schuster, 2002), p. 49.
3. Ibid., p. 83.
4. Ibid., p. 99.
5. Michael Gordon and Bernard Trainor, *Cobra II: The Inside Story of the Invasion and Occupation of Iraq* (London and New York: Atlantic/Pantheon Books, 2006), pp. 3–4.
6. White House, "Radio Address of the President to the Nation", News Release, 6 October 2001, http://www.whitehouse.org/news/relase/2001/10/20011006.html.
7. White House, "President Welcomes Aid Workers Rescued from Afghanistan", News Release, 26 November 2001, http://www.whitehouse.org/news/release/2001/11/20011126-1.html.

axis of evil".[1] He set three essential elements for the role of the US in the world. The first was active US global leadership, and in this he noted: "Our enemies view the entire world as a battlefield." Bush vowed "to pursue them wherever they are". Second was regime change. Here, Bush was determined to include rogue regimes as targets in the war on terrorism. "We cannot stop short," he said. The third element was the promotion of liberal democratic principles: "No nation is exempt" from the "non-negotiable demands" of liberty, law and justice. Bush saw, in the war, an opportunity to spread US political principles especially into the Muslim world.[2]

On 11 May 2002, *Al-Sharq al-Awsat* reported Crown Prince 'Abdullah as saying: "The Americans know our position concerning Iraq." The crown prince explained that as long as Iraq abided by international law there was no need to declare war against it, and emphasized that the position of the Kingdom was to endeavour "... to calm and improve matters". He added: "We are against any attack on Iraq, and hope that matters will not come to this point."[3]

It is worth noting that, according to the "Military Balance 2002–2003" put out by the International Institute of Strategic Studies, Iraq did not have much of an army and was probably not much of a real threat to its neighbours.[4] It is also important to note that the CIA's estimates of Iraq's chemical and biological weapons were not significantly different from the agency's pre-9/11 assessment. Therefore, Iraq's capabilities or programmes did not constitute an imminent threat.[5] In addition, the CIA's 2002 report on nuclear threat from Iraq concluded: "Iraq is unlikely to produce indigenously enough weapons-grade material for a deliverable nuclear weapon until the last half of this decade."[6] Rohan Gunaratna, Director of Terrorism Research at Singapore's

---

1. White House, "The President's State of the Union Address", News Release, 29 January 2002, http://www.whitehouse.org/news/releases/2002/01/20020129-11.html.
2. PNAC, "The Bush Doctrine: Memo from Gary Schmitt and Tom Donnelly to Opinion Leaders", 30 January 2002, http://www.newamericancentury.org/defense-20020130.htm.
3. *Al-Sharq al-Awsat*, 11 May 2002.
4. International Institute for Strategic Studies (IISS), *Military Balance 2002–2003* (London: Oxford University Press for the IISS, 2002), pp. 241–79.
5. CIA, "Unclassified Report to Congress on the Acquisition of Technology Relating to Weapons of Mass Destruction and Advanced Conventional Munitions, 1 January–30 June 2000", http://www.cia.org/publications/bian/bian_jan_2002.htm.
6. CIA, "Iraq's Weapons of Mass Destruction Program", p. 6.

Institute of Defence and Strategic Studies and one of the world's foremost experts on al-Qa'ida, was reported in *Washington Monthly* in 2003 as saying that he "could not find any evidence of an al-Qa'ida link to Saddam Hussein or the Baghdad administration".[1]

Throughout the winter of 2002 and into the spring, endless conversations took place in the US about how the world had and had not changed. The events of 11 September had reopened large questions in a way that was both confusing and liberating. The writer Paul Berman suggested that the hijackers were not "products of an alien world" – their ideology was shaped in the West, just as Germans and Italians and Spaniards and Russians had committed similar acts of mass slaughter at earlier times. Berman claimed that in all cases it stemmed from a totalitarian ideology, which was in effect a revolt against liberalism. Ba'thism was one of the "Muslim totalitarianisms", as was Islamism. The war of terror that was thus waged was an ideological war, and victory required that people across the Muslim world change their political ideas. The overthrow of Saddam and the establishment of an Iraqi democracy would put the US on the side of liberal-minded Arabs, and against the totalitarian ideas that had previously held sway.[2]

In 2002, Bernard Lewis and the scholar Fouad Ajami of the Johns Hopkins School of Advanced International Studies were summoned to a meeting with Cheney. They told him that US power had helped to keep the Arab world in decline by supporting "sclerotic tyrannies". Only if the US broke with its own history in the region could it reverse this. The Arabs needed to be jolted out of their stupor by some foreign-administered shock, such as that which would be provided by the overthrow of the Iraqi regime.[3]

For Saudi Arabia, the big issue was the Israeli-Palestinian peace process. 'Abdullah offered "full withdrawal from all the occupied territories, in accordance with UN resolutions, including Jerusalem, for full normalization of relations" with Israel. Regarding the possible US military strike against Iraq, 'Abdullah said: "Any attack on Iraq or Iran should not be contemplated

---

1. Spencer Ackerman, "The Weakest Link", *Washington Monthly*, November 2003, p. 18.
2. Paul Berman, *Terror and Liberalism* (New York: W. W. Norton, 2004), pp. 103-128.
3. Packer, *The Assassins' Gate*, p. 51.

at all, because it would not serve the interests of America, the region, or the world."[1]

During an Arab summit in Beirut in March 2002, 'Abdullah tried to reconcile the differences between Kuwait and Iraq by arranging for a meeting in his presence between leading figures from both sides. According to Kuwaiti Minister of State for Foreign Affairs Sheikh Muhammad Al Sabah, Iraq submitted a written pledge not to invade Kuwaiti territory. The crown prince also presented his proposal for peace with Israel at the conference. The proposal was adopted and launched as an Arab initiative for peace.[2]

On 26 April, Saud announced that 'Abdullah had presented Bush with an eight-point list of proposed agreements for peace in the Middle East, saying that these were intended "as a comprehensive outline of how to move towards a long-term resolution of the Israeli-Palestinian crisis".[3] The Kingdom argued that terrorists were exploiting the struggle of the Palestinians to agitate people against the US and its allies in the region. Therefore, the Saudis urged the US to consider the Palestinian issue and not Iraq as the cause of terrorism in the Middle East. On 24 June Bush announced a new plan for a two-state solution, stating that, with certain conditions, "the US will support the creation of a Palestinian state".[4]

On 4 August, Saud told reporters: "We have always opposed any attack against an Arab or Muslim country and that also means Iraq."[5] Saudi officials had little confidence in the efforts of the US to bring down Saddam's regime. Because of US policy toward Iraq over the past decade, few in Saudi Arabia at that time believed the US had a convincing plan to drive Saddam from power and reshape Iraq. Moreover, they were not confident that a post-Saddam Iraq would ultimately be a friendly state. According to Cordesman, it would take years of proven moderation by a new Iraqi regime before Saudi Arabia could relax its guard. Part of that concern was that the Iraqi military threat differed fundamentally from that posed by Iran. The Kingdom did not share a common

---

1. Thomas L. Friedman, "An Intriguing Signal from the Crown Prince", *The New York Times*, 17 February 2002.
2. *Al-Sharq al-Awsat*, 29 March 2002.
3. Saudi Embassy, Washington, "Crown Prince Abdullah Presents 8-point Mid East Proposal to US President Bush at Crawford, Texas", 26 April 2002, http://www.saudiembassy.net/2002News/Press/PressDetail.asp?cYear=2002&cIndex=33.
4. White House, Press Office, "President Bush Calls for New Palestinian Leadership", 20 June 2002.
5. *Arab News*, 4 August 2002.

border with Iran, and the Iranians had very limited amphibious capabilities. Iraq and Saudi Arabia, however, did share a border, and Iraq was the only power with land forces strong enough to pose a major threat.[1]

On 29 August Saud was reported as saying: "It is unwise of the international community to overthrow the Iraqi president." He also asserted that it was up to the Iraqi people to do so or not, pointing out: "History never recalls that overthrowing and appointing from the outside brings stability." Saud suggested that there was a chance for diplomacy and also indicated the Saudi intention to protect the integrity of Iraqi territory. Furthermore, he said, pressure on Saddam from the US might strengthen the resolve of ordinary Iraqis: "If they [Iraqis] do not have the choice [of leader], the attack and the strong pressure will force them to support their government."[2] On the same day, Bush received Bandar. After their meeting, White House spokesman Ari Fleischer said the president considered Saddam "a threat to world peace, but he [Bush] has not taken any decision about the best way to dispose of him". Fleischer added that Bush would "continue consultation with Saudi Arabia".[3]

On 12 September, Bush made a speech to the UN General Assembly in which he outlined Iraq's violations of UN resolutions. He then stated: "My nation will work with the UN Security Council to meet our common challenge."[4] Saud welcomed Bush's call, and called upon Saddam to allow UN weapons inspectors (who had been thrown out of Iraq in 1998) back into the country. "The president has shown great leadership in turning this issue over to the UN," said Saud.[5]

In September 2002, Bush promulgated a new National Security Strategy based on the belief that the best and only way to achieve US security was by forcibly creating a better and safer world in the image of the US itself. It outlined a doctrine of pre-emption: "As a matter of common sense and self-defense, America will act against such emerging threats before they are fully

---

1. Cordesman, *Saudi Arabia Enters the Twenty-first Century*, pp. 52–7.
2. *Al-Watan*, 29 August 2002.
3. *Al-Hayat*, 29 August 2002.
4. White House, Press Office, "President's Remarks at the UN General Assembly", 12 September 2002.
5. Saudi Embassy, Washington, "Saudi Foreign Minister Welcomes US President's Address to the UN", 15 September 2002, http://www.saudiembassy.net/2002News/Press/PressDetail.asp?cYear=2002&cIndex=49.

formed."[1] It was a global security strategy to "defend liberty and justice because these principles are right and true for all people everywhere".[2]

The guiding principle seemed to be "to stop rogue states and their terrorist clients before they are able to threaten or use WMD against the US and our allies and friends".[3] Thus the litmus test was the plausible allegation of a potential threat, not the convincing proof of the existence of such a threat. The strategy boldly asserted: "Our best defense is a good offense."[4] Bush talked of pre-emption, but the argument was actually about prevention.

The policy was pursued by the US after the collapse of the Taliban had begun to drive a wedge between Washington and the rest of the world. The easy collapse of the Taliban inclined the US toward a more unilateral policy that threatened the vital interests of others. The most troubling aspect for the US was that many who opposed its foreign policy were friends.[5]

According to *The New York Times*, a top-secret Pentagon war game called "Prominent Hammer" revealed that expanding the campaign against terrorism to include Iraq would place severe strains on personnel and cause deep shortages of certain critical weapons.[6]

Also that September, the Institute for National Strategic Studies issued a report about US interests in the Gulf that stated that the US military posture toward the region would become increasingly brittle unless it adapted to changes in the region in a creative way. The elimination of the Iraqi regime would confront the US with complex policy choices: Saudi Arabia's role in US regional security strategy; the degree to which a friendly Iraq could become the focus of US regional defence strategy; and the type of US military presence in the region.[7] The report argued that three realities confronted the continuing long-term containment:

---

1. The White House, George. W. Bush, "The National Security Strategy of the U.S.A.", Washington, DC, 17 September 2002, p. iv.
2. Ibid., p. 3.
3. Ibid., p. 14.
4. Ibid., p. 6.
5. Shibley Telhami, "Between Faith and Ethics", *Liberty and Power: A Dialogue on Religion and U.S. Foreign Policy in an Unjust World*, The Pew Forum Dialogues on Religion and Public Life (Washington, DC: Brookings Institution Press, 2004), p. 81.
6. Thom Shanker and Eric Schmitt, "Military Would Be Stressed by a New War, Study Finds", *The New York Times*, 24 May 2002.
7. Richard D. Sokolsky, et al., *Beyond Containment: Defending U.S. Interests in the*

1. Sanctions were already almost impossible to enforce;
2. Iraq would eventually possess and deploy WMD and longer-range ballistic missiles;
3. The US military presence, in Saudi Arabia in particular, was a source of growing resentment.

The report concluded that containing a hostile Iraq under these circumstances over the long term would require a much larger and more open-ended US military presence.[1]

According to *The New York Times*, on 11 October the president's Special Assistant for Near Eastern, Southwest Asian, and North African Affairs Zalmay Khalilzad justified the effort to get rid of Saddam in terms of democracy. He advocated US intervention "to get Iraq ready for a democratic transition and then through democracy over time".[2]

On 8 November the UN Security Council, urged by the US, adopted Resolution 1441 giving Iraq a "final opportunity" to comply with the disarmament obligations imposed under previous resolutions or face "serious consequences".[3] Saudi Arabia and other GCC members issued a statement on 22 December urging Iraq to accept UNSCR 1441. The statement also confirmed the GCC's firm stance on the importance of preserving Iraq's security, sovereignty and territorial integrity.[4]

On 15 November, Saud told reporters that the use of Saudi bases was "a sovereign decision ... and I am not going to speculate on how we're going to decide".[5] On 18 November he was reported as saying: "The Kingdom is troubled by the calls for war, especially when there is hope and optimism for peace."[6]

According to Woodward, Bandar, with instructions from 'Abdullah, went

---

    Persian Gulf (Washington, DC: INSS, National Defense University, September 2002), p. 4.
1. Ibid., p. 6.
2. David E. Sanger and Eric Schmitt, "U.S. Has a Plan to Occupy Iraq, Officials Report", *The New York Times*, 11 October 2002, p. 14.
3. UN Security Council Resolution 1441, 2002.
4. Saudi Embassy, Washington, "GCC Urges Iraq to Accept UN Resolution 1441", 12 November 2002, http://www.saudiembassy.net/2002News/News/RelDetail.asp?cIndex=1154.
5. *The Washington Post*, 17 November 2002.
6. *Ukaz*, 18 November 2002.

to see Bush on 15 November. Bandar told the president: "Since 1994, we have been in constant contact and touch with you on the highest level regarding what needs to be done with Iraq and the Iraqi regime." He informed Bush that in 1994 Fahd had suggested, to Clinton, a joint Saudi-US covert action to remove Saddam. Bandar reminded Bush, too, of 'Abdullah's April 2002 proposal to spend up to US $1 billion in such joint operations with the CIA. The ambassador expressed his surprise that the US was now asking the Saudis for their thoughts on how to deal with Saddam, something that caused the Kingdom to "begin to doubt how serious America is about the issue of regime change".[1] Bandar added: "If you are serious, we will take the right decision to make the right support." In return for its support, Bandar explained, Saudi Arabia would expect to have a major role in shaping the regime that would emerge after the fall of Saddam.[2] Bush informed Bandar that he would contact 'Abdullah for his final decision. If accurate, Woodward's claim can presumably have only one explanation – that the Saudis wanted only a covert "regime change" operation in which Saddam would be replaced by another Sunni military officer and control of Iraq would be kept in the hands of the Sunni community. They were afraid that any military action might cause the country to disintegrate into three states – Sunni, Shi'i and Kurdish – and also feared the possibility of Iran's control and intervention through Iraqi Shi'is.

By the end of November, the White House was reported to have settled on a war plan that called for the massing of between 200,000 and 250,000 troops for attacking Iraq by air, land and sea.[3] However, in order to carry out the most effective plan possible, the US needed access to bases and the right to fly over the territories of other states.

Cheney had visited Saudi Arabia and other Middle Eastern countries in March 2002. As part of the war plan, the US wanted to continue to use the Prince Sultan command centre; to station aircraft in and launch attacks from Saudi territory; to carry special operations missions into Iraq from Ara'r, a small town on the Iraq-Saudi Arabia border; and to use Al-Jubayl, a Saudi port, to relieve dependence on the port of Kuwait. At this early stage, the Saudi position was still unclear,[4] but Cheney was urged by Saudi leaders to

---

1. Woodward, *Plan of Attack*, pp. 228–9.
2. Ibid., pp. 229–30.
3. *The New York Times*, "War Plan for Iraq Calls for Big Force and Quick Strikes", 10 November 2002, p. 1.
4. Gordon and Trainor, *Cobra II*, pp. 38–41.

convince Bush to get involved in the Israeli-Palestinian conflict and through his political weight to start some sort of process for resolving it.[1]

According to Gordon and Trainor, the war plan had envisioned that Special Forces Task Force 20 (TF20) would attack secretly by helicopter from Saudi Arabia to secure Saddam International Airport. Paratroopers from the 82nd Airborne would attack the following night in order to reinforce the TF20. At the end of November, General Tommy Franks, CENTCOM commander, visited Saudi Arabia to meet Deputy Defence Minister Prince Khalid bin Sultan. Franks told Prince Khalid: "We just want to let you know that if we have the war we want it to be short. The contribution of our friends will determine the length of the war." Khalid expressed his hope that the Iraqi people would get rid of Saddam, but Franks told him that this was wishful thinking and that it was essential to obtain Saudi cooperation. Khalid said he was willing to set up a liaison office at CENTCOM headquarters in Tampa, Florida, but that the office would be established in the context of the Afghan war, not the war in Iraq. He also informed Franks that Saudi Arabia rejected the request to use the port of Al-Jubayl.[2]

By the end of the year, the dissonance between the US and members of the international community opposed to war on Iraq had reached a critical point. The White House was insisting that war was to be a last resort even as it continued the deployment of troops into the region.[3] *Al-Sharq al-Awsat* reported that Prince Saud urged the US not to launch a unilateral attack on Iraq. He said: "I don't envisage a US unilateral war [on Iraq], because at present the issue is in front of the UN." When asked about Saudi permission for the US to use military bases in the Kingdom against Iraq, he replied: "If war is through the UN and based on consensus, then we have to seek a decision in the Saudi national interest." Saud insisted Bush had indicated that "the decision to go to war would be the last resort."[4]

According to Gordon and Trainor, the "Cobra II" strategy for an Iraq war had been approved in principle by Rumsfeld and Franks in December. Under Cobra II, the attack was to start before all the forces had arrived in the

---

1. Woodward, *Plan of Attack*, p. 112.
2. Gordon and Trainor, *Cobra II*, pp. 85–91.
3. Irene Gendzier, "Oil, Iraq and U.S. Foreign Policy in the Middle East", *Situation Analysis* 2 (spring 2003), p. 26.
4. *Al-Sharq al-Awsat*, 23 December 2002.

region.¹ On 9 January 2003, Franks briefed Bush on the war plan. Bush wanted CENTCOM to be ready to attack as early as 15 February.² On 20 January, Jay Garner, a retired army lieutenant-general, was named head of the US Defense Department's Office of Reconstruction and Humanitarian Assistance (ORHA). The staff of ORHA designed and began to implement the administration of post-war Iraq. The ORHA plan called for a US-led occupation government of Iraq that was to last no more than three months. ORHA was dissolved as the Coalition Provisional Authority took shape, with Garner still at the helm. In May, on account of interdepartmental rivalry between the State and Defense Departments, Garner was replaced by L. Paul Bremer III.³

On 7 January, Saud told reporters: "If the UN asks Saudi Arabia to join, depending on the material breach and the proof that they show, Saudi Arabia will decide."⁴ *Al-Yaum* reported the Saudi foreign minister as saying that it was not permissible for the US to intervene in Iraq without a broad international consensus. He explained that Bush's decision to take the issue through the UN was wise, and that Saudi Arabia was therefore optimistic about avoiding war. Saud expressed his anxiety about the catastrophic results for the Iraqi people in the event of a war.⁵

According to Woodward, Cheney wanted personally to communicate the US decision to go to war to the Saudis, and invited Bandar to meet him on 11 January. Rumsfeld and General Richard B. Myers, Chairman of the Joint Chiefs of Staff, were also present. The intention was to convince Bandar that US forces would have to be sent through and from Saudi territory into Iraq. For Bandar, the Saudis would lose significantly if Saddam survived. Woodward claimed Bandar wanted some assurances that this time the US was serious enough to topple Saddam. "What is the chance of Saddam surviving this?" Bandar asked. Cheney reassured Bandar that once they started they would not stop until they had finished Saddam. Bandar insisted on hearing this directly from Bush. Two days later, Bandar met Bush, and emphasized that if Saddam was attacked one more time by the US and survived, he would become larger than life. The Saudis therefore needed assurances that the US would finish

---

1. Gordon and Trainor, *Cobra II*, p. 95.
2. Ibid., pp. 97–8.
3. David Leigh, "General Sacked by Bush Says He Wanted Early Elections", *The Guardian*, 18 March 2004.
4. Prados, "Saudi Arabia: Current Issues and U.S. Relations", p. 5.
5. *Al-Yaum*, 7 January 2003.

Saddam once and for all. Bush asserted: "That is the message I want you to carry for me to the Crown Prince."[1] On 13 January, however, *Ukaz* reported 'Abdullah's statement that "there will be no war".[2] The contradiction between Woodward's claim and the *Ukaz* report may be attributed to the crown prince having received some strong assurances from the US that war would not be launched without the approval of the UN.

On 8 March, Sultan said his government was allowing US troops to use two airports in northern Saudi Arabia to help in a technical matter. Prince Sultan said emphatically: "The Kingdom is against the war, but it has no power to prevent it."[3] According to Gordon and Trainor, Franks summoned his commanders to his Qatar headquarters for a final briefing on 14 March. The war was scheduled to begin on the evening of 19 March, and Special Forces would attack from Saudi Arabia, Jordan and Kuwait. The major "Shock and Awe" air campaign would begin two days later. The Marines' V Corps would begin to cross into Iraq on 22 March from Kuwait. This nearly simultaneous air and ground attack would surprise the Iraqis.[4] The air campaign and the Special Forces eventually started on schedule; the main land assault started on the evening of 20 March.

The White House's allies in Washington were confident in predicting that the Iraqis would greet the US troops as liberators, and that government functions would be turned over as quickly as possible to the Iraqis themselves.[5] Finally, according to Gordon and Trainor, Saudi Arabia allowed the US to run the air campaign from the Prince Sultan command centre and to dispatch aircraft that would facilitate the strike; but it drew the line at bomber aircraft being launched from its territory.[6]

On 19 March, Bush announced the beginning of "Operation Iraqi Freedom" to compel Iraq to adhere to the UN Security Council resolutions.[7] On the same day, Saudi Arabia issued a communiqué insisting that it "will not participate in any way in the war".[8] Although Saudi Arabia continued to avoid public

---

1. Woodward, *Plan of Attack*, pp. 262–7.
2. *Ukaz*, 13 January 2003.
3. *Al-Riyadh*, 9 March 2003.
4. Gordon and Trainor, *Cobra II*, pp. 164–5.
5. Ibid., pp. 168–9.
6. Ibid., p. 174.
7. Prados, "Saudi Arabia: Current Issues and U.S. Relations", p. 6.
8. CRS, "Saudi Arabia", 24 February 2006, p. 6.

confirmation of any support it was providing, according to *The Washington Post* the Kingdom had agreed to provide logistical support to US-led forces, including permission to conduct refuelling, reconnaissance, surveillance and transport missions from Saudi Arabia. In addition, the Kingdom gave landing and over-flight clearance, and allowed the US to use a military facility known as the Combat Air Operations Centre to coordinate military operations.[1] On 1 May, Bush declared an end to major combat operations in Iraq.[2]

The Saudi position can be explained as a result of two considerations. First was that the US had decided on launching the war, and in the aftermath of 9/11, the Saudis could not but side with the US. Second was that the differences were only about methodology, not about conclusion; therefore, the Saudis had to acquiesce to the US decision. However, having decided to assist the US, the Kingdom could not publicly acknowledge its role, as doing so would have caused vehement criticism from both domestic and external opponents.

Al-Sharq al-Awsat reported on 23 March that Saud was urging the US to stop the war: "The armies, US and British, don't have the necessary knowledge to reconstruct Iraq or unite its complex community setting." He added: "The UN must be left able to define the conditions to be implemented in Iraq." The minister advised the US to consider the possibility of "members of the existing Ba'th government participating in the restructuring process".[3]

On 1 April, the Saudi Council of Ministers issued a statement that it "followed with regret and extreme care the war's consequences and destructive effects on Iraq and its people", and urged "the Islamic nation and peace-loving people and nations to initiate action quickly to stop the war".[4] The next day, Saud expressed his "anxiety about the war extending to other places in the region, due to persisting instability in the Middle East". He reiterated the Saudi position on the war and on the military occupation of Iraq, and insisted: "The Iraqi people have the sole right to determine their country's destiny and to call on the international community to support the people's choice." Moreover, Saud denied that any use had been made of the Prince Sultan command centre in Al-Kharj or that any military operations had been initiated from Saudi

---

1. *The Washington Post*, 26 February 2003.
2. George W. Bush, *We Will Prevail: President George W. Bush on War, Terrorism and Freedom* (New York: Continuum International Publishing Group, 2003), pp. 259–63.
3. *Al-Sharq al-Awsat*, 23 March 2003.
4. *Al-Sharq al-Awsat*, 1 April 2003.

territories. He stated: "The US had not requested permission in the matter, and the Kingdom had not given its permission."[1]

On 30 April *The New York Times* reported that the US was planning to withdraw its troops from Saudi Arabia and move its Combat Air Operations Centre to Qatar.[2] The last US troops finally left Saudi Arabia in early September.

In reality, the war never ended. Saddam's regime did not stay around to surrender but simply melted away, and by June the justifications of Saddam's alleged WMD and his ties to al-Qa'ida had also evaporated. In addition, the lack of any effective coordination between US government agencies led to inadequate planning for the postwar reconstruction of Iraq.[3]

A security vacuum took hold immediately after the war. Sporadic firefights continued throughout Iraq, and looting broke out in Baghdad and other cities. As the months passed, these activities turned into much more serious and long-term security problems. As early as July, US military officials began to characterize them as guerrilla warfare. Throughout the first year US troops continued to be attacked and killed on a regular basis.[4] The Saudis had warned the US prior to the war about the grave consequences that were likely to occur, and the results were as the Kingdom had expected; as 'Abdullah insisted: "The war had served Iran's interest."[5]

The Washington Post reported on 26 August that a senior State Department official described how pro-Saddam Arab volunteer fighters had been infiltrating into Iraq through Iran, Syria and Saudi Arabia to mount attacks against US-led coalition forces in Iraq.[6] A statement by the Saudi embassy in Washington declared that the Kingdom had "not been presented with evidence that supports media reports of illegal movement across its 500-mile border with Iraq". The statement acknowledged that the issue had been raised with the US and that discussions had been held between the two countries on "possible US redeployment of border patrols on the Iraqi side of the boundary".[7]

1. *Al-Hayat*, 2 April 2003.
2. *The New York Times*, 30 April 2003.
3. CSIS and Association of the US Army (AUSA), *Play to Win: Final Report of the Bi-Partisan Commission on Post-Conflict Reconstruction* (Washington, DC: CSIS Press, 2003), pp. 10–2.
4. Ibid., *Winning the Peace: An American Strategy for Post-Conflict Reconstruction* (Washington, DC: CSIS Press, 2004), pp. 268–9.
5. *Al-Hayat*, 27 November 2005.
6. *The Washington Post*, 26 August 2003.
7. Saudi Embassy, Washington, "Saudi Information Office Issues Clarification",

The 'Abdullah Era (2001–6)

In September, Saud stated in an interview with *Time*: "All the discussions that we had [with the US] on Iraq were on our concerns about what happens after the attack." For Saudi Arabia, keeping Iraq secure and its government running were the most important elements. Saud explained that Iraq had been ruled by perhaps two million military personnel and a million Ba'thists, and that without them "Iraq would become unmanageable … We told you … that things won't work out".[1] In a 2005 interview, he would say: "There seems to be no dynamic now which pulls the country together" and emphasize that with the breakdown of the country, with food shortages and salaries nonexistent, the population had turned to resistance groups. To improve the situation, the Sunnis had to be persuaded "that they are equal citizens in the new Iraq … Unless something is done to bring the people of Iraq together, a constitution alone or an election alone won't do it." Saud would also express his government's worry about Iraq's disintegration: "It would bring the countries of the region into conflict."[2]

By November 2003, the US was an occupying power where it was not wanted, in a place that did not really matter to its strategic interests. The Bush administration had no real plans for getting the troops out of Iraq. The war had derailed the Israel-Palestine peace process and generated strong resentment, thereby enabling al-Qa'ida and other terrorist group to capitalize on it. The US military occupation had become a lightning rod that would enable anti-US terrorists in Iraq to expand their operations against troops in their area and ultimately to the shores of the US. Furthermore, the US presence in Iraq weakened the forces of democratic reform by undermining the authority and credibility of the indigenous government.

The Bush neoconservatives' prosecution of the war was becoming so dire that even right-wing political commentators like Pat Buchanan could argue that US policy had been hijacked, that a war was being fought to further Israel's needs, not those of the US and that "our country is in a series of wars that are not in America's interests". (He also echoed the commonly growing

---

28 August 2003, http://www.saudiembassy.net/2002News/Press/PressDetail.asp?cYear=2003 & cIndex=121.
1. Saudi Embassy, Washington, "The Saudis Respond: Foreign Minister Prince Saud Interviewed by Scott Macleod".
2. Saudi Embassy, Washington, "Transcript of Prince Saud Interview with U.S. Print Journalists", 22 September 2005, http://www.saudiembassy.net/2005News/Statements/TransDetail.asp?cIndex=553.

suspicion that the neocons had exploited 9/11 to "steer America's rage into an all-out war to destroy their despised enemies".)[1]

The guiding principle for US foreign policy must be that if core national security interests are not threatened, it can minimize the risk of terrorism by being less involved in the problems of other countries. Iraq is not a threat to US national security today. Therefore, it must hand over the country to the Iraqi people, allow them to decide the form of a new government and withdraw US forces as expeditiously as possible.

The Reconstruction of Good Relations since April 2005

Many observers believe that after the successful meeting in April 2005 at Bush's ranch in Crawford, Texas between Crown Prince 'Abdullah and the president, Saudi-US relations improved greatly. To believe so is misleading. The crucial change had begun earlier, after the terrorist attacks in Saudi Arabia in May, September and November 2003. After these incidents, it was easier for the Saudi regime to hit hard at the militant element inside the Kingdom. With support from the religious establishment and the public, the Saudis could now openly join the "war on terrorism" without fear of stirring up and damaging the domestic social fabric. This was the critical element that changed US attitudes to Saudi Arabia.

The Crawford meeting simply reinforced the trend. A statement after the meeting declared: "Momentous changes in the world call on us to forge a new relationship between our two countries – a strengthened partnership that builds on our past partnership." It acknowledged that both countries had "proud and very distinct histories", and emphasized the respect of the US for the Kingdom "as the birthplace of Islam ... and as the symbolic centre of the Islamic faith". The Kingdom, in turn, recognized "the principle of freedom upon which the US was founded" and appreciated "the historic role of the US in working to end colonialism and imperialism". Both countries pledged to continue their cooperation so that "the oil supply from Saudi Arabia will be available and secure". The statement also held: "Both our nations assert

---

1. Patrick J. Buchanan, "A Neoconservative Clique Seeks to Ensnare Our Country in a Series of Wars That Are Not in America's Interests", *The American Conservative*, 24 March 2003.

our determination to continue to improve upon our close cooperation to combat terrorism."[1]

Prince Saud said afterward that the result of the meeting "would have a positive impact on Saudi-American relations".[2] Some US sources reportedly claimed that the US had asked the Kingdom during the discussion to convince other oil producers to increase production and reduce prices. The Saudis focused on urging the US president to work on the Israel-Palestine peace process, and on establishing a Palestinian state. Many political and press observers in the US, according to *Al-Sharq al-Awsat*, claimed that the visit, with Washington's acknowledgement of the important Saudi role in the fight against terrorism, had returned warmth to the relationship.[3] *Ukaz* reported that the summit had also pledged US support for Saudi membership of the World Trade Organization (WTO), and announced the foundation of a joint foreign ministerial committee to follow up on discussion of strategic issues.[4]

One of the signs of improved relations was the establishment of a strategic dialogue between the Kingdom and the US. On 13 November that same year, Saud and Secretary of State Rice inaugurated the first of these formal meetings. Saud affirmed that the dialogue "establishes a new mechanism of co-ordination between the two states", adding: "The joint will, the sincere will and the hard work, will achieve the intended objectives of the Strategic Dialogue." Rice said it would allow the US "to have regular discussions about a number of issues of interest to us".[5]

Strategic dialogue is designed to institutionalize the relationship between the two countries. Working groups meet on a continuous or "as needed" basis to deal with functional issues and to provide an institutional framework through which officials from a number of departments and ministries from

---

1. Saudi Embassy, Washington, "Joint Statement by Crown Prince Abdullah and President George W. Bush", 25 April 2005, http://www.saudiembassy.net/2005News/Statements/StateDetail.asp?cIndex=517.
2. Saudi Embassy, Washington, "Foreign Minister Gives Press Conference in Dallas, Texas", 26 April 2005, http://www.saudiembassy.net/2005News/News/USDetail.asp?cIndex=5238.
3. *Al-Sharq al-Awsat*, 24 April 2005.
4. *Ukaz*, 26 April 2006.
5. Saudi Embassy, Washington, "Joint Press Conference of Prince Saud and Secretary Rice Following the First Strategic Dialogue", 14 November 2005, http://www.saudiembassy.net/2005News/Statements/Trans Detail.asp?cIndex=562.

both governments work to address, constructively and comprehensively, a range of issues of importance to both countries. The objective is to institutionalize relationships across government departments in both countries to ensure that issues are dealt with effectively.[1]

At the Brookings Institution on 16 June 2006, now-ambassador to the US Prince Turki stressed that the two countries were beginning to rebuild their relationship. He said that after 9/11, "relationships, understanding, and security all fell apart", and emphasized that Saudi-US relations had in fact changed considerably: "… We have endured the challenges and we have come very far in that time." The ambassador explained that prior to 9/11 the relationship had worked because both sides had a lot in common: "We were military allies, reliable energy partners and good friends." After 9/11 the relationship plunged into crisis: "There now existed deep suspicions, mistrust, and misperception."

Turki suggested that both countries address the challenges facing the relationship. Doing so would first involve putting stronger links in place between both governments. (The clearest example of this was the strategic dialogue.) Second, it would mean increasing face-to-face contact by encouraging more delegations between the two countries. Third, better relations would be developed between Saudi Arabia and the US Congress. Fourth, the way in which the US criticized politicians or public figures or leading thinkers caused the Saudis great concern and had to be tackled. Turki suggested: "We often hear political rhetoric and not constructive commentary." He suggested: "Why not engage us productively instead of engaging in rhetoric that seems designed to drive us away?" The ambassador concluded by stating: "If you look at the problems we're facing today … the US cannot deal without us. And we cannot deal with them without you."[2]

The relationship will need a substantial effort on the part of both governments, and deeper understanding of each other's needs and of the obstacles facing their facilitation. The relationship is still blighted by the weeds of suspicion and the ramifications of finger-pointing. These will need to be remedied with time, and with sincere intentions when dealing with the problems that face its long-term prospects.

---

1. Saudi Embassy, Washington, "US-Saudi Strategic Dialogue Joint Statement", 18 May 2006, http://www.saudiembassy.net/2006News/Statements/StateDetail.asp?cIndex=615.
2. Saudi Embassy, Washington, "Saudi Ambassador's Speech at the Brookings Institution", 19 June 2006, http://www.saudiembassy.net/2006News/Statements/SpeechDetail.asp?cIndex=623.

Conclusion: Future Prospects

This book has covered four crucial phases in the Saudi-US relationship, beginning with the Faisal era (1962–1979). The two countries then had formed a regionally based partnership and worked together against the threats of Arab Nationalism and communism to their interests in the region. Faisal urged the US to cooperate with the Kingdom, but maintained his own agenda, which included a wish to develop an Islamic bloc to provide a further hedge in the Middle East against the aforementioned ideological threats. The king's agenda, in many cases, ran counter to the policies and specific interests of the US.

Other elements of the relationship included oil and the Israel-Palestine conflict. The latter brought the two sides into confrontation. Faisal considered the US as the leader and protector of the Free World, but the relationship between the two countries was held back by US support for Israel. The Kingdom had greatly contributed to US interests in the sphere of oil supplies, but in 1973–4 Faisal imposed an oil embargo after failing to convince the US to adopt a more accommodating policy to the Arab stance.

Nasser's Egypt, meanwhile, had aimed to replace imperialist influence with Egyptian hegemony. Saudi Arabia at first bandwagoned with Egypt, but after the latter's involvement in Yemen, the Kingdom attempted to rely on a different ideological appeal: Islamism. The 1967 war signalled the decline of Egyptian hegemony, reducing its threat to Saudi Arabia. The recovery of territories lost during the war emphasized the need to establish inter-Arab coalition. An axis of Egypt, Saudi Arabia and Syria replaced the model of Egyptian hegemony as a new basis for Arab cohesion, for a while at least. The 1973 war and the Arabs' ability to inflict a high cost on Israel using oil as a political weapon forced US intervention and a negotiated settlement. But Egypt's separate peace shattered the "Arab Triangle".

The US and Saudi Arabia collaborated in the face of mutual threats, and worked to avoid conflicts of interests and connections. Under Faisal the Kingdom worked skilfully along the thin line of cooperation with the US, while simultaneously preserving its standing in the Arab and Muslim worlds.

During the first Fahd era (1979–90), cooperation mutated into a compulsive dependence as domestic and regional threats multiplied. Radical Islamist threats, heightened Soviet activities in the region and the Iran-Iraq War necessitated a strong reliance on the US by the Saudis, albeit one that was "over the horizon". The cooperation expanded to cover many other fields.

The Soviet invasion of Afghanistan combined with the Iranian threat heightened feelings of vulnerability in Saudi Arabia and the Gulf. The Kingdom's need to balance against these dangers led to the enhancement of the US presence and influence in the Gulf.

The US encouraged and supported Saudi proselytizing to combat communist expansionism. The Kingdom also played a major role in facilitating US foreign policy in areas where Saudi financial assistance could influence developments. A largely secretive partnership arose between the two countries to counteract communist menace in the region.

The dynamics of the relationship were now based on Saudi Arabia's inclination to promote US foreign policy neutralizing the Soviet "evil empire" – in many instances with scant regard for Saudi national interests. The US manipulated and in many instances abused the Saudi willingness to be of help.

The later Fahd era (1990–2001), witnessed Iraq's invasion of Kuwait, which presented a grave danger to Saudi Arabia's existence. The US response to this threat generated enormous political problems for the Saudi government; the US military presence unleashed a radical religious current that posed many difficulties for both sides.

The collapse of pan-Arab solidarity as a result of the Gulf War hastened fragmentation of the Arab core. US penetration of the region reached levels comparable to that of Britain and France during the colonial era. No security system emerged, and Saudi Arabia continued to rely on US protection. The US was provided with an unprecedented opportunity to project its influence in to the region.

The relationship was now radically different from what it had been. The end of the Cold War weakened justification for close Saudi-US ties, and oil interests alone could not maintain their once-high level. Opposition within Saudi Arabia viewed the relationship with suspicion and alarm. The US failure

Conclusion

to resolve the Israel-Palestine conflict placed Saudi Arabia under additional pressure to adopt a position counterproductive to the interests of the two countries. The double standard inherent in US policies toward Arab states made a closer relationship difficult to sustain.

The 'Abdullah era (2001–6) saw earlier policies supporting Islamic extremism in the fight against communism return to haunt both the US and Saudi Arabia: the events of 9/11 cast doubt and distrust with regard to their cooperation. US accusations of Saudi tolerance and support of terrorism, and the Kingdom's delay in acknowledging the Saudi nationality of most of the 9/11 perpetrators, infuriated an already inflamed public on both sides. The "war on terrorism" effectively put both countries on a collision course. The US's demands for the closure of some Saudi businesses and bank accounts, and for the handover of Saudi citizens for interrogation, were sometimes seen as unreasonable by the Saudi side and were sometimes met with Saudi insensitivity. The Saudi government was in an awkward position. On one hand it could not, because of its Islamic responsibilities, help the "infidels"; on the other hand, it wanted to preserve and protect the relationship with the US by assisting in defusing terrorism.

The two countries were now portrayed in the media as being in confrontation, and to some extent this was true; the US and Saudi Arabia struggled to calmly restructure their ties in order to cope with the challenges of the post-9/11 era.

The reconstructed Saudi-US relationship must acknowledge that the events of 9/11 will not be forgotten, and that there is no way to return to the past. The US must understand that, by selecting the majority of the suicide bombers from Saudi Arabia, bin Laden had chosen to identify the attack with Saudi Arabia in order to undermine Saudi-US relations. Blaming the whole country for the attack only plays into bin Laden's hands. Both countries must define their interests and reaffirm them, looking for points of congruence. The two sides have to learn to tolerate differences. The US must recognize that the Kingdom may disagree on matters secondary to the relationship, and that it does have vital interests at stake that do not necessarily coincide with US interests. Saudi Arabia must promote its vital interests and those of the region regardless of where US interests lie.

The US would also be wise to take account of Saudi advice regarding issues in the Middle East. Both the US and the Kingdom need to work together as much as possible to push the peace process forward and to reduce support for violent extremism on both sides. There will never be truly shared common objectives or perceptions without resolution of the Israeli-Palestinian conflict. The US attitude toward the Kingdom since 9/11 and its apparent indifference to Palestinian suffering cause huge difficulties for the relationship.

Nor can the US expect social change in Saudi Arabia to follow the pattern of US social transformation. The US must recognize that the Kingdom needs to move at its own pace, and that the wrong kind of pressure can be counter-productive. Expecting the Kingdom to create a liberal democracy within a short period of time is unreasonable and can lead only to a conflicting result. The US should encourage a gradual transition toward democracy in the Kingdom and promote constitutional liberalism. The presence of a vibrant civil society increases the likelihood that the democratization process will succeed.

By neglecting scientific research and technological development, the Kingdom is wasting the economic potential of its population and ignoring an opportunity to provide jobs and livelihoods to frustrated young Saudis who will otherwise turn toward extremism. The US can assist in this regard by supporting Saudi economic reform and diversification to help ease the economic and demographic conditions that provide an impetus for terrorism.

The two countries must be involved in a joint strategy for winning the "war on terror". Saudi Arabia needs to manage its Islamic affairs in a manner that will project the moderate reality of Islam. The Kingdom must start to encourage moderate elements in its religious establishment.

The US, too, needs a more extensive and intensive bilateral dialogue with the Kingdom. It must be willing to broaden the focus of its high-level dialogue with Saudi Arabia so that it can deal forthrightly with expectations and modalities for the encouragement of reform within the Kingdom.

Saudi Arabia, for its part, needs to be more positively responsive to requests by the US with regard to the "war on terror" that do not conflict with Saudi national interests. The Kingdom must neutralize Saudi conservatives who continue to oppose what they perceive as the pernicious social influences emanating from the US.

Saudi Arabia, through the religious establishment, must demonstrate and explain to the Saudi and Muslim public that Islam is not against others, and that terrorist attacks clash with the principles of Islam. Saudi Arabia must take a greater role in debate in the Muslim world, promoting tolerant and less extremist interpretations of Islam. The Saudi regime must use its influence in Saudi-supported international Islamic organizations to combat extremist ideas.

Riyadh must expedite its review programme of the educational curriculum and implement a more robust educational system that focuses on science and technology to better prepare the Saudi youth to face the challenges of the future. Saudi Arabia must implement a programme of student exchanges with the US to enhance cultural awareness and understanding in both societies.

The wider development of the Saudi political system will also be of relevance to the relationship with the US. Saudi Arabia must develop new avenues for political participation in society. This includes expanding the role of the Saudi Consultative Council, which should be permitted to monitor and check the affairs of all non-sovereign ministries. Saudi Arabia must be more forthcoming and more accountable in its financial affairs. Financial transparency should be adopted to eliminate corruption and to plan the economic future of the country more effectively. A new formula should be created to meet the future financial needs of the Saudi royal family without resorting to corruption and wastefulness.

Saudi Arabia must allow gradual freedom of speech, a free press and public discussion by intellectuals.

Finally, for the country's continued stability and progress, the Saudi royal family must, in the short term, find a way to hand over power to the second generation to run the affairs of the country. In the long term, it should draw up a plan to become a symbol of unity for the nation, and thereby turn itself into a constitutional monarchy.

Saudi Arabian and US interests overlap, but are not identical. Saudi Arabia can work with the US where these interests are held to be in common, and it must find its own separate direction where interests diverge. In order to preserve and protect their oil connection, the two countries will have to attempt to maximize their own profits without damaging the overarching, economically beneficial relationship. The Kingdom must preserve and enhance its traditional role as the key, and most reliable, energy supplier to the West.

There are several serious challenges facing the relationship in this century. These challenges again reflect the determinant of the relationship: Israel; the security of oil supplies, in particular with regard to Iran; security in Iraq; and the ever-present threat of Islamist terror. The collapsed peace process and the failure to find a just and lasting solution to the Palestinian problem – and in particular the question of Jerusalem – will be an obstacle for developing a strong and solid partnership between the two countries. Iran's radicalism and its likely attempts to obtain WMD, plus the possibility of US military strikes against it, all threaten oil security and even Saudi domestic security; these issues can further restrict the relationship.

The failure of the US to preserve peace and security in Iraq, and Iranian penetration of the internal domestic politics of that country, have placed the Kingdom in an awkward position. Saudi Arabia desires a stable and a governable Iraq, but at the same time cannot accept Iranian interference and recruitment of support inside the country. In facing this situation, the Kingdom may be compelled to intervene, and would thus find itself in a counterproductive position with regard to US interests. The grievances of the Palestinians and the Iraqis can be exploited by al Qa'ida and other terrorist groups, which will continue to strike against the US and its interests in the region. The threat imposed by Islamist terror will hinder any improvement of the relationship as long as failure to solve the problems of the Middle East continues.

Postscript: Obama – Continuation or Change?

US President Barack Obama took office on 20 January 2009. The country was facing its worst economic situation since the Great Depression; internationally, Obama had to contend with the US's loss of prestige in the eyes of both friend and foe alike as people's admiration and respect for it continued to decline. The events of 11 September 2001 had initially provided the US with the world's sympathy and readiness to cooperate. However, instead of using this goodwill to advance its leadership and pre-eminent position throughout the world, the Bush administration chose to undertake reckless and disastrous policies that contributed to a unilateralist and belligerent foreign policy.

Saudi Arabia and the Arab Middle East as a whole had to bear the full burden of this policy. The Kingdom was depicted as the breeding ground for terrorism, and its long and beneficial relationship with the US was suddenly put on a collision course from which it has yet to recover. Iraq, and with it the rest of the Arab Middle East, was unwisely handed to the Iranians. Saudi Arabia and the Gulf are currently facing the threat of substantially strengthened Iranian influence and power. (The only significant regional obstacle to Iran's schemes is Egypt.) One needed only to listen to the speeches of Hizbullah's leader Hassan Nasrallah during the December 2008 invasion of Gaza by Israel, and to his vigorous attacks on Egypt, to apprehend the full picture. Bush's strong support for Israel and his neglect of the suffering of the Palestinians left the latter with no other choice but to turn to the Iranians.

Thus Obama inherited an economy in crisis and a country with few friends owing to the despised foreign policy of his predecessor, whose neo-imperialist ambitions turned so rapidly to ashes. Obama's decisive success in winning the presidency filled the need for a national leadership that would be capable of defining objectives that are politically and morally compelling, and that might offer some hope to the Arab world.

Arabs and Muslims have high hopes that, after Bush's catastrophic engagement with the region, the US will take a more balanced, intelligent and collaborative approach to the Middle East. But in truth, the new administration is not going to be able to deliver on all its promises, let alone on everyone else's expectations. President Obama's historic speech at Cairo University on 4 June 2009 did not represent a dramatic break from the longer perspective of US foreign policy; he had defined his mission, but did not accomplish it. The speech was outstanding, and addressed the world's Muslims frankly yet respectfully. However, as Obama accepted, "no single speech can eradicate years of mistrust". Ultimately his administration will be judged by its deeds and not – or not only – by his words.

The Arab world celebrated Obama's victory, and expressed its hopes that in his handling of the Israeli-Palestinian conflict he would take a different path from that of his predecessor. However, pragmatists took the view that Arab jubilation was motivated more by hope than by reality, as Obama would find his hands tied by the overwhelming support Israel enjoys in Congress.

While Obama's prime focus will be to revive the ailing US economy, an immediate strategic objective will be to strengthen the Iraqi government to ensure stability. However, with regard to foreign policy and other strategic objectives, it is Afghanistan and Pakistan that will consume his energies. In addition, the US will wish to engage Iran in order to curb its nuclear ambitions, and will try to use the connection to maintain stability in Iraq and Afghanistan and prevent future escalation in the Israel-Palestine situation.

The Obama administration will therefore be tackling three interlocking challenges in the Middle East: Iran's nuclear programme, continued tensions between Israel and Syria and the Israeli-Palestinian conflict. Seeking an understanding with Syria will increase pressure on Iran to respond to the US offer of an alternative line of talks, as, in the words of former NSC advisor Martin Indyk, "We've got a Syrian government that wants to engage."[1] Yet given the crucial strategic depth that Iran provides for Syria, it makes no sense from Syria's perspective to change its strategy. As such, to believe that Syria will abandon this alliance is to misconceive its interests and worldview.

---

1. Mark Landler, "After Overture to Syria, Clinton Meets West Bank's Leaders", *International Herald Tribune*, 4 March 2009.

Postscript

In the months since the election of President Obama, new dynamics have begun to emerge in the way the US approaches the Middle East. It has begun to embrace a more pragmatic posture in dealing with the mass of intractable problems that engulfs its relations with the Arab world. The US seems finally to have grasped the key notion in international politics that diplomacy remains the *raison d'état* of states, and that the use of force is but one way of serving it.

In the Middle East, the US should focus on negotiating with Iran as well as on coaxing Israel to withdraw from the Golan Heights and make peace with Syria; it also needs to persuade the Israelis to leave the West Bank and East Jerusalem, as doing so would contribute to fostering the creation of a Palestinian state. The US should view the region's problems as interconnected.

Many people in the Middle East are disappointed by Obama's cabinet choices. Instead of sparkling new lights, he chose many remnants of the old guard. Secretary of State Hillary Clinton, an avowed supporter of Israel, along with other familiar, pro-Israel faces, is a key figure in the new administration. In particular, Obama's Chief of Staff Rahm Emanuel, whose father was a member of the Zionist, terrorist Irgun organization, is a dedicated pro-Israel defender. However, in an interview with the Arabic-language Al-Arabiya television channel, Obama signalled a shift from the former administration when he offered a new readiness to listen rather than to dictate.[1]

The success of the US plan for the region will depend on the role Iran chooses to play. The US needs Iran in order to stabilize Iraq and to secure a speedy and responsible withdrawal of its troops from that country. The US also needs to coordinate with Iran regarding the situation in Afghanistan.

Obama's invitation of direct talks with Iran defines the new administration's first engagement with the rest of the world. On 9 February 2009, Obama spoke about "looking for areas where we can have constructive dialogue, where we can engage directly with them" – although he also cautioned that "there's been a lot of mistrust built up over the years", and that openings are "not going to happen overnight".[2] However, several developments seem to be driving the US and Iran toward the negotiating table. Of those, the most important is probably Iran's progress in enriching uranium. Another is a joint interest in stabilizing the region. Iran wants a pacified Iraq on its border under friendly

---

1. A transcript of the interview can be found at http://www.alarabiya.net/articles/2009/01/27/65096.html (retrieved 22 March 2009).
2. David Sanger, "Iranian Overture Might Complicate Relations with Israel", *The New York Times*, 10 February 2009.

Shi'i leadership; a peaceful, friendly Afghanistan; and acceptance as a member of a Gulf security structure. Above all, it wants to contain Israel's aggressive militarism, and to contribute to the emergence of an independent Palestinian state. If Iran is to consider halting its uranium enrichment programme, the US will certainly have to meet some of these ambitions.

In its negotiations with the Iranians, the US must insist that Iran suspend its efforts to enrich uranium; yet Iran calculates that it can eventually force the world to accept its enrichment programme. Time is on Iran's side, and while the US negotiates, the Iranians will continue to install more centrifuges. However, as long as its nuclear programme remains illegal and subject to international censure, it cannot serve as an attractive model for other regional governments.

Bush's failed policies left Iran with enormous regional influence and very close to building a nuclear weapon. Through a mixture of incentives, including a credible offer to improve relations along with security guarantees, the US may be able to wean Iran away from its nuclear ambitions. It also needs to remind Iran that is clearly in that country's interests for the Taliban to be defeated and Afghanistan stabilized. Furthermore, the US can argue that it is in Iran's strategic interests to join regional negotiations that intended to guarantee Iraq's long-term stability and sovereignty.

Iran's drive for dominance and toward filling the gap created by the US wars against the Taliban and Saddam has clearly transformed it into a regional superpower by default, which is why several Arab leaders have expressed concerns about Iranian designs in the region. King 'Abdullah was clear about this in his speech at a summit in Kuwait in January 2009, when he stated that Arab disputes, division and fragmentation "helped the Israeli enemy and those who want to split the Arab ranks to advance their regional designs". Although the king did not mention Iran by name, he was clearly referring to it.[1] The lack of any balance of power between Iran and the Arab countries, and the dependence of the West on Iran's influence to assist it, were significant factors in contributing to Iran's confidence, boldness and ambitious designs.

The launch of Iran's Omid satellite could be seen as a pre-emptive Iranian step in kicking off the new era of relations between Iran and the US. Obama criticized Iranian leaders for acting in ways that "are not conducive to peace

---

1. *Arab News*, "Excerpts from an Impassioned Appeal", 20 January 2009.

and prosperity in the region". However, he also emphasized his willingness to talk to the Iranians, and to explore "where there are potential avenues for progress".[1] Iran's presidential election on 12 June 2009 left many analysts in doubt about its results. The White House expressed concern about "reports of irregularities". According to the journalist Seymour Hersh, Congress had agreed to a request from Bush (while he was president) to fund a covert operation against Iran designed to destabilize the country's religious leadership and undermine its nuclear ambitions.[2] It remains, however, to be seen who will prevail and what will happen next.

In any case, the re-election of Mahmoud Ahmadinejad put the Obama administration in an awkward position, following its course of nuclear diplomacy with Iran without appearing to accept the Iranian authorities' suppression of dissent. Obama is under renewed pressured at home to issue a tougher line. But Vice President Joe Biden indicated that the administration had no intention of abandoning its Iran policy; eventually, the US will have no choice but to talk to Tehran.

New US policy will eventually ease tensions in the region, and may give incentives to the Iranians to open up internationally and de-radicalize their regional policies. Even so, the US must be careful not to strike deals with Iran that do not take account of, and protect, the vital interests of Saudi Arabia and the other Gulf states. The relationship between Saudi Arabia and Iran has long been strained, amid concerns about Iran's nuclear programmes. At the UN General Assembly in 2008, Prince Saud urged Iran to comply with its nuclear obligations in order to spare the Middle East from "devastating conflicts, futile arms races and serious environmental hazards".[3]

Iran is bidding for hegemony in the Arab world, and in the process is challenging both Egypt and Saudi Arabia. By aiding Hizbullah and Hamas, it is painting itself as the true protector of the Palestinians. Iran is imposing itself as the regional power, and to achieve this objective it is using these groups as valuable proxy forces – trump cards to be played with Washington and to alienate it further from the Arab world. Hamas in particular represents a very

1. Alan Cowell, "On Arab TV Network, Obama Urges Dialogue", *The New York Times*, 27 January 2009.
2. Seymour M. Hersh, "Preparing the Battlefield", *The New Yorker*, 7 July 2008.
3. Saudi Embassy, Washington, "The Kingdom's Address to the 63rd UN General Assembly, 27 September 2008", http://www.saudiembassy.net/2008News/Statements/SpeechDetail.asp?cIndex=73.

practical and useful tool for Iran, whose relationship with that organization is one of shared interests. Iran provides money and training while Hamas acts to undermine US interests in the region. Iran sponsors both Hamas and Hizbullah not only to torment Israel but also to spread its influence in the Arab world.

In the same Al-Arabiya interview, Obama remarked that he believed the path that Israelis and Palestinians were following "was not going to result in prosperity and security for their people". Instead, he declared: "It's time to return to the negotiating table." He also said the Israel-Palestine conflict should not be seen in isolation, but "in terms of what's happening with Syria or Iran or Lebanon or Afghanistan and Pakistan".

Obama's willingness to deal with the Israeli-Palestinian crisis so early in his term represents a clean break with the catastrophic neglect of his predecessor. Yet the US political system is not given to sudden and significant shifts in foreign policy. Rather, it is characterized by evolution, typically at a slow pace. To adopt any new policy, a consensus is needed among competing interests in the system, and the president's role is limited to formalizing rather than to catalyzing this process.

The Israeli attacks on Gaza were clearly aimed at subduing Hamas, delegitimizing its leadership in the eyes of the Palestinian people and wiping out its power in order to prevent a two-state solution to a supposedly intractable problem. In some ways, the attacks were reminiscent of Israel's attack on Lebanon in 1982, when the Israeli objective was to drive the Palestinians into exile. But in the meantime, a new and virulently anti-Israel movement was born in Lebanon in the form of Hizbullah; Israel's northern border remains insecure, and Iran's influence has grown.

Hamas feels it has emerged from the invasion of Gaza more or less intact, and retained its popularity among Palestinians and Arabs. Many analysts believe Hamas gained politically from the attacks, and has a strong likelihood of doing well in future Palestinian elections. The fighting certainly pushed the Arab-Israeli conflict firmly back to the forefront of the US agenda. For the US to ignore the rising power of Hamas would be a fatal political mistake; but it will require a US commitment to be more even-handed, creative and energetic in encouraging Israelis and Palestinians toward peace.

The new administration should help in creating a credible, unified Palestinian government that can negotiate and enforce a state-to-state relationship with Israel. Putting such a government together will not be easy, and Hamas's demands now will be tougher than they were before the attacks. The US must recognize that Hamas is a reality, and engage with it and other factions – isolating Hamas has proved counterproductive. With no tangible return from signing up to democracy, it had no reason to modify its stance on Israel. Furthermore, division among the Palestinians has further complicated the already stumbling Middle East peace process.

The Palestinians should recognize that no peace process can gain traction as long as Gaza remains separated from the West Bank, and as long as Hamas and Fatah remain divided. The US should stop rejecting Hamas and help the Palestinians form a national unity government. It should also demand an end to the siege of Gaza. Yet, as mentioned, the composition of the Obama administration would seem to indicate otherwise. Obama has appeared to content himself with the sort of flawed negotiations of the Clinton years.

The Arab-Israeli conflict remains central to the way most Arabs view the US. Hence Arab-Israeli peacemaking needs to become a priority for the new administration. However, there are other dimensions to consider: Saudi Arabia has become irritated in recent years by the strengthening alliance between Syria and Iran. During the meeting of Arab foreign ministers on 3 March 2009, Prince Saud demanded a common perspective in dealing with the Iranian challenge and interference in Arab affairs.[1]

The Iran-Syria-Hizbullah-Hamas axis is an arc that starts in Tehran, passes through Baghdad and continues through Syria to Lebanon and into the Palestinian Authority. Its true purpose, as far as Iran is concerned, is less to destroy Israel or end the influence of the US than to gain power in Saudi Arabia and the Gulf. The Gulf states recognize the danger of this alliance. A drastic situation will ensue if this axis becomes nuclear: a nuclear Iran will subject the countries of the region to pressure and blackmail. Moreover, conflicting interests between Iran and Saudi Arabia regarding oil policies and the Middle East conflict may also provoke tension.

Some analysts suggest that Saudi Arabia contemplate cooperation with Iran. However, ideological differences and Saudi-Iranian contention for Islamic leadership will always complicate any attempt to cooperate. The military

---

1. Saudi Embassy, Washington, "Arab Foreign Ministers Meet", 3 March 2009; http://www.saudiembassy.net/2009News/News/NewsDetail.asp?cIndex=8460

imbalance between the two countries, and the regional tensions, will give the Iranians an advantage with which to advance their agenda in the region.

Saudi Arabia in concert with the Gulf states should create an axis of their own with Egypt, Turkey and Pakistan. The Gulf states can tempt these countries with economic aid and by urging the Gulf business community to invest in those economies. Pakistan can serve as a balance against Iran's nuclear threat, while Turkey and Egypt, using their ties with the Israelis, could separate the Syrians and Palestinians from the Iranians. Iran's role in the region certainly suffered a blow after Turkey embarked on active cooperation with moderate Arab countries to confront some of the major issues that faced them.

Following 9/11, the tendency to carry out massive military intervention to promote the expansion of US power became part of the consensus among the dominant ruling class in the US. In practice, there was a tacit agreement that it was in the general interest of US capitalism to extend its control over the world. It was necessary, according to the Project for the New American Century, to seize the "unipolar moment".[1] The new administration must acknowledge that outright hegemony is beyond its means. Being the most powerful nation on Earth, the US does not need to dominate the world to live in it safely.

During the Bush administration, US policies in the Middle East assumed a new direction, as the president rejected and reversed the stability-oriented principles and cautiousness of his predecessor Clinton. In Saudi Arabia, according to a survey by Lieven and Hulsman, this new direction led to hostility toward the US.[2] Thus Obama requires new policies that will attend to the changes, distinct interests and needs of the differing peoples of the region. Such policies must move ahead with reform, adopting even-handed approaches and ending state-sponsored terrorism.

There is a perception in the Middle East that Obama will adjust relations with Iran and Syria, soothe the grievances that have led to the rise of Islamism and resolve the Arab-Israeli conflict. For the Palestinian-Israeli peace process, the picture is not very encouraging. Binyamin Netanyahu, once again Prime Minister of Israel, does not favour the establishment of a Palestinian state in the Occupied West Bank and besieged Gaza Strip. He will face some pressure from the US to move forward with the peace process, but will find it more

1. PNAC, *Report on Rebuilding America's Defenses*.
2. Anatol Lieven and John Hulsman, *Ethical Realism: A Vision for America's Role in the World* (London: Pantheon Books, 2006), p. 125.

politically palatable to engage Syria than to alienate his coalition allies and the settler movement by slowing or halting settlements as a concession to the Palestinians.

Saudi Arabia expects from the new administration an engagement that is capable of acting strongly to solve the region's problems. Saudi Arabia needs the US to act decisively by rebuffing any challenges to the stability of the Gulf, particularly encroachment by Iran. The Kingdom's comparative vulnerability and weakness relative to Iran impose a certain obligation on the part of the US not to compound the insecurity by leaving its commitment uncertain or by making excessive intrusions into Saudi domestic structures.

Saudi Arabia should not indulge in a useless and costly nuclear race. Yet it is the duty of the regime to gain knowledge of and expertise in the technology. Therefore, Saudi Arabia and the Gulf should maintain a small and low-cost civil nuclear programme with international supervision.

The Kingdom is caught between its private security concerns and its public position of Muslim solidarity and criticism of the West. The special place that Saudi Arabia holds, psychologically and symbolically, in the lives of Muslims worldwide cannot be underestimated. A strategic engagement between the US and Saudi Arabia should allow for true give-and-take over the strategic needs of both sides. The Kingdom should also accept the fact that if major energy companies continue to be locked out of the Middle East, they will look for substitutes and turn away from conventional oil to manufactured fuel or unconventional oil, outside the Middle East. Alternatives are available, and the costs of producing them are dropping, while technologies exist to effect a gradual transition. Capital accumulation and innovation will be made available to develop these alternatives.

With the new administration promoting, among other things, the use of alternative energy sources, it is imperative that Saudi Arabia consider a limited and controlled opening of its oil sector to foreign investment. Hence "asymmetrical dependence" has developed. Due to the prevailing global economic crisis, the US needs Saudi Arabia to keep oil prices low, and Saudi Arabia needs the US to suspend its efforts to develop new fuel alternatives.

Being a nation without either a great industrial base or military power, Saudi Arabia must find ways of advancing its interests that do not require the application of such power. Therefore it needs to cut deals, to duck and weave in order to remain secure. Saudi Arabia and the Arab world as a whole should heed President George Washington's words:

The nation which indulges towards another a habitual hatred or a habitual fondness is in some degree a slave. It is a slave to its animosity or to its affection, either of which is sufficient to lead it astray from its duty and its interest.[1]

---

[1]. George Washington, "Farewell Address", 1796.

Bibliography

Books, Articles and Speeches

Ackerman, Spencer, "The Weakest Link", *Washington Monthly*, November 2003.
Ahmad, Ahmad Yusif, *Al-Dur al-masri fi al-yaman*. Cairo: Al-Hay'a al-Masriyya al-Amma li al-Kitab, 1981.
Prince Turki Al-Faisal, Speech at Georgetown University, Washington, DC, 26 February 1975.
Alnasrawi, Abbas, *Arab Nationalism, Oil, and the Political Economy of Dependency*. New York: Greenwood Press, 1991.
Anwar, Raja, *The Tragedy of Afghanistan: A First-Hand Account*. London: Verso, 1988.
Arab News, "Saud Decries Move to Sour Saudi-US Ties", 8 August 2002.
Arab News, "Al-Rasheed Vows to Correct Defects in Education System", 7 January 2003.
Arab News, "Excerpts from an Impassioned Appeal", 20 January 2009.
Arabian American Oil Company (ARAMCO), *ARAMCO Handbook: Oil and the Middle East*, rev. ed. Dhahran, SA: Arabian American Oil Company, 1969.
Arnold, Anthony, *The Fateful Pebble: Afghanistan's Role in the Fall of the Soviet Empire*. Novato, CA: Presidio Press, 1993.
Aruri, Naseer H., *Dishonest Broker: The U.S. Role in Israel and Palestine*. Cambridge, MA: South End Press, 2003.
Assah, Ahmed, *Miracle of the Desert Kingdom*. London: Johnson, 1969.
Association for Diplomatic Studies and Training (ADST), *Frontline Diplomacy: The US Foreign Affairs Oral History*. Arlington, VA: ADST, 2000.
Ayoob, M., *The Third World Security Predicament, State Making, Regional Conflict and the International System*. Boulder, CO.: Lynne Rienner Press, 1995.
Badeau, John S., *The American Approach to the Arab World*. New York: Harper & Row, 1968.

Badeeb, Saeed M., *The Saudi-Egyptian Conflict over North Yemen, 1962–1970*. Boulder, CO: Westview Press, 1986.
Baker, James A., III, with Thomas M. De Frank, *The Politics of Diplomacy: Revolution, War and Peace, 1989-1992*. New York: G. P. Putnam's Sons, 1995.
Baram, Amatzia, "U.S. Input into Iraqi Decision-making, 1988–1990", in David W. Lesch, ed., *The Middle East and the US: A Historical and Political Assessment*. Boulder, CO: Westview Press, 1996.
Baram, Amatzia, and Barry Rubin, *Iraq's Road to War*. New York: St. Martin's Press, 1993.
Barnett, Michael, "Institutions, Roles, and Disorder: The Case of the Arab State", *International Studies Quarterly* 37 (1993).
Barnett, Michael N., and Jack S. Levy, "Domestic Sources of Alliances and Alignments: The Case of Egypt 1962–73", *International Organization*, vol. 45, no. 3 (summer 1991).
Batatu, Hanna, *The Old Social Classes and the Revolutionary Movements of Iraq: A Study of Iraq's Old Landed and Commercial Classes and of Its Communists, Baathists, and Free Officers*. Princeton, NJ: Princeton University Press, 1978.
Beattie, Kirk J., *Egypt During the Sadat Years*. New York: Palgrave, 2000.
Bergen, Peter L., *Holy War, Inc.: Inside the Secret World of Osama bin Laden*. London: Weidenfeld & Nicolson, 2001.
Berman, Paul, *Terror and Liberalism*. New York: W. W. Norton & Company, 2004.
Blood, Thomas, *Madam Secretary: A Biography of Madeleine Albright*. New York: St. Martin's Press, 1997.
Bin Laden, Usama, "Declaration of War Against the Americans Occupying the Land of the Two Holy Places", 23 August 1996. Online translation at www.terrorismfiles.org/individuals/declaration_of_jihad1.html.
Bodansky, Yossef, *Bin Laden: The Man Who Declared War on America*. Roseville, CA: Prima Publishing, 2001.
Boykin, John, *Cursed Is the Peacemaker: The American Diplomat Versus the Israeli General, Beirut 1982*. Belmont, CA: Applegate Press, 2002.
Bradsher, Henry, *Afghanistan and the Soviet Union*, 2nd ed. Durham, SC: Duke University Press, 1985.
Bromley, Simon, *Rethinking Middle East Politics*. Oxford: Polity Press, 1994.
Bronson, Rachel, *Thicker Than Oil: America's Uneasy Relationship with Saudi Arabia*. Oxford: Oxford University Press, 2006.
Brookings Institution, *Toward Peace in the Middle East: Report of a Study Group*. Washington, DC: Brookings Institution Press, 1975.
Brown, Carl L., *International Politics and the Middle East: Old Rules, Dangerous Game*. Princeton, NJ: Princeton University Press, 1984.
Brown, Sarah, and Chris Toening, "Why Another War? A Background on the

Iraq Crisis", *Middle East Report* (publication of the Middle East Research and Information Project [MERIP]), 2nd edn, December 2002, pp. 10-11.

Brzezinski, Zbigniew, *Power and Principle: Memoirs of the National Security Adviser, 1977–81*. New York: Farrar, Straus and Giroux, 1983.

Buchanan, Patrick J., "A Neoconservative Clique Seeks to Ensnare Our Country in a Series of Wars That Are Not in America's Interests", *The American Conservative*, 24 March 2003.

Bush, George H. W., and Brent Scowcroft, *A World Transformed: The Collapse of the Soviet Empire, the Unification of Germany, Tiananmen Square, the Gulf War*. New York: Alfred A. Knopf, 1998.

Bush, George W., *We Will Prevail: President George W. Bush on War, Terrorism and Freedom*. New York: Continuum International Publishing Group, 2003.

Carter, Jimmy, *Keeping Faith: Memoirs of a President*. New York: Bantam, 1982.

The Cato Institute, *Cato Handbook for Congress*. Washington, DC: Cato Institute, 2005.

Cave Brown, Anthony, *Oil, God, and Gold: The Story of Aramco and the Saudi Kings*. New York: Houghton Mifflin, 1999.

Center for Strategic and International Studies (CSIS) and Association of the US Army (AUSA), *Play to Win: Final Report of the Bi-Partisan Commission on Post-Conflict Reconstruction*. Washington, DC: CSIS Press, 2003.

CSIS and AUSA, *Winning the Peace: An American Strategy for Post-Conflict Reconstruction*. Washington, DC: CSIS Press, 2004.

Chace, James, "The Turbulent Tenure of Alexander Haig", *The New York Times*, 22 April 1984.

Champion, Daryl, "The Kingdom of Saudi Arabia: Elements of Instability Within Stability", *Middle East Review of International Affairs*, vol. 3, no. 4 (December 1999).

Champion, Daryl, *The Paradoxical Kingdom: Saudi Arabia and the Momentum of Reform*. London: Hurst & Co., 2003.

Chubin, Shahram, *Soviet Policy Towards Iran and the Gulf*. Adelphi Papers, no. 157. London: International Institute for Strategic Studies, 1984.

Chubin, Shahram, and Charles Tripp, *Iran and Iraq at War*. Boulder, CO: Westview Press, 1988.

Citino, Nathan John, "Eisenhower, King Saud, and the Politics of Arab Nationalism: U.S.-Saudi Relations, 1952-1960", unpublished PhD dissertation, Ohio State University, 1999.

Clarke, Richard A., *Against All Enemies: Inside America's War on Terror*. London: Free Press, 2004.

Clinton, William J., "Advancing Our Interest Through Engagement and Enlargement: A National Security Strategy of Enlargement and Engagement" (White House, July 1994), in Alvin Z. Rubinstein, Albina Shayevich and Boris Zlotnikov, eds, *Clinton Foreign Policy Reader: President's Speeches with Commentary*. New York: M. E. Sharpe, Inc., 2000.

Clinton, William J., "A New Covenant for American Security", an address at Georgetown University, *Harvard International Review* (summer 1992).

Cohen, Bernard C., "The Influence of Special Interest Groups and Mass Media on Security Policy in the United States", in Charles W. Kegley, Jr. and Eugene R. Wittkopf, eds, *Perspectives on American Foreign Policy*. New York: St. Martin's Press, 1983.

Cohen, Roger, and Claudio Gatti, *In the Eye of the Storm: The Life of General H. Norman Schwarzkopf*. London: Bloomsbury, 1991.

Coll, Steve, *Ghost Wars: The Secret History of the CIA, Afghanistan, and bin Laden from the Soviet Invasion to September 10, 2001*. New York: Penguin Group, 2005.

Cooley, John K., *Unholy Wars: Afghanistan, America, and International Terrorism*. London: Pluto Press, 2000.

Commins, David, *The Wahhabi Mission and Saudi Arabia*. London: I. B. Tauris, 2006.

Cordesman, Anthony H., *The Gulf and the Search for Strategic Stability: Saudi Arabia, the Military Balance in the Gulf, and Trends in the Arab-Israeli Military Balance*. Boulder, CO: Westview Press, 1984.

Cordesman, Anthony H., *Saudi Arabia: Guarding the Desert Kingdom*, Boulder. CO: Westview Press, 1997.

Cordesman, Anthony H., *Saudi Security and the War on Terrorism: International Security Operations, Law Enforcements, International Threats, and the Need for Change*. Washington, DC: Center for Strategic and International Studies, March 2002.

Cordesman, Anthony H., *Saudi Arabia Enters the Twenty-first Century: The Political, Foreign Policy, Economic, and Energy Dimensions*. Westport, CT: Praeger/Greenwood, 2003.

Cordovez, Diego, and Selig Harrison, *Out of Afghanistan: The Inside Story of the Soviet Withdrawal*. New York: Oxford University Press, 1995.

Cowell, Alan, "On Arab TV Network, Obama Urges Dialogue", *The New York Times*, 27 January 2009.

Cronin, Thomas E., "A Resurgent Congress and the Imperial Presidency", *Political Science Quarterly* 95 (summer 1980).

David, Steven, "Explaining Third World Alignment", *World Politics*, vol. 43, no.2 (1991).

Davies, Barry, *Terrorism: Inside a World Phenomenon*. London: Virgin Books, 2003.

Dayan, Moshe, *Breakthrough: A Personal Account of the Egypt-Israel Peace Negotiations*. London: Weidenfeld & Nicolson, 1981.

De Borchgrave, Arnaud, "Next, a 'Shock' by Sadat?", *Newsweek*, 23 April 1973.

Al-Deeb, Fathi, *'Abd al-Nasser wa harakat al-teharere al-yemeni*. Cairo: Dar Al-Mustaqbal al-'Arabi, 1990.
De Gaury, Gerald, *Faisal: King of Saudi Arabia*. London: The Trinity Press, 1966.
Dekmejian, R. Hrair, "The Rise of Political Islamism in Saudi Arabia", *Middle East Journal* (autumn 1994).
De Onis, Juan, "A Multibillion Purchase of Treasury Issue Due", *The New York Times*, 7 September 1974.
Eddy, William A., *FDR Meets Ibn Saud*. New York: American Friends of the Middle East, 1945.
Emory University, The Carter Center, "Comments by Carter", Middle East Consultation, Atlanta, GA, 6–9 November 1983.
Eran, Oded, and Jerome Singer, "Exodus from Egypt and the Threat to Kremlin Leadership", *New Middle East* 40 (January 1972).
Al-Faisal, Prince Saud, "The Fight Against Extremism and the Search for Peace", Address to Council on Foreign Relations, New York, 20 September 2005.
Fandy, Mamoun, *Saudi Arabia and the Politics of Dissent*. New York: St. Martin's Press, 1999.
Frankel, Glenn, "Lines in the Sand", in Micah Sifry and Christopher Cerf, eds, *The Gulf War Reader*. New York: Times Books, 1991.
Frankel, Glenn, *Beyond the Promised Land: Jews and Arabs on the Hard Road to a New Israel*. New York: Simon & Schuster, 1994.
Free, Lloyd, and William Watts, "Internationalism Comes of Age ... Again", *Public Opinion* 3 (April/May 1980).
Friedman, Thomas L., "An Intriguing Signal from the Crown Prince", *The New York Times*, 17 February 2002.
Gaddis, John Lewis, "A Grand Strategy of Transformation", *Foreign Policy* (November-December 2002).
Galtung, Johan, "A Structural Theory of Imperialism", *Journal of Peace Research*, vol. 8, no. 2 (1971).
Gamlen, Elizabeth, and Paul Rogers, "US Reflagging of Kuwaiti Tankers", in Rajaee Farhang, ed., *The Iran-Iraq War: The Politics of Aggression*. Gainesville, FL: University Press of Florida, 1993.
Garthoff, Raymond, *Détente and Confrontation: American-Soviet Relations from Nixon to Reagan*, rev. ed. Washington, DC: Brookings Institution Press, 1994.
Gates, Robert, *From the Shadows: The Ultimate Insider's Story of Five Presidents and How They Won the Cold War*. New York: Simon & Schuster, 1996.
Gause, F. Gregory, III, "The Foreign Policy of Saudi Arabia", in Raymond Hinnebusch and Anoushiravan Ehteshami, eds, *The Foreign Politics of Middle East States*. London: Lynne Rienner, 2002.
Gause, F. Gregory, III, "From Over the Horizon to into the Backyard: The

US-Saudi Relationship and the Gulf War", in David W. Lesch, ed., *The Middle East and the United States: A Historical and Political Reassessment*. Boulder, CO: Westview Press, 2003.

Gelvin, James L., *The Modern Middle East: A History*. New York: Oxford University Press, 2004.

Gendzier, Irene, "Oil, Iraq and U.S. Foreign Policy in the Middle East", *Situation Analysis* 2 (spring 2003).

George, Alexander L., "The Gulf War's Impact on the International System", in Stanley A. Renshon, ed., *The Political Psychology of the Gulf War: Leaders, Publics, and the Process of Conflict*. Pittsburgh: University of Pittsburgh Press, 1993.

Gerges, Fawaz, *The Superpowers and the Middle East: Regional and International Politics, 1955–1967*. Boulder, CO: Westview Press, 1994.

Gerner, Deborah, *One Land, Two Peoples: The Conflict Over Palestine*. Boulder, CO: Westview, 1991.

Ghaus, Abdul Samad, *The Fall of Afghanistan: An Insider's Account*. Washington, DC: Pergamon-Brassey, 1988.

Glazov, Jamie, "Symposium: The Future of U.S.-Saudi Relations", *FrontPage Magazine*, 11 July 2003.

Golan, Galia, *The Soviet Union and the Israeli War in Lebanon*, Research Paper 46, Jerusalem: Soviet and East European Research Centre, 1982.

Gordon, Michael, and Bernard Trainor, *Cobra II: The Inside Story of the Invasion and Occupation of Iraq*. London and New York: Atlantic/Pantheon Books, 2006.

Gordon, Michael R., and Bernard E. Trainor, *The General's War: The Inside Story of the Conflict in the Gulf*. Boston: Little, Brown and Company, 1995.

Graeber, Daniel J., "The United States and Israel: The Implications of Alignment", in Jack Covarrubias and Tom Lansford, eds, *Strategic Interests in the Middle East: Opposition or Support for US Foreign Policy*. Aldershot, UK: Ashgate, 2007.

Grayson, Benson Lee, *Saudi-American Relations*. Washington, DC: University Press of America, 1982.

Gulick, Edward V., *Europe's Classical Balance of Power*. New York: W. W. Norton & Company, 1955.

Hadar, Leon, *Sandstorm: Policy Failure in the Middle East*. New York: Palgrave Macmillan, 2005.

Haig, Alexander M., Jr., *Caveat: Realism, Reagan, and Foreign Policy*. New York: Macmillan, 1984.

Hajjar, Sami G., "U.S. Military Presence in the Gulf: Challenges and Prospects". Carlisle Barracks, PA: The Strategic Studies Institute, Army War College, March 2002.

Handel, Michael I., *The Diplomacy of Surprise*. Cambridge, MA: Harvard University Center for International Affairs, 1981.

Harik, Iliya, "The Origins of the Arab State System", in Ghassan Salame, ed., *The Foundation of the Arab State*. London: Croom Helm, 1987.

Hart, Parker T., *Saudi Arabia and the US*. Bloomington, IN: Indiana University Press, 1999.

Al-Hawali, Safar, *Haqaiq hawl azmat al-khalij* [*Realities Behind the Gulf Crisis*]. Cairo: Dar Makka al-Mukarama, 1991.

Hawthorne, Amy, *Political Reform in the Arab World: A New Ferment?* Publication of the Carnegie Endowment for International Peace, Carnegie Papers, no. 52, October 2004.

Heikal, Mohamed Hassanein, *The Road to Ramadan*. London: Collins, 1975.

Heikal, Mohamed Hassanein, *The Sphinx and the Commissar: The Rise and Fall of Soviet Influence in the Arab World*. London: Collins, 1978.

Heikal, Mohamed Hassanein, *Iran: The Untold Story*. New York: Pantheon Books, 1982.

Heikal, Mohamed Hassanein, *Autumn of Fury*. New York: Random House, 1983.

Heikal, Mohamed Hassanein, *Sanawat al-ghalayan*. Cairo: Al-Ahram Centre for Political and Strategic Studies, 1988.

Hinnebusch, Raymond, and Anoushiravan Ehteshami, eds, *The Foreign Policies of Middle East States*. Boulder, CO: Lynne Rienner Publisher, 2002.

Hinnebusch, Raymond, *The International Politics of the Middle East*. Manchester, UK: Manchester University Press, 2003.

Holden, David, and Richard Johns, *The House of Saud*. London: Sidgwick & Jackson, 1981.

Huntington, Samuel P., "The Clash of Civilizations?", *Foreign Affairs* 72 (summer 1993).

Institute for Advanced Strategic and Political Studies, "A Clean Break: A New Strategy for Securing the Realm" (Study Group on a New Israeli Strategy Toward 2000); see http://www.israeleconomy.org/strat.1htm.

International Institute for Strategic Studies, *Military Balance 2002–2003*. London: Oxford University Press for the IISS, 2002.

The Islamic Review and Arab Affairs, vol. 57, no. 2, 1969.

Jehl, Douglas, "Holy War Lured Saudis as Rulers Looked Away", *The New York Times*, 21 December 2001.

Jentleson, Bruce W., *American Foreign Policy: The Dynamics of Choice in the 21st Century*, 3rd ed. New York: W. W. Norton & Company, 2007.

Juergensmeyer, Mark, "Terror Mandated by God", *Terrorism and Political Violence*, vol. 9, no.2 (summer 1997).

Jungers, Frank, "From Construction Engineer to CEO and Chairman of Aramco, 1948–1978", an oral history conducted in 1992 by Carol Hicke, in *American Perspectives of Aramco, the Saudi-Arabian Oil-Producing Company, 1930s to*

1980s. Berkeley, CA: University of California, Bancroft Library, Regional Oral History Office, 1995.

Kamrava, Mehran, *The Modern Middle East: A Political History since the First World War*. Berkeley, CA: University of California Press, 2005.

Karsh, Efraim, *The Iran-Iraq War: A Military Analysis*, Adelphi Papers, no. 220, London: International Institute for Strategic Studies, 1987.

Karsh, Efraim, and Inari Rautsi, *Saddam Hussein: A Political Biography*. London: Brassey's, 1991.

Kegley, Charles W., Jr., and Eugene R. Wittkopf, eds, *Perspectives on American Foreign Policy*. New York: St. Martin's Press, 1983.

Kepel, Gilles, *Jihad: The Trail of Political Islam*. London: I. B. Tauris, 2004.

Khadduri, Majid, *Political Trends in the Arab World*. Baltimore, MD: Johns Hopkins University Press, 1970.

Kissinger, Henry, *The White House Years*. Boston: Little, Brown and Company, 1979.

Kissinger, Henry, *Years of Upheaval*. Boston: Little, Brown and Company, 1982.

Kissinger, Henry, *Diplomacy*. New York: Simon & Schuster, 1994.

Kissinger, Henry, *Years of Renewal*. New York: Touchstone/Simon & Schuster, 1999.

Korany, Bahgat, "Alien and Besieged Yet Here to Stay: The Contradictions of the Arab Territorial State", in Ghassan Salame, ed., *The Foundations of the Arab States*. London: Croom Helm, 1987.

Kristol, William, "Testimony Before the House Committee on International Relations Subcommittee on Middle East and South Asia", 22 May 2002, http://www.newamericancentury.org/saudi-052302.htm.

Kyle, Keith, *Suez*. New York: St Martin's Press, 1991.

Landau, Jacob M., *The Politics of Pan-Islam: Ideology and Organization*. Oxford: Clarendon Press, 1990.

Landler, Mark, "After Overture to Syria, Clinton Meets West Bank's Leaders", *International Herald Tribune*, 4 March 2009.

Lansford, Tom, *All for One: Terrorism, NATO and the US*. Aldershot, UK: Ashgate Publishing, 2002.

Laqueur, Walter, *Confrontation: The Middle East and World Politics*. London: Wildwood House, 1974.

Legum, Colin *et al*, eds, *Middle East Contemporary Survey*, vol. III (1978–79). New York: Holmes and Meier, 1978–1982.

Leigh, David, "General Sacked by Bush Says He Wanted Early Elections", *The Guardian*, 18 March 2004.

Lesch, David W., *Syria and the United States: Eisenhower's Cold War in the Middle East*. Boulder, CO: Westview Press, 1992.

Lesch, David W., ed., *The Middle East and the United States*. Boulder, CO: Westview Press, 1996.

Lewis, Bernard, "The Roots of Muslim Rage", *The Atlantic Monthly*, vol. 266, no. 3, September 1990.

Liakhovskii, A. A., *The Tragedy and Valour of the Afghani*. Moscow: GPI "Iskon", 1995.

Lieven, Anatol, and John Hulsman, *Ethical Realism: A Vision for America's Role in the World*. London: Pantheon Books, 2006.

Lindsay, James M., *Congress and the Politics of US Foreign Policy*. Baltimore, MD: Johns Hopkins University Press, 1994.

Little, Douglas, *American Orientalism: The U.S. and the Middle East Since 1945*. London: I. B. Tauris, 2003.

Lockman, Zachary, *Contending Visions of the Middle East: The History and Politics of Orientalism*. Cambridge: Cambridge University Press, 2004.

McCormick, James M., *American Foreign Policy and Process*. Itasca, IL: F. E. Peacock Publishers, 1992.

MacFarquhar, Neil, "Aviation Challenged: Education, Anti-Western and Extremist Views Pervade Saudi Schools", *The New York Times*, 19 October 2001.

Mamdani, Mahmood, *Good Muslim, Bad Muslim: America, the Cold War, and the Roots of Terror*. New York: Pantheon Books, 2004.

Mansur, Abdul Kasim, "The American Threat to Saudi Arabia", *Survival*, January-February 1981.

Matar, Fuad, *Saddam Hussein: The Man, the Cause and the Future*. London: Third World Centre, 1981.

Matar, Fuad, ed., *Gulf War Panorama: A Factual Documented Account*. Beirut: Arab Institute for Research & Publishing, and London: Fouad Matar Consultancy for Media, Documentation and Research, 1994.

Melhem, Hisham, *Dual Containment: The Demise of a Fallacy*. Washington, DC: Georgetown University Center for Contemporary Arab Studies, Edmund A. Walsh School of Foreign Service, 1997.

Moon, Bruce, "The State in Foreign and Domestic Policy", in L. Neack, J. Hey and P. Haney, eds, *Foreign Policy Analysis Continuity and Change in Its Second Generation*. Englewood Cliffs, NJ: Prentice Hall, 1995.

Moran, Theodore H., "Modeling OPEC Behavior: Economic and Political Alternatives", *International Organization*, vol. 35, no. 2 (spring 1981).

Morgenthau, Hans J., *Politics Among Nations: The Struggle for Power and Peace*. New York: Alfred A. Knopf, 1978.

Morgenthau, Hans J. and Eugene R. Wittkopf, eds, "Defining the National Interest – Again: Old Superstitions, New Realities", in Charles W. Kegley, Jr., *Perspectives on American Foreign Policy* (New York: St. Martin's Press, 1983), pp. 32–9.

Morris, Dick, *Off with Their Heads: Traitors, Crooks and Obstructionists in American Politics, Media and Business*. New York: Reagan Books, 2003.

Mufti, Malik, *Sovereign Creations: Pan-Arabism and Political Order in Syria and Iraq*. Ithaca, NY: Cornell University Press, 1996.

Munro, Alan, *Arab Storm: Politics and Diplomacy Behind the Gulf War*. London: I. B. Tauris, 2006.
The New York Times, "Soviet Build-up Seen at Afghan Border", 22 December 1979.
The New York Times, "Afghan President Ousted and Executed in Kabul Coup with Soviet Help", 28 December 1979.
The New York Times, excerpts from Pentagon's Plan: "Prevent the Re-emergence of a New Rival", 8 March 1992.
The New York Times, "Sept. 11 Families Join to Sue Saudis, Banks, Charities and Royals Accused of Funding al Qaeda Terrorists", 16 August 2002.
The New York Times, "War Plan for Iraq Calls for Big Force and Quick Strikes", 10 November 2002.
The New York Times, "How the Holy Warriors Learned to Hate", 18 June 2004.
The New York Times, *Report of the Congressional Committee's Investigation: The Iran-Contra Affair, with the Minority View*. New York: Times Books, 1994.
Niblock, Tim, *Saudi Arabia: Power, Legitimacy and Survival*. London: Routledge, 2006.
Noman, Ahmed, and Kassim Al Madhagi, *Yemen and the U.S.: A Study of a Small Power and Super-State Relationship, 1962–1994*. London: Tauris Academic Studies, 1996.
Le Nouvel Observateur, "Interview with President Jimmy Carter's National Security Adviser, Zbigniew Brzezinski", 15–21 January 1998.
O'Ballance, Edgar, *The War in Yemen*. Hamden, CN: Archon Books, 1971.
Olayan, Suliman S., "Saudi Arabia: The Burden of Moderation", *The Washington Quarterly* 4 (autumn 1983).
Oppenheim, V. H., "We Pushed Them", *Foreign Policy* (winter 1976–77).
Organization of the Islamic Conference (OIC), *Declarations and Resolutions of the Conference of the Organization of the Islamic Conference from Rabat to Kuala Lumpur*, statement; Jeddah: OIC General Secretariat, 1974.
Packer, George, *The Assassins' Gate: America in Iraq*. London: Faber & Faber, 2005.
Palmer, Michael A., *Guardians of the Gulf: A History of America's Expanding Role in the Persian Gulf, 1893–1992*. New York: Macmillan, 1992.
Palmer, Monte, and Princess Palmer, *At the Heart of Terror: Islam, Jihadists, and America's War on Terrorism*. New York: Rowman & Littlefield, 2004.
Parker, Richard B., *The Politics of Miscalculation in the Middle East*. Indianapolis: Indiana University Press, 1993.
Pauly, Robert J., Jr., *US Foreign Policy and the Persian Gulf: Safeguarding American Interests through Selective Multilateralism*. Aldershot, UK: Ashgate Publishing, 2005.
Paz, Reuven, "Islamists and Anti-Americanism", *Middle East Review of International Affairs*, vol. 7, no. 4 (December 2003).

Perlez, Jane, "Saudis Uncooperative, White House Aides Say", *International Herald Tribune*, 12 October 2001.

Peterson, J. E., *Saudi Arabia and the Illusion of Security*. London: Oxford University Press for the International Institute for Strategic Studies, 2002.

Pierre, Andrew J., *The Global Politics of Arms Sales*. Princeton, NJ: Princeton University Press, 1982.

Pipes, Daniel, "The Muslims Are Coming, the Muslims Are Coming", *National Review*, 19 November 1990.

Pollack, Josh, "Saudi Arabia and the U.S., 1931–2002", *Middle East Review of International Affairs*, vol.6, no.3 (September 2002).

Powell, Colin L., with Joseph E. Persico, *My American Journey*. New York: Random House, 1995.

Prados, John, *Presidents' Secret Wars: CIA and Pentagon Covert Operations from World War II through the Persian Gulf*. Chicago: Ivan R. Dee, Publisher, 1986.

The Project for the New American Century, "A Letter to Clinton", 26 January 1998, http://www.newamericancentury.org/iraqclintonletter.htm.

The Project for the New American Century, *Report on Rebuilding America's Defenses: Strategy, Forces and Resources for a New Century*. Washington, DC: PNAC, September 2000.

The Project for the New American Century, "The Bush Doctrine: Memo from Gary Schmitt and Tom Donnelly to Opinion Leaders", 30 January 2002, http://www.newamericancentury.org/defense-20020130htm.

Provop, Michaela, "The War of Ideas: Education in Saudi Arabia", in Paul Aarts and Gerd Nonneman, eds, *Saudi Arabia in the Balance: Political Economy, Society, Foreign Affairs*. London: Hurst & Co., 2005.

Quandt, William B., *Decade of Decisions*. Berkeley and Los Angeles: University of California Press, 1977.

Quandt, William, *Saudi Arabia in the 1980s*. Washington, DC: Brookings Institution Press, 1981.

Quandt, William, *Saudi Arabia's Oil Policy*. Washington, DC: Brookings Institution Press, 1982.

Quandt, William B., *Peace Process: American Diplomacy and the Arab-Israeli Conflict Since 1967*. Washington, DC: Brookings Institution Press, 2005.

Qureshi, Emran, and Michael A. Sells, *The New Crusades: Constructing the Muslim Enemy*. New York: Columbia University Press, 2003.

Rabin, Yitzhak, *The Rabin Memoirs*. Boston: Little, Brown and Company, 1979.

Rahmy, Ali Abdel Rahman, *The Egyptian Policy in the Arab World: Intervention in Yemen, 1962–1967: A Case Study*. Washington, DC: University Press of America, 1983.

Rasanayagam, Angelo, *Afghanistan: A Modern History*. New York: I. B. Tauris, 2005.
Al-Rasheed, Madawi, *A History of Saudi Arabia*. Cambridge: Cambridge University Press, 2002.
Rashid, Ahmed, *Taliban: Militant Islam, Oil and Fundamentalism in Central Asia*. London: Yale University Press, 2000.
Rashid, Jamal, "Pakistan and the Central Command", *Middle East Report*, July-August 1986.
Reagan, Ronald W., *An American Life: The Autobiography*. New York: Simon & Schuster, 1990.
Ricks, Thomas E., "Briefing Depicted Saudis as Enemies", *The Washington Post*, 6 August 2002.
Ridgeway, James, *The March to War*. New York: Four Walls Eight Windows, 1991.
Ridgeway, James, *The Five Unanswered Questions About 9/11: What the 9/11 Commission Failed to Tell Us*. New York: Seven Stories Press, 2005.
Ross, Dennis, *The Missing Peace: The Inside Story of the Fight for Middle East Peace*. New York: Farrar, Straus and Giroux, 2004.
Rouleau, Eric, "Interview with Nourridine Kianouri, Secretary General of Iran's Pro-Soviet Communist 'Tudah' Party", *Le Monde*, 18 April 1980.
Rubin, Barnett, *The Fragmentation of Afghanistan: State Formation and Collapse in the International System*. New Haven: Yale University Press, 1995.
Rubinstein, Alvin Z., *Red Star on the Nile: The Soviet-Egyptian Influence Relationship since the June War*. Princeton, NJ: Princeton University Press, 1977.
Rusciolelli, Philip C., *Can America Remain Committed? U.S. Security Horizons in the 1990s*. Boulder, CO: Westview Press, 1992.
Rustow, Dankwart A., "US-Saudi Relations and the Oil Crisis of the 1980's", *Foreign Affairs*, vol. 55, no. 3 (April 1977).
Rustow, Dankwart A., "Realignment in the Middle East", *Foreign Affairs*, vol. 63, no.3 (1984).
El-Sadat, Anwar, *In Search of Identity: An Autobiography*. London: Collins, 1978.
Sadowski, Yahya, "Revolution, Reform or Regression? Arab Political Options in the 1990 Gulf Crisis", *Brookings Review*, vol. 9, no. 1 (winter 1990–91).
Safran, Nadav, *Saudi Arabia: The Ceaseless Quest for Security*. Ithaca: Cornell University Press, 1988.
Said, Amin, *Tarikh al-dawla al-saʻudiyya*, vol. 3. Beirut: Dar al-Katib al-ʻArabi, 1965.
Saikal, Amin, *Modern Afghanistan: A History of Struggle and Survival*. London: I. B. Tauris, 2004.
Salame, Ghassan, ed., *The Foundations of the Arab State*. London: Croom Helm, 1987.

Sanger, David E., and Eric Schmitt, "U.S. Has a Plan to Occupy Iraq, Officials Report", *The New York Times*, 11 October 2002.
Sanger, David, "Iranian Overture Might Complicate Relations with Israel", *The New York Times*, 10 February 2009.
Saudi Press Agency, *The Echoes of the Saudi Position During the Events of the Arab Gulf, 1990–1991*. Riyadh, KSA.
Saunders, Harold H., "The Iran-Iraq War: Implications for US Policy", in Thomas Naff, ed., *Gulf Security and the Iran-Iraq War*. Washington, DC: National Defense University Press, 1985.
Schiff, Ze'ev, and Ehud Ya'ari, *Israel's Lebanon War*. New York: Simon & Schuster, 1984.
Schmidt, Dana Adams, *Yemen: The Unknown War*. New York: Holt, Rinehart and Winston, 1968.
Schwarzkopf, H. Norman, with Peter Petre, *It Doesn't Take a Hero: The Autobiography: General H. Norman Schwarzkopf*. London: Bantam Press, 1992.
Schweizer, Peter, *Victory: The Reagan Administration's Secret Strategy That Hastened the Collapse of the Soviet Union*. New York: The Atlantic Monthly Press, 1994.
Sela, Avraham, *The Decline of the Arab-Israeli Conflict: Middle East Politics and the Quest for Regional Order*. Albany, New York: State University of New York Press, 1998.
Sepehri, Saman, "The Geopolitics of Oil", *International Socialist Review* 26 (November-December 2002).
Sewell, John W., and John A. Mathieson. *The Third World: Exploring US Interests*, Headline Series no. 259. New York: Foreign Policy Association, May 1982.
Seymour, Ian, *OPEC: Instrument of Change*. London: Macmillan, 1980.
Shanker, Thom, and Eric Schmitt, "Military Would Be Stressed by a New War, Study Finds", *The New York Times*, 24 May 2002.
Sheehan, Edward R. F., *The Arabs, Israelis, and Kissinger: A Secret History of American Diplomacy in the Middle East*. New York: Reader's Digest Press, 1976.
Shultz, George P., *Turmoil and Triumph: Diplomacy, Power and the Victory of the American Ideal*. New York: Charles Scribner's Sons, 1993.
Simmons, Mathew R., *Twilight in the Desert: The Coming Saudi Oil Shock and the World Economy*. New Jersey: John Wiley & Sons, Inc., 2005.
Simpson, William, *The Prince: The Secret Story of the World's Most Intriguing Royal, Prince Bandar bin Sultan*. New York: HarperCollins, 2006.
Sindi, Abdullah M., "King Faisal and Pan-Islamism", in Willard A. Beling, ed., *King Faisal and the Modernization of Saudi Arabia*. Boulder, CO: Westview Press, 1980.
Singh, Ashok Kumar, *Saudi-US Relations: The Oil Factor*. New Delhi: Classical Publishing Co., 2000.

Smith, Charles D., *Palestine and the Arab-Israeli Conflict*. New York: St. Martin's Press, 1996.
Sokolsky, Richard D., et al., *Beyond Containment: Defending U.S. Interests in the Persian Gulf*. Washington, DC: Institute for National Strategic Studies (INSS), National Defense University, September 2002.
Spechler, Dina R., "The USSR and Third-World Conflicts: Domestic Debate and Soviet Policy in the Middle East, 1967–73", *World Politics*, vol. 38, no. 3 (April 1986).
Spiegel, Steven L., *The Other Arab-Israeli Conflict: Making America's Middle East Policy, from Truman to Reagan*. Chicago: University of Chicago Press, 1985.
Stein, Janice G., "Deterrence and Compellence in the Gulf, 1990–91: A Failed or Impossible Task?" *International Security*, vol. 71, no. 2 (1992).
Stein, Kenneth, *Heroic Diplomacy: Sadat, Kissinger, Carter, Begin, and the Quest for Arab-Israeli Peace*. New York: Routledge, 1999.
Sultan, HRH General Khaled bin, with Patrick Seale, *Desert Warrior: A Personal View of the Gulf War by the Joint Forces Commander*. London: HarperCollins, 1995.
Tarock, Adam, *The Superpowers' Involvement in the Iran-Iraq War*. New York: Nova Science Publishers, Inc., 1998.
Taylor, Alan, *The Arab Balance of Power*. Syracuse, NY: Syracuse University Press, 1982.
Teitelbaum, Joshua, *Holier Than Thou: Saudi Arabia's Islamic Opposition*. Washington, DC: Washington Institute for Near East Policy, 2000.
Telhami, Shibley, "Between Faith and Ethics", *Liberty and Power: A Dialogue on Religion and U.S. Foreign Policy in an Unjust World*, The Pew Forum Dialogues on Religion and Public Life. Washington, DC: Brookings Institution Press, 2004.
Thompson, William R., "The Arab Sub-System and the Feudal Pattern of Interaction: 1965", *Journal of Peace Research*, vol. 7 (1970).
Timmerman, Kenneth R., *The Death Lobby: How the West Armed Iraq*. London: Fourth Estate, 1992.
Tolchin, Martin, "Foreigners' Political Roles in US Grow by Investing", *The New York Times*, 30 December 1985.
Trice, Robert, "Congress and the Arab-Israeli Conflict: Support for Israel in the US Senate, 1970–73", *Political Science Quarterly* 92 (summer 1977).
Tuson, Penelope, and Anita Burdett, eds, "Joint Saudi-Egyptian-Syrian Communiqué, 24 September 1956.", *Records of Saudi Arabia 1902–1960*. London: Archive Editions, March 1992.
Tyler, Patrick E., and E. Sciolino, "Bush Advisers Split on Scope of Retaliation", *The New York Times*, 20 September 2001.
US News and World Report, Triumph Without Victory: The Unreported History of the Persian Gulf War. New York: Times Books, 1992.

Vance, Cyrus, *Hard Choices: Critical Years in America's Foreign Policy*. New York: Simon & Schuster, 1983.
Vatikiotis, P. J., *Islam and the State*. London: Routledge, 1987.
Vassiliev, Alexei, *The History of Saudi Arabia*. London: Saqi Books, 1998.
Wallerstein, Immanuel, "The Rise and Future Demise of the World Capitalist System: Concepts for Comparative Analysis", *Comparative Studies in History and Society*, vol. 16, no.4 (1974).
Walt, Stephen M., *The Origins of Alliances*. Ithaca, NY: Cornell University Press, 1987.
Washington, George, "Farewell Address", 1796.
Weinberger, Caspar W., *Fighting for Peace: Seven Critical Years in the Pentagon*. New York: Warner Books, 1990.
Weinstein, Franklin B., "The Concept of a Commitment in International Relations", *Journal of Conflict Resolution*, vol. 13, no.1 (March 1969).
Wittkopf, Eugene R., *The Domestic Sources of American Foreign Policy: Insights and Evidence*, 2nd ed. New York: St. Martin's Press, 1994.
Woodward, Bob, *Veil: The Secret Wars of the CIA 1981–87*. London: Headline Books, 1987.
Woodward, Bob, *The Commanders*. New York: Simon & Schuster, 1991.
Woodward, Bob, *Bush at War*. New York: Simon & Schuster, 2002.
Woodward, Bob, *Plan of Attack*. New York: Simon & Schuster, 2004.
Yaqub, Salim, *Containing Arab Nationalism: The Eisenhower Doctrine and the Middle East*. Chapel Hill, NC: University of North Carolina Press, 2004.
Yergin, Daniel, *The Prize: The Epic Quest for Oil, Money and Power*. New York: Barnes & Noble, 1992.
Yizraeli, Sarah, *The Remaking of Saudi Arabia: The Struggle Between King Saud and Crown Prince Faysal, 1953–1962*. Tel Aviv: Moshe Dayan Center, 1998.
Young, Oran, "Political Discontinuities in the International System", *World Politics*, vol. 20, no.3 (April 1968).

US Government Sources

Central Intelligence Agency

CIA Briefing Materials, Counter-Terrorist Center (CTC) Briefing for the NSC Small Group, 2–3 December 1999.
CIA Cable, "Intelligence Community Terrorist Threat Advisory", 30 March 2001.
CIA, Directorate of Intelligence, "The Soviet Invasion of Afghanistan: Five Years After", May 1985.
CIA, Directorate of Intelligence, "The Cost of Soviet Involvement in Afghanistan", February 1987.
CIA, "Iraq's Weapons of Mass Destruction Program".

CIA, Memorandum from Cofer Black, Director of CTC, to Clarke, "NSC Requests on Approaches for Dealing with Problems in Afghanistan", 29 December 2000.

CIA, "Mohammad Daud: President of Afghanistan", 13 August 1973.

CIA Report, *Additional Background on the Saudi Discovery of an UBL Network in Saudi Arabia*, undated.

CIA, Senior Executive Intelligence Brief, "Bin Laden Planning Multiple Operations", 20 April 2001.

CIA, Senior Executive Intelligence Brief, "Bin Laden Planning High-Profile Attacks", 30 June 2001.

CIA, Senior Executive Intelligence Brief, "Bin Laden Plans Delayed but Not Abandoned", 13 July 2001.

CIA, "Unclassified Report to Congress on the Acquisition of Technology Relating to Weapons of Mass Destruction and Advanced Conventional Munitions, 1 January–30 June 2000",

NA II, CIA, CIA-RDP 79 B00457A000600040001-3, CIA Records Search Tool (CREST), CD-ROM, 2, "Trends in OPEC Economic Assistance, 1976".

Congress, House of Representatives

Committee on Appropriations, Subcommittee on Military Construction Appropriations, "Military Construction Appropriations for 1984", 98th Cong., 1st sess., 1983.

Committee on Armed Services, "Hearings on Military Posture, H.R. 2970 (H.R. 3519), Department of Defense Authorization for Appropriations for FY1982", Part 1, 97th Cong., 1st sess., 1981.

Committee on Armed Services, Subcommittee on Military Installations and Facilities, "Hearings on H.R. 1816 (H.R. 2972) to Authorize Certain Construction at Military Installations for FY 1984", 98th Cong., 1st sess., 1983.

Committee on Foreign Affairs, "The Soviet Union and the Third World: Watershed in Great Power Policy", 97th Cong., 1st sess., 1977.

Committee on Foreign Affairs, *Foreign Assistance Legislation, Fiscal Year 1981*, Part 1.

Committee on Foreign Affairs, "Proposed Arms Sales to Saudi Arabia, Hearing Before a Subcommittee on Foreign Affairs and its Subcommittee on Europe and the Middle East", 99th Cong., 2nd sess., 1986.

Committee on Foreign Affairs, Subcommittees on Arms Control, International Security and Science, and on Europe and the Middle East, "Proposed Sales to Saudi Arabia in Association with the Conduct of Operation Desert Storm", 101st Cong., 2nd sess., 31 October 1990.

Committee on Foreign Affairs, Subcommittee on Europe and the Middle East,

Bibliography

"U.S. Interests in, and Policies toward, the Persian Gulf, 1980", 96th Cong., 2nd sess., 1980.

Committee on International Affairs, Subcommittee on Europe and the Middle East, "Saudi Arabia and the United States: The New Context in an Evolving Special Relationship", Staff Report by Richard M. Preece, 97th Cong., 1st sess., Aug. 1981.

Communication from the President of the US, "Military Assistance to Saudi Arabia: A Report on the Deployment and Mission of the US Armed Forces in Response to the Request Received from the Government of Saudi Arabia", 101st Cong., 2nd sess., 5 September 1990.

Congress, Senate

Committee on Armed Services, "Department of Defense Authorization for Appropriation for Fiscal Year 1981", 96th Cong., 2nd sess., 1980.

Committee on Armed Services, "Military and Technical Implications of the Proposed Sale to Saudi Arabia of Airborne Warning and Control System (AWACS) and F-15 Enhancements, 1981", 97th Cong., 1st sess., 1981.

Committee on Armed Services, Subcommittee on Sea Power and Force Projection, "Department of Defense Authorization for Appropriations for Fiscal Year 1982", Part 4, 97th Cong., 1st sess., 1981.

Committee on Finance, "Financial War on Terrorism: New Money Trails Present Fresh Challenges", 107th Cong., 2nd sess., 9 October 2002.

Committee on Foreign Relations, "Arms Sales Package to Saudi Arabia", Part 2, 97th Cong., 1st sess., 1981.

Committee on Foreign Relations, "War in the Persian Gulf: The US Takes Sides", Senate Staff Report, S PRT 100-60, November 1987.

Committee on Foreign Relations, Subcommittee on International Economic Policy, Export and Trade Promotion, "U.S. Economic and Strategic Interests in the Caspian Sea Region: Policies and Implications", 105th Cong., 1st sess., 23 October 1997.

Committee on Foreign Relations, Subcommittee on Multinational Corporations, "Multinational Petroleum Companies and Foreign Policy", 93rd Cong., 2nd sess., 20 and 21 February, 27 and 28 March 1974.

Committee on Foreign Relations, Subcommittee on Multinational Corporations, "US Oil Companies and the Arab Oil Embargo: The International Allocation of Constricted Supplies", Report Prepared by the Federal Energy Administration, Office of International Energy Affairs, 93rd Cong., 2nd sess., 27 January 1975.

Committee on Foreign Relations, "War in the Gulf", A Staff Report, Print 98-225, 98th Cong., 2nd sess., 1984.

"Multinational Corporations and US Foreign Policy", Hearing, 94th Cong., 1st sess., 1975.

Congressional Research Service Reports

Collins, John M., "Petroleum Imports from the Persian Gulf: Use of US Armed Forces to Ensure Supplies", 1 May 1979.

Grimmett, Richard F., "Arms Sales to Saudi Arabia: AWACS and the F-15 enhancements", 12 May 1981.

Prados, Alfred B., "Saudi Arabia: Current Issues and U.S. Relations", 4 August 2003.

Department of State

1971 Policy Assessment: Policy Review – A US Strategy for the 1970s, 26 June 1971.

Afghanistan in 1977: An External Assessment, 30 January 1978.

Bulletin, 7 January 1963.

Bulletin, 8 April 1974.

Bulletin, 12 September 1977.

Bulletin, February 1980.

Bulletin, December 1980.

Cable, Nairobi 7020, "Sudan: Foreign Minister on Developments Re Terrorism and Peace", 21 May 1996.

Current Policy N. 978, US Undersecretary Michael Armacost, "US Policy in the Persian Gulf and Kuwaiti Reflagging", June 1987.

"Iran-Iraq War: Analysis of Possible US Shift from Position of Strict Neutrality", 7 October 1983.

Office of the Coordinator for Counterterrorism, "Patterns of Global Terrorism 2003". Washington, D.C.: State Dept., Publication 11124, April 2004.

Office of Intelligence Research (Declassified Documents), 1994, "The Cairo-Riyadh Axis: Second Thoughts in Saudi Arabia", 10 August 1956.

Office of Intelligence and Research, "The Outlook for Saudi Arabia", 13 January 1956.

Records, Afghanistan and Pakistan, March 1980.

Records, Lot 58 D776, Box 10, Folder: "Near & Middle East – 1955–56".

Records, Central Files (786A. 00/11-1755), American Embassy, Jeddah, to State Dept., 17 November 1955.

Records, Central Files, reel 1, US Army Attaché, Beirut, to State Dept., CX 158, 21 November 1956.

Records, Central Files (780.00/4-1757), Ralph Lewis, American Consul, Dhahran, to State Dept., 17 April 1957.

Records, Central Files, Egypt, Reel 7, US Embassy, Cairo, to State Dept., 26 April 1957.

Records, Central Files (786A. 11/6-457), US Embassy, Baghdad, to State Dept., 4 June 1957.

Bibliography

Records, Central Files (783.00/8-2357), Strong to State, 19 August 1957.

Records, Central Files, Egypt, (674.83/9-357), US Ambassador, Egypt, to State Dept., 3 September 1957.

Records, Central Files (783.0010/1557), Memorandum of conversation, Yohanan Meroz and John Dorman, 15 October 1957.

Records, Central Files (786A. 00/12-1957), US Embassy, Jeddah, to State Dept., 19 December 1957.

Records, Central Files (786A.11/8-958), Sec. of State, to US Embassy, Jeddah, 9 August 1958.

Records, Central Files (786A.11/8-1258), US Ambassador, Jeddah, to Sec. of State, 12 August 1958.

Records, Central Files (786A.11/8-1258), US Embassy, Jeddah, to State, 12 August 1958.

Records, Central Files (786.A 00/9-358), US Embassy, Jeddah, to State Dept., 3 September 1958.

Records, Central Files, (786A. 00/6-2591), King Saud to President Kennedy, 25 June 1961.

Records, Central Files (786B.00/9-2861), State Dept. to Embassy, Jordan, 28 September 1961.

Records, Central Files (811.0086B/12-161), Memorandum of Conversation between Egyptian Ambassador and NEA Talbot, 1 December 1961.

Records, Central Files, (786A. 11/2–1362), Memorandum of Conversation between King Saud and President Kennedy, 13 February 1962.

Records, Central Files, (611.86A/6-462), Memorandum from the Dept. of State Executive, William Brubeck, to Bundy, 4 June 1962.

Records, Central Files (786H. 00/9-6, 2762), Circular telegram from the State Dept. to Certain Posts, 27 September 1962.

Records, Central Files (786A. 11/10-562), Memorandum of Conversation between Faisal and JFK, Washington, 5 October 1962.

Records, Central Files (786H. 00/10-962), Memorandum of Conversation between British Ambassador, Washington, Sir David Ormsby Gore, and Sec. of State Dean Rusk, 9 October 1962.

Records, Central Files, (786H. 00/10-962), Memorandum from Talbot to Rusk, 9 October 1962.

Records, Central Files, (786H. 00/10-1062), US Embassy, Cairo, to State Dept., 10 October 1962.

Records, Central Files, (786H. 00/10-1162), US Embassy, Cairo, to State Dept., 11 October 1962.

Records, Central Files, (786H. 00/10-1062), State Dept. to US Embassy, Cairo, 13 October 1962.

Records, Central Files, (786H. 02/10-1762), Paper by the Office in Charge of

Arabian Peninsula Affairs, State Department's division of NEA, Talcott Seelye, 17 October 1962.

Records, Central Files, (786A. 11/11-162), Memorandum from William Brubeck, State Dept., Executive Sec. to Bundy, 1 November 1962.

Records, Central Files, (786A. 11/10-2562), State Dept. to US Embassy, Jeddah, 2 November 1962.

Records, Central Files, (786H. 00/11-462), US Embassy, Jeddah, to State Dept., 4 November 1962.

Records, Central Files, (786A. 5486B/11-462), US Embassy, Jeddah, to State Dept., 4 November 1962.

Records, Central Files, (786A. 5622/11-562), US Consulate, Dhahran, to State Dept., 5 November 1962.

Records, Central Files, (786A. 54866/11-762), Sec. of State Dean Rusk to US Embassy, Jeddah, 7 November 1962.

Records, Central Files, (786A. 5811/11-762), US Embassy, Jeddah, to State Dept., 7 November 1962.

Records, Central Files, (786H. 00/11-1062), State Dept. to US Embassy, Jeddah, 10 November 1962.

Records, Central Files, (785.00/11-1362), Memorandum from Talbot to Rusk, "Rationale for Our Proposed Course of Action on Yemen", 13 November 1962.

Records, Central Files, (786H. 00/11-2062), Telegram from US Embassy, Jeddah, to State Dept., 19 November 1962.

Records, Central Files, (786H. 00/12-1862), US Legation, Sanaa, to State Dept., 18 December 1962.

Records, Central Files, (786-02/12-1962), US Embassy, Cairo, to State Dept., 19 December 1962.

Records, Central Files, (686A. 86B/12-3162), Memorandum of Conversation between Khayyal and Talbot, 31 December 1962.

Records, Central Files, (686A. 86B/12-3162), Memorandum of Conversation between Talbot and Saudi Ambassador, Washington, Ibrahim Khayyal, 31 December 1962.

Records, Central Files, (786A. 5486B/12-1362), State Dept. to US Embassy, Jeddah, 31 December 1962.

Records, Central Files, (786A. 5486B/12-3162), State Dept. to US Embassy, Cairo, 31 December 1962.

Records, Central Files, (786A. 5486B/12-3162), US Embassy, Jeddah, to State Dept., 31 December 1962.

Records, Central Files, (786A. 5622/1-1563), State Dept. to US Embassy, Cairo, 8 January 1963.

Records, Central Files, (786A. 5486B/1-863), State Dept. to US Embassy, Jeddah, 8 January 1963.

Bibliography

Records, Central Files, (611.86B/1-963), US Embassy, Cairo, to State Dept., 9 January 1963.

Records, Central Files, (786H.02/1-1163), US Embassy, London, to State Dept., 11 January 1963.

Records, Central Files, (641.86A), US Embassy, London, to State Dept., 16 January 1963.

Records, Central Files (786H. 02/1-1963), State Dept. to US Embassy, Cairo, 19 January 1963.

Records, Central Files, (POL 26 YEMEN), Memorandum of Conversation Between Saudi Arabia's Ambassador al-Khayyal with State Sec., 23 February 1963.

Records, Central Files, (POL 27 YEMEN), State to US Embassy, Jeddah, 25 February 1963.

Records, Central Files, (POL 26 YEMEN), State to US Embassy, Cairo, 2 March 1963.

Records, Central Files, (POL 27 YEMEN), US Embassy, Cairo, to State Dept., 5 March 1963.

Records, Central Files, (POL 27 YEMEN), US Consulate, Dhahran, to State Dept., 7 and 8 March, and Memorandum from Talbot to Rusk, undated.

Records, Central Files, (POL 7 US/BUNKER), State to US Embassy, Jeddah, 14 March 1963.

Records, Central Files, (POL 7 US/BUNKER), State to US Embassy, Cairo, 18 March 1963.

Records, Central Files, (POL 26 YEMEN), US Embassy, Lebanon, to State Dept., 19 March 1963.

Records, Central Files, (POL 16 YEMEN), US Embassy, Cairo, 3 April 1963.

Records, Central Files, (POL 27 YEMEN), US Embassy, Jeddah, to State Dept., 7 April 1963.

Records, Central Files, (POL 27 YEMEN), Telegram 1706 and 1707 from US Embassy, Cairo, 9 April, and Telegram 831 from US Embassy, Jeddah, 10 April 1962.

Records, Central Files, (POL 27-14 YEMEN/UN), US mission to UN, 10 and 12 April 1963.

Records, Central Files, (DEF 6-3 US), US Embassy, Jeddah, to State Dept., 8 June 1963.

Records, Central Files, (POL 27 SAUD-UAR), US Embassy, Jeddah, to State Dept., 10 June 1963.

Records, Central Files, (POL 27-5 US), Memorandum from Rusk to Kennedy, 12 June 1963.

Records, Central Files, (DEF 6-3 US), State Dept. to US Embassy, Jeddah, 14 June 1963.

Records, Central Files, (DEF 19-2 SAUD-US), Circular Telegram, 29 June 1963.
Records, Central Files, (POL 27-10 YEMEN), Kitchen to Johnson, 5 July 1963.
Records, Central Files, (POL 27 SAUD-UAR), US Embassy, Cairo, to State Dept., 6 July 1963.
Records, Central Files, (POL 27 UAR-YEMEN), US Embassy, Cairo, to State Dept., 11 July 1963.
Records, Central Files, (POL 26 YEMEN), State to US Embassy, Cairo, 23 July 1963.
Records, Central Files, NEA/NE Files: Lot 66 D 218, UAR. POL. UAR-YEMEN, 24 July 1963.
Records, Central Files, (POL 27 YEMEN), US Embassy, Jeddah, to State Dept., 2 August 1963.
Records, Central Files, (POL 27 SAUD-UAR), US Embassy, Cairo, to State Dept., 9 August 1963.
Records, Central Files, (POL 27 SAUD-UAR), US Embassy, Jeddah, to State Dept., 13 August 1963.
Records, Central Files, State-JCS Meetings, Lot 70 D 328, Memorandum on the substance of discussion at a Dept. of State-JCS Meeting, 16 August 1963.
Records, Central Files, (POL 27 YEMEN), US Embassy, Jeddah, to State Dept., 20 August 1963.
Records, Central Files, (POL 27 YEMEN), US Embassy, Jeddah, to State Dept., 30 August 1963.
Records, Central Files, (POL 27 YEMEN), US Consulate General, Istanbul, to State Dept., 18 October 1963.
Records, Central Files, (POL 27 YEMEN), US Embassy, Cairo, to State Dept., 21 October 1963.
Records, Central Files, (POL 27-14 YEMEN), US Consulate, Dhahran, to State Dept., 24 October 1963.
Records, Central Files, (POL 27 YEMEN), US Embassy, Cairo, to State Dept., 27 October 1963.
Records, Central Files, (POL 27-14 YEMEN), State to US Embassy, Jeddah, 28 October 1963.
Records, Central Files, (POL 27 YEMEN), State to US Embassy, Cairo, 6 November 1963.
Records, Central Files, (POL 15-1 SAUD), US Embassy, Jeddah, to State Dept., 7 November 1963.
Records, Central Files, (POL 32-1 SAUD-UAR), US Embassy, Jeddah, to State Dept., 19 November 1963.
Records, Central Files, (POL 27 US-UAR), State to US Embassy, Cairo, 20 November 1963.

Bibliography

Records, Central Files, (POL 26 YEMEN), State to US Embassy, Jeddah, 1 December 1963.

Records, Central Files (POL 26 YEMEN), State to US Embassy, Jeddah, 9 December 1964.

Records, Central Files, 1964-66 (POL 2 ISLAMIC), State to Certain Posts, 20 May 1966.

Records, Decimal Files (890F. 6363), Standard Oil Company / 123, Memorandum from Patchin to Murray, 24 December 1940.

Records, Decimal Files (980F. 24/32), Roosevelt to Stettinius, 18 February 1943.

Records, Decimal Files (890F. 248/8-845), Eddy to the Secretary of State, 8 August 1945.

Records, Decimal Files (890F. 11/12-447), Childs to State Dept., 4 December 1947.

Records, Decimal Files (78A.00/11-1956), US Embassy, Jeddah, to State Dept., 9 October 1956.

Records, Decimal Files (773.00(W)/11-2656), US Embassy, Tripoli, to State Dept. Dept., 26 November 1956.

Records, Decimal Files (786A.00/5-2257), US Embassy, Jeddah, to State Dept., 22 May 1957.

Records, Group Records-State, Political-UAR, Egypt, 1970–1973, Entry 1613, Box 2251, US Interests, Cairo, to Sec. of State, 25 July 1972.

Records, Group Records-State Political-UAR, Egypt, 1970–1973, Entry 1613, Box 2249, Memorandum for Kissinger, 25 July 1973.

Records, Group Records-State, Political-UAR, Egypt, 1970–1973, Entry 1613, Box 2250, Bureau of Intelligence and Research Note, 30 August 1973.

Records, NEA Files, Lot File 62D435, Box 7, Operation Hard Surface, Deputy Assistant Sec. of Defense for International Security Affairs K. Sloan to Talbot, 4 March 1963.

Records, NEA/NE Files: Lot 65 D 28, Syrian Coup, Memorandum from Roger Hilsman Jr., Director of Intelligence and Research, State Dept., to Rusk, 8 March 1963.

Records, National Security Action Memorandum Files: Lot 72 D316, NSAM 105, 16 October 1961.

Records, PPS Files: Lot 67D 548, Egypt, Talbot to McGhee, 30 May 1961.

Records, Record Group 59, Lot 66D487, "Program to Counter Soviet Penetration in the Middle East," 15 December 1956, "Policy Planning Staff Office Files," Box 113, Folder: "S/P Working Papers, Dec. 1956".

Records, Record Group 59, SN 70-73, POL 15-1 US/Nixon, Joseph Sisco, Assistant Secretary of State to Kissinger, "Proposed Presidential Message to King Faisal", 12 October 1973.

Records, Records of Henry Kissinger, Box 25, Cat C Arab-Israeli War, Memorandum of Conversation Between Hafiz Ismail and Henry Kissinger, 20 May 1973.

Records, Records of Henry Kissinger, 1973–1977, Box 25, Cat C 1974, Arab-Israeli War, Memcon Between Simcha Dinitz, Israeli Ambassador, and Kissinger, 7 October 1973.

Records, Records of Henry Kissinger, Subject-Numeric Files 1970-1973, POL Isr-US, Memcon Between Dinitz and Kissinger, 9 October 1973.

Records, SN 70-73, POL 27 Arab-Isr, Memcon Between Deputy Secretary of State Kenneth Rush and Petroleum Company Executives, 10 October 1973.

Records, SN 70-73, POL 27 Arab-Isr, William B. Quandt to Kissinger, Memorandum of Conversation with Arab Foreign Ministers, 17 October 1973.

Records, S/S-NSC Files: Lot 72 D 316, NSAM, National Security Action Memorandum No. 227, 27 February 1963; and ibid., (POL 26 YEMEN), Memorandum from Brubeck to Bundy, 28 March 1963.

Records, S/S-NSC Files: Lot 72 D 316, NSAM 262, National Security Action Memo No. 262, "Yemen Disengagement", 10 October 1963.

Records, S/S-NSC Files: (Presidential Correspondent: Lot 66 D 204, UK-OFFICIALS-SEC. RUSK, 1962–64), State Dept. to US Embassy, London, 22 October 1963.

"S/CT Update on Critical Issues", Memo, Sheehan to Albright, 9 July 1999.

Department of State Declassified Documents

Declassified Documents, State Dept. Records, Haig to All Near Eastern and South Asian Diplomatic Posts, "Military Equipment for Iran and Iraq", 16 February 1981.

Declassified Documents, State Dept., Cable from Haig to the US Interests Section in Iraq. "De-designation of Iraq as Supporter of International Terrorism", 27 February 1982.

Declassified Documents, State Dept., Sec. of State George P. Shultz, Cable to the State Dept., "Sec.'s May 10th Meeting with Iraq Foreign Minister Tariq Aziz", 11 May 1983.

Declassified Documents, State Dept., Bureau of Near Eastern and South Asian Affairs Information, Memorandum from Jonathan T. Howe to Lawrence S. Eagleburger, "Iran-Iraq War: Analysis of Possible US Shift from Position of Strict Neutrality", 7 October 1983.

Declassified Documents, State Dept., US Embassy in UK to State Dept., "Rumsfeld Mission: December 20 Meeting with Iraqi President Saddam Hussein", 21 December 1983.

Department of State Series: Foreign Relations of the United States (FRUS) 1945, vol. 8, "Great Bitter Lake Conversation", Memorandum of Conversation

Bibliography

Between the King of Saudi Arabia (Abdul Aziz al Saud) and President Roosevelt, 14 February 1945.

1945, vol.8, "President Roosevelt to King of Saudi Arabia (Abdul Aziz Ibn Saud)", 5 April 1945.

1948, vol. 5.

1955–7, vol. 15, Diary Entry by the President, 28 March 1956.

1955–7, vol. 15, "United States Policy in the Near East," 28 March 1956.

1955–7, vol. 16, US Consulate, Dhahran, to State Dept., 23 August 1956.

1955–7, vol. 17, US Embassy, Cairo, to State Dept., 28 February 1957.

1955–7, vol. 13, "Memorandum by Sherwood", 29 August 1957.

1955–7, vol. 12, "Memorandum by Dulles", 21 October 1957.

1955–7, vol. 12, "US Objectives and Policies with Respect to the Near East", 30 October 1957.

1955–7, vol. 12, "Memorandum Presented to the NSC Planning Board", 4 November 1957.

1958–60, vol. 12, "National Security Council Report", NSC 5801/1, 24 January 1958.

1958–60, vol. 12, "Memorandum of conversation by Reinhardt", 30 January 1958.

1958–60, vol. 12, US Consulate, Damascus, to State Dept., 3 March 1958.

1958–60, vol. 12, State Dept. to US Embassy, Jeddah, 4 March 1958.

1958–60, vol. 12, "Memorandum of Discussion at the 358th Meeting of the National Security Council", 13 March 1958.

1958–60, vol. 12, Assessment of Current Situation in the Near East", 24 March 1958.

1958–60, vol. 12, "Special National Intelligence Estimate: Implications of Recent Government Changes in Saudi Arabia.

1958–60, vol. 12, Rountree to J. F. Dulles, 14 March 1958.

1958–60, vol. 12, Assistant Sec. William Rountree to Dulles with Attachments, 24 March 1958.

1958–60, vol. 12, Deputy Undersecretary of State Douglas Dillon to the Acting Sec. Christian Herter, 30 June 1958, and attachment "Transport of Oil from the Middle East (Joint Report by US-UK Officials)", 12 May 1958.

1958–60, vol. 12, NSC 5820/1, 4 November 1958.

1958–60, vol. 12, US Embassy, Cairo, to State Dept., 1 April 1959.

1958–60, vol. 12, State Dept. to US Embassy, Cairo, 2 April 1959.

1958–60, vol. 12, Rountree to Deputy Undersecretary of State Douglas Dillon, 29 April 1959.

1958–60, vol. 13, US Embassy, Cairo, to State Dept., 1 December 1959.

1958–60, vol. 13, n. 5, Reply from State Dept. with Acceptance.

1961–63, vol. 17, NIE 36-61, 27 June 1961.

1961–63, vol. 17, SNIE 36.1-62, 28 March 1962.

1961–63, vol. 18, JFK letter to Sallal, Hussain, Nasser, Faisal, 16 November 1962.

Foreign Broadcast and Information Service

Daily Report, 8 December 1978.
Middle East Edition, 15 September 1979.
Middle East Edition, 17 September 1979.
Middle East Edition, 28 December 1979.

National Archives and Records Administration

RG59, Central Files 1964–66 (POL 7 SAUD), Memorandum of Conversation, 15 May 1964.
RG59, Central Files 1964–66 (POL 27 YEMEN), Memorandum of Conversation, 11 December 1964.
RG59, Central Files 1964–66 (POL 27 YEMEN), US Embassy Jeddah to State Dept., 19 August 1964.
RG59, Central Files 1964–66 (POL 27 YEMEN), State to US Embassy, Jeddah, 22 August 1964.
RG59, Central Files 1964–66 (POL 1 SAUD-UAR), State to the US Embassy in the UK, 28 August 1964.
RG59, Central Files 1964–66 (POL 27 YEMEN), Editorial Note.
RG59, Central Files 1964–66 (POL 27 YEMEN), US Embassy, Cairo, to State Dept., 25 August 1965.
RG59, Central Files 1964–66 (POL 15-1 SAUD), US Consulate General, Dhahran, to State Dept., 20 February 1966.
RG59, Central Files 1964–66 (POL 27 YEMEN), Memo of Conversation Between Prince Sultan and Rusk, "Yemen, Communism in the Middle East", 23 February 1966.
RG59, Central Files 1964–66 (POL 23-7 NEAR E.), State to US Embassy, Jeddah, 26 February 1966.
RG59, Central Files 1964–66 (POL 23-7 NEAR E.), US Embassy, Jeddah, to State Dept., 4 May 1966.
RG59, S/S Visit, Files: Lot 67 D 587, Visit of King Faisal of Saudi Arabia, 21–23 June 1966, Vol. II, Memcons, Admin and Sub. Misc.. "Proposed Strategy for Visit of King Faisal", 1 June 1966.
RG59, Central Files 1967–69 (POL SAUD-US), US Embassy, Jeddah, to State Dept., 10 January 1967.
RG59, Central Files 1967–69 (POL SAUD-US), State to US Embassy, Jeddah, 16 January 1967.
RG59, Central Files 1967–69 (POL 27-10 YEMEN), State to the Mission to the European Office of the UN, 25 May 1967.

Bibliography

National Security Archive

CIA, Presidential Daily Briefing, 6 August 2001.
Director of Central Intelligence "DCI", SNIE 34/36 2-82, "Implication of Iran's Victory over Iraq", 8 June 1982.
Director of Central Intelligence–National Intelligence Officer, "NIO"/Middle East DCI/NIO 1039-75, "The Implications of the Iran-Iraq Agreement", 1 May 1975.
Defense Dept., Estimate Center, April 1980.
Defense Intelligence Agency, Intelligence Report, "Defense Estimative Brief: Prospects for Iraq", 25 September 1984.
George Bush, National Security Directive 45, "U.S. Policy in Response to the Iraqi Invasion of Kuwait", 20 August 1990.
George Bush, National Security Directive 54, "Responding to Iraqi Aggression in the Gulf", 15 January 1991.
Interagency Intelligence Memorandum (IIM), *Soviet Options in Afghanistan*, 28 September 1979.
Interagency Intelligence Memorandum (IIM), *The Soviet Invasion of Afghanistan: Implications for Warning*, October 1980.
National Security Council, Bush Administration, First Memo on al-Qa'ida, "Presidential Policy Initiative/Review – The Al-Qaeda Network", 25 January 2001.
National Security Council, *A National Security Strategy for a New Century*, Washington, DC: December 1999.
National Security Council, National Security Study Memorandum 198, "Joint US-Saudi Economic, Military and Technological Cooperation", 12 March 1974.
National Security Council, Memorandum from Mary McCarthy, NSC senior director responsible for intelligence programs, to CIA, December 1999.
National Security Council, Memorandum from Paul Kurtz, member of the White House counterterrorism team, to Berger, "Roadmap for March 10th Principals Committee (PC) Meeting", 8 March 2000.
National Security Council, "Strategy for Eliminating the Threat from Jihadist Networks of al-Qaeda: Status and Prospects", December 2000, attached to NSC memo, Clarke to Condoleezza Rice, the NS advisor for President Bush, 25 January 2001.
National Security Decision Directive 139, from Ronald W. Reagan, "Measures to Improve US Posture and Readiness to Respond to Developments in the Iran-Iraq War", 5 April 1984.
Nobel – Compendium, "15 October Situation Report", 15 October 1979.
Nobel – Compendium, Additional Materials, "Brzezinski Memo", 20 September 1979.
Nobel – Compendium, "Record of the Meeting of the Special Coordination Committee", 17 December 1979.

A Report from JCS, "Guerrilla Use of Stinger Missiles and Their Effect on Soviet Tactics in Afghanistan", undated.

State Dept., Bureau of Intelligence and Research, Assessments and Research, "The Afghan Resistance Movement in 1981: Progress, But a Long Way to Go", 12 January 1982.

State Dept., Bureau of Public Affairs, Policy No. 152, "Persian Gulf, Southwest Asia, Indian Ocean: Developing a Cooperative Security Framework", 24 March 1980.

State Dept., Bureau of Public Affairs, Report No. 72, "Soviet Dilemmas in Afghanistan", June 1980.

State Dept., Cable, "Afghanistan: Meeting with the Taliban", 11 December 1997.

State Dept., Cable, "Dealing with the Taliban in Kabul", 28 September 1996.

State Dept., Cable, "Osama bin Laden: Taliban Spokesman Seeks New Proposal for Resolving bin Laden Problem", 28 November 1998.

State Dept. Records, Briefing Memorandum from Harold Sanders to Vance, "Situation in Afghanistan", 30 April 1978.

State Dept. Records, Briefing Memorandum from William Bowdler to Warren Christopher, "The Coup in Afghanistan", 1 May 1978.

State Dept. Records, Briefing Paper, "Soviet Perspective on Iran/Iraq War", 24 September 1980.

State Dept. Records, Bureau of Near Eastern and South Asian Affairs, Memorandum "Issue Paper: Gulf War Update" and "Issue Paper: US Attitude Toward Iran" attached, 27 February 1986.

State Dept. Records, (POL 7 US/KISSINGER), Memorandum of Conversation between Fahd and Kissinger, 8 November 1973.

State Dept. Records, (POL 7 US/KISSINGER), Memorandum of Conversation between Saqqaf and Kissinger, 8 November 1973.

State Dept. Records, (POL 27 ARAB-ISR), Memorandum of Conversation between Faisal and Kissinger, 14 December 1973.

State Dept. Records, Memorandum to Different Posts, "Staunching Iran's Imports of Western Arms and Urging Restraint on Iraq", 14 December 1983.

State Dept. Records, "Iran-Iraq War: US Responses to Escalation, Scenarios and Threats to Persian Gulf States", 24 March 1984.

State Dept. Records, State to Intsum Collective Priority, "Intelligence Summary 914 – October 11, 1979", October 1979.

State Dept. Records, State to US Embassy, Baghdad, "Memcon: Secretary's Meeting with Iraqi Deprimmin Tariq Aziz", 26 November 1984.

State Dept. Records, US Embassy, Baghdad, to State Dept., "Iraq Exults in Fao Victory, Barely Mentions US Actions", April 1988.

State Dept. Records, US Embassy, Jeddah, to State Dept., 15 June 1963.

State Dept. Records, US Embassy, Jeddah, to State Dept., 16 June 1963.

Bibliography

State Dept. Records, US Embassy, Jeddah, to State Dept., "Saudi View on Iran", January 1979.

State Dept. Records, US Embassy, Jeddah, to State Dept., "Dialogue on Afghanistan", October 1979.

State Dept. Records, US Embassy, Jeddah, to State Dept., "Meeting with Crown Prince Fahd – October 2", October 1979.

State Dept. Records, US Embassy, Jeddah, to State Dept., "Islamic Foreign Ministers Conference on Afghanistan", January 1980.

State Dept. Records, US Embassy, Jeddah, to State Dept., "Saudi Official Commands, US/Iraqi Contacts", 7 December 1983.

State Dept. Records, US Embassy, Kabul, to State Dept., June 1979.

State Dept. Records, US Embassy, Kabul, to State Dept., "Prime Minister Amin Reiterates That He Wants Friendly Relations with the US", September 1979.

State Dept. Records, US Embassy, Kabul, to State Dept., "Charge's Call on President Amin", September 1979.

State Dept. Records, US Embassy, Kabul, to State Dept., "Meeting with President Amin", October 1979.

State Dept. Records, US Embassy, Kabul, to State Dept., "Signs Continue of Strained Relations between President Hafizullah Amin and the Soviets", October 1979.

State Dept. Records, US Embassy, London, to State Dept., "Saudi Arabian Oil Production", January 1979.

State Dept. Records, US Embassy, Paris, to State Dept., "Gromyko Press Conference in Paris", April 1980.

State Dept. Records, US Embassy. Paris, to State Dept., "France to Send Five Super-Étendard Aircraft", 24 June 1983.

State Dept. Report, "US Engagement with the Taliban on Usama Bin Laden", 16 July 2001.

State Dept., US Embassy, Islamabad, Cable, "SITREP 6: Pakistan/Afghanistan Reaction to US Strikes", 25 August 1998.

State Dept., US Embassy, Islamabad, Cable, "SITREP 7: Pakistan/Afghanistan Reaction to US Strikes", 26 August 1998.

State Dept., US Embassy, Islamabad, Cable, "Usama bin Laden: High-Level Taliban Official Gives the Standard Line on bin Laden with a Couple of Nuances, in October 11th Meeting with Ambassador", 12 October 1998.

State Dept., US Embassy, Islamabad, Cable, "Usama bin Laden: Coordinating our Efforts and Sharpening Our Message on bin Laden", 19 October 1998.

Transcripts of Sec. of State Henry Kissinger, Staff Meetings, 1973–1977, Box 1, Transcript, "Secretary's Staff Meeting", 23 October 1973.

US Central Command, "Operation Desert Shield/Desert Storm", Executive Summary, 11 July 1991.

US Embassy, Moscow, Cable, "A/S Raphel Consultation with Deputy FM Chernyshev", 13 May 1996.

The White House, Memorandum of Conversation between Faisal and Kissinger, 8 November 1973.

The White House, Memorandum of Conversation between Saqqaf and Fahmi and Vice President Gerald Ford and Kissinger, 18 February 1974.

The White House, Memorandum of Conversation between Assad and Kissinger, 26 February 1974.

The White House, Memorandum of Conversation between Fahd and Kissinger, 2 March 1974.

The White House, Memorandum of Conversation between Saqqaf and Kissinger, 2 March 1974.

The White House, Memorandum of Conversation between Saud and Ford, 18 September 1975.

The White House, Memorandum of Conversation between Saud and Kissinger, 6 October 1976.

The White House, NSC, National Security Decision Directive, "US Policy Toward Iran", 11 June 1985.

The White House, NSC, National Security Study Directive 7-84, "US Security Relationship with Saudi Arabia", 6 November 1984.

The White House, Office of the White House Press Secretary, "Text of the President's Address to the Nation", 4 January 1980.

Nixon Presidential Materials Project

Nixon Presidential Materials Project, NSCF, Box 1173, 1973 War (Middle East), 6 October 1973, File No. 1 (1 of 2), Memorandum from William B. Quandt, NSC Staffer, to Brent Scowcroft, 6 October 1973.

Nixon Presidential Materials Project, NSCF, Box 1174, 1973 Middle East War, 10 October 1973, File No. 5, State Dept., Operation Center, Middle East Task Force, Situation Report #18.

Nixon Presidential Materials Project, NSCF, Box 1174, 1973 Middle East War, 12 October 1973, File No. 7, State Dept., Operation Center, Middle East Task Force, Situation Report #22.

Nixon Presidential Materials Project, NSCF, Box 1174, 1973 Middle East War, October 15th, 1973, File No. 9., State Dept. to US Embassy, Jeddah, 14 October 1973.

Nixon Presidential Materials Project, NSCF, Box 1174, 1973 Middle East War, 16 October 1973, File No. 11, US Embassy, Jeddah, to State Dept., 16 October 1973.

Nixon Presidential Materials Project, NSC Institutional Files, Box H-92, WSAG

Bibliography

Meeting Middle East 10/17/73, Folder 6, Memcon, "WSAG Principles: Middle East War", 17 October 1973.

Nixon Presidential Materials Project, NSC Institutional Files, Box H-117, WSAG Minutes 10-2-73 to 7-23-74, Minutes of WSAG, 17 October 1973.

Nixon Presidential Materials Project, NSC Files, Subject Files, Box 321, Folder: "Energy Crisis, November 1973–74", Memorandum from Pentagon to the White House, 30 November 1973.

Presidential Libraries

Dwight D. Eisenhower Library (DDEL), AWF, DDE Diary Series, Box 18, Folder: "Oct. 56 Phone Calls", Telephone Conversion between Eisenhower and US Ambassador to UN Henry Cabot Lodge, 31 October 1956.

DDEL, AWF, International Series, Box 46, Folder: "Saudi Arabia, King Saud 1957 (1)", US Embassy, Cairo, to State Dept., 28 February 1957.

DDEL, AWF, NSC Series, Box 9, "Memorandum of Discussion at the 357th Meeting of the National Security Council", 6 March 1958.

DDEL, ACW, NSC Series, Box 10, "Memorandum of Discussion at the 363rd Meeting of the NSC," 24 April 1958.

DDEL, White House Office, Staff Secretary papers, State Dept., Subseries, Subject Series, Box 3, Memorandum by Goodpaster of conference with the President, 23 December 1958, State Dept. (September 1958–January 1959).

John F. Kennedy Library, Countries Series, Yemen, 10/1/62-10/8/62, Memorandum from the Office of National Estimates, CIA, to Director of Central Intelligence McCone, 8 October 1962.

John F. Kennedy Library, NSC, Meetings and Memoranda, Staff Memoranda, Robert W. Komer, Memorandum from Komer to Kennedy, "Aid to the UAR", 15 February 1962.

John F. Kennedy Library, NSC, UAR, 09/63-11/63, State Dept. to US Embassy, Cairo, 19 October 1963.

John F. Kennedy Library, NSF, Countries Series, Yemen, 8/61-9/62.

John F. Kennedy Library, NSF, Box 45, Komer Papers, UAR 1961-1962, White House Memorandum from Komer to Rostow, 2 June 1961.

John F. Kennedy Library, NSF, Box 169, Nasser Correspondence, UAR, Nasser Letter to Kennedy, 21 June 1961.

John F. Kennedy Library, NSF, UAR, 7/61-10/61, Memorandum from Komer to Rostow, 30 June 1961.

John F. Kennedy Library, NSF, Meeting and Memoranda Series, Staff Memoranda, Robert W. Komer (11/61-12/61), 3 November 1961.

John F. Kennedy Library, NSF, UAR, 11/61-12/61, Memo from Komer to Bundy and its attachment Memorandum for the President "A Shift in Policy Toward Nasser", 8 December 1961.

John F. Kennedy Library, NSF, Box 169, UAR, Memorandum from George Ball to Kennedy, 31 January 1962.

John F. Kennedy Library, NSF, White House Memoranda, Komer papers, UAR 1961-62, Komer memo to Bundy, 10 July 1962.

John F. Kennedy Library, NSF, Box 443, Komer Papers, Saudi Arabia, Faysal Visit 10/4/62-10/8/62, (Folder 1 of 3), Memorandum of conversation between Crown Prince Faysal and Sec. of State, 27 September 1962.

John F. Kennedy Library, NSF, Box 443, Komer Papers, Saudi Arabia, Faysal Visit 10/4/62-10/8/62, (Folder 1 of 3), Memorandum of Conversation Between Talbot and Dr. Fir'awn, 3 October 1962.

John F. Kennedy Library, NSF, Box 158, Saudi Arabia, Faysal Briefing Book, 10/3/62-10/5/62, Komer Memorandum to the President, 4 October 1962.

John F. Kennedy Library, NSF, Box 443, Komer Papers, Saudi Arabia, Faysal Visit 10/4/62-10/8/62, (Folder 1 of 3), Memorandum of Conversation Between Crown Prince Faysal and the President, 5 October 1962.

John F. Kennedy Library, NSF, White House Memoranda, Box 445, Komer papers, UAR 1961-62, Komer memo to JFK, 5 October 1962.

John F. Kennedy Library, NSF, Meeting and Memoranda Series, Staff Memoranda, Komer papers, Komer memo to Kennedy, 18 October 1962.

John F. Kennedy Library, NSF, Box 169, UAR, Memorandum from Komer to Bundy, 2 January 1963.

John F. Kennedy Library, NSF, Yemen, Memorandum for the Record: Presidential Meeting on Yemen, 25 February 1963.

John F. Kennedy Library, NSF, Countries Files, Yemen, Bunker/Bunche Missions. Letter from Kennedy to Faisal, 1 March 1963.

John F. Kennedy Library, NSF, White House Memoranda, Box 44, Komer Files, Yemen, 1961–64, Memcon: JFK Meeting on Yemen, 11 March 1963.

John F. Kennedy Library, NSF, Box 446, Komer Papers, UAR 1/63-11/63, William S. Gaud to Hollis B. Chenery, 25 April 1963.

John F. Kennedy Library, NSF, Countries Series, Saudi Arabia, 6/1/63-6/14/63.

John F. Kennedy Library, NSF, Countries Series, Yemen, 6/63, Memorandum from Komer to President, 7 June 1963.

John F. Kennedy Library, NSF, Countries Series, Saudi Arabia, 6/1/63-6/14/63, Memorandum from Komer to Kennedy, 13 June 1963.

John F. Kennedy Library, NSF, Countries Series, Saudi Arabia, JCS Telegram 1512, DTG 032235Z, July 1963.

John F. Kennedy Library, NSF, Countries Series, Saudi Arabia, 7/63-8/63, Memo from Komer to Kennedy, 2 July 1963.

John F. Kennedy Library, NSF, Countries Series, Saudi Arabia, JCS Telegram 3520, DTG 09 1747Z, November 1963.

John F. Kennedy Library, NSF, Countries Series, UAR, 6/63-8/63, Helms to Bundy, 12 July 1963.

Bibliography

John F. Kennedy Library, NSF, Countries Series, Yemen, 7/63, Komer to Kennedy, 12 July 1963.

John F. Kennedy Library, NSF, Countries Series, UAR, 6/63-8/63, Komer to Bundy, 15 July 1963.

John F. Kennedy Library, NSF, Countries Series, Yemen, 7/63, "Estimate of Soviet Involvement in Yemen" by the Office of National Estimates of the CIA, 24 July 1963.

John F. Kennedy Library, NSF, Countries Series, Yemen, 9/63, Paper by Komer, "The Next Round in Yemen", 20 September 1963.

John F. Kennedy Library, Oral Histories, Robert W. Komer, NSC *Chargé* of Middle Eastern Affairs, 16 July 1964.

Lyndon B. Johnson Library, NSF, Country File, Yemen, Cables & Memos, vol.II, 6/64-12/68, Special Memorandum Prepared in the CIA, 18 February 1965.

Lyndon B. Johnson Library, NSF, Country Files, Saudi Arabia, Memos, Vol. I, 12/63-4/67, Memorandum of Conversation, 21 February 1966.

Lyndon B. Johnson Library, NSF, Country Files, Saudi Arabia, Memos, Vol. I, 12/63-4/67, Memorandum of Conversation, "President's Meeting with King Faisal", 21 June 1966.

Lyndon B. Johnson Library, NSF, NIE 36.6, Saudi Arabia, National Intelligence Estimate NIE 36.6-66, 8 December 1966.

Ronald Reagan Presidential Library, Public Paper, "Statement on US Measures Taken Against the Soviet Union Concerning its Involvement in Poland", 29 December 1981.

George Bush Presidential Library, The White House, NS Directive 26, "US Policy Toward the Persian Gulf", 2 October 1989.

Public Papers of the Presidents of the United States (PPP)

Bush, George, 1991, Book I, 1 January–30 June 1991, Washington, DC: US Government Printing Office, 1992.

Bush, George W., Books I and II, 2001, "Address Before a Joint Session of the Congress on the U.S. Response to the Terrorist Attacks of September 11", 20 September 2001.

Nixon, Richard, The President's News Conference, 25 February 1974. Washington DC: US Government Printing Office.

Carter, Jimmy, 1977. Washington, DC: US Government Printing Office.

White House, Press Office

"Visit of President Heydar Aliyev of Azerbaijan", 1 August 1997.

"Radio Address of the President to the Nation", News Release, 6 October 2001, http://www.georgewbush-whitehouse.archives.org/news/relese/2001/10/20011006.html.

"President Welcomes Aid Workers Rescued from Afghanistan", News Release,

26 November 2001, http://www.georgewbush-whitehouse.archives.org/news/release/2001/11/20011126-1.html.
"The President's State of the Union Address", News Release, 29 January 2002, http://www.georgewbush-whitehouse.archives.gov/news/releases/2002/01/20020129-11.html.
"President Bush Calls for New Palestinian Leadership", 20 June 2002.
"President's Remarks at the UN General Assembly", 12 September 2002.
"The National Security Strategy of the U.S.A.", Washington, 17 September 2002.
"US-Middle East Free Trade Area", 9 May 2003.

Miscellaneous US Government Sources

Chief of Naval Operations (CNO) Records, serial 0005P30, file: A16-3(5) War plans, OP 30 files, Memorandum "Resume of Pincher Panning", Rear Adm. Cato D. Glover, 21 January 1947.
Department of Defense, News Briefing, The Pentagon, Office of Assistant Sec. of Defense, Ref. No. 266-95, 17 May 1995.
Council on Foreign Relations, Task Force Report, *Terrorist Financing*, 2002.
Final Report of the National Commission on Terrorist Attack Upon the United States, *The 9/11 Commission Report*. New York: W. W. Norton & Company, 2004.
Library of Congress, Area Handbook, *Iran*.
Library of Congress, Federal Research Division, Area Handbook Series, *Iran: A Country Study*, Helen Chapin Metz, ed., December 1987.
National Defense University (NDU), Institute for National Security Studies (INSS), *Strategic Assessment 1999*. Washington DC: NDU/INSS, 1999.
National Energy Policy Development Group (NEPD), *National Energy Policy: Reliable, Affordable, and Environmentally Sound Energy for America's Future*, Report of the NEPD. Washington, DC: US Government Printing Office, 2001.
Navy Department Records, Record Group 80, Memorandum: "The Problem", Folder: "Oil", Duffield Office File, 13 March 1944.
Treasury Department, The Office of Public Affairs, JS-1257, "Testimony of Juan C. Zarate, Deputy Assistant Secretary Executive Office for Terrorist Financing and Financial Crimes, Before the House of International Relations Subcommittee on the Middle East and Central Asia", 24 March 2004.
US Army, "Impact of the Stinger Missile on Soviet and Resistance Tactics in Afghanistan", March 1989.
US Defense Intelligence Agency, Intelligence Commentary, 7 January 1980.
US Defense Intelligence Agency, Directorate for Research, "Afghan Resistance", 5 November 1982.

Bibliography

Washington National Records Center, RG330, OASD/ISA Files:FRC 67 A 4564, Iraq 000.1-1963, Memorandum from Stephen O. Fuqua of the Bureau of International Security Affairs, Dept. of Defense, to Frank K. Sloan, Deputy Assistant Sec. of Defense for International Affairs, 8 February 1963.

Washington National Records Center, RG330, OASD/ISA Files: FRC 65 A 3501, Yemen, 000.1-1963, Memo from Glass to Bundy "S-18, 373/P-3", 21 June 1963.

Washington National Records Center, RG 330, OSD Files: FRC 69 A 3131, Saudi Arabia 1963, JCSM-1003-63, 24 December 1963.

Saudi Government Sources

Saudi Embassy, Washington, "Looking Ahead: The Oil Market and Its Future", Ali I. Al-Naimi, Saudi Minister of Petroleum and Mineral Resources at the Los Angeles World Affair Council, 8 May 2000, http://www.saudiembassy.net/archive/2000/speeches/Page11.aspx.

Saudi Embassy, Washington, "Crown Prince Abdullah presents 8-point Mid East Proposal to US president Bush at Crawford, Texas", 26 April 2002, http://www.saudiembassy.net/archive/2002/press/page30.aspx.

Saudi Embassy, Washington, "Embassy Issues Summary Report on Fight Against Terrorism", 27 August 2002, http://www.saudiembassy.net/archive/2002/statements/page7.aspx.

Saudi Embassy, Washington, "Saudi Foreign Minister Welcomes US President's Address to the UN", 15 September 2002, http://www.saudiembassy.net/archive/2002/press/page15.aspx.

Saudi Embassy, Washington, "FBI, Treasury Department Praise Saudi Efforts to Stop Terrorist Financing", 20 September 2002, http://www.saudiembassy.net/archive/2002/press/page14.aspx.

Saudi Embassy, Washington, "Response to CFR Report", 17 October 2002, http://saudiembassy.net/archive/2002/press/page10.aspx.

Saudi Embassy, Washington, "Saudi Actions to Crack Down on Terrorist Financing", 18 October 2002, http://saudiembassy.net/archive/2002/press/page9.aspx.

Saudi Embassy, Washington, "GCC Urges Iraq to Accept UN Resolution 1441", 12 November 2002, http://www.saudiembassy.net/archive/2002/news/page22.aspx.

Saudi Embassy, Washington, "Saudi Information Office Issues Clarification", 28 August 2003, http://www.saudiembassy.net/archive/2003/press/page29.aspx.

Saudi Embassy, Washington, "The Saudis Respond: Foreign Minister Prince Saud Interviewed by Scott Macleod", *Time* exclusive, Paris, 10 September 2003, http://www.saudiembassy.net/archive/2003/statements/page2.aspx.

Saudi Embassy Washington, "Saudi Arabia's Progress on Economic, Education and Political Reforms", 7 November 2003, http://www.saudiembassy.net/archive/2003/press/page11.aspx.

Saudi Embassy, Washington, "Statement on Creation of a Charity Commission", 28 February 2004, http://www.saudiembassy.net/archive/2004/statements/page23.aspx

Saudi Embassy, Washington, "Prince Saud's Address to US-Saudi Arabian Business Council", New York, 26 April 2004, http://www.saudiembassy.net/archive/2004/speeches/page11.aspx.

Saudi Embassy, Washington, Address by Minister of Foreign Affairs HRH Prince Saud Al-Faisal to the Council on Foreign Relations, "The US and Saudi Arabia: A Relationship Threatened By Misconceptions", New York, 27 April 2004.

Saudi Embassy, Washington, Information Office, "Saudi Arabia and the US Take Joint Action Against Terror Financing", 2 June 2004.

Saudi Embassy, Washington, "FATF Releases Evaluation of Kingdom's Mechanism Against Terrorism Financing and Money Laundering", 2 July 2004, http://www.saudiembassy.net/archive/2004/press/page21.aspx.

Saudi Embassy, Washington, Prince Saud Al-Faisal Interview with *Newsweek/The Washington Post*, "Changes in the Kingdom – On Our Timetable", Lally Weymouth, 27 February, 2005, http://www.saudiembassy.net/archive/2005/statements/page25.aspx.

Saudi Embassy, Washington, "Joint Statement by Crown Prince Abdullah and President George W. Bush", 25 April 2005, http://www.saudiembassy.net/archive/2005/statements/page20.aspx.

Saudi Embassy, Washington, "Foreign Minister Gives Press Conference in Dallas, Texas", 26 April 2005, http://www.saudiembassy.net/archive/2005/news/page567.aspx.

Saudi Embassy, Washington, "Transcript of Prince Saud Interview with U.S. Print Journalists", 22 September 2005, http://www.saudiembassy.net/archive/2005/transcript/Page5.aspx.

Saudi Embassy, Washington, "Joint Press Conference of Prince Saud and Secretary Rice Following the First Strategic Dialogue", 14 November 2005, http://www.saudiembassy.net/archive/2005/transcript/Page0.aspx.

Saudi Embassy, Washington, "US-Saudi Strategic Dialogue Joint Statement ", 18 May 2006, http://www.saudiembassy.net/archive/2006/statements/page9.aspx.

Saudi Embassy, Washington, "I Think We Need to Talk", New Saudi Ambassador to the US Prince Turki Al-Faisal at the Brookings Institution", Washington 19 June 2006, http://www.saudiembassy.net/archive/2006/speeches/page31.aspx.

Saudi Embassy, Washington, "Political and Economic Reform in the Kingdom of Saudi Arabia", December 2006.

Saudi Embassy, Washington, "The Kingdom's Address to the 63rd UN General

Assembly, 27 September 2008", http://www.saudiembassy.net/latest_news/news09270801.aspx.

Saudi Embassy, Washington, "Arab Foreign Ministers Meet", 3 March 2009, http://www.saudiembassy.net/latest_news/news03030902.aspx.

Communist Party of the Soviet Union

Archive of the President, Russian Federation, f.3, op.82, d.149, ll.120-122, trans. by M. Kramer, Ustinov, Report to CPSCU CC on Mission to Afghanistan by Pavlovskii, 5 November 1979.

Archives of the General Staff of the USSR Armed Forces, *Znamya*, no. 4, 1991, Report from Soviet Deputy Defence Minister Army Gen. Ivan Pavlovskii during visit to Afghanistan, 25 August 1979.

Archive of the President, Russian Federation (APRF), f. 3, op. 82, d. 173, ll. 72-75, trans. by M. Kramer, CPSU CC Politburo Decision, with report by Gromyko, D. F. Ustinov, S. K. Tsvigun, 15 September 1979.

Cold War International History Project, Archive of the President, Russian Federation, from notes taken by A. F. Dobrynin and provided to Norwegian Nobel Institute by Odd Arne Westad, Director of Research, Nobel Institute, trans. Daniel Rozas, Personal Memorandum, Andreopov to Brezhnev, n.d. [early December 1979].

Cold War International History Project, Memorandum from Brzezinski to Carter, "Reflections on Soviet Intervention in Afghanistan", 26 December 1979.

Tsentr Khraneniia Sovremennoi Dokumentatsii (The Center for the Storage of Contemporary Documentation), Moscow, fond "f." 5, opis "op." 75 delo, "d." 1179, listy "ll." 2-17, notes taken by Odd Arne Westad, Letter from Soviet Ambassador to Afghanistan to Soviet Foreign Minister, 31 May 1978 (Communist Party Archives).

Tsentr Khraneniia Sovremennoi Dokumentatsii (The Center for the Storage of Contemporary Documentation), f. 5, op. 75, d. 1181, ll. 36040, Notes of O. A. Westad, Conversation between Puzanov and Taraki, 18 July 1978.

Tsentr Khraneniia Sovremennoi Dokumentatsii (The Center for the Storage of Contemporary Documentation), f. 89, perechen "per." 14, document "dok." 24, document provided by Mark Kramer, Harvard University, trans. by Daniel Rozas, "Communist Party of the Soviet Union (CPSC), Central Committee (CC), Politburo Decision on Afghanistan", 7 January 1979.

Tsentr Khraneniia Sovremennoi Dokumentatsii (The Center for the Storage of Contemporary Documentation), f. 89, per. 25, dok.1, ll. 1, 12-25, document provided by M. Kramer (Harvard University), trans. by Carter-Brezhnev Project, Transcript of CPSC CC Politburo Discussions on Afghanistan, 17–19 March 1979.

Tsentr Khraneniia Sovremennoi Dokumentatsii (The Center for the Storage of

Contemporary Documentation), f. 89, per. 25, dok. 2, documents provided by M. Kramer, trans. by Carter-Brezhnev Project, Transcript of CPSC CC Politburo Session on Afghanistan, 22 March 1979.

Tsentr Khraneniia Sovremennoi Dokumentatsii (The Center for the Storage of Contemporary Documentation), f. 89, per. 42, dok.16, provided by M. Kramer, trans. by D. Rozas, CPSU CC Politburo transcript, 13 November 1986.

United Nations Sources

United Nations, Department of Public Information, *The Blue Helmets: A Review of United Nations Peace-Keeping*. New York: UN, 1985.
UN Document (S/5298).
UN Security Council Resolution 660, 1990.
UN Security Council Resolution 1267, 15 October 1999.
UN Security Council Resolution 1441, 2002.
UN Security Council 12/67 1333/1390 Mandate blocking Usama bin Laden and associates, including al Qaʻida and the Taliban.

Newspapers and Related

Agence France-Presse (AFP)
Al-Ahram
ʻAin al-Yaqeen
Al-Anouar (Lebanon)
Arab News
Al-Bilad (Saudi newspaper)
Daily Star (Lebanon)
Financial Times
The Guardian
Guardian Unlimited
Gulf News (United Arab Emirates)
Al-Hawadith
Al-Hayat
International Herald Tribune
Al-Iqtisadiyya
Al-Jazirah (Saudi Arabia)
Al-Madina
Al-Majallah
Al-Manhal (Saudi Arabia)
Middle East Contemporary Survey
Middle East Economic Digest
Middle East Economic Survey

Bibliography

Middle East Journal
Newsweek
The New Yorker
The New York Times
Oil and Gas Journal
Al-Qabas (Kuwait)
Al-Quds al-'Arabi
Al-Riyadh (Saudi Arabia)
Saudi Gazette
Saudi Press Agency
Al-Siyasah (Kuwait)
Al-Sharq al-Awsat (Saudi Arabia)
US News and World Report
Ukaz (Jeddah: *Mu'assasat 'Ukāz* – Saudi newspaper)
'Um al-Qura
The Washington Post
The Washington Times
Al-Watan (Kuwait)
Al-Watan (Saudi Arabia)
Al-Yaum (Saudi Arabia)
BBC Summary, ME/6144/A5, 8 June 1979, ME/6145/A7, 9 June 1979.
Voice of America, Washington, DC, Transcript of the Editorial, 15 February 1990.

Interviews Conducted by the Author

Prince Bandar bin Sultan, October 2006.
Prince Saud Al-Faisal, December 2005.
Prince Turki Al-Faisal, November 2005.

Miscellaneous

Arabic & World Selected News Agency, Beirut, [Lebanon's Invasion (*Ijtiyah Lebanon*)], undated.
Central Command, Posture Statement, 1995.
Headquarters Rapid Deployment Joint Task Force (RDJTF), Fact Sheet, 1981.
US v. bin Laden, "Closing Statement by Assistant US Attorney Ken Karas", 2 May 2001.

Index

'Abd Al-Rahman, 'Umar, 267
Abu Dhabi, 159
Abu Ghazala, Talal, 163
Abu Musa Island (Iran), 153
Abu Al-Nasser, 'Abd Al-Karim, 286
Abu Rudeis oilfields (Sinai), 107
Aden, 49–51, 54, 57, 61, 64, 74–5, 258
Adham, Kamal, 84
"Afghan Arabs", 249–50
Afghanistan, 117, 123–35, 161, 165, 251, 255, 257–60, 262, 268, 275, 284, 292, 316–18, 320 *see also* Democratic Republic of Afghanistan
   1980 Soviet invasion of see USSR, invasion of Afghanistan in 1980 and aftermath
   2001 US invasion of see US, invasion of Afghanistan and aftermath
   Afghanistan Revolutionary Council, 134
   Usama bin Laden in, 254–7, 260
   Communist Party of, 128, 134
Africa, 190, 192, 196, 234, 291
Imam Ahmad [Ahmad bin Yahya Hamidaddin], 42
Ahmed, Wakil, 259
Ahmedinejad, Mahmoud, 319
Ajami, Fouad, 294

Akhtar, Abdur Rahman, 137, 146
Akins, James, 91
Albright, Madeleine, 252
Alexandria (Egypt), 71, 73
Algeria, 82, 156, 185, 250
Algiers, 97
Algosaibi, Ghazi, 270
Aliyev, Heydar, 234
Amer, 'Abd al-Hakim, 72
American Israel Public Affairs Committee (AIPAC), 26
Amin, Hafizullah, 127–9, 131–4
Amman, 150, 155
Amstutz, J. Bruce, 133
Anderson, Robert B. 32, 34
Angola, 126, 190
al-Aqsa Mosque (Jerusalem), 81, 238
Arab Cooperation Council, 201
Arab League, 114, 176, 185, 187, 203, 216
Arabian Gulf, 117, 122–3, 127, 135–6, 138, 151, 154–6, 158–60, 163–5, 170–3, 175–7, 183, 196–201, 203–4, 207–8, 214, 216, 221, 223, 233–4, 242–3, 290, 297, 315, 318, 321, 323 *see also* Persian Gulf
   First Gulf War *see* Iraq, invasion of Kuwait

365

Second Gulf War *see* US, invasion of Iraq
    as key US interest, 24
    oilfields of, 30, 198, 231
    US military presence in, 21, 310
Arabian Peninsula, 48, 51, 52 (n.), 73, 80, 127, 155, 168, 200
Arabian Sea, 257
Arafat, Yasser, 105, 109–10, 182–3, 185, 187–9, 224, 237–8, 240
ARAMCO [Arabian American Oil Company], 32, 88, 94–5, 118 *see also* California Arabian Standard Oil Company
Ara'r (Saudi Arabia), 299
Argentina, 192
Argov, Shlomo, 182
Al-Asaf, Nasser, 277
Ashcroft, John, 254, 274
al-Assad, Hafiz, 87, 97–8, 104–6, 109, 179–80, 186, 225–8, 236–7
Atherton, Alfred, 113, 191–2
Austria, 106
al-'Awdah, Salman, 232, 247
Azerbaijan, 234–5
Aziz, Tariq, 166–7, 174, 178, 201, 203, 219–20

Badeau, John S., 50–1, 55–6, 58, 65, 69–70
Badeeb, Ahmed, 137, 140
al-Badr, Imam Muhammad, 47–8, 50, 65
Baghdad, 149, 153, 202, 204–7, 218–19, 290, 304, 321
    1978–9 Arab summits in, 114–16, 121
Bahrain, 152
Baker, Howard, 161
Baker, James [A. III], 208–9, 218–20, 222–30
Baluchistan (Afghanistan), 125
Banisadr, Abolhassan, 157–8

Barre, Siad, 191
Basra, 164, 178
Ba'th Party *and* Ba'thism, 57, 76, 149, 165, 214, 265 [de-Ba'thification], 294, 303, 305
Begin, Menachem, 110, 114, 179–80, 182–4, 188
Beijing, 169
Beirut, 166, 182–9, 295
Bekaa Valley (Lebanon), 179, 180 (n.), 183
Ben-Gurion [David], 179
Bennett, William, 289
Bentsur, Eytan, 223
Berger, Samuel R. "Sandy", 240, 254, 257, 262
Berman, Paul, 294
Biden, Joe, 319
Boland, Edward P., 193
Bonn (West Germany), 183
Borchgrave, Arnoud de, 87
Bosnia, 250, 264, 278
Boumédienne, Houari, 97
Bremer, L. Paul III, 301
Brezhnev, Leonid, 129
Brookings Institution, 109, 308
Brown, Harold, 118, 120, 134–5, 139
Brzezinski, Zbigniew, 119, 128–31, 134–5, 138–40, 150–1, 191
Bubiyan Island (Kuwait), 173
Buchanan, Pat, 305
Buckley, James, 144, 161
Bundy, McGeorge, 42, 44, 47, 55, 65
Bundy, William P., 64
Bunker, Ellsworth, 58–62, 66, 71
Buraimi Oasis [Oman], 33
Bush, George H. W., 184–5, 199, 202, 205, 209–11, 214–20, 222, 224–5, 227–9, 240–1, 254, 288
Bush, George W. (Jr), 25, 238–40, 262, 265–7, 269, 270–1, 274, 280, 285–6, 289, 291–3, 295–7,

299–301–3, 305–6, 315–16, 318–19, 322
Butler, Richard, 73
Byrd, Robert, 117

Cairo, 35, 40, 56, 84, 190, 225
Cairo University, 316
California Arabian Standard Oil Company (CASOC), 28 *see also* ARAMCO
California Texas Oil Company (CALTEX), 28
Camp David (US), 113, 238
    Accord signed at, 112–16, 118, 120, 192
Canada, 234
Carter, Jimmy, 22, 24, 109–15, 117, 129–31, 135–6, 139, 154, 156, 159, 161, 179, 190, 192, 199, 210–11
Casey, William, 142–6, 165, 194
Caspian Sea, 234–5
Celler, Emanuel, 63
Central America, 194
Central Asia, 143, 145, 291
Chad, 191
Chechnya, 250, 264
Chehab, Fuad, 42
Cheney, Richard, 209, 211–13, 218, 288, 291, 294, 299, 301
Chernyshev, Albert, 255
China, 27, 74, 77, 83, 127, 133, 135, 140, 169–70, 266
Christopher, Warren, 139, 237
Clarke, Richard A., 200, 257, 262–3, 265, 291
"The Clash of Civilizations" (S. Huntington), 246
Clement, Bill, 94
Clinton, Bill, 234, 236, 238, 240–2, 245, 252, 254, 257–60, 262, 265, 289–90, 299, 321–2
Clinton, Hillary, 317

Commodity Credit Corporation, 165, 201
Communist Bloc, 44 *see also* Eastern Bloc; Soviet Bloc; USSR
Contras, the (Nicaragua), 192–5
Cooper, Sherry, 241
Council on Foreign Relations (US), 279–80
Crawford (US), 306
Cuba, 24, 131, 190, 192–3, 212

Dam, Kenneth, 278
Damascus, 38, 179, 226
Dammam (Saudi Arabia), 59
Daoud Khan, Mohammed, 124–7
Dar es Salaam, 257
Dayan, Moshe, 111–12
Democratic Republic of Afghanistan, 134–5
Dhahran (Saudi Arabia), 53, 64, 252
Diego García (Indian Ocean), 208
al-Din, Hassan Hamid, 50
Djibouti, 196
al-Douri, Izzat Ibrahim, 207
Dubs, Adolph, 129
Dulles, Allen, 32
Dulles, John Foster, 32, 39

Eagleburger, Lawrence, 211
East Jerusalem *see* Jerusalem
Eastern Bloc, 64 (n.) *see also* Communist Bloc; Soviet Bloc; USSR
Eastern Europe, 83, 144
Eastham, Alan W., Jr, 259
Egypt, 35, 38, 40–2, 44–7, 86–8, 92, 121, 139, 155, 163–4, 168, 190–2, 196, 204–5, 214, 240, 268, 285, 309, 315, 319, 322
    1967 war with Israel 75, 82, 309
    1973 war with Israel, 89–91, 96, 309

decline in standing in Arab world, 121–2, 152, 309
Egyptian Third Army, 104
involvement in Yemen War *see* United Arab Republic, involvement in Yemen War
peace with Israel, 27, 86, 103–16, 118–19
relationship with USSR, 36, 43, 80, 82–5, 91, 107
and Suez Crisis *see* Suez Crisis
Egyptian Islamic Jihad, 256
Eilts, Hermann, 76–8, 80, 114
Eisenhower, Dwight D., 21, 30–5, 42–3
Eizenstat, Stuart, 234
El Salvador, 192–3
Emanuel, Rahm, 317
Erkowit (Sudan), 73
Ethiopia, 123, 126, 190–1
Europe, 32–3, 120, 143–4, 148, 233 *see also* Western Europe
Exxon, 90

Fahmi, Ismail, 97
King Faisal I of Iraq [Faisal bin al-Hussein bin Ali al-Hashemi], 37 *see also* Hashemites
Fao Peninsula (Iraq), 175–6, 178
Fawzi, Mohamed, 56
Feith, Douglas, 289
Financial Action Task Force (FATF), 281–2
Fir'wan, Rashad, 49, 71, 80
Fleischer, Ari, 296
Ford, Gerald R., 106–07
Fortune magazine, 142
France, 30, 33–5, 45, 86, 167, 171 (n.), 190–1, 226, 310
  Service de Documentation Extérieure et de Contre-Espionnage (SDECE), 190

Franks, Tommy, 300–2
Freeh, Louis, 253–4
Fulbright, James, 97

Gailani, Ahmad, 127
Garner, Jay, 301
Gaza, 115, 223, 315, 320–2 *see also* Israel, conflict with Arab states *and/or* Palestinians; Occupied Territories; Palestine *and* Palestinians; Palestinian Authority; West Bank
Gemayel, Bashir, 179–80, 188–9
Gemayel, Pierre, 179
Geneva, 88, 106, 111, 147, 178, 220
Georgetown University, 234
Ghazzawi, Abbas, 136
Gidi pass (Sinai), 107
Glaspie, April, 205
Glass, Robert, 63
Glenn, John, 161
Golan Heights, 89, 98–9, 104, 108, 236, 317 *see also* Israel, 1967 Arab-Israeli war; Syria
Gorbachev, Mikhail, 148–9, 228–9
Gorelov, L. N., 129
Great Bitter Lake [Egypt], 29, 235
Great Britain, 21, 29–30, 33–5, 48, 50, 52, 57, 73, 79, 134, 174, 182, 201, 205, 214–15, 303, 310
  interests in Aden, 49, 51, 54, 57, 74
Greenhill, Denis, 73
Gromyko, Andrei, 111, 127, 141, 154
Group of Twenty Finance Ministers and Central Bank Governors, 279
Gulf, the *see* Arabian Gulf
Gulf of Aqaba, 37
Gulf Cooperation Council (GCC), 159, 174–5, 203, 227, 229, 236, 298
  Supreme Council of, 159
Gulf Oil, 90
Gulf states, 127, 136, 138–9, 141, 150–2,

154, 156, 159, 162, 164, 167–8, 170–1, 173–4, 176–7, 197–8, 200, 205–6, 216, 243–4, 319, 321–2
Gunaratna, Rohan, 293

Habib, Philip, 180–2, 184–9
Haddad, Saad, 182
Haggani, Hussein, 157
Haig, Alexander, 159–62, 179, 182, 185–6
Hamas, 319–21
Hammadi, Sa'dun, 203
Hammarskjöld, Dag, 32
Harad (Yemen), 74
Al-Haramain Islamic Foundation, 278, 281
Hare, Raymond, 40–1, 77
Harib (Yemen), 57
Hart, Parker T., 53–4, 56, 62–3, 66, 69–70, 72
Harvard University, 246
Hashemites, 30 (n.), 33, 36–7, 289 *see also* King Faisal I of Iraq
King Hassan [II] of Morocco, 191
al-Hawali, Safar, 231, 246–7
al-Hazmi, Nawaf, 261
Heath, Donald R., 39
Heikal, Mohamed Hassanein, 50–1, 82, 86–7
Hekmatyar, Gulbuddin, 127
Helms, Richard, 65
Herat (Afghanistan), 129–30
Hersh, Seymour, 319
Hilsman, Roger, 47
Hitler [Adolf], 210
Hizbullah, 166, 289, 315, 319–21
Hodeida (Yemen), 50, 64 (n.), 74–5
Hoover, Herbert, 32
von Horn, Carl, 67
Horn of Africa, 64 (n.)
Huntington, Samuel, 246

King Hussein of Jordan [Hussein bin Talal], 42, 105, 109, 210
Hussein, Saddam, 150, 152–3, 156, 158, 163–5, 168–9, 172–3, 177–8, 200–15, 217–22, 225, 233, 242–4, 250, 289–90, 294–6, 298–302, 304, 318

Ibn Saud, 19, 29–30, 235
Ikhwan-i-Shaytin ("Brotherhood of Satan") [Saudi Arabia], 129
Imam Muhammad Ibn Saud University (Saudi Arabia), 232
Inderfurth, Karl, 256, 260
Indian Ocean, 94, 135, 208
Indyk, Martin, 242, 316
Inman, Bobby Ray, 134
Institute for Advanced Strategic and Political Studies (Israel), 289
Institute of Defence and Strategic Studies (Singapore), 294
Institute for National Strategic Studies (US), 297
International Bank for Reconstruction and Development (IBRD), 41
International Institute of Strategic Studies (Great Britain), 293
International Monetary Fund (IMF), 45
Iran, 18, 21, 27, 78, 99–100, 103, 117–18, 124–7, 135–6, 138, 149–50, 152, 190, 199–200, 205, 208, 214, 216–17, 221, 234, 242–3, 248, 253–4, 256, 289–90, 292, 294–6, 299, 304, 313–15, 317–22, 323
  1979 Islamic Revolution in, 101, 114, 119–20, 132, 151
  1979 US embassy hostage crisis, 123, 139, 150
  1980–88 war with Iraq, 153–78, 183, 196, 309

Communist (Tudeh) Party of, 154
Iranian Defence Supreme Council, 157–8
Parliament of, 163
supply of aid to Iraqi Kurds, 149
Iraq, 18, 21, 32–4, 37, 40–2, 59, 76, 82, 93, 114, 120, 122, 138, 150–2, 223, 242, 313–15, 318
   1963 coup, 57
   1980–88 war with Iran, 153–78, 183, 196, 309
   1991 invasion of Kuwait (First Gulf War), 13, 21, 196, 199, 201–22, 230–1, 233, 243, 250–1, 290, 310
   2003 US invasion of see US, invasion of Iraq (Second Gulf War)
   Coalition Provisional Authority (2003–4), 301
   Iraqi National Assembly, 153
   King Faisal of, see Faisal I of Iraq
   Kurds of, 149
   Republican Guard of, 203, 219
   Revolutionary Command Council, 207
Islamabad, 137
"Islamic Army for the Liberation of the Holy Places", 257
Islamic Conference of Foreign Ministers, 136–7, 157–8
Islamic world, the, 20, 78–9, 81, 239, 247, 249–50, 267, 275, 277, 309
Ismail, Hafez, 86
Israel, 35, 37 (n.), 71, 83, 86, 93–4, 121–2, 137, 157, 161, 168–9, 196, 201–2, 219, 286, 289, 305, 313, 315, 317–18, 320–2
   1967 Arab–Israeli war, 75, 81, 82, 88, 95
   1973 Arab–Israeli war, 89–91, 96–9

1982 invasion of Lebanon, 165, 179–89
1991 Madrid peace conference, 222–30
conflict with Arab states and/or Palestinians, 17, 22, 25, 27, 42, 89, 99, 103, 141, 160, 173, 222–5, 236–42, 266, 284, 294–5, 300, 305, 307, 309, 311–12, 316, 320–1
Israeli Defence Forces (IDF), 189
peace with Egypt, 27, 86, 103–16, 118–19
peace with Jordan, 237
and US Jewish community, 22, 26
US support for, 20, 22, 24–7, 42, 84–5, 88, 90, 92, 99, 105–6, 160, 181, 197, 239–40, 245, 247, 270, 274, 309, 316–17
Italy, 294

Jalalabad (Afghanistan), 255
Japan, 233
Al-Jarf, Reima, 283–4
Jeddah, 74, 122, 157, 168, 203, 207–8
Jerusalem, 27, 81, 96, 98, 108, 111, 113–15, 118, 229–30, 238, 294, 313, 317
Al-Jibeir, 'Adel, 281
bin Jibrin, 'Abdullah, 275
Jizan (Yemen), 65
Johns Hopkins School of Advanced International Studies, 294
Johnson, Lyndon B., 71, 75, 77, 80
Johnson, Ural Alexis, 65
Joint Commission on Economic Cooperation (Saudi Arabia/US), 101
Jones, David, 155
Jordan, 30 (n.), 32–3, 37, 40, 42,

Index

49–54, 92, 150–1, 164, 223, 228, 236–8, 302
Jordan River, 71
Al-Jubayl (Saudi Arabia), 299–300
Julaidan, Wa'el Hamza, 278
Jungers, Frank, 88, 94–5

Kabul, 124–5, 128–32, 134–5, 142, 255
Kagan, Robert, 289–90
Kaissouni, 'Abd al-Moneim, 68
Kamel, Mustafa, 44, 66, 70
Kandahar, 255
Karmal, Babrak, 124, 127, 134
Katanga (Zaire), 191
Kaysen, Carl, 45
Kelly, John, 207
Kelly, P. X., 197
Kennedy, John F., 23, 40–3, 45, 47, 49, 51–3, 55–66, 68–70
Kenya, 196, 257
Khaddam, Abdel Halim, 187
Khaddouri, Majid, 76
Al-Khafji (Saudi Arabia), 216
Khaibar, Mir Akbar, 126
Khairallah, Adnan, 157
Khales, Yunus, 127
Al Khalifa, Muhammad Mubarak, 152
Khalilzad, Zalmay, 298
Khalq (party, Afghanistan), 124, 126–7, 130, 141
Khamene'i, Ali, 158
Khamis Mushait (Saudi Arabia), 122, 152
Kharg Island (Iran), 167, 172, 176
Al-Kharj [Saudi Arabia], 37, 303
Khashoggi, Jamal, 275
Khomeini, Ayatollah Ruhollah, 122, 158, 164, 248
Khrushchev, Nikita, 41
King 'Abdul 'Aziz Centre for National Dialogue (Saudi Arabia), 287

King Saud University (Saudi Arabia), 284
Kingdom of Saudi Arabia *see* Saudi Arabia
Kissinger, Henry, 17, 83, 86, 89–101, 104–5, 107–9, 125, 190
Kitchen, Jeffrey, 65
Komer, Robert W., 43–5, 47, 52, 55, 63–5, 67, 199
Kristol, William, 289–90
Kurdistan, 178
Kuwait, 92, 151, 175–7, 181, 185, 295, 299, 302, 318
    Iraqi invasion of *see* Iraq, invasion of Kuwait (First Gulf War)

Labour Party (Israel), 186, 237
bin Laden, Usama, 250–2, 254–62, 265–8, 272–5, 278, 291–2, 311
Lake, Tony, 240
Larak (Iran), 176
Larson, Alan, 278
Latin America, 117, 190
Lebanon, 37, 40, 42, 60, 108, 210, 292, 320–1
    1982 Israeli invasion of, 179–89
Lewis, Bernard, 245, 294
Lewis, Samuel, 180
Libby, I. Lewis, 292
Libya, 82, 112, 155–6, 191
Likud Party (Israel), 226, 237
Lloyd, Selwyn, 32
London, 118
Los Angeles World Affairs Council, 291

Madrid, 229
    1990 peace conference in, 230, 236–7
Majnoun Islands (Iraq), 178
Mansouri, 'Abdul Rahman, 180
de Marenches, Alexandre, 190, 192

Marib (Yemen), 57
Masoud, Muhammad, 175
McCone, John, 49
McFarlane, Robert, 146, 194–5
McGhee, George, 44
McMahon, John, 146
Mecca, 67, 137, 231, 255
　　Grand Mosque of, incident in 1979, 123
Medina, 255
Mediterranean Sea, 94
Meese, Edwin, 184
Meyer, Herb, 142
Middle East, the, 15–16, 39–41, 56, 89, 94, 96, 99, 108–10, 112, 115, 135, 141, 161, 165, 196, 206, 218, 220, 222, 224–5, 228, 239, 242, 247, 266, 269, 273, 277 (n.), 283, 285–6, 289, 295, 299, 303, 310, 314, 319–20, 322–3
　　communism in, 76–8, 80, 100
　　oil and, 22, 30–2
　　political identity in, 14
　　regional politics of, 19, 31, 79, 106, 236, 239, 309
　　Soviet influence in, 16, 44, 46, 76, 82, 92
　　US interests/power in *and/or* policy toward, 20–6, 31, 34, 41, 44, 46, 77, 83–4, 100, 155, 160, 230, 233, 315–17
al-Midhar, Khalid, 261
Milam, Will B., 259
Mitla pass (Sinai), 107
Mobutu Sese Seko, 191
Mohammadi, Mohammad Nabi, 127
Mojaddedi, Sibghatullah, 125, 127
Montazeri, Hossein Ali, 158
Morgenthau, Hans J., 18, 22
Morocco, 81, 112, 190–1
Morris, Dick, 258
Moscow, 74, 85, 129, 131, 133, 148–9, 228

Mosul (Iraq), 41
Mount Lebanon (Lebanon), 179
Mubarak, Hosni, 204–5, 210, 215, 225–6, 228
Mueller, Robert, 278
Mujahid, Abdul, 260
mujahideen, the (Afghan), 140–4, 146–8, 250
Mullah [Mohammad] Omar, 256–8
Murawiec, Laurent, 269
Muskie, Edmund, 154
The Muslim Brotherhood, 251
The Muslims Are Coming, the Muslims Are Coming (D. Pipes), 246
Myers, Richard B., 301

Najibullah, Mohammad, 149
Najran (Saudi Arabia), 55–6
Al-Naimi, Ali, 291
Nairobi, 257
Nasrallah, Hassan, 315
Nasser, Gamal Abdel, 31–4, 36–7, 39–41, 44–6, 76–7, 79, 83
　　death in 1970, 82, 84
　　defeat by Israel in 1967 war, 75, 82
　　as embodying Arab nationalist resistance against Western power, 35, 38, 42–3
　　role in Yemen War, 47, 49–51, 55, 57–63, 64 (n.), 65–71, 73–5
Nazer, Hisham, 203
Netanyahu, Binyamin, 289, 322
Newbold, Greg, 292
Newsom, David, 128
New York, 50, 108, 152, 154, 167, 178, 261
　　attacks of 11 September 2001, 21, 261, 267, 291
Nicaragua, 192–4
al-Nimeiry, Gaafar, 192

Index

Nixon, Richard M., 22, 83–4, 90–4, 96–9, 104, 190
Non-Aligned Movement, 260
North Atlantic Treaty Organization (NATO), 196
North Korea, 292
North, Oliver, 194
North Sea, 234
North Yemen *see* Yemen Arab Republic
Northern Alliance (Afghanistan), 262, 268
Nye, Joseph, 243

Obama, Barack, 315–22
Occupied Territories, 223–4, 229 *see also* Gaza; Israel, conflict with Arab states *and/or* Palestinians; Palestine *and* Palestinians; Palestinian Authority; West Bank
Ogaden (Ethiopia), 191
Oman, 208
O'Neill, Paul, 277
Organization of Arab Petroleum-Exporting Countries (OAPEC), 92
Organization of the Islamic Conference, 136, 260
Organization of the Petroleum-Exporting Countries (OPEC), 99–103, 162, 203, 234–5

Pakistan, 78, 124–7, 130, 132, 134–7, 139–41, 143, 145–6, 149, 158–9, 169, 196–7, 249, 254–5, 259–61, 316, 320, 322
    Inter-Services Intelligence (ISI), 137, 140, 142, 146, 249
    Special Forces, 260
Palestine *and* Palestinians, 25, 29, 42–3, 81, 88, 90, 92–3, 95–6, 104, 106, 108–11, 113, 115, 118, 120, 137, 168, 182, 185, 187–9, 197, 216, 223–5, 228–9, 235–40, 283, 289, 295, 307, 312, 314–15, 317–19, 320–3 *see also* Gaza; Israel, conflict with Arab states *and/or* Palestinians; Palestinian Authority; Occupied Territories; West Bank
Palestine Liberation Organization (PLO), 105, 109–11, 113, 121–2
    Fatah (party), 321
    as target of Israel in 1982 invasion of Lebanon, 179–89
Palestinian Authority, 236, 321
Palestinian National Council (PNC), 110
Panjsher Valley (Afghanistan), 145
Pankin, Boris, 229
Parcham (party, Afghanistan), 124–8, 141
Paris, 141, 166, 239
Pastora, Edén, 193–4
Pavlovskii, Ivan, 130, 133
Peay, J. H. Binford III, 243
Peircy, Charles, 161
People's Democratic Party of Afghanistan (PDPA), 124, 126–8, 130, 134, 141
People's Democratic Republic of Yemen (PDRY), 119, 138–9, 156, 191, 199 *see also* People's Republic of South Yemen (PRSY); Yemen
People's Republic of South Yemen (PRSY), 74–5, 119 *see also* People's Democratic Republic of Yemen (PDRY); Yemen
Peres, Shimon, 186
Pérez de Cuéllar, Javier, 178
Perle, Richard, 289
Persian Gulf, 135, 156, 212 *see also* Arabian Gulf
Peshawar, 140
"Peshawar Seven", the, 128

Phalange Party (Lebanon), 179, 181, 183–4, 189
Pipes, Daniel, 246
Poland, 143
Powell, Colin, 203–4, 209, 211, 218, 239, 268–9, 280, 285
Prince Sultan Command Centre (Saudi Arabia), 299, 302–3
Princeton University, 245
Project for the New American Century (PNAC), 26, 289–90, 322
Puzanov, Aleksandr M., 127

Qadir, Abdul, 128
al-Qa'ida, 250, 255–8, 260–3, 265–8, 272–3, 275, 277–9, 281, 284, 291–2, 294, 304–5
Qasim, 'Abd al-Karim, 40–2, 57
Al-Qassem, 'Abd al-'Aziz, 284
Qatar, 302, 304
Quayle, Dan, 289
Qutb, Muhammad, 251
Qutb, Sayyid, 251

Rabat (Morocco), 81, 112
Rabbani, Burhanuddin, 125, 127
Rabin, Yitzhak, 106, 109, 237
Radio Baghdad, 153
Radio Cairo, 36, 84
Radio Kabul, 131–2, 134
Radio Sana'a, 74
Rafsanjani, Ali Akbar Hashemi, 163, 208
RAND Corporation, 142, 269–70
Raphel, Robin, 255
Ras Mishab (Saudi Arabia), 216
Al-Rashed, 'Abd Al-Rahman, 285
Al-Rasheed, Ahmed, 283
Reagan, Ronald, 22, 24, 136, 142–3, 146, 159–62, 166, 168, , 170, 174, 180, 182–5, 187–9, 192–4, 210, 240, 289, 291

Red Sea, 47, 77, 191
Rhodesia, 191
Rice, Condoleezza, 265–66, 307
Riskhor (Afghanistan), 132
Riyadh, 72, 95, 98, 100, 104, 106–7, 114, 117–19, 157, 159, 161, 170, 175, 180, 224, 231–2, 252, 276, 288
Roberts, Pat, 271
Rochefort (France), 86
Rogers, William, 85
Roosevelt, Franklin Delano, 24, 29, 235
"The Roots of Muslim Rage" (B. Lewis), 245
Ross, Dennis, 220, 222–3, 225–7, 229
Rostenkowski, Dan, 26
Rostow, Walt, 42–3
Rountree, William, 41
Rowen, Henry, 142
Rumeilah oilfield (Kuwait), 203
Rumsfeld, Donald, 168–9, 270, 289, 292, 300–1
Rush, Kenneth, 90
Rusk, Dean, 46, 59, 63, 68, 76–7
Russia, 255, 291, 294

Sa'ada (Yemen), 65
Al Sabah, Muhammad [Al Salim], 295
Al Sabah, Sa'ad [Al Abdullah Al Salim], 206–7
Al Sabah, Sabah Al Ahmad Al Jaber, 151–2
Sabra and Shatila refugee camps (Lebanon), 189
Sabri, Ali, 61, 65
Sadat, Anwar, 51, 82, 84–6, 89, 94, 97, 104–07, 109, 111–15, 140, 152
Saddam International Airport (Iraq), 300
Safari Club, 190–2
Safwan (Iraq), 212

Index

sahwa ("awakening sheikhs"), the (Saudi Arabia), 232
al-Sallal, 'Abdallah, 47–8, 54, 62, 65
Salzburg, 106
Sana'a, 47–8, 50, 64 (n.), 75
Sana'a–Hodeida Road (Yemen), 71
Sandinistas [Sandinista National Liberation Front; Nicaragua], 192–3
Sandino Harbour (Nicaragua), 193
Sandino Revolutionary Front (FRS) [Nicaragua], 193
San Juan del Norte (Nicaragua), 194
Saqqaf, Omar, 53, 63, 66, 76, 78, 90, 92, 96–8
Sarkis, Elias, 182
Sarraj, 'Abd al-Hamid, 38
Al-Saud, 'Abdul 'Aziz Ibn Abdul Rahman (King) *see* Ibn Saud
Al-Saud, 'Abdullah bin 'Abdul 'Aziz (King), 212, 238–9, 242, 256, 259, 270, 286, 293, 299, 304, 306, 311
    attempts to renew the Middle East peace process, 294–5
    as *de facto* ruler following Fahd's incapacitation, 238, 241, 264
    response to 9/11 attacks on US, 264, 267
    response to 2003 US invasion of Iraq (Second Gulf War), 293, 298, 302
Al-Saud, Bandar bin Sultan bin 'Abdul 'Aziz (Prince), 109, 148, 152, 155, 169–70, 172, 174, 178, 187–8, 192, 194–5, 202, 204–5, 210–12, 215, 219–21, 224–9, 236, 239–41, 252–4, 267–9, 271–2, 276, 279–80, 288, 296, 298–9, 301
Al-Saud, Fahd bin 'Abdul 'Aziz (King), 100–1, 104, 108–9, 113, 115, 118, 121–2, 132, 137–9, 143–5, 147–8, 158, 170, 174, 176, 178, 190, 197, 231, 233, 236, 241, 264, 281, 286–7, 299, 310
    advice to Saddam Hussein against attacking Iran in 1980, 152
    incapacitation due to major stroke in 1996, 238, 241, 264
    response to 1990 Iraqi invasion of Kuwait, 202–6, 208–15, 218–19
    rift with Khalid in favour of US orientation, 119–20
    role in 1991 peace process negotiations 222, 224–9
    role in negotiations following 1982 Israeli invasion of Beirut, 180–9
    three-month absence abroad in 1979, 120
Al-Saud, Faisal bin 'Abdul 'Aziz (King), 31, 34, 42, 46, 84–5, 87–8, 90–1, 94–9, 101, 104–06
    assassination, 106 (n.)
    assumption of kingship, 74
    assumption of power as prime minister, 39
    attempt to establish closer ties to Nasser and UAR, 40
    control of foreign policy ceded to Saud, 42
    death in 1975, 82
    first-ever interview on US television, 88
    leadership during Yemen War, 48–9, 52, 54–64, 66–75
    power struggle with Saud, 71–2
    resumption of dominant political role under Saud, 73
    strategic adoption of pan-Islamism as an alternative to pan-Arabism, 75–82
Al-Saud, Faisal bin Musa'id bin 'Abdul 'Aziz, 106 (n.)

Al-Saud, Khalid bin 'Abdul 'Aziz (King), 106, 119, 153, 180, 184
  rift with Fahd in favour of Arab bloc orientation, 119–20
Al-Saud, Khalid bin Sultan bin 'Abdul 'Aziz (Prince), 202, 205, 208, 212–13, 217, 221, 300
Al-Saud, Naif bin 'Abdul 'Aziz (Prince), 269, 272
Al-Saud, Nawaf bin 'Abdul 'Aziz (Prince), 275
Al-Saud, Saud bin 'Abdul 'Aziz (King), 32–6, 38, 43, 45, 52
  extensive absence abroad and return in 1963, 71
  isolation within Arab (nationalist) world, 39, 73
  power struggle with Faisal, 71–2
  resumption of foreign-policy prerogative from Faisal, 42
  suspected assassination plot against, 37
Al-Saud, Saud bin Faisal bin 'Abdul 'Aziz ("Saud al-Faisal") (Prince) 91, 103, 106–9, 113–15, 118, 137–8, 180, 183–4, 186–7, 204, 206, 215–16, 225, 237, 267–9, 271–4, 283–7, 295–6, 298, 300–1, 303, 305, 307, 319, 321
Al-Saud, Sultan bin 'Abdul 'Aziz (Prince), 53, 77, 138–9, 159, 217, 243–4, 251, 269–70, 302–3
Al-Saud, Turki bin Faisal ("Turki al-Faisal") (Prince), 137, 143, 145, 192, 250, 255–6, 258, 261, 284, 287, 308
  first public Saudi response to Iran–Iraq war given on US television by, 156
Saudi Arabia
  anti-communist outlook/policy of, 36, 76–7, 95 (under Faisal); 122, 132, 190–2, 194–5, 197, 230, 248 (under Fahd)
  anti-Zionist outlook/policy of, 36, 78, 81, 88, 90, 92, 96, 98, 104 (under Faisal); 118, 120, 137, 197 (under Fahd); 238–9, 269, 272, 294, 318 (under 'Abdullah)
  arms purchase from China, 169–70
  arms purchase from Great Britain, 174
  attempts to secure AWACS from US in 1980, 24, 26, 139, 155, 160–2
  Coalition Coordination Communications and Integration Cell (C3IC) [with US CENTCOM [during the First Gulf War], 217
  Combat Air Operations Centre (CAOC), 303–4
  Consultative Council, 286–7, 313
  controversy over stationing of US forces on territory of, 231–2, 242–4, 251–2, 298–9, 302–4
  cooperation with US in combating terrorism, 278–82, 288, 306, 312
  Council of Ministers, 119, 204, 270, 303
  Council of Senior *Ulama*, 231–2, 275
  denials of assisting US in 2003 invasion of Iraq, 302–3
  dependence on US for security, 18, 30, 53, 55, 58, 63, 68–9, 72, 100, 116, 119, 121, 136, 139, 155, 161–2, 173–4, 183, 198–200, 209, 211–12, 216, 231–2, 242–4
  see also Saudi Arabia, social contract inhibiting institution of national service requirement in

divergence of interests with US
  after Cold War, 230, 239
Eastern Province, 208
Egyptian-backed sabotage bombings in 1966 in, 75
funding Nicaraguan Contras at request of US, 194–5
General Intelligence Department (GID), 137, 140, 146, 249, 261
Grand Mufti of, 72
Gulf Coast, 208
investment in US, 100–01
involvement in Yemen War, 47–75
Joint Directorate of Planning (with US CENTCOM during the First Gulf War), 216
Khobar Towers bombing, 252–3, 259
membership in Group of Twenty Finance Ministers and Central Bank Governors, 279
membership in World Trade Organization, 307
Ministry of Defence of, 199
National Commission for Relief and Charity Work Abroad, 281
National Guard of, 180, 252
official censure of 9/11 attacks, 264, 267, 269, 272, 288
oil embargo of 1973, 86–100, 103–4, 106 (n.), 120, 198, 309
opposition to Baghdad Pact, 33
political and economic reform in, 286–7, 312
as protector of Islam, 19–20, 232
relations with UAR, 40, 46, 53, 55–6, 66–7, 71–2
reparation of ties with US since 2005, 306–8
response to 1980 Soviet invasion of Afghanistan, 132–49, 176
response to 1980–88 Iran–Iraq War, 153, 155, 157–9, 172, 174–8
response to 1990 Iraqi invasion of Kuwait, 201–22
response to 2001 terrorist attacks on the US, 267–73, 275
response to 2001 US invasion of Afghanistan, 268, 275, 300
response to *and* involvement in Israel–Egypt peace process, 103–16
response to rise of post-Cold War Islamism, 230–3, 251, 255–6, 258–9, 261
response to terrorism, 275–8
revision of educational curriculum in, 283–5, 313
role in Israel–Palestine peace process, 224–8, 236, 238–41, 294–5
role in PLO withdrawal from Beirut during 1982 Israeli invasion, 185–9
social contract inhibiting institution of national service requirement in, 198
stability of monarchy, 38
suspicion of, on account of Saudi nationality of 9/11 hijackers, 268, 272
"trilateral alliance" with Egypt and Syria, 87
Sayyaf, Abdul Rabb-ur-Rasul, 125, 127
Schlesinger, James, 91, 97
Schmidt, Dana Adams, 48
Schwarzkopf, H. Norman, Jr, 200, 207, 209, 216–19
Schweizer, Peter, 142–3, 145
Scowcroft, Brent, 204–6, 211, 218, 222
Sea of Galilee, 237
Al-Shaer, 'Ali, 181–2
Shah of Iran [Mohammad Reza

Pahlavi], 99, 103, 114, 117–18, 122, 127, 149–50, 192, 198, 210
Shamir, Yitzhak, 225–9
Sharif, Nawaz, 259–60
Sharon, Ariel, 182–3
Shatt al-'Arab waterway, 149, 153, 157–8
Shevardnadze, Eduard A., 223
al-Shifa pharmaceutical plant (Khartoum), 257
Al-Shirian, Daoud, 270
Shultz, George, 166–7, 169, 174, 186 (n.), 187–9, 289
Al-Shura, Ismail, 132
Sick, Gary, 150
Sinai Peninsula, 35, 37 (n.), 82–3, 88, 105, 107, 112
Sirri Island (Iran), 176
Somalia, 191, 196, 278
Somoza Debayle, Anastasio, 192
South Asia, 129
South Lebanon Army, 182
South Yemen *see* People's Democratic Republic of Yemen (PDRY); People's Republic of South Yemen (PRSY)
Southwest Asia *see* Middle East
Soviet Bloc, 48 *see also* Communist Bloc; Eastern Bloc; USSR
Soviet Union *see* USSR
Spain, 120, 294
Standard Oil Company of California (SOCAL), 28 *see also* Exxon
Straits of Bab El-Mandeb, 191
Straits of Hormuz, 156, 166–8, 172, 176
Strong, Robert, 38
Sudan, 73, 78, 82, 192, 254
Suez Canal, 29–35, 82, 84, 86, 89–90, 107
Suez Crisis, 35, 38, 43, 76
Syria, 30 (n.), 31, 33, 37–9, 45, 47, 57, 59, 76, 82, 87, 89, 92, 104–08, 110–12, 114, 120, 150, 155–6, 165, 167–8, 214, 223, 227, 229, 236–7, 289, 304, 309, 316–17, 320–3
   1973 war with Israel, 89, 91, 97–9
   departure from UAR, 44
   reaction to 1982 Israeli invasion of Lebanon, 179–83, 185–7

Taif (Saudi Arabia), 152, 185
Ta'iz (Yemen), 75
Talbot, Phillips, 44, 49, 57, 59, 70–1
Taliban, the, 255–6, 258–62, 268, 275, 297, 318
Tampa (US), 300
Tanzania, 257
Taraki, Nur Mohammad, 124, 127–32
Tarasenko, Segei, 223
Tehran, 66, 99, 150–4, 321
Tehran University, 157–8
Tel Aviv, 237
Tenet, George, 256, 266
Thacher, Nicholas, 66–7
Thant, U, 62, 68–70
Thatcher, Margaret, 204
Al-Thawrah (Iraq), 158
Third World, 23, 27, 46, 141–2, 147, 165, 222
Transjordan *see* Jordan
Tripoli (Lebanon), 186
Tripoli (Libya), 112
Truman, Harry S., 21, 29
Tuhami, Hassan, 112
Tunb Islands (Iran), 153
Tunis, 181, 185
Tunisia, 188
   Congress of, 79
Turkey, 167, 169, 196, 322
Turner, Stansfield, 130, 134
Tutwiler, Margaret, 205
Al-Twarji, 'Abdul 'Aziz, 180

Index

Umm Khisheiba (Sinai), 106
Umm al-Qara University (Saudi Arabia), 231
United Arab Emirates (UAE), 203, 208
United Arab Republic (UAR), 31–2, 38–41, 43–6, 76–7
    détente with Saudi Arabia, 66
    intervention in Yemen (Yemen War), 47–75
    National Assembly, 51
    use of chemical warfare in Yemen War, 75
United Kingdom (UK) *see* Great Britain
United Nations (UN), 32, 50, 58, 64, 68, 96, 107, 122, 136, 165, 167, 178, 184, 186–7, 209, 219–20, 226, 229, 243–4, 260, 294, 296, 300–3
    General Assembly, 35, 42, 108, 111, 152, 222, 296, 319
    Security Council, 35, 55–6, 62, 95, 209, 296, 298, 302
        Sanctions Committee, 278
    United Nations Yemen Observation Mission (UNYOM), 67–71
US [United States of America]
    and Arab nationalism, 39, 43
    arms transfers to Saudi Arabia, 16
    Central Intelligence Agency (CIA), 24, 32, 49, 65, 124, 130–2, 134, 140–3, 145–9, 165–6, 190, 192–4, 209, 249, 250, 257, 260–2, 266, 299
        Counter-Terrorism Center (CTC), 261–2
        Near East Division, 194
        Office of National Estimates (ONE), 49, 64
    and Cold War, 21
    Congress of, 23–5, 53, 59, 94, 146, 154, 161–2, 170, 174, 177, 193–4, 199, 213, 215, 217, 219, 222, 224, 234–5, 274, 278, 285, 290, 308, 316, 319
    House of Representatives, 193, 290
        Committee on Foreign Affairs, 160
        Financial Services Committee, 278
        International Relations Committee, 281
        Judiciary Committee, 63
    Senate, 24, 162, 193
        Armed Services Committee, 197
        Foreign Relations Committee, 97, 108, 161, 166
        Select Committee on Intelligence, 271
    cooperation with Saudi Arabia in in combating terrorism, 278–82, 288
    Counterterrorism Security Group, 266
    Department of Defense, 32, 62, 64, 94, 147–8, 151, 161, 198, 200, 207, 210, 267, 269–71, 288, 291, 297, 301
        Defense Intelligence Agency (DIA), 63, 133, 135, 144, 149, 173
        National Security Agency (NSA), 134
        Office of Reconstruction and Humanitarian Assistance (ORHA), 301
        Rapid Deployment Joint Task Force (RDJTF), 151
    US Air Force, 62, 155, 161, 200, 252
    US Army, 200

82nd Airborne [Division], 300
Special Forces, 302
Task Force 20 (TF20), 300
US Central Command (CENTCOM), 166, 196–7, 199–200, 204, 217, 243, 292, 300–1
   Coalition Coordination Communications and Integration Cell (C3IC) [with Saudi forces during the First Gulf War], 217
   Joint Directorate of Planning (with Saudi forces during the First Gulf War), 216
US Joint Forces Command, 217
US Marine Corps, 200
V Corps, 302
US Navy, 183, 200, 257
US Sixth Fleet, 94
US Seventh Fleet, 94
détente with USSR, 84, 89
domestic politics of, 23–7
Federal Bureau of Investigation (FBI), 253–4, 257, 278
focus on Iraq threat at the expense of al-Qa'ida, 291–2
hegemony of, 16, 21
increase in geopolitical power of, as a result of Suez Crisis, 35
intervention in Lebanon in 1958, 40
invasion of Afghanistan in 2001, 265, 268, 275, 300, 316–18
invasion of Iraq (Second Gulf War) and aftermath, 13, 26–7, 288–306
Israel lobby in, 25–6, 269
Jewish community of, 22, 26

Joint Chiefs of Staff, 30, 64, 70–1, 148, 155, 203, 207, 292, 301
and Middle East *see* Middle East, US interests in *and/or* policy toward
National Energy Policy Development Group (NEPD), 291
National Intelligence Council (NIC), 142
National Security Council (NSC), 32, 39, 43, 45, 47, 55, 62, 89, 194, 209, 211, 242, 262, 265, 269, 276, 280, 292, 316
   Special Coordination Committee, 130
   Washington Special Action Group (WSG), 89, 93
National Security Planning Group (NSPG), 142, 146
Pentagon *see* Department of Defense
relations with the UAR, 43–7, 51, 54, 56
reparation of ties with Saudi Arabia since 2005, 306–8
response to 9/11 terrorist attacks, 21, 25–6, 264, 267–75
response to 1979 Islamic Revolution in Iran, 150–1
response to Iran–Iraq War, 154–6, 159–74, 177
response to pan-Islamic solidarity, 79–81
speculated encouragement of Saddam Hussein's invasion of Kuwait by, 206
State Department, 32, 34, 36, 40–2, 44–50, 54, 58, 60, 62–4, 66, 70–2, 79, 81, 88, 90–2, 122, 125, 132, 139–41, 143, 147, 154,

163, 167–71, 173, 176, 179, 205, 234, 255, 261, 273, 276, 285, 304
  Antiterrorism Assistance Program, 261
  Bureau of Near Eastern Affairs (NEA), 34, 44, 66, 77
  Intelligence and Research Bureau (INR), 47
  Middle East Partnership Initiative, 285
  Office in Charge of Arabian Peninsula Affairs, 51
  Strategic Petroleum Reserve, 139
  and strategy of pre-emptive war, 296–7
  support for Israel, see Israel, US support for
  Treasury Department, 145, 276–8, 281
  White House, the, 89, 94, 141, 170, 184–5, 194, 202, 267, 272, 276, 279, 296, 299–300, 302, 319
US–Middle East Free Trade Area, 286
US–Saudi Arabian Business Council, 272
USSR [Union of Soviet Socialist Republics], 35, 38, 55, 66, 74, 77, 80, 83, 89, 91–3, 95, 98–9, 105, 111, 117, 121, 123–35, 155, 160, 163, 169, 175, 177, 179, 191–3, 196, 198–200, 207, 222, 228, 230, 249–50, 264, 273
see also Communist Bloc; Eastern Bloc; Russia; Soviet Bloc
  arms transfers to Saudi Arabia, 16, 33
  détente with US, 84, 89
  influence in Middle East, 16, 20, 30, 44, 46, 76
  invasion of Afghanistan in 1980 and aftermath, 27, 135–50, 155, 196, 200, 248–50, 264, 310
  involvement in Yemen War, 54, 62–4, 74
  Politburo of the Central Committee of the Communist Party of, 129, 133, 147
  relations with Egypt, 36, 43, 45, 82–5, 91, 107
  relations with UAR, 41, 44
  response during 1979 Iran hostage crisis, 150
  response to Iran–Iraq War, 153–4, 165
  Soviet General Staff, 146
University of Virginia, 265
Uzbekistan, Republic of, 262

Vance, Cyrus, 109–11, 113–14, 119, 126, 128, 135
Vattel, Emerich de, 17 (n.)
Velayati, Ali Akbar, 175
Venezuela, 100, 235
Vienna, 99, 103

Wahhad, Muhammad 'Abdul, 48
Warban Island (Kuwait), 173
Washington, DC, 76, 80, 84, 87, 89, 94, 96, 98, 106–07, 109, 115, 119, 129, 169, 187, 219, 256, 259–60, 267, 280, 289, 301, 304
Washington, George, 324
Webster, William H., 208
Weinberger, Caspar, 161–3, 177, 184
West, the, 80, 83, 101, 141, 143, 154–5, 161, 164, 168–9, 171 (n.), 172, 176, 201, 213, 231–2, 246–7, 276, 283, 313, 323
West Bank, the, 115, 223, 317, 320, 322
see also Gaza; Israel, conflict with Arab states and/or Palestinians;

Occupied Territories; Palestine *and* Palestinians; Palestinian Authority
West Beirut *see* Beirut
West Germany, 294
West, John C., 118, 122, 132–3, 161
Western Europe, 98–9
Wilson, W. W., 53
Wolfowitz, Paul, 213, 288–9, 291–2
World Bank, 32
"World Islamic Front", 256 see also bin Laden, Usama; al-Qa'ida; al-Zawihiri, Ayman
World Trade Center (New York), 267, 291

Yamani, Ahmed Zaki, 87, 90, 97, 99, 103
Yassin, Yusuf, 35
Yazdi, Ibrahim, 152
Yemen, 27, 42, 76–7, 117, 210, 212, 309 *see also* Yemen Arab Republic; People's Democratic Republic of Yemen (PDRY); People's Republic of South Yemen (PRSY)
   Yemen War 47–75, 82
Yemen Arab Republic, 48, 52, 54–7, 58 (n.), 59, 61–2, 64 (n.), 68, 73, 75, 119
Yeosock, John, 217
Young, Andrew, 122

Zahir Shah, Mohammed, 124
Zahle (Lebanon), 179–81
Zaire, 191
Zarate, Juan C., 281–2
al-Zawahiri, Ayman, 256
Zelikow, Philip, 265
Zia ul-Haq, Muhammad, 137, 140, 145–6